Jurji Zaidan
and the Foundations of Arab Nationalism

Modern Intellectual and Political History of the Middle East
Mehrzad Boroujerdi, *Series Editor*

Other titles in Modern Intellectual and Political History of the Middle East

Becoming Turkish: Nationalist Reforms and Cultural Negotiations in Early Republican Turkey (1923–1945)
Hale Yılmaz

The Essentials of Ibadi Islam
Valerie J. Hoffman

The International Politics of the Persian Gulf
Mehran Kamrava, ed.

Mirror for the Muslim Prince: Islam and the Theory of Statecraft
Mehrzad Boroujerdi, ed.

Modernity, Sexuality, and Ideology in Iran: The Life and Legacy of a Popular Female Artist
Kamran Talattof

Pax Syriana: Elite Politics in Postwar Lebanon
Rola el-Husseini

Pious Citizens: Reforming Zoroastrianism in India and Iran
Monica M. Ringer

Raging Against the Machine: Political Opposition under Authoritarianism in Egypt
Holger Albrecht

The Urban Social History of the Middle East, 1750–1950
Peter Sluglett, ed.

JURJI ZAIDAN
and the Foundations of Arab Nationalism

◆ ◆ ◆

A STUDY BY THOMAS PHILIPP

Selected Writings by Jurji Zaidan
Translated by Hilary Kilpatrick and Paul Starkey

Published in Cooperation with and
Foreword by the Zaidan Foundation

Syracuse University Press

The Zaidan Foundation for Enhancing Intercultural Understanding, Inc.
7007 Longwood Drive, Bethesda, MD 20817
Email: george@zaidanfoundation.org Website: www.zaidanfoundation.org

First Edition 2014
14 15 16 17 18 19 6 5 4 3 2 1

∞ The paper used in this publication meets the minimum requirements of the American National Standard for Information Sciences—Permanence of Paper for Printed Library Materials, ANSI Z39.48-1992.

For a listing of books published and distributed by Syracuse University Press, visit www.SyracuseUniversityPress.syr.edu.

ISBN: 978-0-8156-3358-7 (cloth) 978-0-8156-5271-7 (e-book)

Library of Congress Cataloging-in-Publication Data

Philipp, Thomas, 1941–

Jurji Zaidan and the foundations of Arab nationalism : a study / by Thomas Philipp ; selected writings by Jurji Zaidan translated by Hilary Kilpatrick and Paul Starkey. — 1st ed.

pages cm. — (Modern intellectual and political history of the Middle East)

"Published in Cooperation with and Foreword by the Zaidan Foundation."

Includes bibliographical references and index.

ISBN 978-0-8156-3358-7 (cloth : alk. paper) — ISBN 978-0-8156-5271-7 (ebook) 1. Zaydan, Jirji, 1861–1914—Political and social views. 2. Arab nationalism—History—20th century. 3. Arabic language—Political aspects. I. Kilpatrick, Hilary. II. Starkey, Paul, 1947– III. Zaydan, Jirji, 1861–1914. Works. Selections. English. 2014. IV. Zaidan Foundation. V. Title.

PJ7876.A9Z833 2014
892.7'35—dc23 2014027907

Manufactured in the United States of America

To the memory of Choucri Jurji Zaidan and his brother Emile for carrying on the legacy of their illustrious father.

—The Zaidan Foundation

Contents

◆ ◆ ◆

Foreword

Jurji Zaidan and His Works

Jurji Zaidan (1861–1914) was a prolific writer whose objective was to inform and educate his Arab contemporaries about the modern world, their shared past, and their national identity. He is considered to be one of the intellectual leaders who laid the foundation for a pan-Arab secular national identity.

Zaidan was the archetypical member of the Arab Nahda (Awakening) at the end of the nineteenth and early twentieth centuries. He belonged to a new intellectual elite whose education was not based on traditional or religious learning. Jurji Zaidan was an autodidact whose only college training was one year spent in the medical department of the Syrian Protestant College in Beirut. It came to an abrupt halt because of a strike resulting from a schism between the administration and some teachers over the firing of a faculty member for having expressed favorable views about the theory of evolution. The young Zaidan was a student leader and a strong proponent of reinstalling the professor in his position.

His writings as a historian, linguist, and political and social commentator bore the strong imprint of his scientific and evolutionary outlook and shaped his analytic approach in all these areas. His works gave a distinctly secular outlook to the emergence of the Arab nationalism of the times. Many other Arab writers both Christian (like Zaidan) and Muslim promoted similar political and social values, but Zaidan was one of the movement's leaders. His multivolume works on Arab literature and Islamic civilization as well as his monographs on history and language testify to his scholarly endeavors in all these areas. He was especially concerned about spreading education to as many people as possible—as his efforts to establish a simplified, modern form of standard written Arabic show. This concern led him to the innovative idea of writing historical novels in simple prose to inform and educate the public about Arab and Islamic civilization. He founded the monthly magazine *al-Hilal* in 1892, which has been published without interruption to this day. *Al-Hilal* remains a treasure trove for the student of intellectual and social history of the time and is a source of much of the material for this book.

Zaidan may be best remembered today as one of the pioneers in the composition of historical novels within the modern Arabic literary tradition and in their serialization in magazines. The twenty-one historical novels he wrote are popular to this day. They were regularly reprinted every decade or so since they were first serialized. To date more than one hundred translations of his novels into twelve languages were made—and many were translated into several languages. The novels cover an extensive period of Arab history, from the rise of Islam in the seventh century until the decline of the Ottoman Empire in the nineteenth. The particular manners, lifestyles, beliefs, and social mores of those periods, as well as political events, provided the context within which Zaidan wove adventure and romance, deception and excitement. They were therefore as much "historical" as "novels," reminiscent of the historical novels of Alexandre Dumas in France and Sir Walter Scott in Britain, though Jurji Zaidan's novels more closely reflect actual historical events and developments.

About This Book

The central theme of this book is to demonstrate how Jurji Zaidan's secular analysis of history and language influenced the evolution of his pan-Arab nationalist thought. It traces the manifold relationships linking Zaidan's thinking as a historian and linguist and his views on Arab nationalism. The seminal contribution of this work is that it is the first to analyze Zaidan's thought on history, language, and nationalism as an integrated whole.

The volume consists of three parts. The first and main part consists of an essay that demonstrates Jurji Zaidan's secular approach to the analysis of Arab and Islamic history and the evolution of language, especially the Arabic language. It goes on to assess how this approach influenced the secular pan-Arab nationalism that Zaidan spearheaded, which was the defining characteristic of the Nahda. The essay draws on articles published in *al-Hilal* between 1892 and 1914 as well as Zaidan's scholarly works. The second part consists of twenty-nine articles and excerpts from his scholarly works that were translated for this book. They were chosen for their relevance to the topics covered in the essay. The third section constitutes the first comprehensive bibliography of Jurji Zaidan's works, both in Arabic and all the languages into which his works have been translated over the past century, along with a compilation of works about Zaidan.

Heavily influenced by his exposure to science in general and evolution in particular during his sole year at university, Zaidan's writings make numerous references to natural laws, evolution, and other scientific principles. But with few exceptions Zaidan left it to the reader to determine how these laws specifically apply to social phenomena. There are, of course, basic differences between scientific laws, which can be tested and reduced to broad and simple axioms that are predictable and measurable, and social laws that are complex, imprecise, and neither general nor simple. But these differences should not obscure what scientific laws have in common with Zaidan's secular interpretations of social phenomena—namely that neither relies on metaphysical or divine explanations. In Zaidan's view, historical and linguistic changes resulted from human actions—either those of individuals or of groups motivated by a common interest. The notion that human actions were responsible for change according to rational explanations was similar to, and no less revolutionary than, moving from creationism to evolution. In both cases the influence of God—as creator, driving force, or provider of higher meaning to natural or human events—became limited. This was a world where man could influence his destiny more than ever before and where dynamic change therefore became desirable.

The modern world that Jurji Zaidan and his contemporaries in the Nahda were exposed to was characterized by orderly progress within a stable framework. Newtonian physics reflected a certain, predictable, and orderly world; the uncertainties of twentieth-century physics were yet to come. The theory of evolution and the survival of the fittest were applied to social phenomena by social Darwinists who believed that things were being perfected in response to a changing environment. In the international arena the Western model of political and economic development with its liberal values provided the best model for the developing world to emulate in order to become part of the civilized world. There were no competing models of progress that the twentieth-century ideologies of communism and fascism would bring. With few exceptions, conservatives and progressives agreed on the need for modernization but differed on its pace and the need for compromise with traditional values. For the Arab intelligentsia of the times, certain progress toward Western ideals was in the air.

This was Jurji Zaidan's political, cultural, and scientific environment and it may explain both the revolutionary and the evolutionary aspects of his work. The secular approach to social phenomena—explaining change in purely human terms without divine intervention—was indeed revolutionary, even though Zaidan was always a theist who believed in the afterlife. His secular approach to history and language made Arab identity the predominant bond among Arab-speaking peoples, displacing both religion and regional nationalisms as the primary bonds. In this view Arabs needed to consider themselves as Arabs, first; and as Moslems, Christians, or Jews; or Egyptian, Syrian, Phoenician, or Ottoman; second. His secular pan-Arab nationalism was seen as a threat by religious purists, both Moslems and Christians. That is why when he was attacked—and attacked he was—the attacks were directed much more at the secularism of his approach than at the findings and conclusions of his works. Zaidan was also attacked by Egyptian nationalists, such as Mustafa Kamel who rejected Zaidan's pan-Arabism, notwithstanding their own secular outlook. Zaidan's analysis was revolutionary but the implications he drew were moderate and evolutionary—perhaps influenced by the gradualism he saw in the natural world as well as his nonconfrontational nature and his desire to promote peaceful change. Whatever the reasons, even though Jurji Zaidan's thought was revolutionary, he himself, like most of his contemporaries, argued forcefully in his writings for a measured and gradual approach to political and social change based on factual information and rational analysis.

This secular pan-Arab nationalism, spawned by the Nahda, evolved and thrived in the twentieth century. It prevailed as an ideology and legitimization for political power in the nation-states that came into being with the breakup of the Ottoman Empire. It then reached an apogee after World War II when it was adopted and strongly promoted by a number of military republican revolutionary regimes that rebelled against the Western liberal model that had been espoused by most Arab states in the early years of their independence. Its influence waned in the closing decades of the twentieth century when regional nationalisms reasserted themselves and especially and more recently when nonsecular Islamic fundamentalist forces increasingly challenged established authority.

Jurji Zaidan and The Zaidan Foundation—A Personal Note

Jurji Zaidan was my grandfather—a heritage that is a source of great honor as well as humility. He died many years before I was born. When I have been asked on more than one occasion if I knew him, I routinely answered "no" without giving the question further thought. However, one surprising and unintended consequence of the present work was to discover how much I really did know him after all. His beliefs and values were passed on to me through his two sons—my father Choucri and my Uncle Emile, sometimes quoting him directly, but more often not. I recall on so many occasions my father arguing strongly for the existence of the Hereafter and God: he did not refer to his father but he could have been reading from some of his articles translated for this volume! One of my Uncle Emile's favorite sayings was, "In the end truth always prevails." This saying was even inscribed on his desk—but it never occurred to me that it was also the title of one of the articles translated in this book! It forcefully conveyed my grandfather's business ethic, which was reinforced by attributes of objectivity—balance, perspective, good judgment, and never letting one's own personal considerations influence what was or was not published. All this, in addition to his hard work and erudition, did much to explain his success in so many different fields.

For a variety of reasons, the United States became my adopted country. Though my professional life did not touch on either literature or journalism, I decided after my retirement to establish the Zaidan Foundation with the mission of enhancing intercultural understanding in general and between the Western and Arabo-Islamic cultures in particular.

Whether we are in the midst of something as dramatic as a "clash of civilizations" is debatable. What is not is that many of the misunderstandings between the Western and Arab and Islamic worlds often begin and are greatly magnified by the limited, or erroneous, knowledge that each culture has about the other. To this end the Foundation's first program is the international dissemination of the secular and progressive view of the Arab and Islamic heritage through the study and translation of the works of Jurji Zaidan. This is particularly timely and has a distinctly modern flavor more than a century after these views were being developed. And it is a fitting tribute to Zaidan's legacy that new studies and translations are being published around the hundredth anniversary of his death.

More specifically, the Zaidan Foundation is supporting the following projects:

1. One writer aptly described Jurji Zaidan as being "many men within one man": not only a historian and linguist but also a historical novelist, an educator, a proponent for strengthening the role of women, a journalist, a publisher, and a successful businessman. The current work is designed to spark debate on these themes, which the Foundation is happy to sponsor and invite other scholars to pursue. This initial work should encourage a broadening of studies on Zaidan's works into areas that go beyond history and language to cover his contributions in the social areas—education, the role of women, his political views, his assessment as a historical novelist, and the like. A recent Symposium on Jurji Zaidan's Contributions to Modern Arab Thought and Literature, which was sponsored by the Library of Congress and the Zaidan Foundation, is a first step in this direction.[1]

2. The Foundation has so far sponsored the translation of five of Zaidan's twenty-one historical novels into English by translators who are all eminent literary scholars in their own right. In the hundred years since they were written almost all these novels were translated into one or more languages—there were more than one hundred translations but surprisingly none of the novels was translated into English. Of the five novels two are set in Spain, two others are set during the 'Abbasid period, and the fifth novel deals with Saladin.[2]

Acknowledgments and Thanks

The Zaidan Foundation was fortunate to have Professor Thomas Philipp, a leading expert on the life and thought of Jurji Zaidan, undertake this work. He continues to write on the development of Arab thought in the nineteenth and early twentieth centuries and has an abiding interest in the economic, social, and intellectual history of the Eastern Arab provinces during Ottoman rule. His doctoral thesis was published in 1979 as *Gurgi Zaidan: His Life and Thought.* He has written a history of the Syrian emigration to Egypt between 1725 and 1975 and also an economic and political history of the city of Acre between 1730 and 1831. He organized and edited the proceedings of three international conferences in Erlangen on the history of Greater Syria during Ottoman times. Most recently we coedited the Proceedings of a Symposium held at the Library of Congress in June 2012, *Jurji Zaidan's Contributions to Modern Arab Thought and Literature,* published by the Zaidan Foundation. He has taught at universities in the Middle East and the United States of America. Thomas Philipp held the position of Professor of Politics and Modern History of the Middle East at the Friedrich-Alexander Universität, Erlangen until his retirement in 2008.[3]

The Foundation was also fortunate to have two noted scholars, Professors Hilary Kilpatrick and Paul Starkey, translate the *al-Hilal* articles and the other selected writings of Jurji Zaidan. Dr. Hilary Kilpatrick lives and teaches in Lausanne; she has published on modern and classical Arabic literature and is currently researching Arabic literature in the early Ottoman period. She is the translator of Ghassan Khanafani's *Men in the Sun* (Boulder, CO: Lynne Reinner, 1999). Professor Paul Starkey was the Head of the Arabic Department at Durham University, UK, until his retirement in 2012. He is the author of several books on Arabic literature, most notably *Modern Arabic Literature* (Edinburgh: Edinburgh University Press, 2006), and has translated many Arab literary works, most recently a historical novel by Jurji Zaidan, *Saladin and the Assassins* (Bethesda, MD: Zaidan Foundation, 2013).

While the Foundation is happy to sponsor various studies on Zaidan it does not necessarily endorse all the findings or conclusions of those works and invites others to pursue the analysis and interpretation of Jurji Zaidan's multifaceted contributions.

1. *Jurji Zaidan (1861–1914).*

Many persons too numerous to mention have helped in various aspects of the Zaidan Foundation's work from its original inception to advising on its program and reviewing its products. Foremost among these are Ambassador Hussein A. Hassouna, until recently the ambassador of the Arab League to Washington, DC; Ambassador Clovis F. Maksoud, Professor of International Relations and Director of the Center of the Global South at American University; and Edmond Asfour and Bassem Abdallah—all members of the Foundation's Advisory Council.

2. Jurji Zaidan with his family circa 1908. From left to right: wife Maryam, daughter Asma, son Emile, and Jurji holding in his lap his youngest son Choucri (Shukri).

Professor Thomas Philipp was instrumental in helping launch the Jurji Zaidan project following a fortuitous meeting after several decades. Last but not least my greatest debt is to my wife Hada Zaidan and our son George Zaidan Jr. for their support of all aspects of this project. Indeed, the original idea of the Jurji Zaidan program came from Hada, who had more than a marital interest in this project as her grandfather, Jabr Dumit, was one of Jurji Zaidan's closest friends. In addition to their general and unstinting support, both she and George Jr. aided in the design of the program and made detailed reviews and many suggestions on the projects sponsored by the Foundation.

George C. Zaidan
President
The Zaidan Foundation
Bethesda, Maryland

Notes

1. The Zaidan Foundation published the Proceedings of this Symposium, held in June 2012 at the Library of Congress, in a volume titled *Jurji Zaidan's Contributions to Modern Arab Thought and Literature,* which was edited by George C. Zaidan and Thomas Philipp (Bethesda, MD: Zaidan Foundation, 2013). It is available at amazon.com. More information about the Zaidan Foundation and its activities can be found on the Foundation's website at *www.zaidanfoundation.org.*

2. The following lists these five translated novels in historical chronological order, which were published by the Zaidan Foundation and are available at *www.amazon.com*:

The Conquest of Andalusia, translated by Roger Allen. Bethesda, MD: Zaidan Foundation, 2011.

The Battle of Poitier: Charles Martel and Abd al-Rahman, translated by William Granara. Bethesda, MD: Zaidan Foundation, 2012.

The Caliph's Sister: Harun al-Rashid and the Fall of the Persians, translated by Issa J. Boullata. Bethesda, MD: Zaidan Foundation, 2012.

The Caliph's Heirs: Brothers at War: The Fall of Baghdad, translated by Michael Cooperson. Bethesda, MD: Zaidan Foundation, 2012.

Saladin and the Assassins, translated by Paul Starkey. Bethesda, MD: Zaidan Foundation, 2012.

3. *Ǧurǧī Zaidān: His Life and Thought,* Beiruter Texte u. Studien 3 (Beirut: F. Steiner, 1979). References to other works written or edited by Thomas Philipp mentioned in this paragraph are given in the Bibliography of Sources Quoted in This Book.

◆ ◆ ◆

Preface

To revisit after almost four decades one's earliest attempts at scholarly work and research is a unique opportunity. The result is, of course, a mixed one. Some insights still seem to stand, and parts of those have been included in this essay. Scholarship on the Middle East, however, has developed substantially, as has our knowledge. The theory of nationalism has received fresh impulses from new questions and innovative research. This has certainly made it possible to analyze Zaidan's nationalist thought in greater depth. Rereading my own earlier study and Jurji Zaidan's work, I have realized that nationalism per se was not as central to his work as I had thought earlier. However, I found that the disengagement of Arab history from Islamic history through using evolutionary theory for a secular analysis was the innovative achievement of Zaidan's work. Applying such secular analysis not only to the history but also to the language and culture of the Arab people led almost by necessity to the reconstruction of an Arab cultural history, an Arab identity, and the idea of Arabism.

The shift from an Islamic history, in which the Arabs play a certain role in the manifestation of the divine will, to an Arab history, in which Islam constitutes one of several Arab civilizational phases, occurring before and after Islam, is the focus of this volume. Since nothing of Zaidan's scholarly work has—with one exception—ever been translated into a Western language, it was decided early on to include translations of relevant essays or passages of Zaidan's writings in order to familiarize the reader with Zaidan's own texts and to illustrate the arguments and interpretations made in the essay. The translations were chosen with care as representative of Zaidan's thought on specific subjects. The reader is seriously invited to refer to the relevant translations while reading the essay.

This is not to say that the texts are representative of all of Zaidan's thought. They only illuminate the topics of history and language in the context I spoke of above. In fact, a great number of topics are not included, such as Zaidan's sociological thought; his political ideas; his support of the emancipation of women; and his enormous role in the development of modern Arabic literature, especially the development of the Arabic novel. Their omission does not imply that they are not important but only that there are physical limits to a book. The hope for this study is that it will further the interest in Zaidan's work and will lead to more studies on a whole range of other topics.

Innovative concepts, novel questions, and the passage of time can open different approaches to research, enabling scholars to gain new insights from the same materials. I am indebted to Dr. George C. Zaidan and the Zaidan Foundation for providing me with the opportunity to immerse myself anew in the subject, which I thought I had left behind a generation ago. For the pleasure of this experience and for our fruitful cooperation I would like to thank George Zaidan.

Special thanks go to Professor Jens Hanssen for reading through the whole manuscript, offering constructive criticism, and sharing generously his own thoughts on the subject with me. I think back with much pleasure to our conversations—long-distance and personal—during the two last years. I would also like to thank Professor Anne-Laure Dupont for reading the manuscript. She herself has written a brilliant study on Jurji Zaidan, and I thank her for catching a number of factual errors. I am also obliged to the two anonymous readers for pointing out flaws and raising pertinent questions. Mary Starkey did a marvelous proofreading job. My thanks go to her and all those who helped edit the text. Needless to emphasize, any remaining mistakes are mine.

Last but not least it is difficult to express the full measure of my gratitude toward my wife, Mangol Bayat. She encouraged me to join this venture and with much patience and love kept me going through some difficult times.

Thomas Philipp

A note on transliteration in this work: To make the reading less cumbersome, Arabic book and journal titles as well as proper nouns and names have been rendered in the English text of the essay, the footnotes, and the translated articles in a simplified form of transliteration. However, Arabic technical terms and those expressing particular concepts have been rendered in full transliteration. Arabic book titles, quotations, and also names appear in full transliteration in the footnotes and bibliographies. The transliteration follows the rules suggested by the *International Journal of Middle Eastern Studies* with one exception: the silent alif in the article *al-* is shown by a straight single quotation mark thus ['] and not by a dash.

Jurji Zaidan
and the Foundations of Arab Nationalism

PART ONE

◆ ◆ ◆

Jurji Zaidan's Secular Analysis of History and Language as a Foundation of Arab Nationalism

Thomas Philipp

I

◆ ◆ ◆

Introduction

Jurji Zaidan was one of the great pioneers of the Nahda Movement. As a scholar and scientist he was a relentless promoter of new ideas, concepts, and knowledge; he considered it his mission to enlighten and educate society. Zaidan was also a creative interpreter of language and an innovative historian. He was one of the first and certainly among the most important and prolific authors to write historical novels and serialize them. A self-made man, he was also an entrepreneur and a businessman. As a member of the bourgeoisie, Zaidan was well accepted and respected in modern Cairene society, and nothing would have been further from his mind than the thought of radical or violent revolutionary change. Yet his radical new thought, which he so successfully spread through his innovative journal *al-Hilal*,[1] his novels, and his scholarly works, contributed in essential ways to the transformation of Arab society.

Today Zaidan is mainly remembered in the Arab world for his historical novels. Several generations of Arabs were introduced to their own history through these novels, and even to this day, over a hundred years after their initial publication, they are periodically reprinted. However, by contrast, Zaidan's scholarly works on Arab history, the Arabic language, and Arab literature, as well as his reflections on society, are hardly acknowledged today.[2] In Anglo-European scholarship on the modern Middle East, Zaidan is practically unknown and his contribution to the articulation of Arab nationalism is hardly perceived, although recently a new interest in his novels can be observed in the field of comparative literature. Various reasons can be given for this situation, and we will discuss some of them later. But certainly the most important one is to be found in the historiography of Arab nationalism or, to be precise, in its two narratives, the English and the Arabic.

The English narrative of Arab nationalism was for a long time determined by George Antonius's book on the subject.[3] Antonius himself was the child of Syrian immigrants in Egypt. He later took employment with the British Mandate's authorities in Palestine and became a prominent member of the Arab Palestinian movement.[4] In his book, he located the origins of Arab nationalism in Syria—and especially in Beirut—among Christian Arabs educated by the missionaries. But according to Antonius, they learned many languages and lost touch with Arabic; hence, they lost their interest in Arab nationalism. The decisive moment for this development, Antonius said, was the switch from Arabic to English as the language of instruction at the Syrian Protestant College. The education of Muslim Arabs was much poorer than what was offered in the missionary schools, but it was in Arabic. In this way, according to Antonius, the Muslim Arabs became the torchbearers of Arab nationalism against the 'Abdülhamidian tyranny. From here Antonius continued directly to individuals such as Kawakibi[5] as among the torchbearers.[6] The whole structure of his narrative later focuses on political events during and after World War I in geographical Syria, where he worked, was politically engaged, and, presumably, had access to documents. Clearly Egypt did not belong to this narrative, including by implication everything that happened in Egypt—for instance the whole Arab Nahda Movement that was developed and promoted predominantly by the Syrian immigrants in Egypt. Zaidan, of whom and of whose work Antonius certainly must have been aware, is not even mentioned in the index of his book. One generation later Sylvia Haim also failed to mention Zaidan or include him in her anthology, which was published in 1962 and republished in 1976.[7] Yet she was by 1954 very critical of Antonius as a historian.[8]

Also in 1962, Albert Hourani published his seminal work, but he made only a fleeting reference to the role of the journals *al-Muqtataf* and *al-Hilal*. He remarked somewhat later: "But perhaps it was Jurji Zaidan who did more than any other to create a consciousness of the Arab past."[9] Cleveland observed in 1971: "In conjunction with al-Husri's contributions, Constantine Zurayq's *The National Consciousness*[10] and Ali Nasir al-Din's

The Arab Question[11] are generally recognized as the outstanding initial [*sic*] attempts to introduce the basic concepts of nationalism and unity to the Arabs."[12] Note here that there is not a word about Zaqi al-Arsuzi,[13] Antun Sa'adeh,[14] or Michel 'Aflaq,[15] national thinkers and contemporaries of al-Husri; nor is there any mention of their predecessor Jurji Zaidan.

In the late 1970s monographs about persons as well as intellectual history became unpopular in historiography.[16] Class analysis and structuralism were the new approaches. Ernest Dawn demonstrated how such approaches could be used with excellent results.[17] His work dealt mainly with Arab ruling elites before and after the collapse of the Ottoman Empire, and it did not show much interest in the intellectuals and ideologues of Arab nationalism. In 1991 a book appeared that looked specifically at the beginnings of Arab nationalism. But it, too, continued what had by now become a tradition: Zaidan's name cannot even be found in the index, his works are not mentioned in the general bibliography on primary sources, and there is no mention of him in the footnotes of any article.[18] This tradition was continued in 2003 by Yasir Suleiman.[19] He deals summarily with the period before World War I and chooses, of all people, Ibrahim al-Yaziji as an example for the development of language, although al-Yaziji[20] was highly critical of the language simplifications made by the Nahdawis. Suleiman then moves to Sati' al-Husri as the "most important exponent of the ideology of Arab nationalism"[21] and deals with his approach to Arabic.

The Arabic version of the narrative of Arab nationalism is quickly summarized—and Cleveland was its first victim by taking Sati' al-Husri too much at face value. Al-Husri liked to quote German Romantic and nationalist thinkers of the early nineteenth century such as Johann G. Fichte, Friedrich E. D. Schleiermacher, and Ernst M. Arndt. By the time al-Husri became a proponent and spokesman of Arab rather than Turkish nationalism, some twenty-five volumes of Zaidan's journal *al-Hilal* along with his scholarly works were readily available to him. But he never discussed particular positions of Zaidan or even mentioned him in his work, though there were many themes of common interest he shared with Zaidan, such as the role of the Arab language and the reinterpretation of the *Jahiliyya*.[22] This is especially peculiar since we can assume that al-Husri was familiar with the works of Zaidan, even if only through reading *al-Hilal*. But al-Husri does not mention his contemporary Zaqi al-Arsuzi either, and the latter returns the favor.[23] Al-Arsuzi, when discussing the importance of the Arabic language in Arab nationalism, referred frequently to his professor at the Sorbonne, Henri Bergson, but never to Zaidan. Antun Saadeh and, to my knowledge, Michel 'Aflaq also never referred to the works of Zaidan. These writers' motives in not mentioning Zaidan in their works might differ: for example, Antonius simply was not interested in the Arab Nahda beyond certain—limited—aspects of it in Beirut. Others apparently felt that deriving arguments for Arab nationalism from European thinkers would invest them with more legitimacy than quoting other Arab intellectuals.

The present volume is an attempt to rectify the neglect of Zaidan's scholarly work and to evaluate his intellectual contribution to the "Arab Awakening."[24] On the surface he is today vaguely known as a thinker on Arabism and a promoter of Arab nationalism. Though this observation is not false, his real intellectual contribution lay in the way he came to view and promote Arabism. The theme of this study is to show how Zaidan replaced a religious model of explanation for historical change with a secular one borrowed from the modern natural sciences, in particular the theory of evolution. Zaidan was able thereby to separate Arab history and the Arabic language from Islamic history or, to be more precise, to transform the latter into one phase of Arab history, which, in his view, stretched from antiquity until his own days. The influence of the Enlightenment's vision of man as a thinking, responsible individual guided by reason and even more by the natural sciences and the theory of evolution led him to a secularized analysis of history and culture. A radically secular view lay at the root of Zaidan's nationalism and his vision of the development of Arab society. His analyses of Arab history and literature provided an Arab identity that in turn constituted the basis for Arab nationalism.

Since the French Revolution, nationalism was a driving power to restructure empires, tribes, ethnicities, and enlightened absolutist states into modern nation-states. The basic idea of nationalism is as simple and attractive as it is historically highly questionable: "The doctrine holds that humanity is naturally divided into nations, that nations are known by certain characteristics which can be ascertained, and that the only legitimate type of government is national self-government."[25] It should be added that one of this doctrine's most important characteristics was the assumption that every such nation lived exclusively in a well-circumscribed, contiguous territory with inhabitants that spoke the same language. Much ink and more blood were spilled over the next two hundred years to make this doctrine a physical and historical reality.

Historically, there existed two principal ways of establishing a nation-state. In the first case a centralized sovereign state already existed with its own infrastructure and defined borders and an "official"—that is, administrative—language. An absolute monarch was deposed by a class or group, with the claim of the right of the people to self-government. It was the task of intellectuals before and after the revolution to establish the fact that subjects indeed constituted one nation and that its members were citizens with inalienable rights. Given the territorial circumscription of the state and its centralized organization, this was not so difficult. The real task of the new political elite was to convert the existing institutions of the state into forms that would enable self-government and political participation by the citizen. France is the obvious example for this case, even though it would take a full century after the Revolution for Parisian French to become firmly established as the official language, while the true separation of state and church came only at the beginning of the twentieth century. In the Middle East, Egypt under Muhammad 'Ali,[26] until the 'Urabi Rebellion in 1882, was the perfect example of this case. His state was very comparable to states of Enlightened Absolutism in Europe. He established a centralized administration; Arabic gradually became the official language and Cairo was the seat of power. The borders of Egypt also were definitively established, albeit much against the will of Muhammad 'Ali, when the European powers forced Egypt out of Syria in 1840. In the years after Muhammad 'Ali's rule the army became increasingly Egyptianized and the first Egyptians entered the officer corps. One of them was 'Urabi, who, in alliance with key members of the recently established parliament, tried to reduce the powers of the ruler. The rebellion of 1882 led to the British occupation and ended the first attempt to establish a measure of self-rule.

In the second case there is no centralized sovereign state that can easily form a nation-state. Here the task of the intellectual and the national ideologue was to establish a consciousness among a certain population—not defined territorially by political borders. That population would acquire a national identity that eventually would enable it to stake out a territory on which to build a nation-state. Here the emphasis must be much more on common origins, culture, language, and history precisely because a state that coincided with the spread of the population as a structural frame is missing. In this case a much larger value is attached to the emotional unity of the nation than to the rights of the individual and the participatory structure of power. The borders of the territory to be converted into a nation-state are typically fairly vague. In Europe, the first example was Germany, which because of its strategic position in central Europe and the vagaries of history never had formed a single centralized state. The German national movement was consequently characterized by its preoccupation with language and German history, real or imagined, and a heavy emphasis on the emotional unity of the people.

In the Middle East the relevant example is, of course, Bilad al-Sham[27] or, as it was increasingly called in the second half of the century, "Syria." Though geographically a relatively well-defined territory, this entity had never coincided with a single political entity in its long history. The region had always been either part of a larger empire because of its geostrategic importance or had been split into a number of mini-states, often playing proxy for one or the other neighboring empire. Hence the uncertainty in the early Arab nationalist movement about whether "Syria" referred to all the Arab lands, to Bilad al-Sham, or perhaps only to Lebanon. This uncertainty, however was counterbalanced by the construction of a national Arab history, stretching from Hammurabi to modern civilization, and the successful creation of a profoundly reformed modern Arab print language understood by all literate Arabic speakers.

This short and somewhat schematic sketch of the course of national movements is not designed to create the impression that national movements were neat affairs with clear-cut results. Too many other factors, such as internal power struggles and international relations, interfered with such a linear development. For the doctrine of nationalism to have any semblance of realism required that nations and their territories be made to coincide. This happened more in the twentieth century than in the nineteenth with mass migrations, expulsions, deportations, and ethnic cleansing of whole population groups. Sometimes formal administrative actions were taken, such as the transfer of populations between Turkey and Greece in 1923. The results were always the same: many lost lives and massive streams of refugees in both the Middle East and Europe.

The point I want to make with this sketch is to clarify the link between national ideology and national political action. The doctrine of nationalism was such a radical break with past experiences that it needed the work of scholars and ideologues to construct secular histories and national languages, to legitimize national movements, to create a new national identity, and to claim a specific territory as their own. To be effective, every national program and political action needed the work of scholars and ideologues.

Other aspects of Zaidan's work, such as the development of his political thought after the Young Turk Revolution, his position on gender issues, or his literary work (the historical novels), have been largely left out of this essay. The reason for this is not that secularization did not touch them (it did) but rather due to the mundane limits of space. One of the purposes of this study is to familiarize the English reader with Zaidan's own writings that are pertinent to the issues dealt with in the essay. Considering the enormous scope and output of his writings, those that will be discussed here can only be a very small, but hopefully representative, selection of the topics he covered and of his thought. It is hoped that additional studies will deal with other aspects of Zaidan's work and will help to define and establish even more the role he played in modern Arab thought and the impact the Nahda had upon him.

The term "Nahda" comes from the Arabic root *n-h-ḍ*, which means "a single act of rising, a motion or movement . . . also power, ability, strength."[28] In 1870 the term lacked any particular abstract meaning or connotation of a specific historical event.[29] When in 1868 al-Yaziji addressed his famous ode to the Arabs, "Arise Ye Arabs and Awake," he did not use the term.[30] During the following twenty years, however, the term with this specific connotation must have become accepted. In 1888 *al-Muqtataf* used the term in connection with the contemporary development of Arab medicine.[31] In 1892 an article by Zaidan titled "The Latest Egyptian Nahda" appeared in the first volume of his magazine *al-Hilal*.[32] Neither in 1888 nor in 1892 is the term explained, which implies that readers were by then familiar with it.

The term *al-Nahḥa* is most often translated as "Renaissance" or "Arab Renaissance," just as the European Renaissance is translated in Arabic as *al-nahḍa al-urubbiyya*. To speak of the Nahda as a Renaissance suggests a European frame of history as a reference and as a normative standard of historical development. Such terminology, ironically, has always implied a European denial of historical development in Arab society or, for that matter, in the entire non-European world. The "normative" sequence of Renaissance, Humanism, Reformation, Revolution, and so on could not be recognized in non-European histories. Therefore Europeans considered only their own historical sequence to represent valid phases of progress. This denial of historical progress led in the worst case to a racist sense of European superiority and in its most benign version to the claim these historical phases had taken centuries to develop in Europe and would take as long in the non-European world. Following the assumed normative character of European historical development was expected as a development that each culture had to experience on its own. If the European experience was not available to them, historical maturity of these cultures would be pushed into an uncertain future.

The Arab Nahda—henceforth I shall use the Arabic term—is also often described as a movement of renewal and innovation in Arabic literature.[33] This is true; but it was much more than that. It referred to, reproduced, and analyzed in the widest sense all aspects of modernity as it was developing in Europe and America—in contrast to the European Renaissance, which referred to a classical period of the past. But it would be wrong to reduce the Nahda to a mere "translation movement" and a copying of the concepts and ideas of modernity. In the process of translating, summarizing, or adapting texts into Arabic, the works were analyzed, criticized, and put into a relevant Arab societal context. More than that, they were publicly debated by the newly introduced literary genre of periodicals, which created a new educated and politically savvy public.[34]

The antecedents of the Arab Nahda can be traced to the first half of the nineteenth century in Egypt and Syria, and possibly to the eighteenth century in the latter region. Al-Jayyusi identifies Aleppo as the first center of a classicist revival of Arabic, where Christians attended classes with Muslim shaykhs. She claims that in Syria—in contrast to Egypt, where education was monopolized by al-Azhar—clerks and secretaries, too, played a role in poetry and *belles-lettres*.[35] In the first generation she includes Jirmanus Farhat (1670–1732), a Maronite patriarch, lexicographer, grammarian, and poet, "first of the arabized Syrians [Christians] to achieve classical purity and style." He studied in Aleppo with Christian and Muslim scholars.[36] In 1789 a Maronite priests' seminary was established in 'Ayn Waraka, Mount Lebanon, where the language of instruction was Arabic. Some participants in this early Nahda, like Butrus al-Bustani and Ahmad Faris al-Shidyaq, received their first training at the new seminary, though they never entered the priesthood.[37]

Immediate precursors, which then overlapped with the Nahda, strictly speaking, were a group in Mount Lebanon consisting of Butrus al-Bustani,[38] Ahmad Faris al-Shidyaq,[39] and Nasif al-Yaziji;[40] and in Egypt, 'Abdallah Nadim.[41] They all came from educated families and were trained in Arabic language and literature, in contrast to the later Nahdawis, who often had hardly any formal education, like Zaidan himself.[42] Their concern was the perceived decay of the Arab language, and they attempted a revival of the classical language. Composing dictionaries of the Arabic language (al-Bustani) or grammars (al-Shidyaq), reviving classical forms of Arabic literature such as the rhymed rhythmic prose of the *maqāma* (Nadim and al-Yaziji)—all were attempts to preserve the classical forms of language and literature. One could speak of an early Nahda, feeding on a neoclassicist revival. Though, without a doubt, those who had participated in one or the other form in the Bible translation projects[43] were aware of and had to acknowledge the need for a simplified language to address a wider and often uneducated public. The issue arose not only with the composition of simple textbooks for schools but also with the publication of a new genre of literature in Arabic, the journal, to which most Nahdawis contributed in one way or another. Clarity of style and readability became another issue for the early participants of the Nahda.

The difference between the early Nahda, or neoclassicist revival, and the later Nahda Movement is perhaps best explained in terms of their aims for the Arabic language. The former wanted to revive classical forms of literature, and the elaborate classical style of writing was meant to express learnedness or poetic refinement. The later Nahda Movement saw its main goal as the simplification of the written language to make it also accessible to the poorly educated reader. In time these two tendencies overlapped considerably. Even the aforementioned Bible translation project raised the issue of stylistic simplicity. Ahmad Faris al-Shidyaq, for instance, was much more innovative than other classicists: he adopted a highly elaborate and decorative style. Its exaggerated use of synonyms led Zaidan to claim that it "made our educated people shy away from him."[44] Zaidan was a relentless protagonist of a simple and clear style, which should explain content to the reader rather than impress him with the learnedness of the author. But as late as 1910 Ibrahim al-Yaziji wrote a long essay against what he considered to be the faulty use of Arabic in newspapers.[45] This was a direct attack on the lack of formal training in Arabic literature of the members of the later Nahda Movement.

New research is elaborating the point of how far the representatives of the early Nahda distinguished themselves from the subsequent Nahda not only by their formal education in the Arabic language and literature but also in holding onto their interest in aesthetics, drawn from the classical literature and their search for harmony in nature. This contrasted sharply with the haphazard educational experience of the Nahdawis, their orientation toward modern civilization coming from Europe, and a profound concern with the marketability of their print product to new classes of readers.[46]

Even the early Nahdawis, who studied in the priests' seminary 'Ayn Waraka, such as Butrus al-Bustani and Ahmad Faris Shidyaq, would not pursue theological studies or careers as priests. Hardly any converted to Protestantism. Most often the Nahdawis were instead attracted to the Freemasons. They believed in the Enlightenment and relied on rational thought, took an interest in the modern sciences, and discussed theories explaining the phenomena of nature. They had no vested interest in the classical Arabic language or literature, either emotional or intellectual. As Zaidan observed in his autobiography:

> At that time, i.e., after the unrest of the sixties, there developed a third class amongst the people of Beirut [in addition to the elite and the masses] educated in the Christian missionary schools. . . . This third social group was determined to change the social norms from what they were to what they became, so that the contemporary morals of Beirut became comparable with the most advanced habits and customs of the Europeans.[47]

And, we might add, they also changed the meaning and content of education.

Zaidan had discussed various aspects of the Nahda ever since 1892, when he first published his journal *al-Hilal*. He was the first to make the Nahda a topic of his historical studies.[48] He believed that the movement had started in Egypt under Muhammad 'Ali, who wanted to reform his army and most other aspects of society. It is with Muhammad 'Ali's rise to power that Zaidan dated the end of Ottoman Egypt and the beginning of the modern history of Egypt. In the Egyptian context he recognized Rif'at al-Tahtawi[49] as one of the pioneers of this Nahda. At the same time, though, he also mentioned the Syrian contemporaries of al-Tahtawi—Butrus al-Bustani, Nasif al-Yaziji, and Ahmad Faris al-Shidyaq—as being part of the Nahda Movement. In his opinion the Nahda came into its own in Syria only after sectarian unrest in 1860.

The Nahda started to gain its own momentum after the unrest in Mount Lebanon in the 1840s and 1850s, and especially after the large sectarian unrest in 1860 in Damascus and the Syrian hinterland. Eventually its center shifted from Beirut to Cairo in the early 1880s, where it flourished for another generation. Several reasons can account for this shift: the missionary schools of the Americans in Lebanon provided more young men (and some young women) with a modern education than the region could absorb; the Syrian Protestant College, which was the focal point of this new intelligentsia, switched in 1882 from Arabic to English as a teaching language; censorship under Sultan 'Abdülhamid II became more repressive; and, at the same time in Egypt under British control, the cotton-driven economy stabilized and expanded and job opportunities for people with modern skills increased. It also helped that Lord Cromer, Britain's consul in Egypt and its de facto ruler, was apparently of the opinion that in a population with a 90 percent illiteracy rate, journalists and other indigenous writers were not dangerous and were therefore not worth the trouble of censoring.

The development of a secular educated class, the intelligentsia, constituted a clear departure from traditional society. Its members were no political radicals—they never clamored for the overthrow of the Ottoman Empire, and even the voices against the British occupation were few and far between. The vision of most was for a very gradual change of society that they themselves were called upon to guide. However, the ideas, concepts, and worldviews that they so successfully introduced and established were of an explosive character, questioning and challenging just about everything that had characterized and distinguished premodern society. From the sources of the legitimacy of political power to systems of education, the structure of society, and the concepts of knowledge and science—every aspect of premodern society was questioned.

The transitions between premodern and modern society differ according to time and place, leading to endless debates. In a global sense a decisive transition is one that proceeds from a worldview determined by a metaphysical teleology to one in which the belief of progress in this world grows out of the assumption that man is capable of rational action to improve his lot and that of society, as well as an understanding of and reliance on the power of the laws of nature. Marxism in Christian society and Zionism in Jewish society are typical examples of shifting salvation from a metaphysical place to one on earth. All national movements, claiming the right to sovereignty and self-rule, reflect this transfer. The Enlightenment and the French Revolution may be considered as the beginnings of this transition. In the Middle East the first formal step in this direction was taken in 1839 with the Hatt-i Humayun of Gülhane, the document that initiated the first Tanzimat period in the Ottoman Empire and promised among other things the equality of all subjects before the law, regardless of religion. In the Arab world it was the later Nahda Movement, starting in the middle of the nineteenth century, that created a mental earthquake felt throughout society. The Nahda was a revolutionary movement, the political results of which became evident during and after World War I.

Secularization has been and is a long-drawn-out process. Without necessarily going as far back as Harvey Cox, claiming that "the *disenchantment of nature* begins with Creation; the *desacralization of politics* with the Exodus,"[50] it is safe to say that secularization is a major defining characteristic of a modern society (perhaps even *the* defining characteristic). "Secularization is man turning his attention from worlds beyond and toward this world and this time (saeculum = this present age)," Cox says. Religion no longer provides the dominant interpretation of the events of this world. Even though, according to Cox, "the forces of secularization have no serious interest in persecuting religion . . . secularization simply bypasses and undercuts religion and goes on to other things. It has relativized religious world views and thus rendered them innocuous."[51] Differently formulated, secularization is the "assertion of autonomy of large aspects of life, for instance, politics, law, science, art, and customs vis-à-vis religion."[52] Secularization is the process of the disengagement of man's interpretation of this world from religion.

The dichotomy between the secular and the sacred has often been exaggerated. In all recognizable human history, as opposed to myth, the secular and the sacred existed next to each other and were intertwined. The separation of church and state existed, de facto, since the early Middle Ages in Europe. Despite the claim that Islam permeated all aspects of society and a separate church was therefore not needed, the state and its regions were typically centered around powerful, secular elites and not based on consensus of the Muslim community. Most often the representatives of religion were even dependent on the state run by secular elites, as only the latter could guarantee security. Yet, the overall perception of the world order, the interpretation of life and its meaning in this world, was shared by all as resting in a transcendental God who could at any moment show His immanence in this World, as had been the case with the Ten Commandments given on Mount Sinai or the revelations to the Prophet Muhammad.

Secularism goes far beyond the secular character of political power or of any incidental action by human beings, that is to say, action that has no sacred quality. Secularism also challenges directly the authority of the sacred to interpret the cosmic order, the order of society, and the life of the individual. Secularism thereby becomes an essential part of modernity, asserting legitimate autonomy of various aspects of human life and nature. Recently Talal Asad has contributed to the debate on the understanding of secularism. He observes in the Christian worldview an increasing separation of God from this world:

> But there is more at stake here than the immanence or transcendence of divinity in relation to the natural world. The idea of "nature" is itself internally transformed. For the representation of the Christian God as a being sited quite apart in "the supernatural" world signals the construction of a secular space that begins to emerge in early modernity. Such a space permits "nature" to be reconceived as manipulatable material, determinate, homogenous, and subject to mechanical laws. Anything beyond that space is therefore "supernatural"—a place for fanciful extension of the real world peopled by irrational events and imagined beings. This transformation had a significant effect on the meaning of myth.[53]

Beginning in the seventeenth century, during the scientific revolution, nature became the first major subject of scientific studies in the search for observable and testable laws in nature—hence the expression "natural sciences." Asad shifts from the preoccupation with studying nature, whose full development he locates in the eighteenth century, to the politics of secular liberalism in the nineteenth century, an ideology that was extremely influential in the Nahda Movement and, not surprisingly, is also reflected in Zaidan's thought. He ascertains that the central principles of liberalism rest on assumptions about the nature of mankind and of society, which are frequently questioned, such as the equality of all humans and the existence of certain rights within human nature.[54] With Canovan he points out that in the eighteenth century ideas of liberalism were attached to a distinctive conception of nature as deep reality. Subsequently in the nineteenth century, liberals invoked nature as a realm more real than the social world, an understanding that gave them grounds for optimism about political change. The terminology of natural rights referred not simply to what men (and later, women too) *should* have but to what they *did in fact* possess in the reality of human nature that lies beneath the distorted world as it now appears.[55]

He then poses the question of why the early liberal thinkers relied so much on nature as a point of reference. He assumes that in their thinking nature itself was a source of explanation and justification. But I would suggest that for most of the nineteenth century the modern scientific knowledge of nature and its laws was far more advanced than that of any of the social or human sciences. Hence it seemed that the natural sciences were by far more reliable as a source of reference of authoritative knowledge.

According to Asad the idea of human freedom and equality actually implied a counterworld—a mythical world—that provided freedom and equality, just because it was "natural" and without civilizational distortions.[56] Quoting Canovan he shows how the founding myth of secular liberalism about the nature of human beings is essential to legitimize secular liberalism as a project to be realized, rather than as a truth in need of discovery.[57] Expressed differently, the sacred and the secular remain interwoven because secular liberalism, too, relied on a myth for its legitimization. The secular and the sacred remained intertwined, as reflected in Fritz Stern's astute observation, speaking of imperial Germany, where he notes a process of "the secularization of religion and a sacralization of the throne."[58]

Asad believes that the new science of sociology, using the theory of evolution, provided evidence of a cruel and hierarchical nature. This weakened secular liberalism at the end of the nineteenth century was to be revived, according to Asad, only after World War II in its confrontation with fascism and communism. It seems, though, that secular liberalism had a longer lease on life if we look at the various constitutional revolutions in the Middle East and elsewhere before World War I. They were driven by the ideas of equality, freedom for all human beings, and democratic rule based on constitutionalism. The above-mentioned optimism found in nature could also be found in the theory of evolution or, more precisely, in a misunderstood yet very popular version of evolution. In this version, the concept of the survival of the fittest—meaning nothing more than what best fits an incidental mutation in the environment—was confused or replaced with the idea of the best, strongest, most virtuous, intelligent, and just values, which promised to raise society to higher levels of progress. This became the basis for an unshakeable faith in progress, which was only destroyed, for different reasons, in Europe as well as in the Middle East, during and after World War I.

Jurji Zaidan relied heavily, as we will see in what follows, on the laws of nature and, more specifically, on the laws of evolution as a point of reference and source of legitimization for the approach he developed to the history of culture, language, and even religion, albeit somewhat more discreetly for the latter. He was a firm believer in the idea of progress, which for him not only was possible but followed inevitably from the laws of evolution. At the same time, though, he had his doubts about human nature. These doubts became acute with the Constitutionalist movement, an expression of secular liberalism, which led to the Young Turk Revolution in 1908, of which he became an enthusiastic supporter. Asad articulates this ambivalence, which was felt not only by Zaidan but by most of his Nahda contemporaries and many thinkers in Europe:

> In fact liberal democracy . . . expresses the two secular myths that are, notoriously, at odds with each other: The Enlightenment myth of politics as a discourse of public reason whose bond with *knowledge* enables the elite to direct the education of mankind, and the revolutionary myth of universal suffrage. . . . The secular theory of state toleration is based on these contradictory foundations: on the one hand elite liberal clarity seeks to contain religious passion, on the other hand democratic numbers allow majorities to dominate minorities, even if both are religiously formed.[59]

This was precisely the greatest bone of contention for the supporters of the Young Turk Revolution in the multiethnic and multisectarian Ottoman Empire. For a long time they believed—somewhat naively—in the efficacy of the newly established constitution to overcome these contradictions. Kurzman elaborates the point somewhat differently:

> Positivist Liberalism faced a theoretical problem: . . . how to reconcile openly desired rule of the intellectuals with the often-proclaimed sovereignty of the people? The solution lay in the belief that an enlightened population would freely choose enlightened leaders. With proper

> education the voters would be able to identify and surely prefer the expounders of truth and progress, namely the intellectuals.[60]

In the "solution" Kurzman offers to the predicament, he touches upon the same issue as Asad, mentioning the "discourse of public reason." It is basically the "free space," which Habermas believes to be necessary for the public venting and exchange of ideas and the formulation of a workable degree of consensus. Here Asad raises an important question that troubled Zaidan and his contemporaries enormously: "If the performance of free speech is dependent on free listening, its effectiveness depends on the kind of listeners who can engage appropriately with what was said, as well as the time he or she has to live in."[61] We find repeatedly the question asked by Zaidan and other Nahdawis, implicitly and explicitly, namely whether the public they spoke to was prepared for the great changes the educated elite planned for society. Most often the answer was that more education of the masses was needed before they could participate in the political discourse. Sometimes, as in the case of Zaidan, it meant a somewhat hesitant return to the idea of a constitution limiting the ruler rather than granting political rights to the masses.

Jurji Zaidan was perhaps more willing than his counterparts in Europe to support the notion that liberal democracy and nationalism were related projects, that is to say, people had to be educated about these projects and trained so as to become effective participants in the political discourse. The colonized citizen already faced a European model with regard to the public space of politics. With his faith in progress—evolutionary or otherwise—he could believe that his own society would join this modern world in the foreseeable future. As a nationalist he was in need of his own history, as was his European counterpart, to legitimize his claim to a nation. The longing for an idealized past that would show the way into a utopian future was not part of the secular colonial citizen's liberal nationalism before World War I. Such longing was rather typical for European Romantic and conservative nationalists. In the Middle East its appearance was typically associated with religious fundamentalism. It was precisely the emancipation from religion-dominated worldviews that enabled Zaidan to construct a secular, national Arab history.

Unabashedly, Zaidan traced the historical origins of modernity to Europe as did the majority of the Nahdawis of the second generation. They felt they could fully adopt and participate in this European modernity and the progress it promised. Well before the British occupation of Egypt in 1882 there existed a tension in the thinking of the Nahdawis between the admiration for Europe and the fear of domination by European imperialism. But a global resentment against Europe was restricted to traditional religious scholars until World War I. Zaidan was fully aware of the profound changes this Nahda brought about. It shows how far he had gone in his lifetime of work to disengage Arab culture from Islamic history. For him it confirmed the ability of the Arab people to participate fully in a civilization (modern civilization) that was distinct from the Islamic one. To trace the mental path he took to reach this conclusion will be a major theme of the following essay.

II

◆ ◆ ◆

Jurji Zaidan

A Short Biography

There is a wealth of information on Zaidan's childhood and youth, perhaps more than for any other notable Arab personality before him.[62] We have information not only on his parents, education, and apprenticeships but also about his feelings, relationships, ambitions, and likes and dislikes. The major reason for this abundance of information is the fact that Zaidan is, as far as we know, the first Arab to write an autobiography in the modern meaning of the term. A "modern autobiography" is actually an oxymoron. Autobiographical information abounds in European and Islamic medieval literature, but it tends to occur in texts accidentally or implicitly. When it is presented as a coherent narrative, the focus is not on the narrator himself but, for instance, on the manifestation of God's will. In the classical Arabic literary genre of *ṭabaqāt,* bio-bibliographical dictionaries, the author often includes his own biography, *tarjama,* at the alphabetical or chronological place where it belongs. It generally follows the normative patterns of all the others in that particular work, and its purpose is to supply all the relevant information relevant for the purpose of the study. A late but typical example is to be found in 'Ali Pasha Mubarak's geographical work on Egypt, where his own biography appears under the entry "Birinbal," his own birthplace, simply to offer all the information worth knowing about the village.[63] The autobiography proper is a modern phenomenon, and it presupposes a radically new worldview that positions the self as a reasonable, responsible being at the center of events and in possession of his own history. A sense has to develop for what Franz Rosenthal calls the "awareness of the intrinsic value of the uniquely personal."[64] Or, as a more recent formulation states, "the curiosity of the individual about himself, the wonder he feels before the mystery of his own destiny, is thus tied up with the Copernican revolution."[65] Two formal characteristics of the autobiography follow from this self-awareness: the author, the narrator, and the main subject of the narrative are the same; and the structure of the narrative will almost always be chronological.[66]

A precursor of the autobiography in Arabic is *Muntakhabāt al-jawāb 'ala 'qtirāḥ al-aḥbāb* by Mikha'il Mishaqa,[67] a contemporary of 'Ali Pasha Mubarak. Mishaqa's own life is not the main topic of his book, but he does attempt to link the fate of his family and his own development in a meaningful causal relationship to the events of his time. When Zaidan wrote a full-fledged autobiography in 1908, he knew of Mishaqa and his work. Though Zaidan was a pioneer in the genre of autobiography, he hardly can be called the founder of autobiographical writing in Arabic. Selected parts of his autobiography were published in *al-Hilal* during 1954.[68] The full manuscript was not published until 1968, when Taha Husayn had already influenced a whole generation of autobiographical writings with his *Ayyam*, published in 1926.[69]

The immediate impetus for Zaidan's decision to write his autobiography was perhaps his son Emile's departure in 1908 to study at the Syrian Protestant College in Beirut,[70] the very place where Zaidan *père* had started his own studies some thirty years earlier The autobiography covers the first twenty-two years of Zaidan's life, breaking off in the middle of a sentence; we know of no reason why he did not return to it. Nevertheless, as far as it goes, it is a real autobiography in the modern sense of the term and thus differs radically even from Mishaqa's work.

Zaidan was born in Beirut on 14 December 1861. Beirut found itself in a century-long growth trend that expanded its population from 6,000 inhabitants in 1820 to 150,000 in 1905. It belonged, with Alexandria, Haifa, Mersin, Izmir (Smyrna), Trieste, and Odessa, to those Mediterranean cities that grew in the nineteenth century from villages or small towns to trading ports with several hundred thousand inhabitants. They were part of the European-dominated world economic system, opening up inland markets to European goods and supplying Europe with raw materials such as cotton, tobacco, silk, grain, leather, and so on. In 1861 Beirut was just emerging from twenty years of sectarian unrest in Lebanon and Syria, which climaxed in the 1860 massacre of Christians in Damascus during which some 5,000 were killed. The European powers had taken an active part in the sectarian unrest. The French had supported the Maronites and the British, the Druze. French troops had landed in Beirut following the massacre in Damascus and, just a few months before Zaidan was born, a new political order was established that made Mount Lebanon an autonomous province of the Ottoman Empire.

The Zaidan family had fled the unrest in Mount Lebanon, moving to Beirut just as the first outbursts of violence erupted in the 1840s. They were not alone. Future close friends had experienced a similar fate. In 1860 Faris Nimr's mother had fled with her son to Jerusalem after his father was killed during the unrest. Later they moved to Beirut. The family of Shahin Makarius also fled in 1860 to Beirut. Ya'qub Sarruf,[71] however, did not come as a refugee. In 1866 he applied to the Syrian Protestant College as a regular student.[72] With the influx of refugees from the fighting in Mount Lebanon, the population of Beirut roughly doubled between the early 1850s and mid-1860s to about 60,000 inhabitants.[73] "The post-war period from 1860 to the creation of the provincial capital of Beirut in 1888 was a foundational moment in Beirut's history in which local notables, merchants, and public moralists joined forces in an attempt to formulate a modern vision for Beirut."[74]

Those were the years of Zaidan's childhood and youth described in his autobiography. He provides the details of the modest circumstances of his family, the small and frequently changed apartments, and his mother's attempts to add to the family income by baking bread for others while his father was running various eateries. The boy Jurji was required to work in them, and he obtained a close-up view of the lower classes. He hated his smelly job, the vulgarity of the customers and the storytellers. His environment is not, however, the real focus of his narrative. The main theme remains the emotional and intellectual growth of the boy, a process convincingly described from his own point of view. In his search for role models, for instance, Jurji first looked to the ruffians and young toughs who hung out at his father's eatery. But soon he had to admit to the discomfort he felt in their company. Try as he might, he was not cut out to be a "tough guy." Formal education was provided by an ignorant priest who made his pupils learn psalms by heart without any understanding of the text. The application of a collection of different-sized sticks established the priest's authority in class. The limits of this sort of education were quickly reached, and Jurji's parents attempted to launch him in a career as a shoemaker. It was a reflection upon the changing times that they insisted he should become a shoemaker for "European" shoes. This apprenticeship did not work out, and he was sent to a shopkeeper as bookkeeper and manager—without success. It was only when he had made the acquaintance of students and members of the new intelligentsia in Beirut that he felt he had found himself. Then he could admit his distaste for the bad manners, boorishness, and vulgarity that seemed the norm in his own social surroundings. The boy's intellectual gifts and his hunger for knowledge had been disregarded by his father, who believed that any education beyond reading, writing, and basic arithmetic was a waste of time. Only Jurji's mother, of whom he always spoke with tenderness, had recognized his potential and tried to steer him away from working in his father's restaurant. In the end it was the boy himself who found the channels through which he could direct his intellectual curiosity and drive, and finally he was accepted as a medical student at the Syrian Protestant College.

Zaidan was an autodidact. He had no formal training in Arabic language and literature, not to speak of the canon of Koranic studies and its ancillary sciences. His first encounter with education was the school of the neighborhood priest, of which he only remembered the threat of being beaten and the mindless recitation by heart of psalms. After "graduating" from this school, he was sent to a school set up by refugees from Damascus after 1861, where he was to learn the basics of writing and arithmetic, so as to be able "to write a name [of a client] and put next to it what he owed."[75] The principal of the school was a self-taught mason who nevertheless was able to awaken Zaidan's interest in learning. After the school was closed down he continued in a new school founded by the former principal. When he was eleven his father took him out of this school, apparently feeling that he had learned enough for the keeping of accounts and the running of the eatery. Four years passed in this environment "during which I did not read a book and did not learn a word until

I forgot what I had learned in the school."[76] Only when he made friends with some students of the new missionary schools and was accepted into their circle did he begin to read. He read voraciously and haphazardly whatever happened to be available on the market. Of particular interest to him were the natural sciences. For the classics, he read the works of al-Mutanabbi and Ibn al-Farid, which had just reached the market in printed form.[77] Of their contemporaries he mentioned Nasif al-Yaziji and Asad Ibrahim al-Shududi.[78] He read *Lisan al-Hal,*[79] a biweekly on politics, literature, and sciences, and subscribed to the monthly *al-Muqtataf,* dealing mainly with science and technology; both had a pioneering role in the development of journalism in Arabic. With the possible exception of Nasif al-Yaziji, none of the authors had training in classical Arabic language or literature, and all were sooner or later involved in the educational enterprise of the American missionaries in Lebanon. In preparation for his entry exams to the medical school Zaidan also read a number of books on science in Arabic translation and, most importantly for him, he read Samuel Smiles's book *Self-Help.*[80] He probably read many more books but even this short list, which he supplied himself, makes a salient point: here was a new educational elite in the making that came most often from no distinct social background, had very little knowledge of classical Arabic literature, and had hardly any training in the religious sciences—the mainstay of traditional education. Frequently they were gifted autodidacts and all were influenced by their friendships, studies, and collaboration with the American missionaries.

Zaidan tells us of the fears and anxieties of the boy and adolescent, his excitement on reading books, his guilt feelings about masturbation, his friendships, and his admiration for his mother. His growth, the events that shaped him, the widening of his emotional and intellectual horizons, and his coming to terms with himself— all are described convincingly from the boy's point of view.

Yet at the same time, it is the almost fifty-year-old author of the autobiography who is speaking, looking back on his youth, interpreting it and giving it meaning in the context of his whole life. Jurji Zaidan, the well-established bourgeois in Cairo, recognized and respected in intellectual circles, had indeed come a long way. The message and the meaning of the autobiography are clear: it is the story of the self-made man. The *motif* of the story, if not a "rags to riches" theme, was at least the tale of a journey from lowly social origins to a respected bourgeois life, which threads itself through the whole autobiography. It is the story of life as a journey, but a journey made under one's own willpower and intellectual drive.[81]

Even though Zaidan never continued his autobiography beyond his childhood and youth in Beirut, he not only provides us with historical facts and biographical data but also gives meaning to his life by interpreting it for the reader. His life was the story of a journey from Beirut to Cairo, from humble beginnings to material comfort and respectable social status, from the narrow confines of his father's eatery and the priest's modest education and crudeness to his own journalistic enterprise and the scholarly expansion of his intellectual horizons. It was a tale of the triumph of moral values and a model for a modern life. The story was well worth telling, if only to his son, who just then was striking out on his own.

Three aspects described in Zaidan's autobiography bear closer scrutiny: the theme of the self-made man, the strike at the Syrian Protestant College in 1882, and the role of knowledge and education in his life and that of society. Having read unsystematically but widely, as a nineteen-year-old he came across a book freshly translated from English into Arabic by Ya'qub Sarruf that shook him profoundly: *Self-Help* by Samuel Smiles, translated into Arabic as *The Secret of Success*. Only three years before Darwin published his *On the Origin of Species* and just when Spencer began to develop what would later be called "social Darwinism," Smiles formulated some concepts that were typical of the laissez-faire liberalism of mid-century Victorian society: any individual could improve his position in society if he had talent and the disciplined willpower to use it. It was a kind of individualist social mobility that stood, of course, in complete contrast to any socialist or Marxist concept of improving the lot of a whole class collectively. Though Zaidan read a great deal, he hardly mentions the names of books, and only in the case of *Self-Help* does he tell us of the impact it had:

> Vigor and zeal sprang up in me. Too great was the enthusiastic impact it had on me to read about the lives of men who reached the highest

> achievements by their own diligence and efforts and self-reliance. Among them barbers and shoemakers, servants, artisans and maids who rose through their eagerness and vigilance to the station of great people. When I read a few pages I would be so agitated that I could not sleep any longer or be calm, and, finding myself tied down, [self-]pity would overcome me and I would get depressed. So I would put the book aside and until today I have not finished reading it.[82]

Terms such as "hard work," "punctuality," "discipline," "self-reliance," and "perseverance" abound in his autobiography. These social values became, if anything, even more pronounced in his later life. In 1897 a book by E. Demolins, very much in the same moral vein as Smiles's book, appeared in French and within only one year was translated into Arabic: *A quoi tient la supériorité des Anglo-Saxons?*[83] Only weeks after its appearance in Arabic, Zaidan wrote an essay in *al-Hilal* called "The Eastern Youth" in which he discouraged young people from seeking government employment. What was needed for the country was a young generation concentrating on agriculture, trade, and industry. Dedicated hard work would make up for an initial lack of money. Entrepreneurs were needed, not government employees.[84] Ten years later he would make the same argument, when writing the biography of the Damascene Salim Sidnawi, owner of the largest department store in Cairo:

> As far as scholars, merchants or professionals are concerned who achieved their wealth or greatness through their own efforts and faith, their biographies set a good example for the young generation—an ounce of example is better than a pound of instruction . . . we are in greater need of biographies of merchants who are self-made men and who became rich by lawful means befitting the conditions of success.[85]

Clearly he also perceived his life story as such an example of the self-made man.

The second episode, the student strike at the Syrian Protestant College in 1882, was equally of formative importance in the life and thought of the young Zaidan.[86] Soon after the foundation of the college in 1866 a dispute had broken out over the introduction of English as the teaching language. In the academic year 1879–1880 English was introduced throughout the college with the exception of the medical school. The issue divided the faculty into "liberal" and "conservative" camps, the latter demanding the elimination of Arabic as a teaching language. But this division was not only about the language of instruction. It also included the more basic question as to the role Protestant doctrine should play in the education provided by the college. This discussion came to a head over the issue of the validity and admissibility of Darwin's theory of evolution. The liberal camp centered on Cornelius van Dyck,[87] who was a physician and the only nontheologian among the missionaries—who were not exactly the avant-garde of modern thought in the Western world. He was supported by his son William, who joined the faculty in 1880. He held evolutionary views and had brought Darwin's book with him to Beirut. His colleague in medical school E. R. Lewis, a physician and ordained minister, also belonged to the circle, as did Faris Nimr and Ya'qub Sarruf, who had been hired as "native tutors" in the college—Sarruf for Arabic, mathematics, and physics, Nimr for astronomy and Latin.[88] In 1876 they had started the journal *al-Muqtataf*, in which the themes of modern science, and especially the natural sciences, were prominent from the beginning. Articles about Darwin and the theory of evolution had already appeared there before Lewis's speech triggered a crisis.

In 1882 Lewis gave the commencement speech, in which he spoke positively about the theory of evolution.[89] This provided an excuse for the conservative camp to take action against the liberals. Lewis was dismissed. Students who went on strike in protest were locked out of the campus. Eventually Cornelius van Dyck and some liberal colleagues resigned. Many of the students refused to return to the college.

It is noteworthy that during the whole dispute between the faculty and the students in connection with the students' right to protest and go on strike, Darwin's theory of evolution was hardly mentioned and freedom of speech only indirectly. The students' argument turned around a legalistic point that they had joined the college and paid their fees under the assumption that Lewis would be their chemistry teacher. In a similar manner the faculty never argued that Lewis did anything objectionable by speaking favorably about Darwinism. They simply claimed that students had no right whatsoever to interfere with the hiring and firing policies of the college.

Unequivocal proof that the real issue had been the theory of evolution and its suppression in the Syrian Protestant College can be found in the college's annual reports, which reveal that from January 1883 on, every teacher appointed to the college had to sign a Declaration of Principles. The declaration was a manifesto of Protestant dogma that implied the incompatibility of support for any part of the theory of evolution and a teaching position in the college. In 1884 the appointments of Nimr and Sarruf were not renewed. With this last step the college finally lost its role as a center for the rapidly evolving new intelligentsia of the Arab world.

Zaidan commented in his autobiography on Lewis's speech, which was about Darwin's theory that "in no regard did his lecture oppose religion."[90] But his view was altogether new and the men of religion thought it contradictory to the fundamentals of Christianity.[91] Zaidan never tells us whether he was by that time already a supporter of Darwinism. For the participants of the Nahda, Darwinism was more than just another scientific theory. It seemed to promise the key to a scientific explanation and analysis not only of nature but of human society and its history. The importance of modern science in general and Darwinism in particular for the new Arab intelligentsia was that it seemed to provide a secular, rational alternative to tradition and religion: "The religion of science was a declaration of war on older religions."[92] Zaidan had been an early subscriber to *al-Muqtataf*, and became a close friend of Nimr and Sarruf. They all were in close contact with Cornelius van Dyck and E. R. Lewis. They also met at places such as *Shams al-Birr*, a branch of the British YMCA, and in the Freemason lodges. The same enthusiastic belief in science and rationality that made the new educated classes adopt Darwinism made them join the Freemasons. The latter provided, like the early scientific and literary societies, a space where people could meet regardless of religious affiliation and join in the enlightened vision of universal rationality. When the students organized their protest against the college, Zaidan, who had been elected chairman of the organization, had this to say about the solidarity of the students: "All were acquainted with each other and accustomed to meetings in the College itself and in the Society *Shams al-Birr* and some of them in the Freemasons."[93] Zaidan had been a very active participant in this protest movement. Through his activities, he had joined with a fraternity of students and some professors who were committed to the primacy of the natural sciences and increasingly considered scientific truth the way to improve society. This network of literary societies and Freemasonry would provide him with social and intellectual support and personal friendships all his life, in Lebanon as well as in Egypt: "In 1888 a good number of people, tied to each other by their stay at the American College in Beirut, their love for Arabic literature and the experience of emigration, found themselves in the same lodge in Cairo."[94] Dupont summarizes the role the Freemasons played in Zaidan's life and that of others: "To be a Freemason meant making a choice of adhering to modernity while reinventing at the same time a tradition of learned or mystic sociability, typical for the Arab and Muslim world."[95] Later Zaidan would even write a history of the Freemasons.[96] But his membership seems to have become rather passive, just as was the case with his membership in the Greek Orthodox Church.

The third aspect concerns education. The importance of education was, of course, closely linked to the image the Enlightenment had developed of the human being, possessing reason, able to acquire knowledge, and using both to make responsible decisions and shape the world around him. The image of the self-made man, so important to Zaidan, was quite close to the idea of the survival of the fittest *individual* rather than of the fittest group, not owing anything to society. Zaidan disdained any form of socialism and class loyalty. Self-reliance was decisive. But Zaidan's survival had heavily depended on his ability to acquire an education. It had been his means to gain bourgeois respectability. Yet, education was much more than the achievement of respectability. The Enlightenment had endowed each individual with reason and the ability of learning. In principle, education was to be universally accessible. Such premises led to a new educational project whose task was to transform the whole of society through education. It was to change society from a situation of weakness, mired in tradition, to taking its full place among modern and "progressive" societies. The self-made man who by his own virtues rose in society without any debt to others contrasted sharply with the teacher and reformer whose mission was to elevate the whole society to a new level of civilization and progress. Who else but the talented, the knowledgeable, and those familiar with modern sciences, the educated and intellectual members of the Nahda, were able to fulfill this role of teacher and reformer? Zaidan embraced both roles—that of the self-made man and that of the teacher/reformer—and with that an intellectual tension that would accompany him throughout his life. Though the two roles were linked through the function that education played individually or generally in both, in the end the role of the teacher of society became the dominant, more creative, and productive one.[97]

The strike at the college ended in defeat for the students. The faculty did not concede anything, and the liberal element was purged; some students submitted to the new demands of the college, others refused and never returned. In 1883 Zaidan, following so many of his contemporaries both in and outside the college, left for Egypt, recently occupied by the British. Once in Egypt he quickly gave up the idea of continuing his medical studies. He worked for a while as editor of the newspaper *al-Zaman*.[98]

In the fall of 1884, after two years in Egypt, occupied with various jobs, he joined the Wollesley expedition as a translator[99] together with his friend Jabr Dumit.[100] This military adventure to defeat the Mahdi and save General Gordon ended in failure sometime in the middle of 1885. Zaidan had to look for a job once more. Together with his friend he decided to go back to Beirut and study languages. The year 1885–1886 must have been intellectually a very intense period for him. Not only did he immerse himself in the study of Semitic languages (Hebrew and Syriac),[101] he also resumed contact with his former friends and teachers, first and foremost Cornelius van Dyck, and he participated actively in the debates in such groups as *al-Majma' al-'Ilmi al-Sharqi*,[102] whose leading members were Cornelius van Dyck, Ya'qub Sarruf, Faris Nimr, and Butrus and Salim al-Bustani.[103] It had been founded in 1882 as a successor to the defunct *al-Jam'iyya al-'Ilmiyya al-Suriyya*,[104] which was founded in 1852 by Butrus al-Bustani. The new society, however, also included American and European members.[105]

In the summer of 1886 Zaidan traveled to London, again joined by his friend Jabr Dumit. They spent a few months in the reading rooms of the British Museum where Zaidan acquainted himself with the works of European Orientalists. They had planned to stay longer, but with the oncoming winter Zaidan's health deteriorated and he returned to Cairo, which he was to make his permanent home. The next five years were a restless time for Zaidan, as he tried to find his way professionally. He worked for over a year as an administrative manager in the office of *al-Muqtataf,* which Nimr and Sarruf had in the meantime transferred from Beirut to Cairo. Even though his father criticized him harshly for not choosing a "remunerative" profession such as medicine or law,[106] he continued to develop his career as a writer. He wrote a book on the history of the Freemasons and on the modern history of Egypt; he accepted a job as head teacher of Arabic in a Greek Orthodox school; and in 1890 he published his *History of the World* with the equally grandiloquent subtitle *From Creation till Today.*

In 1891 things came together for Zaidan. With Najib Mitri, a compatriot from Beirut, he founded a printing enterprise that they called *Matba'at al-Ta'lif.* It was a small affair in a few rooms with a hand-driven printing machine. Their collaboration soon ended, and Najib Mitri opened a new publishing house, which he called *Dar al-Ma'arif.*[107] Zaidan kept the press and called it *Matba'at al-Hilal.* During the same year he came out with his first historical novel, *The Fugitive Mamluk,*[108] which was so successful that he felt he could give up teaching in the Greek Orthodox School. From that time on he worked as an independent writer, journalist, novelist, linguist, and historian, all fields in which he was an autodidact.

In 1891 he also finally married Maryam, a girl he had met four years earlier. She was an orphan, a trained teacher, and from Lebanon like himself. His parents bitterly opposed this liaison because they felt it was a mismatch. Friends had to intercede and in 1888 the parents finally agreed to the marriage.[109] Yet it took another three years before they actually married. Apparently there existed objections on the other side as well. Maryam's family felt that Zaidan was not good enough for Maryam because he came from a lower social class, and it was only through Jabr Dumit's intervention that they changed their minds.[110] Some of Zaidan's experiences during this difficult time flowed into his only nonhistorical novel *The Lovers' Struggle.*[111]

Maryam and Jurji had four children: Farid, Emile, Asma, and Choucri, born in 1891, 1893, 1895, and 1900, respectively. The firstborn died in infancy. The last two surviving grandchildren are George C. Zaidan, son of Choucri; and Nadim, son of Emile. Two great-grandchildren survive: George Jr., son of George C. Zaidan, and Bassem Abdallah, grandson of Asma. From Jurji Zaidan's letters to his son Emile in Beirut and from the reminiscences of his children, expressed in many conversations with this author in the early 1970s, one gains the impression that the family was very close, intimate, and loving.

After Zaidan had established himself permanently in Cairo he helped bring his brothers and three sisters from Beirut. Two of his brothers, Mitri and Ibrahim—the latter for only a few years—worked with him at *Matba'at al-Hilal.* A third one, Yusif, became a successful businessman in Cairo. Work, indeed, must have become the keynote of Zaidan's life. Since his earliest childhood it had been impressed upon him that one should never waste one's time.[112] His capacity for work was astounding. In 1892 he started his single most important project, the publication of the journal *al-Hilal.* A large part of his time must have been consumed by this enterprise. For a long time he was not only its sole author but also combined manager, editor, and sales agent. From 1891 on he also wrote a novel every year. After a certain routine had established itself, and he had delegated the managerial aspects of the journal to his brothers, he found time and energy to write scholarly works; beginning in 1899 he wrote one volume almost every year until his death.

Whenever he had time left over from his work, Zaidan spent it with his family and friends. Salama Musa describes him as an "extrovert, stout, jocular man with a great many friends."[113] In the letters Zaidan wrote to his son Emile while the latter was studying in Beirut, one finds the names of a veritable stream of friends and visitors who frequented Zaidan's home, especially on Tuesday nights when a regular *soirée* was held. Members of the Cairene cultural elite would attend, including journalists, writers, and sometimes even teachers from al-Azhar. European Orientalists visiting Cairo would also join on these occasions.

Zaidan might have been, in the words of Musa, an "extrovert" but only with respect to his friends. On the whole, he was a very private man who shied away from active participation in political organizations and public appearances. For a while he had been an active member of the Freemasons (not exactly a public organization) but it was not of great importance to him. Later he left the Masons. Perhaps he did not care much for organized forms of socializing. Though he was baptized in the Greek Orthodox Church, he was not active either in the Greek Orthodox community or church activities.[114] He became an enthusiastic supporter of the Young Turk Revolution, but when asked to run in elections to the reestablished Ottoman parliament he declined, claiming others were better suited than he.[115]

Zaidan was inclined to accept an offer for a public position only once, in 1910, when he was invited to teach Islamic history at the newly founded Egyptian University. The offer was an official recognition of his scholarly merits and, as one of the first to clamor for the establishment of a university, it vindicated his own views on education. Zaidan considered accepting the position, but the affair ended in disaster. Even before he began teaching, his appointment was canceled by the university, which found itself under pressure from Muslim quarters to dismiss Zaidan from the position.[116] It was a humiliating affair and "left a stain of bitterness in his heart."[117]

The life of a private writer suited his temperament best. He was a man of the written word, not of public speech and organizations. He saw his role as an educator of society, but he spent time in a classroom only in times of economic need. The positive upshot of the "university affair" was a very original book on the history of Ottoman Egypt, which Zaidan composed from notes he had already compiled for lecturing in the university.[118]

By the time he died completely unexpectedly in Cairo on 21 July 1914 at the age of fifty-three, he had established himself in a little over twenty years as one of the most prolific and influential thinkers and writers, educators, and intellectual innovators in the Arab world.

III

◆ ◆ ◆

Religion, Science, and Evolution

By the time Jurji Zaidan's interest in his own education became a driving force in his life, the term *'ilm,* knowledge or science, had already experienced a change in meaning. In particular the plural, *al-'ulūm,* had lost its traditional religious sense and acquired the meaning "modern sciences," especially "natural sciences." As a teenager he had subscribed to the newly founded magazine *al-Muqtataf,* which was subtitled as a "journal for sciences and technology." In it Zaidan read about solar eclipses and the weather, which aroused his curiosity about the laws of nature. It was also in this magazine that he first read about evolutionary theory. When he finally came close to realizing his dream to study at the Syrian Protestant College, he chose medicine, mainly because of its greater financial benefits. There followed his first—and only—year in the medical school, where he studied biology, botany, anatomy, physiology, and pharmacology with great delight—though the science he enjoyed most was chemistry "because through it man sees the world as he has never seen it before."[119] He also enjoyed, after some initial difficulties, the study of Latin, and at year's end he received a prize for best performance in Latin. Regardless of the subject he studied, he was of a sharp mind and quick comprehension. He seemed to learn effortlessly. His first encounter, however, was with the natural sciences. Only in London, in the British Library, would he read the works of Orientalists and thus be introduced to the human sciences such as history and linguistics. He became convinced that the laws of nature, especially evolution, could also be applied to these sciences.

In Zaidan's autobiography, mention of religion is noticeably lacking. The only contact he seems to have had with his Greek Orthodox faith was the painful experience of learning to recite psalms he did not understand.

He never mentions going to church during his childhood. As Dupont points out, the only two times that he mentions his family's membership in the Greek Orthodox community is to establish his Arab origins and urban Beiruti identity.[120] At the college he was, of course, exposed to the tenets of Protestantism. But he did not convert to Protestantism, as did Faris Nimr and Ya'qub Sarruf. Nor did he become an atheist, as did his contemporary Shibli Shumayyil,[121] although he later became strongly critical of the instrumentalization of religion by the political and religious elites.[122] His attitude toward religion was also informed by his awareness that he was living in a society where religious affiliation was still of the utmost importance and where his position as a Christian writing about Islamic history was, to say the least, highly sensitive.[123]

From the time of the strike at the college Zaidan was faced with the question of the relationship between religion and science. He took his cue from Cornelius van Dyck:

> Dr. van Dyck was liberal in thought and word and did not mind speaking out frankly about these things which his colleagues and others in the group of clerics avoided discussing. Dr. van Dyck was a God-fearing man, his conviction being based on understanding and thought. He cared little for the details and trivialities to which some religious zealots cling and which have absolutely nothing to do with religion. But he held fast to the essentials of the Christian religion, unmindful of its external aspects and its superficialities if they contradicted the principles of science. When a new theory of scientific thought appeared and presumably contradicted these superficialities he would nevertheless respect it and examine it from the point of view of the scientist as, for instance, the evolutionary theory and similar theories of the philosophy of natural scientists.[124]

In the third year of *al-Hilal* (1895) Zaidan tackled the issue in a very lengthy article:

> We want to expand here on the pillars of these sciences, the props they are based on. In other words we want to summarize the results which the natural scientists have reached with their research over many generations, which would be attributed to the uniqueness of the Lofty Creator

> for the brilliant wisdom he planted into his creatures. The full comprehension of the research will only add to the admiration for the greatness of the Creator. What is firmly established in science will only add to the solid base of religion. What appears sometimes as contradiction between the two is of no consequence, it is nothing but a summer cloud which does not linger. The light of science will disperse it.[125]

The claim that "true" science does not contradict "true" religion is, of course, a rather facile papering over of the chasm existing between the two. But he hinted at the "true" balance of power between them when he assigned to science the authority to solve contradictions. In answer to a reader's question about the age of the earth, thirteen years later, he did not mince his words:

> The earth is very old, perhaps older than two hundred million years as will become clear to you through geological proof. This seems to be in contradiction to what Genesis says. But this is of little consequence because the theologians adjust in such situations and interpret the text until it fits science. The six days in which God—according to Genesis—created the world are interpreted each as standing for a long period of thousands of years. But the scientific proof of the age of the earth comes from geology.[126]

Religion had to adjust to science because the latter provided proof. Zaidan was a theist believing in the Hereafter, without bothering too much with the details and the various dogmas of organized religion. Twice he made a serious effort to deal with the question.[127] In both cases he intended to provide scientific proof for the existence of God and the Hereafter, respectively. In the first article his argument goes roughly as follows: We know nothing that our senses cannot grasp. The development of the senses differs in intensity with each person. You do not call somebody a liar because he sees things you cannot see. In the same way we cannot call prophets liars. When a whole group agrees on a story—its essentials, not its details—then its truth is superior. The closer opinions are to the correct version, the simpler the interpretation of events. The more comprehensive the explanation, the closer it is to the truth. Some perceptions of events require an explanation by the laws of nature, others by the laws of the intellect and morality. Even many of the natural phenomena cannot yet be explained. God as the original cause is the simplest and most comprehensive explanation for all events, even if our senses cannot experience it. "This is the conclusion we reached investigating by thinking and reading, needing to take the short road and needing above all a learned cognizant guide."[128] The last sentence betrays an uncertainty, and perhaps the inconclusive character of the essay. His whole argument relies on the different capabilities of the senses to perceive things. Here he makes a critical step and enters a circular argument when he accepts that the prophets, whose veracity he does not question, see and hear more than the average person. In other words, he proves the existence of God by an integral aspect of the theology that assumes the existence of God, namely prophecy.

The second article was written sixteen years later in response to a question from a reader as to whether human beings experience another world after death, in which they still have some form of recognizable identity. This time Zaidan took a different tack. He started with the observation of the eternity of matter, which can transform itself into energy, motion, and so forth, but does not disappear. This establishes in principle the possibility of the Hereafter, albeit without discussing dogmatic niceties such as the resurrection, which had always been understood by the Church as a physical one. He then argued that the natural sciences established that the same cause will always deliver the same results. The logic of the laws of nature is always predictable and measurable. But people who start under the same conditions will act differently, unpredictably, and the results of their actions differ. Such observation of human behavior will come only to its expected logical conclusion in the Hereafter. "The existence of the Hereafter does not deny the order of this world but it complements it."[129] The critical step here is the assumption that the transcendental world also functions according to the laws of nature. Yet the emphasis has changed. It is the logic of the laws of nature that demands the existence of a Hereafter. In the next two issues,[130] Shibli Shumayyil and Zaidan, both supporters of the theory of evolution, carried on a dispute over the existence of the Hereafter. "For Shumayyil . . . it is not necessary anymore to believe if one admits [the validity] of the theory of evolution. For Zaidan the religious truth complements the scientific truth."[131]

One passage on the relation between religion and the natural sciences that he published in 1895 seems to give us some indication of his understanding of the issue. To the question of a reader as to whether modern scientists were of the opinion that the laws of society were sent by divine revelation or were manmade, Zaidan answered as follows:

> Some of the natural scientists do not accept divine revelation and claim that those laws, when established, issued from the lawgivers themselves or they took them from others preceding them. For them these are manmade laws of civilization. Their proof is that the revelation cannot be ascertained by the law of nature. Others however accept the divine revelation and argue for it on the basis of the very same laws.[132]

The statement is more self-revealing than the author might have suspected, because he equivocated between both positions. Debating the question of the existence of another world after ours,[133] he actually argued that the laws of nature demanded the existence of such a world. The frame of reference is the same for both: the laws of nature. In the first case revelation remains irrelevant; in the second case it remains subordinated to the law of evolution. On a certain level he wrote more abstractly about the issue, very often in response to questions by readers, but he also dedicated some essays to the topic. Whenever he wrote in general terms about the existence of God or the Hereafter, he argued in favor of the compatibility of revelation and the laws of natural sciences.[134] However, when he discussed specific issues, he relied on modern scholarship, as in the case of the origins of the Code of Hammurabi, where he clearly supported the position that the ancient legal codes were manmade and not dependent on revelation, as the Old Testament suggested. According to Zaidan, even Hammurabi collected different laws from a variety of sources, and collated them; in other words, they were all manmade.[135] He cited the evidence of the natural sciences, for instance, when dating the age of the earth or the distances in the cosmos, explicitly commenting that the interpretation of the Bible had to be fitted to the results of modern science. In the case of both history and language he was convinced that the laws of nature applied to them. Generally, he believed firmly in the veracity of the theory of evolution, associated the growth of human knowledge and the rise of natural sciences with an evolutionary process, and subjected even the development of religions to the law of evolution.

In a long and rather descriptive series on premonotheistic religions[136] he assumed with Darwin that all human beings have a craving for religion. Here and in other articles[137] the terminology of evolutionary theory abounds: *irtiqā'* and *nushū'*, rising and growing; *arqā* and *adnā*, higher and lower; *tafarru'* and *tasha''ub*, ramification and branching off. He had always separated natural science from religion and frequently, though implicitly, subordinated religion to the laws of nature. He repeatedly asserted that the "true" sciences and their laws did not contradict "true" religion, but we have also seen a shift in emphasis on the necessity that religion adapt itself to science and not vice versa. In a one-page answer to a reader he wrote: "The attempt to adapt the facts of nature to the verses of religion is very onerous, leads to doubts, and imposes mental anxiety. The principle in such a situation is rather the adaptation of the verses to the factual evidence. The laws of nature are real events which feelings acknowledge and proofs ascertain. They are not open to interpretation."[138]

He continued pointing out that many teachings of the monotheistic religions, such as miracles, contradict the laws of nature. He hesitated to call these religions false. At the same time he argued that a lot of scientific truth would be destroyed by adapting science to religion. In conclusion he stated the independence of each; science is valid for this world, religion for the Hereafter. Half a year later he went further: religion is the source of guidance, improvement, and character building for the individual. All law and social order come in the last analysis from religion. It sometimes seems that religion is the cause of divisions in society and of many wars but, he argued, that occurs only because religion is misused by other interests.[139] He perceived a role for religion not only in the Hereafter but even for this world.

Rarely did he come out with as clear a statement as the following: "We are not among those who expect religion to disappear, but expect changes in its manifestation, ramifications of its denominations, some overcoming others—*according to the laws of general evolution*" (emphasis mine).[140] If he has to be labeled he probably would be called a deist or theist—that is, one who thought that the Creator did not interfere in the details of the everyday life of the world. He believed in the afterlife as witnessed by his membership in the Freemasons and attested by his articles on the "The Proof of the Existence of God" and "Is there Another World in the Universe?" He also saw the benefits of religion for a virtuous society and believed that religion was a permanent feature of human life. But he was highly critical of the exploitation of religion for political purposes.[141] He carved out an independent space for science, which had its own laws; and he further implied, though rarely pronouncing it as clearly as in the above quote, that even religion was subject to evolution. His belief in evolutionary theory was inconsistent with the belief in the literal biblical version of a spontaneous onetime creation of the world. Also the idea of the immanence of God in the world after Creation would be difficult to harmonize with his observation that the Ten Commandments and other laws in the Old Testament were manmade, pointing out their origin in the laws of Hammurabi.

In a review article on Shumayyil's work in 1910, Zaidan praised him for having presented and defended the theory of evolution to the Arab public. But he also accused him of excessive materialism in dismissing any scholarship dealing with aesthetics, ethics, or issues of morality. Shumayyil only accepted the natural and immediately "useful" sciences such as medicine, chemistry, and mechanical sciences, "which would raise the material conditions of the life of society through inventions and discoveries."[142] He disregarded the arts and human sciences such as history, philosophy, literature, and poetry. Zaidan admitted that the natural sciences were the solid foundation, but maintained that the arts and human sciences were the beautiful structure, the source of all social order and of civilization. At the same time Zaidan also accused Shumayyil of an abstract idealism far removed from reality, desiring a harmonious society where unity and equality would rule, which was to Zaidan's mind simply impossible; and here, in a mood of pessimism, he commented that human beings have a natural inclination toward religion and that when they abandon one, they will follow another. Religion will always produce its managers and rulers, its benefits and costs. As long as mothers give birth to both weak and strong children equality will not prevail, but some will always rule over others. In the same spirit Zaidan dismissed Shumayyil's idea of establishing one language for all of mankind as nonsense.

The debate over the relation between religion and modern science, in particular the theory of evolution, was at that point not exactly new. Shumayyil as well as Zaidan were familiar with it because it was generated in the circle of their friends around the editors of *al-Muqtataf*, Sarruf and Nimr, and Dr. Cornelius van Dyck, director of the medical school of the Syrian Protestant College. Especially the latter's son William became an active protagonist of Darwinism. In 1882 a first pro-Darwinian essay was published in *al-Muqtataf*. Two articles followed on the occasion of the death of Darwin in April 1882. Three months later Lewis held his commencement speech at the Syrian Protestant College, which led to the already mentioned crisis in the college, and eventually to the resignation of some of the liberal faculty as well as many students who defended the speech of Lewis. The lecture itself was published in August 1882 in *al-Muqtataf* and engaged an ever-widening public in the debate over Darwinism, with the participation of foreign and local educated people on both sides of the issue. Muslim and Christian voices argued that evolutionary theory was not compatible with religion, hence that it was *kufr* or heresy. Others claimed that the origins of Darwinism were to be found in classical Arabic literature, while a third group argued for the validity of Darwinism as part of the modern sciences. The editors of *al-Muqtataf* participated only rarely in the debate but did not hide their strongly favorable view of Darwinism. The discussion was abruptly cut short by Nimr and Sarruf at the end of the year, apparently fearing for the existence of their journal.[143]

Shumayyil published two years later his translation into Arabic of L. Büchner's *Lectures about Darwin's Theory*.[144] It was the first attempt to make texts, if not by Darwin himself then about Darwin's writings, accessible in Arabic. His introduction was severely criticized by Sarruf and Nimr. They considered it a materialist and atheistic misinterpretation, thereby endangering the acceptance of the theory in religious circles.[145] Many years later Zaidan would still accuse Shumayyil of the same flaws in his work.

Zaidan did not write books on evolutionary theory, as did Shumayyil. Rather, he used the articles in his journal, or elaborated on the subject in answers to questions by readers. But it is noticeable that here—much more than on other topics—he let other writers expound their views in *al-Hilal* and provide explanations of evolutionary theory. The conclusion that he was less of a supporter of evolutionary theory than his contemporary Shumayyil, however, would be wrong. Shumayyil was perhaps the more rigorous, systematic thinker, and Zaidan was less interested in the theoretical details. Zaidan's concern was the applicability of the laws of evolution not only to the natural sciences—which he took for granted—but also to what he called *'ilm al-ādāb*, the human and social sciences, popularly speaking, the "soft sciences."

Before analyzing some of the terminology used in Arabic to discuss Darwinism, it is perhaps useful to point out how problematic this issue is in English and other European languages. Probably the best-known term is "survival of the fittest." It was coined by Herbert Spencer and then entered into the Darwinist vocabulary. The meaning of "the fittest" remains ambivalent. It could refer to what fits best (as in "the screw fits the bolt") or it may mean the most deserving, be it in character, intelligence, virtue, or strength. "Survival of the strongest" is popularly, albeit erroneously, used.[146] In Darwinism only the first meaning can be correct and "the survival of the best adapted" would be the more appropriate, if less attractive, formulation. Behind this ambivalence stands the question of whether "evolution" means—in the case of human beings—also "progress." Though for Herbert Spencer "progress" meant first of all the development of the organism from the simple to the complex, from the homogeneous to the heterogeneous (terms that we encounter frequently in Zaidan's writings: *tafarru'* and *tasha''ub*, "ramification"; *adnā* and *arqā*, "lower" and "higher"), there always was a connotation of "improvement" in it, and Spencer can never quite rid himself completely of the idea of progress, moving society to "higher" or "more developed" levels. As Barzun has pointed out: "Contrary to common belief, Darwin's distinctive contribution . . . is not the theory of evolution as a whole, but a theory which explains evolution by *natural selection from accidental variations* [emphasis in original]. The entire phrase and not merely the words Natural Selection is important, for the denial of purpose in the universe is carried in the second half of the formula—accidental variation."[147]

The shocking fact of Darwin's evolutionary theory—even for Darwin himself—was that evolution was based on random variations, some more adaptive to a given environment than others. The "survival of the fittest" meant indeed only that he who fitted best into a set of random external conditions would survive best. No particular virtue, value, or strength was attached to it. No judgment was made as to the meaning and end result of this process. This aspect of evolutionary theory, however, was lost on those who equated "evolution" with the value-laden term "progress." Thus, the meaning of the term "the fittest" was expanded to mean "the better," "the stronger," or "the superior."

In Arabic either new terms had to be created or new meanings had to be assigned to old ones. *Taqaddum* became the most frequently used term for "progress"; *taraqqin wa-ta'akhkhur,* "progress" and "backwardness," were neologisms; *irtiqā' wa-'nḥiṭāṭ,* "rise and fall," implied in contrast to progress an up-and-down cycle in history, as in "the rise and fall of nations."[148] Though both *taraqqin* and *irtiqā'* could mean "rise" as well as "progress," the latter term was also used for the English term "evolution."[149] Additional terms used for "evolution" were *tasalsul,* descent; *taṭawwur,* development, but also progress and evolution; and *nushū',* for growth.[150] "Shumayyil's phraseology *madhhab al-nushū' wa-'l-irtiqā,* the school of growth and ascent, rendered more aptly in English as the theory of evolution and progress, thus added a completely new layer of meaning to Darwin's ideas by giving them a teleological and politicized character."[151]

Zaidan used most frequently the term *al-nushū' wa-'l-irtiqā',* which he obviously took from Shumayyil but, as we have seen, neither of the two "added a completely new layer of meaning to Darwin's ideas." The ambivalence of meaning occurred already with the extension of Darwinism to social Darwinism in England. The translation for "survival of the fittest" into Arabic carries over this ambivalence: *al-aṣlaḥ,* first to be found in *al-Muqtataf,*[152] means good, right, proper, virtuous, pious, useful, practical, fitting, or appropriate. It has the same ambivalence or potential misunderstanding as the English term "the fittest."[153]

Zaidan used the term *irtiqā'* in the sense of "evolution," as in *nāmūs al-irtiqā',* the law of evolution, but often the meaning of advancement, ascent, or progress is implied in his use of the term. Zaidan never discussed the issue of meaning explicitly, and only the analysis of the context can bring clarity whether he applied the term *al-nushū' wa-'l-irtiqā'* in its ambivalent sense or in either of its two meanings—that is, as signifying progress or merely change devoid of any moral connotation.[154] When he referred to *nāmūs al-irtiqā'* as a synonym for *nawāmīs al-hayāt* or *nāmūs al-ṭabī'a,* the laws of life or the law of nature, their function was different. Typically these terms were meant to emphasize simply the scientific validity of his analysis of language, history, and society. As Khuri-Maqdisi observes: "In the eyes of *Nahḍa* intellectuals the battle over Darwinism as manifested through the Lewis affair epitomized many crucial struggles: for the freedom of speech, for the curbing of clerical and missionary authority in the realm of knowledge . . . and the supremacy of science."[155]

This echoes very closely what Barzun had analyzed two generations earlier as the reason for the intense debates over evolutionary theory and the enthusiastic defense of it even during Darwin's life:

> Darwinism acted as a test case for freedom of scientific inquiry, by which is to be understood not unlimited intellectual freedom but freedom for scientists. It gave over to them everything between heaven and earth without restrictions. They had their way in clerical as well as civil courts, in education as well as the popular mind. The spread of evolution was truly world-wide. . . . The scientists won on vaccination and vivisection, Bible teaching and table rapping. By won I mean that the opposition to their views in all these things put one in a minority even in the opinion of the ignorant. Materialism, conscious or implicit, superseded all other beliefs.[156]

Almost simultaneously the Darwinism debate began to play the same role in the Middle East.

Toward the end of his highly productive but short life, Zaidan's interests shifted increasingly away from literature and culture (but not history) and focused more on political and sociological issues. The change in interests certainly had to do with the Young Turk Revolution, which caused him to rethink issues of political power, institutions, and questions of social structures and their coherence. His professional crisis, triggered by the cancelled appointment at the university and the sharp criticism by Muslim intellectuals,[157] most likely added to this shift of interest. He never doubted that the theory of evolution was the most basic of sciences, providing the key for analyzing all other natural and social sciences. But the last four years of his life were characterized by more pessimistic and critical views of society and human beings, as he commented on the potential for the misuse of religion by selfish ruling elites and the possibilities for misleading the masses.

Zaidan had considered himself to be the first to have called, since 1900, for the establishment of a university in Cairo so that the youth in Egypt would have prospects for a higher academic education.[158] In 1905 the Muslim journal *al-Mu'ayyad* argued that small schools in villages were more important than a university. Zaidan responded that the need was for good teachers rather than more schools. Teachers have to be trained before the school system can expand.[159] A year later he rejoined the now-flourishing debate over the nature of this university with an article in which he insisted on the importance of Arabic as the language of instruction.[160] A university was eventually established in December 1908.[161] After it opened its doors Zaidan again formulated his vision of the university, its tasks, and its aims. Any demand for freedom and independence, a constitution, and participation in politics could only be achieved through knowledge and science—not by just abstractly formulating demands (a jibe directed against Mustafa Kamil and his political agenda). He stressed that teachers of integrity and strength of character were needed as examples for the students to learn from as much as the content of instruction in the natural sciences, history, and other human sciences. He pointed out that he was instrumental in making his studies of Islamic history part of the Nahda; perhaps a discreet hint of his wish to teach at the university.[162]

In the summer of 1910 Zaidan had been invited to teach Islamic history at the university. As we mentioned earlier, he was a very private person and apparently hesitated to take on such a public function. Yet it was a public recognition of his work as a historian, especially in Islamic history. He finally agreed because the invitation appealed to his desire for "service to science and to the benefit of the sons of the fatherland," which, as he claimed, "all our life and energy we had dedicated to this cause." With the contract in his pocket he went to Lebanon for the summer and prepared his lectures on the history of Ottoman Egypt for the coming academic year. In September he heard first from the press and a day later from the university that he had been dismissed before he even had started because, as the newspaper *al-Mu'ayyad* wrote, "it would not be proper for a Christian to teach Islamic history."[163] The rejection itself and the form in which it was communicated were highly humiliating and shocking for Zaidan. This crisis was followed during the next years by sharp attacks on Zaidan's scholarly work by Christian as well as Muslim scholars.[164]

Since 1910 and the beginning of his professional crisis he observed the danger of religious values and sentiments being exploited by the clergy or other elites for their own purposes.[165] While loyalty to the fatherland and the willingness to defend it were based on rational decisions, such as defending one's property for instance, Zaidan argued that in religion the driving forces were emotions: the poor and the weak were given the hope that in the Hereafter they would reap the rewards they never could gain in this world. The poor had more faith than the upper classes. But the latter exploited the religiosity of the former for their own purposes. The elite could manipulate the people in the name of religion. Here so-called holy wars enter the picture. They were as old as known history. The masses were always willing to follow any leader who appealed to religious myths, but whether this was for the good of the people or not depended entirely on whether the leader's interests and goals matched those of the people.

Ever since Voltaire wrote his drama, called *Mahomet*—superficially a virulent attack on Islam and the Prophet, but correctly understood by the Catholic Church as an attack on its clergy and hence immediately put on the index of forbidden books—it became standard for members of the Enlightenment to attack explicitly the clergy and other elites for exploiting the beliefs of the people for their own purposes. Implicitly it was also an attack on the corruptibility of the masses as long as they were uneducated. In Zaidan's time al-Afghani as well as the Muslim reformist Muhammad 'Abduh had made the same arguments on the exploitation of religion. In his *Anthology* article "The Sensitive Matter of Religion and How the Elites Monopolize It at the Expense of the Masses," Zaidan demonstrated how much he was aware of the potential abuse of religious faith and sentiments to fulfill the ambitions of unscrupulous elites.

The same disappointing experiences and shift of interests in the last four years of his life, which we mentioned, also led him to reflect more on society and the laws that might determine its structure, consistency, and patterns of change. To the observation of a reader that Europeans rejected religious fanaticism but indulged in national fanaticism, Zaidan responded that human beings always have to live in groups or communities with each other. But they will choose the group from which they expect the greatest benefits for themselves:

> The most stable social groups are those that give benefits, *manfa'a*, or are useful to its members. People will be loyal to and associate with those groups that promise benefits to the individual. At the height of Islamic rule in the East it was useful for the people of the East to be loyal to Islam and join a counter-movement to the European states. But today it is in the interest of the people of the East to safeguard the national society and they take to it on wings.[166]

In a subsequent issue, he elaborated in an essay on the relation between individuals and a group and the expected benefit from membership in this group.[167] Zaidan started with the observation that association with others is a human instinct, because social groups are the essential instrument for the survival of the individual. After briefly reviewing the primal associations such as the family or the clan, into which the individual is born and which also are mutual help associations, he discussed the societies or groups that individuals would form and join voluntarily, depending on their perceived benefit.[168] The identity-forming elements that would hold such societies together were of almost unlimited variety, from professional associations or racial similarity to language groups or religion—anything that could hold a group together. The perceived benefits could also differ and were not necessarily determined by the common identity. Most important, Zaidan asserted that individuals were simultaneously members in a variety of associations or societies, which might even have contradictory purposes or goals. They would shift the emphasis of membership in one or another group according to their needs at any given moment. They could also join additional societies or leave others, depending on changing circumstances and always according to their perceived benefits. Societies of one form could be replaced by societies of another form. The shapes and structures of such societies and their strength, endurance, and benefits were limitless in their variety, but the driving force behind them remained the *jāmi'at al-manfa'a* or "community of usefulness."

As was his habit, Zaidan used history to provide the evidence for his argument: "When relatives multiplied and the tribes branched off, each would live in a different land and participate in the defense of that land. That is the society of the motherland, even though they might still maintain their kinship group and language association, because they came from one root."[169]

But if people perceived staying with one or the other association as harmful to themselves, they would leave it. Zaidan argued that with the rise of Islam the Arab tribes saw a benefit for joining the religious community, which did not hinder them from reverting to an "Arab" identity when they needed to mobilize Christian Arab tribes and draw them to their side to enhance their strength against Byzantium. The breaking up of the early Islamic empires into territorial states constituted a further shift of perceived benefit.

The question of what holds a group together is now answered with its "usefulness" for each member. This, Zaidan pointed out, was true also for such primordial associations as family, tribe, or nation. Just as important was his observation of the simultaneous existence of such voluntary associations. Each individual belonged to several such associations and would shift his primary loyalty according to his immediate needs and goals. He described the "community of usefulness" as the "source for all other group formations" and said that it was the "first incentive for carrying out any common tasks."[170] In principle, people have an unlimited variety of possibilities from which to choose a group. The individual needs to be part of a group or groups because of his own limits. Which group the individual chooses and to which he will be the most loyal or will identify with depends entirely on the perceived usefulness of the group to the individual. In other words, none of these groups has an essential, inherent value, not even religion. The strength of the group and its survival depends on its usefulness to its members. Even language did not escape the question of usefulness. Almost casually Zaidan could observe on another occasion that if the Ottomans, after conquering the Arab lands, had successfully Turkified the population (and Arabic would have disappeared), the coherence of the Ottoman Empire would have been greater, implying that Arab nationalism would not have developed.[171] Zaidan argued here for an amazing relativity of values: family, motherland, nation, and language are all judged by their perceived usefulness to arrive at certain goals; their worth is determined by their functionality in executing tasks for their members.

This emphasis on "benefit" or "usefulness" in this essay, however, should not be confused with J. S. Mill's utilitarianism, since Mill starts out with society as a given and the general goal of all activity as "happiness," defined as the "greatest good for the greatest number of people." He then puts the question of how individuals can act morally, yet achieve their individual goal of happiness, without disregarding the ultimate goal of societal happiness. There is never a discussion of the individual choosing between different kinds of loyalties and associations.

Zaidan starts altogether with a different question: How can the evolutionary model be applied to the explanation of change in society and of societies, civilizations, and cultures? According to him the process of change in society is not driven by the random variations in nature but by the perceived self-interest of individuals, They form their goals and aims on a voluntary basis, determined by a cost-benefit analysis for joining different human associations, which will flourish or wither, stabilize or disintegrate according to the their capacity to fulfill the needs of their members. The basic pattern is always the "community of usefulness and benefit." Zaidan seems to consider all human associations that constitute society as the species that change—they survive or perish according to their adaptive capabilities in an ever-changing environment over time, differing geographically from each other and with competing human interests and goals. In contrast to the natural environment with its accidental differences and changes, the human environment changes in response to the reflecting mind and activated will of human beings. This could give meaning to an otherwise random process and even assert the idea of progress. Though it must be emphasized that in this essay and also elsewhere

Zaidan perceives the process of the "community of usefulness and benefit" as a completely open-ended process free of any teleological goal.

The application of the concept of the survival of the fittest in its Darwinian meaning to human society typically raises several questions. First, could one apply laws of biology to human society? Second, how could one deal with random variations that drew all meaning from a society, yet whose development was based on it? And third, which units struggle against each other for survival: individuals, families, tribes, civilizations, classes, or nations? Zaidan did not explicitly discuss the first question, but always worked on the assumption that it was feasible and appropriate. Concerning the second question, he reintroduced a certain ambivalence by substituting, in human society, conflicting human goals and active wills for the random variation in nature as the cause for change. The last question he answered clearly by focusing on human associations in all their shapes and forms, which were able in different degrees to fulfill the goals of individuals.

But in the end Zaidan saw also weak points in the concept of the *jami'at al-manfa'a*. The problem arises from the uncertainty as to whom usefulness and benefits would ultimately accrue. Zaidan warned of the possibility that the interests of the people could be easily hijacked by the interests of the leaders and elites. In particular he attacked the religious leadership and, to a degree, political leaders for abusing concepts such as "faith" or "fatherland," employing them for their own personal gain and not for the common goals of society.

In trying to establish rational principles for the functioning of society and human associations without resort to religious or metaphysical interpretations, Zaidan actually was engaged in secular explanations of the influences that affect human affairs.

We shall see how in the two subjects that most concerned Zaidan as a scholar—history and language—he systematically established the theory of evolution as a new point of reference. In this way he could analyze and explain the development of language and history without recourse to religion and divine forces as the cause for historical events. He emancipated history and the Arabic language from religious or divine explanations to establish a secular, that is, "manmade" history of the Arabs and their language that, according to him, followed the laws of nature. In other words, from a sacred history of Islam he could filter out an independent history of Arab civilization subject to human forces, which became the foundation of his Arab nationalist thought.

IV

◆ ◆ ◆

Evolutionary and Historical Approaches to the Arabic Language

On the basis of evolutionary theory Zaidan undertook a radical reinterpretation of the character and role of language. The book title *The Arabic Language: a Living Being Subject to the Law of Evolution*[172] formulated succinctly the general intellectual task Zaidan had set for himself: the application of the laws of nature to cultural and social development. Against the classical view of the Koranic language as the unchangeable ideal, he argued that evolutionary change was what kept language alive and relevant and, with it, the society that used that language. His writings contributed massively to the development of Modern Standard Arabic, a simplified print language that is today understood by all literate Arabs.

Few among Zaidan's generation in the Nahda Movement had had an education in the traditional religious sciences; most often they had little knowledge of the Koranic Arabic language or classical Arabic literature, and none had a vested interest in it as a model for their own writing. Not participating in certain traditions of society does not necessarily mean a lack of identity or rootlessness. It may mean the freedom to choose new concepts, ideas, and models. Not having gone through a formal education before starting to question the meaning of things but, on the contrary, to have awoken intellectually and then acquired an education—often in an unsystematic and autodidactic fashion—had the exhilarating advantage of providing totally new perspectives on religion, society, culture, and history.

In the case of Zaidan, this innovative intellectual energy manifested itself for the first—but not the last—time in the study of language. When he returned to Beirut in 1885 he joined his old friends from the Medical School in the Eastern Scientific Society. He also became a member in the Freemason lodge. We can assume that much of the intellectual debate centered on the questions of evolution, progress, and the modern sciences in its many forms. Many members of these circles had themselves tried their hand at translating textbooks of modern science for the students of the medical school and the Syrian Protestant College. Nimr and Sarruf, owners and editors of *al-Muqtataf* and very much at the center of this group, would have had to deal constantly with the question of how to mold new scientific ideas, concepts, or theories into an Arabic understandable to the reader and also how to develop an urgently needed terminology in Arabic that could replicate unambiguously the meaning of the objects and ideas of modern society.

The generation of Sarruf and Nimr was, of course, not the first to discuss such issues as style and language, the introduction of new terms when translating texts from another language and from a different discourse of science and knowledge, and the role of the reader. At the time of the massive translations from Greek into Arabic during the ninth century, a whole new terminology had to be developed in Arabic, in order to be able to transmit the ideas and knowledge of the Greek philosophers and physicians. In modern times it was under the aegis of Muhammad 'Ali that a school for foreign languages and a bureau for translations were established. Rifa'at Rafi'al-Tahtawi, who spent five years in Paris with a group of students from Egypt, was the first to tackle this problem. He was fully aware of the difficulties of expressing himself in Arabic when the French concepts had no equivalent words in Arabic. He would typically attach glossaries to his translations, which would sometimes take up almost as much space as the text itself. During the same time American missionaries undertook a long-term project in the 1840's to translate the New Testament into Arabic with the help of educated Arabs. They recognized the need to simplify the grammar and use of common words if they wanted to reach their intended audience. Later, the task was rather to write textbooks in Arabic for pupils who had no inkling of the classical written Arabic. For Sarruf and Nimr the question became of the utmost importance. Once they began to publish their own magazine, their livelihood began to depend on the popularity of their print product *al-Muqataf,* in as large a reading market as possible.[173]

Already in the first year of *al-Hilal* Zaidan summarized his ideas on how authors should deal with style and the choice of terms and neologisms. The guiding principle had to be clarity and wherever possible the use of Arabic words. Transliterated or arabized foreign words were not to be used. The style should be pleasing and encourage the reader to read more:

> Where stories, novels, histories and other literary subjects of general interest are concerned, the writer has the task of choosing words which the common people understand while at the same time paying attention to vocabulary and inflexions. . . . The use of two or three words which are common to convey an intended concept is better than using a single obsolete word to convey that same concept. Even if we then somehow violate one of the principles of eloquence, on the other hand we can convey to the reader, whether he is one of the common people or not, what we want him to understand, instead of making him become bored with reading and abandon it. After all, we want him to persevere with it, so as to obtain the intended benefit of what we write.[174]

During his stay in Beirut in 1885 and as a result of all his activities in the various associations, Zaidan began, at the age of twenty-five, to write his first book, *Arabic Vocabulary and the Philosophy of Language*.[175] Not surprisingly, based on his own language studies and discussions with his friends and teachers, it dealt with the evolution of the Arabic language.

Zaidan introduced his book with a discussion on the origin of language, exemplifying his ideas with the Turanic, Aryan, and Semitic language groups that each developed from one original language. He then equated each language with one people or nation (*umma*). Just as the original Semitic language branched out into Arabic, Hebrew, Phoenician, Carthagian, and other languages, the peoples associated with those languages developed into Arabs, Israelites, Phoenicians, Carthagians, and others. The mechanism causing such development was migration and/or separation of various groups from the original population and—over time —the repetition of this mechanism. He concurred with the biblical story that the first human beings lived on the banks of the Euphrates and Tigris rivers but then observed critically that the time period, according to him, between Creation and the Flood was a very long one. Many people must have migrated from Mesopotamia during this period. The Confusion of the Tongues in Babylon indeed reflected the historical division of a language into several branches, but it left out part of the story. According to Zaidan, Babylon referred only to the descendants of Noah after the Flood and not to those who emigrated earlier and escaped the Flood, which Zaidan obviously understood not as a world catastrophe but a Mesopotamian one. Those emigrants he identified in the East as the Chinese and in the West as the Egyptians. On the basis of a perceived etymological similarity between the words *ṣīn,* China, and *qāyīn,* Cain, he made a strong case for the Chinese as direct descendants of Cain. He also thought that arguably the Egyptians were descendants of Cain on the basis of the similarity of the ancient name of Egypt, *Kīm* or *Kīmī,* with *qāyīn,* Cain. But he pointed out that apart from the descendants of Cain there existed other people before the Flood.[176] In any case, both were ancient cultures and contemporaries of Babylon. Their ancient origins, however, meant that their languages were much more primitive than the Semitic languages, and in particular Arabic, which appeared much later, that is, after the Flood, when mankind was already much more developed. Zaidan still cherished the biblical proposition that behind all languages there had existed one original language of mankind. He asserted that by analyzing and comparing the earliest concepts in human linguistic development, for instance personal pronouns or numbers, one could establish some of the words of the earliest language.

He introduced the section titled "What Is the Arabic language?" with the claim—and not without a trace of nationalist pride—that of all the living Semitic languages Arabic was the most developed, benefiting from the achievements of all the older languages and surpassing them.[177] He pointed to the longevity of Arabic, which, in contrast to Latin, did not metamorphose into various national languages. He attributed this to the role of the Koran as a classical standard. As the first written document in Arabic it stabilized the language on a very elevated and refined level. Its crystallization in a written form also slowed down uncontrolled borrowing from other languages.

He also offered an anthropological explanation for the development of language in human society. Human weakness forced human beings to associate with each other. In order for society to function, a high level of interaction and communication was necessary. By imitating descriptive sounds from nature, the first words were formed. From the simple and undifferentiated words, ramifications and complexity grew. The level of such diversity and complexity always reflected the varying needs of each society. The community of language is one of the first "communities of usefulness and benefit."[178] Zaidan made an observation that remains remarkable—namely that even though human beings were better equipped to learn languages than other beings, language was still not an inborn trait of humans but was something acquired and had to be learned. He added, "We only learn to speak what we hear in our surrounding. We only speak Arabic because we grew up in its environment. Had we grown up among the Greeks we would speak their language and among the Indians it would be Hindi."[179]

We are not concerned here with the scientific veracity of his conclusions. Obviously, the state of the art of linguistics has gone far beyond what it was more than a hundred years ago. But the method he used in writing a natural history of language deserves our attention. As a basic concept he introduced an essential aspect of the theory of evolution: development from the simple unit of origin to an increasing complexity of divisions and subdivisions through migration and separation over space and time, with the law of evolution, *nāmus al-irtiqā'*, as the trigger for these changes. However, he never gave a general interpretation of the theory of evolution and all its parts. He referred to aspects of it or simply to the "law of evolution." He apparently assumed that his readers knew what he was talking about and agreed with the validity of the theory.

He accepted the biblical stories of Paradise and the Flood, albeit in a qualified fashion, and seemed to accept the story of the Confusion of Tongues, but was critical of the whole biblical narrative because it left out much of human history and, in particular, of language. He also implicitly dismissed the Confusion of Tongues by providing a "natural" explanation for the development of many languages. His anthropological explanation of how language developed within a society is, needless to say, a direct contradiction of the biblical story in which God teaches man the names of objects and animals. He never raised the issue of this contradiction but clearly gave the impression that his explanations were the scientifically correct ones.

Zaidan diverged somewhat from his evolutionary argument when he repeatedly praised the role of the Koranic language, meaning its immutability, as preventing the ramification of Arabic into a diversity of independent languages whose speakers would no longer understand each other. However, another insight was closely associated with the recognition of the role of the Koran: once a language obtained a written standard, the laws of nature worked much more slowly. It is not clear whether he wanted simply to emphasize the longevity of Arabic or to make an obliging remark about the role of the Koran. The latter seems less likely, as we will see further on. As a thinker coming from a Christian background, he never offered an argument about the sacredness of Arabic as the language of the Revelation and the Prophet. Almost as if to underline in a very subtle way his denial of the sacredness of Arabic terminology and the monopoly Islam had over it, he used the term *umma* not in its well-known context of *ummat al-mu'minīn*, the "community of the believers," but as *ummat al-lugha*, the "community of language," that is, the nation—just as other contemporaries began to speak of *al-umma al-miṣriyya* or *ummat al-'arab*, the Egyptian or the Arab "nation." But at the same time, he did not attempt to sanctify Arabic as the national language. He simply observed that we all learn and speak the language into which we are born, the social environment determining whether we speak Arabic or Greek and that—apart from its evolutionary stage and its benefits as a community of usefulness—there was no inherently greater value in speaking one language over any other.

Over the years he would come back to the issue of the importance of language again and again in essays, answers to letters to the editor, and even in private letters to his son. In 1904 he republished his first book *Philosophy of Language and Arabic Vocabulary* and in the same year published an additional book, *The Arab Language as a Living Being*.[180] His declared intention here was to write a history of the Arabic language rather than a philosophical speculation about the general development of language and its diversification. Implicitly the book is a frontal attack on any classicist attitude toward the Arabic language that declared the Arabic of the *Jahiliyya* and of the Koran as an exemplary standard to be followed. Much bolder than ever before, Zaidan declared already in the book's title that language was a living being, subject to the law of evolution like anything else. Every living organism, he explained, was subject to decay and renewal, whether it was the body and its cells decaying and renewing themselves, or a society where individuals play a similar role to the cells in the body. All were subject to the general laws of evolution. Similarly, all manifestations of the human mind, such as language, habits, religions, laws, sciences, literature, and so on were subject to these laws. The ways in which the laws of decay and renewal applied depended, according to Zaidan, upon the level of evolution, with its diversification and complexity on the one hand, and upon the needs, obstacles, and opportunities of the environment on the other. Writing the history of a language meant writing about how these laws of renewal and decay responded to specific historical situations and thereby directed the development of the language.

Here, unlike in his earlier writings, we find no reference to biblical stories about how language was created and no mention of the role of the Koran in preserving the language but instead a strict application of the laws of decay and renewal. In the case of the language, words, concepts, and specific terms are the "cells." Some slip into oblivion, because they are not needed any more; others are newly developed from the Arabic or imported from other languages and fulfill new intellectual needs. This process not only happened at all times but it was also, in Zaidan's opinion, a positive event, because it proved the language was still alive and could reproduce itself, be creative, adapt to new needs, and thus survive. What was true for the language was equally true for the society using it.

Zaidan directly challenged classicist concepts of exemplary Arabic when he analyzed the condition of Arabic in the late pre-Islamic and early Islamic times. He demonstrated the variety, mixture, and changing character of expressions and composition among the Arab tribes during the

Jahiliyya. The tribes speaking an Arabic most similar to the original Semitic language had also been those most isolated. For the tribes engaged with other people the opposite obtained, "especially the Meccans and above all Quraysh, who were merchants trading and traveling north to Syria, Iraq and Egypt, south to Yemen, east to the Persian Gulf. . . . In addition, different peoples gathered around the Ka'ba. . . . All that led to the Hejazi dialect developing, thanks to the derived words and constructions which were generated or were incorporated through borrowing."[181]

In similar fashion he demonstrated how the new religious, administrative, and scholarly needs during the early Islamic period led to new concepts and terms derived from Arabic itself or imported and Arabized from other languages. All this was not meant as a traditional critique of the "corruption" of classical language but as modern praise for the innovative and re-creative forces of Arabic.

What interested him most was, of course, the Nahda of his own time, which in his book took up much more space than any other section. His reinterpretation of the history of the Arabic language demonstrated that even at the time of the Koran and the time of the Rightly Guided Caliphs, Arabic had not reached a static classical standard but was evolving all the time, transliterating foreign words, Arabizing such imports, or deriving new Arabic words from old roots. This historical precedent legitimized the enterprise of the Nahda, which he compared with the drastic changes and innovations in the language during the early Islamic period constituted for Zaidan a Nahda *avant le mot*. He admitted that at the beginning of that first Nahda mistakes were made concerning terminologies and naming concepts. But principally the two periods were comparable: "In our recent cultural nahda too, new terms and expressions have been coined. To stand still during such a process of growth is contrary to the course of the laws of nature, quite apart from being useless. For language is a living, growing being, subject to the laws of evolution—and disintegration and generation are inevitable whether people like that or not. New words appear and old ones disappear, as circumstances require, according to a rationale common to all existing beings."[182]

Without any false romanticism and without a trace of classicism, he pleaded now with writers to free their pens from the shackles of the

Jahiliyya and to leave the prison of nomadism. "Now is the time for us to free our pens from the chains of the pre-Islamic Age of Ignorance and bring them out of the prison of nomadic life. Otherwise we shall not be able to survive in this new level [of civilization]."[183] Newly developed terms should exactly fit and reflect the meaning of what they name. Arabic derivatives were better than terminology imported from other languages. Precision and clarity was of utmost importance; it was preferable to use three words rather than one to achieve this aim if the latter lacked the desired precision.

Language played an enormous role in Zaidan's thinking concerning the integration of society and its progress in modern civilization; indirectly it provided the foundation for the secularization of society. Language had its own life and development, following the laws of evolution. However, it also needed constant attention against abuse and corruption just as it took a self-conscious effort on the part of the intellectuals and educators of society to develop new terms and whole terminologies in order to cope with the intellectual and scientific challenges of the modern world. Zaidan considered Arabic as one of the most developed languages of the world. But he never fell into the trap of later romantic nationalist thinkers who attributed to it an inherent superiority and essentialist quality. Zaki al-Arsuzi, for instance, spoke of the *'abqariyya* or "genius" of the Arabic language, which had always existed and was waiting to be reawakened.[184] For Sati' al-Husri language and history were—just as for Zaidan—the most important components of nationhood. Since language, meaning the modern printed Arabic, was so essential for him, he—like Zaidan—"had little sympathy for colloquial Arabic."[185] But in contrast to Zaidan's evolutionist approach, he had a mystical-romantic conception of the nation: "Synonymous as the natural and the national are in al-Husri's definition, he asserts that the nationalism which sustains nations operates on a spiritual level distinct from the mechanical actions within the organisms of nature. This romantic emphasis on spiritual forces pervades all of al-Husri's work. Phrases such as *rūḥ al-'urūba*, the spirit of Arabism, and *rawābiṭ ma'nawiyya*, spiritual ties, appear repeatedly."[186]

The nation acquired for him a spiritual aspect, which would by itself drive the nation to unification. Haim speaks of Husri's "genuine metaphysics of nationalism" and points out that Husri used the same term as the Sufis when speaking of the individual as 'losing himself', *yufnī*, in the nation.[187]

Zaidan, faithful adherent of evolutionary theory, saw nothing inherently superior or eternal in the Arabic language. The nationalist essentialism of Zaki al-Arsuzi and Sati' al-Husri contradicted his "community of benefit and usefulness"; and speakers of Arabic constituted exactly such a community. If no benefit could be perceived, there loomed danger of its decay—or even disappearance:

> The Romans spread their language (Latin) in their Western Empire in Southern Europe. The people there took pride in their Roman relations because they spoke Latin. This led to the consolidation of Roman rule. The Portuguese in South America and the English in North America did likewise. Had the Ottomans done this from the beginning of their rule they would have spared themselves the break-up of the various races in their kingdom. This is [today] the reason for their great weakness and for the decay of their position of power. If the people of Syria, Iraq and Egypt had been forced at the time of Ottoman rule to adopt Turkish they would today consider themselves Turks—and defend the Turkish race like the people of Syria and Egypt defended the Arabs, though many of them had no trace of Arab identity by kinship. Some Muslims had Turkish, Circassian, Kurdish or Albanian origins. Some Christians could be identified by their name as Italian, Greek or European—but they spoke Arabic and considered themselves Arabs.[188]

In Zaidan's opinion, political power as much as cultural neglect could mean the disappearance of a language, and he felt that any language, while being flexible and able to change with changing circumstances, also needed to be protected if it was to survive. There had to be limits to change: it should not lead to the abandoning of Arabic in favor of local dialects as the means of formal communication. He was keenly conscious of how Latin dialects had been elevated to national languages. This he wanted to avoid at all cost, because it could cause the Arabs to drift apart from each other. The demand to declare the Egyptian dialect a literary language came typically from foreigners who worked and lived in Egypt and might have learned a smattering of spoken Arabic there but could neither read nor write the classical written language.[189] The Egyptian nationalist Mustafa Kamil, a foe of all educated Syrians in Egypt, also demanded the cultivation of Arabic and the introduction of Arabic in all Egyptian schools as the language of instruction but "his interest in the language is for him a consequence of nationalism rather than a source of it. In spite of the common language he hardly feels a special relationship to the Syrians, the inhabitants of the Arab peninsula, and the North African Arabs."[190]

For Zaidan, in contrast, the relations of Egypt with other Arab lands, or the relationships among all Arabic-speaking populations, was of utmost importance. In response to a speech given in Cairo by the British engineer Willcocks,[191] in which he clamored for the introduction of the Egyptian dialect as a written language, Zaidan offered in 1893 a carefully developed argument as to why such a step would have disastrous consequences.[192] First and foremost it was an argument of cultural politics: elevating the Egyptian or any other Arab dialect to the official written language would mean that 1,300 years of literary heritage would be lost, that is, inaccessible to those who did not learn "classical" Arabic any more. Secondly, if Yemenis wrote in Yemeni dialect, Egyptians in Egyptian dialect, and Maghribis in Maghribi dialect, they would no longer be able to understand each other and read writings in a different dialect. In the last analysis this was also an argument of national politics. As Zaidan put it bluntly: "the unity of the Arabs would be disrupted." Thirdly, there existed an underlying economic argument that Zaidan did not articulate but of which he was, nevertheless, keenly aware: the elevation of vernaculars to written languages would shrink the market for each print product[193] enormously. This touched directly on the issue of his livelihood and that of every Nahdawi. Finally, Zaidan always argued that the written language had to be simplified in its syntax; enriched with new terms, reflecting the meaning of new concepts; and freed from anachronistic verbal ballast. He felt that the dialects were not sophisticated enough to deal with the need for new terminologies and concepts. The purpose of the simplification and clarification of the written language was so that it could reach as many readers as possible, especially those who were educated but did not have a training in religious studies and Koranic interpretation. Here the economic argument for reaching as large a market as possible was joined by an educational one: to inform and instruct society, raise the level of knowledge, and prepare the people for participation in modern civilization and the progress this promised.[194]

V

Secular Analyses of Arab History

The only formal education Zaidan had received pertained to the sciences: medicine, chemistry, and pharmacology. His in-depth knowledge of history was acquired through years of his own extensive reading. Judging from the long list of books that usually preceded his works on history, he was not only familiar with classical authors such as Herodotus, Josephus Flavius, and Strabo but also with the Muslim Arab historians. He also had a solid knowledge of the modern standard works of European scholars' writings on history in general and Near Eastern history in particular. It was probably his stay in London that introduced him to the latter works during his visits to the British Library.

Zaidan developed an inclination for history early on. When he wrote about language, he wrote about its development over time. His book on the Freemasons is about their history. He wrote a *History of Arabic Literature and Culture* rather than an aesthetic or literary critique of it. For him history served to illustrate his arguments, to confirm or reject ideas and theories, to extract general patterns of historical movement, and certainly to legitimize his or other peoples' actions in the present and also define "the position of the Arabs among the rest of the advanced people with respect to their social and intellectual progress."[195]

Methods of Analysis

Zaidan's treatment of history constituted a profound break with traditional Arab Muslim historiography. His studies at the Syrian Protestant College had given him a sense of modern scientific research. European historians of the time were, under the influence of positivist thought,[196] gathering individual "historical facts" and using increasingly refined techniques of research. Zaidan's readings of modern European historiography must have demonstrated to him how the critical reading of sources, the comparative study of texts, and the use of ancillary sciences (such as archaeology and linguistics) all helped to differentiate between the nonsensical, *khurāfa,* and the rationally acceptable, *al-ma'qūl,* in historical writings. It was methodology that led him to consider translation into Arabic of the works of Seignobos,[197] the most worthwhile of all contemporary historians, because he insisted vigorously on "the criticism provided by sincerity and exactitude and the establishment of individual facts."[198]

Zaidan was conscious of the fact that his method was new to Arab historiography.[199] He took pains to indicate his textual sources and explain the use of other types of sources such as inscriptions, coins, dates, anthropological findings, and architectural evidence. He also insisted that the whole cultural context had to be given in order to be able to analyze and interpret individual military events or political developments.[200] He criticized the Muslim historians of the past for always having a bias in favor of the ruling dynasty—the most glaring example being the historians of the Abbasid period on the subject of the Umayyads. He also took exception to their uncritical and sole reliance on the *isnād*[201] and the total absence of the application of common sense—not to mention scientific methods—in their works. As early as the third year of *al-Hilal* (1895),[202] he lashed out at Muslim historians who never provided the dates of birth, death, or length of rule of monarchs but only lists with rulers of different dynasties. They would indicate only the average length of rule for the members on their lists, which could vary from 80 to 180 years, "which no rational mind can accept." They would also accept without question the worst bits of *khurāfa,* superstition or fairy tale, even when constraints of space and time demonstrated their absurdity. In a lengthy answer to a reader's letter[203] discussing Ibn Khaldun's[204] criticism of uncritical, unquestioning Muslim historiography,[205] Zaidan praised Ibn Khaldun for his justified criticism.

At the same time he demonstrated a sophisticated understanding of the conditions and constraints of writing history by contextualizing historiography in the political and cultural conditions of the time. Listing the reasons for the fact that the history of the Tubba' people[206] in Yemen was not known nor explored, in contrast to that of the Babylonians and the Assyrians, he pointed out that they were not mentioned in the Bible and that therefore a European interest to study them did not exist. Only archaeological excavations had provided scientific proof for the existence of the Assyrians and Babylonians. Since there existed no particular religious interest and since the Yemen was a dangerous place, only the Ottoman government could have guaranteed safety for excavations there, but it was not willing to do so; hence Himyarite history remained unexplored.[207]

He always insisted that history required a description and analysis of society in all its aspects. Only in this way could the position of any given society with respect to its intellectual and cultural advancement be defined. His most conscientious effort in this direction remains his *History of Islamic Civilization,* always insisting that he was not writing a history of religion but a history of the culture, *Kulturgeschichte,* of a society in a specific epoch. For Arab historiography this was certainly a new approach, but Zaidan found European examples in the *Culturgeschichte des Orients* by A. von Kremer and in the *Histoire de la Civilisation Arab* by G. Le Bon. He was influenced by both, and borrowed especially from Kremer[208] without, however, sharing the views of the latter about the finality of the downfall of the Arabs, nor agreeing with Le Bon's racial theories.

Models of Historical Development

In one of the very first history books he wrote, *A General History,*[209] he adhered strictly to the biblical story of creation. He then proceeded to divide mankind into four different groups: the nomadic savage, *al-hamajiyya;* the primitive, settled, *al-barbariyya;* those who were civilized but making no use of sciences, *al-ḥadariyya;* and the fully civilized, possessing all modern technological and scientific features, *al-madaniyya.* Even though we find a faint allusion to the concept of one stage evolving from the other in the relation between "civilized" and "fully civilized," it remains a static model and he did not elaborate on the internal mechanisms by which societies moved between the four stages.[210] Zaidan's classification of religions is even more static. Next to the three monotheistic religions he puts a fourth category, paganism, in which he includes everything from tribal totemism to Buddhism. The three monotheistic religions are explained as being based on their Holy Scriptures but any hint of a relationship between them is lacking. It is not surprising, then, that he should have organized his whole book similarly by unhistorical criteria, that is, the five continents, rather than, for instance, by civilizations.

Zaidan also had a genuine interest in other analytical models such as the historical theory of Ibn Khaldun, which itself was much more an attack on the established Islamic religious view of history than is usually recognized. He admired Ibn Khaldun as a critical historian and appreciated his cyclical theory, according to which nomads possessed a high degree of loyalty to the clan or tribe. That loyalty and their desert-hardened bodies enabled them in wave after wave to pour out of the desert and conquer sedentary civilizations, softened by decadence and the loss of loyalty to clan or tribe. But conquest of a civilization bore in itself the seeds of destruction. Once the new rulers had established themselves, they would begin a new cycle of decadence and the loss of loyalty to their own kin. But in the end Zaidan did not believe that the theory of history of Ibn Khaldun was valid for the modern age. Again, responding to a question from a reader about the relation between science and national independence, he became very explicit:

> As far as the independence of some nations before the advent of modern science is concerned, this belongs to ancient civilizations, *al-tamaddun al-qadīm*, where superiority was attached to physical force; therefore one can see that most political transformations, *inqilāb*, took the form of nomadism overwhelming civilization. . . . Thus did the German tribes overcome the Romans . . . and the Arabs in the beginning of Islam overwhelmed the civilized world. There are many examples in ancient history for the vanquishing of civilizations by nomadism, or of science by ignorance, when victory belonged to physical prowess . . . [the nomads] were usually united by religious or racial sentiment or the desire to plunder and to loot. But nowadays people rise in the name of the fatherland, *al-waṭan*, and demand independence based on social and political rights. How could this be feasible without science and education, *'ilm wa-tarbiyya*?[211]

Zaidan equally paid attention to the cyclical concept of a living organism, including biological birth, growth, and decay as a model for history—but also the possibility of reproduction and regeneration. In addition, he was a firm believer in the possibility of educating people in order to reach higher stages of development. As we shall discuss further on, a great part of all his work was focused on his educational enterprise—not exactly the laissez-faire attitude of social-survival-of-the-fittest advocates, but rather reflecting the beliefs of the Enlightenment that humans were rational beings and that through education and knowledge they would be empowered to make rational decisions and thus serve the betterment of mankind. Zaidan never quite resolved the contradiction between the "laws of nature" deciding the fate of society and the role of the intellectual interfering with them through education.

The theory of evolution played an increasingly dominant role in Zaidan's analysis of history and loomed ever larger in his thinking. Answering a question about the age of mankind, he unequivocally followed the evolutionary argument and concluded that the Holy Books needed to be reinterpreted accordingly. He described language as "a living being, subject to the laws of evolution." He would even describe the history of his magazine *al-Hilal* in terms of evolutionary development:

> Whoever contemplates the path *al-Hilal* has taken since its first appearance until now, will see that it has gradually matched in content and form the intentions of its name, proceeding according to the laws of evolution. He will recognize after inspecting its past years, that we have changed its topics, added to them and substituted others according to the needs of our readers, i.e., what entertains them and benefits them—this is the secret of its wide diffusion.[212]

A development from the simple to the complex, as a process of constant adaptation (i.e., removing patterns and structures that had become obsolete and introducing new and more fitting ones), according to changing circumstances (i.e., the wishes of readers, the challenges of modern sciences), and advances in quality—all ensured survivability. History for him was change, and change was good. He did not see innovative change as an ever-increasing departure from an imagined Golden Age in the past or a general deterioration of human and societal life, but rather as proof that society was alive and advancing.

We have seen in the section on religion and science how his position had changed by the mid-1890s when he bluntly declared that the interpretation of holy texts had to be adapted to the findings of modern science. Soon he also applied the laws of evolution to society. This was a nonlinear intellectual development of Zaidan's thought, embracing the evolutionary approach for different topics at different times. Zaidan had, for example, written his first book *Arabic Vocabulary and the Philosophy of Language*,[213] already firmly embedded in evolutionary thought, four years before his *General History*. Though still a challenge to traditional scholarship, language was not such a sensitive topic of creation according to the Bible, the veracity of which was directly and provocatively questioned by the theory of evolution.

Let us summarize the models of history Zaidan had used. He saw the validity of Ibn Khaldun's model of history, but also its obsolescence since the arrival of "true sciences," that is, modern civilization. He applied the model of the development of biological organisms as well as the theory of evolution to history without, however, explicitly facing the issue of evolutionary randomness. The cyclical biological model as well as the evolutionary model seemed to be based on the law of nature, which in turn was the subject of modern natural sciences. Applying these laws to the study of history provided the latter with the status of a "true science." The timing of introducing evolutionary theory into his works seems to have somewhat depended on the sensitivity of the topic to which he wanted to apply it—language, religion, or history.

The application of the biological laws of organisms to the development of society, nations, or institutions seemed to endow the interpretation of history with the legitimacy of scientific laws. But as always when such comparisons with nature are used to explain the historical process, it is left up to the author which particular "law of nature" he chooses and to what entity, precisely, it is to be applied. He can compare an institution, for instance, with a living body which is born, reaches its zenith, eventually dies, and is replaced by another, similar body. But he can also compare the development of an institution with a living organism that consists of cells that go through a constant process of replacement and renewal. In this case change and improvement can be explained and justified, as Zaidan did in the case of language, without condemning the institution, that is, the whole organism, to biological death.

The attempt to apply the laws of evolution to history also does not explain which entity is actually fighting for survival: Is it individuals, classes, groups within societies, or the whole of mankind? It seems that in the age of the dominance of the natural sciences the real role of the laws of nature in the study of what we today call the "soft sciences" was to lend them the cloak of respectability and scientific authority.

Zaidan did not apply the theory of evolution with the same rigor to the history of civilization as he did to that of language; though, on balance, he was inclined toward the evolutionary model. This can be seen in what he said about the forces that drive the development of society. He mentioned the "tribal solidarity," *al-'aṣabiyya*, of Ibn Khaldun, and he cited the greed and violence of human beings. But central to his thinking was the concept of the "community of usefulness or benefit," *jāmi'at al-manfa'a* or *jāmi'at al-maṣlaḥa*, as he called it.[214]

Zaidan admitted the relevance of economic and cultural factors, but he failed to show what impact they had on historical development. His explanation for economic and cultural development refers to the role of individuals, mostly belonging to the political elite, who are the movers of history, the *agentes historia*. True, they were subject to the laws of human nature, but their position of power and influence made their beliefs and actions decisive for the course of history. It was here that Zaidan also saw the danger of abuse in his model of the *jāmi'at al-manfa'a*. Strong personalities, leaders with personal ambitions and desires, could make people believe that their interests would benefit from supporting a particular national group or religious community while in fact they were being used for the egotistical aims of their seducers. He saw the greatest danger for such derailment in societies constructed around religion. Obviously these were not true communities of usefulness, as their aims were usurped and their activities only benefited their leaders: and each would have to be investigated carefully as to its real aims.

In his essay on the *jāmi'at al-manfa'a*, Zaidan did not mention the theory of evolution explicitly. But concepts such as branching out, diversification, complexity, adaptation to new circumstances, and continuous change are evident throughout. The idea of one natural law—in this case, the nature of man, searching for his own greatest benefit—is in its role equivalent to the concept of the fittest in evolutionary theory. This law determines the whole process of human society, that is, the course of history.

Periodization of History

The issue of structuring history into discrete historical periods occupied Zaidan throughout his career as a historian. Again, his thoughts on the topic did not develop in a linear, progressive form, and various options were used almost simultaneously. The way he dealt with these issues might also help us to clarify what role different models of the historical process played in his thinking and how development happened. In his *General History of Freemasonry,*[215] which was probably compiled from a few European sources on the topic, Zaidan gave a rather original twist to the history of the Freemasons. He started with the reign of Roman King Numa Pompilius as the beginning of the Masons. With the rise of Islam and the construction of the Umayyad mosques, he then traced the Freemasons in Islamic civilization.[216] After the decline of the latter, and with the trans-Mediterranean connections of the Crusaders, the Freemasons—supposedly—moved to Europe, where they continued as "active" (i.e., practicing) Masons until, at the end of the seventeenth century, they transformed themselves into, as he called them, "symbolic" Freemasons. Zaidan here used two features that were already much discussed by Muslim thinkers in his time: the triptych of antiquity, Islam, and modern Europe as the core of world history; and the role of Islamic civilization as a link and transmitter between antiquity and modern Europe.[217] This is not the place to investigate the veracity of his claims about the history of the Freemasons. To invent long histories for their group or organization and thereby gain legitimacy and respectability was the favored ploy of all national and other movements in the nineteenth century and was not restricted to the Freemasons. Of relevance here is that Zaidan applied the same triptych model to the history of Freemasonry, attaching great importance to the middle period, thus assuring the preservation and transmission of culture and knowledge. Eight years later he repeated: "Islamic history is the history of the East and the Arabs, nay it is the history of the World in the Middle Ages."[218] He saw the importance of Islamic civilization in its role as a link and conduit, *muwaṣṣil*. In space it linked the regions of the East and the West; in time it linked antiquity with modern Western civilization. In addition, Islamic civilization drew people who had not been heard of before into world history.[219] In twenty-two years of publishing *al-Hilal*, Zaidan hardly ever devoted space to a major article on the European Middle Ages. They seemed to him of little relevance in terms of a contribution to world history and the evolution of mankind. The history of Islamic civilization was for him the world history during the (European) Middle Ages.

In a seminal article that Zaidan had originally drafted as his introductory lecture at the university in his new position as professor of Islamic history in 1910,[220] and which was addressed to a presumably much more sophisticated audience of scholars, he brought together his earlier thought and ideas and revised profoundly the structure of world history as he saw it.[221] He now discarded the triptych of world history—ancient civilizations, Islamic civilizations, and modern civilization—because it was European-centered. Instead, he suggested a division between an Eastern history, including Asia and the Nile Valley, and a Western history, including Europe and America. He then proceeded to divide Western history into the typical triad of antiquity, the Middle Ages, and modern civilization. For Eastern history, too, he suggested three stages, but their periodization was highly original. Antiquity ended here with the conquest of Persia by Alexander the Great, followed by the undistinguished Middle Ages before the modern period of the East began with the rise of Islam.

Zaidan achieved several things with this separation between Eastern and Western history:

1. He established a periodization that was more relevant to the East or, more precisely, to the Middle East, making himself at the same time guilty of a "Middle-East-centeredness." Just as Western history was European-centered, speaking of "world history" but meaning European history, Zaidan spoke of the "history of the East," but Japanese, Chinese, and Indian history had no place in his scheme while African history was not even mentioned.

2. He divided Eastern and Western history into the same pattern of ancient, medieval, and modern stages. But at each stage the earlier

beginning and greater length of time in Eastern history gave it more weight. When he stretched the Eastern antiquity "from the earliest times until the conquest of Persia by Alexander the Great," Zaidan had already offered a radically new interpretation of the pre-Islamic Arabs of the *Jahiliyya* period as a very advanced society. More important, Hammurabi's Code had already been deciphered and Babylonian civilization had been fully integrated by Zaidan as part of the national history of the Arabs, "from earliest times," as he said, referred to the Babylonian civilization.[222]

3. He depicted Islamic history as a modern civilization of the East, an idea that had been hinted at earlier when he declared in the introduction to one of his historical novels that "the history of Islam is tantamount to the history of the modern East and is the history of the world after the Romans and the Persians."[223] He would never waver in his view that between the collapse of the Roman Empire and the European Renaissance, Islamic civilization took on the role of world history, especially in the early part of this period when Arabs were dominantly engaged in that civilization.

Zaidan also attempted to periodize Islamic history itself, showing an ambiguity in the use of models of history that reflects his indecisiveness as to whether Islamic civilization had fulfilled its role in the evolution of world history or still contributed to it. This division of Islamic history into five different phases went as follows:[224]

a. The period of formation, *takawwun* and growth, *numū'*, which started with the Prophet and went as far as the fall of the Umayyads;

b. the period of maturity, *bulūgh*, which covered the Abbasids until the Turks prevailed in the middle of the ninth century;

c. the period of ramification, *tasha''ub,* and diversification, *tafarru',* which ended with the fall of Baghdad in1258;

d. the period of the Islamic Middle Ages, *al-qurūn al-islāmiyya*; and

e. the latest Nahda, which began in the early nineteenth century.

The first three terms—formation, growth, and maturity—are taken from the biological development of a living organism and would be followed by the stages of decay and death and the repetition of the whole cycle. But growth and development that leads to diversification and ramification points rather to an evolutionary process that goes on forever. After those stages, however, Zaidan seems to recognize the continuity of Islamic civilization linking it to the Nahda as a part of the movement. He therefore added—after the stage of diversification and ramification, which should have led to further evolutionary change—a period of "Islamic Centuries" that begins with the fall of Baghdad and that carried for him and the Nahdawis negative connotations of sterility and a lack of culture and creativity, which in fact separated Islamic civilization from the Nahda. The terms "Islamic Centuries" and "Nahda" are not categories of the evolutionary process or the development of organisms; rather, they hark back to the three stages of "classic," "middle," and "modern," similar to Zaidan's organization of Western and Eastern history. These Islamic Centuries, which he does not explain any further, separate the Nahda from the period of "diversification and ramification" but they are also distinct from the Nahda, which, as he explains, "is still going on and is borrowed, *muqtabasa*, from modern Western civilization."[225] Considering the fact that in his periodization of Islamic history the Nahda appears as the most recent of these phases, the last sentence raises questions as to the meaning of "borrowed" in this context and whether the period of the Nahda still belongs to the history of Islamic civilization.

Later, in 1911, Zaidan added an intriguing differentiation in the lectures he had prepared on the history of Ottoman Egypt. He ended the history of Ottoman Egypt with the French occupation of Egypt in 1798 and dated the beginning of the Nahda with the end of the French presence in 1801, which he considered a colonial conquest. He may have even established the later widely accepted dictum by historians that "modern times" started in Egypt with the French invasion. Zaidan shared with Volney the view that the brutality of the Ottoman tyranny had driven Arab culture into an abysmal state of decay in all aspects, and he understood the Nahda as a new beginning for the Arabs. He connected these beginnings closely with the social and cultural politics of Muhammad 'Ali and the active participation of the Arabic-speaking Egyptians,[226] a point he made on many occasions. Politically, though, Zaidan's statement remains somewhat peculiar. In 1911 Egypt was officially still part of the Ottoman Empire, although it had been under the direct but informal control of the

British for almost thirty years—Zaidan himself being at that time (still) an enthusiastic supporter of the Ottoman Empire.[227]

Contemporary and Later Critiques of Zaidan's Historical Work

Contemporary Muslim scholars attacked Zaidan's methodology. They blamed him for not relying exclusively on the transmitters and collectors of *ḥadīth,* [228] for relying more on the stories of Herodotus than on the *Ayyam al-'Arab* in the oral accounts of pre-Islamic Arab battles,[229] and for using the Koran in a critical manner like any other historical source.[230] A sharp criticism of Zaidan's *History of Islamic Civilization* came in 1912 from the Indian scholar Shibli al-Nu'mani. It was a blistering personal attack on Zaidan himself accusing him of cowardice and commercial interests in his writings and denying Zaidan, the Christian, the right to write on Islamic history.[231] Rashid Rida, who had published Nu'mani's attack in *al-Manar,*[232] added insult to injury by publishing a collection of critical reviews, even including one by Père Louis Cheikho, the Jesuit priest. [233] The latter had disqualified Zaidan as a historian of Islamic history because he had never studied Islamic sciences. During his lifetime Christian scholars continued to attack Zaidan's works vehemently. Père Cheikho, publisher of *al-Mashriq* in Lebanon, and Père Anastas-Marie, a Carmelite and publisher of the journal *Lughat al-'Arab* in Baghdad, were his fiercest critics.

> [The problem] raised by Père Cheikho was of a religious nature. Between him and Zaydan two conceptions of the origins of the world and of the relationships between faith and science confronted each other. Père Cheikho blamed Zaydan for saying that the teachings of religion were not in agreement with the discoveries of scientists, especially those of Darwin and his disciples, and accused him of denying any divine intervention in his description of the origins of the human species.[234]

Zaidan applied his critical and methodological approach also to Christian history when discussing the dubious authenticity of the so-called Charter of the Prophet for the Christians, of which a Turkish copy supposedly existed in the monastery of Saint Catherine on Mount Sinai. Zaidan argued that (a) none of the early Muslim writers ever mention it; (b) some of the provisions and stipulations are incompatible with the conditions during the first years of Islam; and (c) it was very likely the Christians fabricated the charter for their own advantage.[235] Christian scholars were not happy with him either, accusing him of a pro-Islamic bias.

The first book of criticism on Zaidan's historical work was al-Hulwani's book, published in India in 1890. It is an intense critique of Zaidan's *History of Egypt.* The new edition contains a preface by Muhammad Sayyid al-Wakil, who states that Zaidan was one of the most famous falsifiers of Islamic history: "He hid behind a cloak of Arabness and was invisible behind national feelings." Al-Wakil claims that Western media arranged for him to write a disfigured and fragmented history of Islam.[236] The book enumerates 101 mistakes that Zaidan made in his history. Typically they are spelling mistakes or factual errors of a technical nature. But in his introduction al-Hulwani, a contemporary of Zaidan, described with obvious hostility the role of Christian Syrian immigrants in Egypt and how they dominated the publishing scene and came to divide the nation, *al-umma*.[237] The Egyptians always underestimated the danger of these immigrants. The latter propagated Freemasonry and preached local chauvinism, *nadā' iqlīmī,* wanting to split the *umma*. There were 500 Syrian government employees in the Egyptian administration, and they collaborated with the foreigners—that is, Europeans—because they knew Arabic but were Christians.[238] Needless to say, al-Hulwani labeled Zaidan as one of them.[239] That some people considered it worth their while to republish this book one hundred and more years after its first publication is demonstrated by the tenor of the books described in the following section, which also deals with Zaidan's historical novels.[240]

Ashmawi—a century later—recognized Zaidan as a literary pioneer but denied the artistic value of his novels, because (a) the central characters are not those mentioned in the title of his book, but fictitious characters; (b) Zaidan overloads descriptions with details, and the reader loses interest; (c) there is no balance between historical truth and the needs of art; (d) the language is plain but faulty; and (e) Zaidan makes historical mistakes and is inconsistent in his narrative.

But beyond these rather technical accusations about the artistic weaknesses of Zaidan's novels, Ashmawi's criticisms are aimed at something totally different. He claimed Zaidan neglected historical figures in his novel and preferred to invent heroes, since he "shied away from the manifest truth of Islamic history because his Christianity prevented him from dealing fairly with Islamic history."[241] Elsewhere he says: "He wrote Islamic history with a Christian pen."[242] Like Ashmawi, Abu Khalil considers these novels a danger for the Muslim and Arab reader: "Veritable poison was provided to two generations of the youth of our Arab nation through Jurji Zaidan's stories, based on the texture of imaginary adventure [but] carrying the title 'Novels of Islamic History.'"[243]

At first sight al-Muhs takes a much more scholarly approach. He quotes Zaidan as saying that his only aim in writing historical novels was to bring history and an interest in history close to the reading public. Al-Muhs comments explicitly that Zaidan did not intend to vilify Islamic history nor was he driven by the need to defend the fatherland or other interests; he was a paragon of fairness and justice in his writings.[244] Zaidan subordinated the romantic story to history, and separated the two clearly.[245] However, he accuses Zaidan of always choosing for his novels periods in Islamic history that were full of crisis and war, as if he wanted to tell the reader, "this is all there is to Islamic history." Al-Muhs also considers his titles sensationalist. For example, the juxtaposition of *Saladin and the Assassins* in a title seemed to him offensive and malicious.[246] Al-Muhs observes that most of the novels are introduced by a long chapter on earlier history preparing the scene, place, and time of the story dealt with in the novel. He admits that they display great historical knowledge but are burdensome and often irrelevant. In the final analysis he accuses Zaidan of denigrating Islamic history because of his Christian prejudices. He also blames this attitude on the close relations that Zaidan cultivated with European Orientalists.[247] He quotes a certain Dr. Mamun Fariz Jarar, who wrote a book on *the characteristics of the Islamic narrative* (emphasis mine),[248] saying that it is no wonder that we do not find an Islamic interpretation of history in the novels of Zaidan, as such an interpretation could only come from a Muslim author.[249]

Ashmawi and his fellow critics differ profoundly from Zaidan in their understanding of the meaning of history and historiography. For them Islamic and Arab history consists of irrefutable and unquestionable "facts" as they were articulated in the early Islamic chronicles by Arab and other Muslim historians, and historiography's task is to be normative, paradigmatic, and pedagogical. The recording of the history of Islam and of the Arabs was to give examples of morality and virtue and to guide the Muslim in his life as a believer or the Arab as a patriot; therefore a Christian could not possibly treat these aspects in the proper manner. It is remarkable that more than a century has passed and yet the Muslim criticism of Zaidan's approach to history has remained the same. This is not surprising since the meaning and role of Islamic history has not changed in fundamentalist Muslim circles, as is also shown by the reprint of books first published more than a hundred years ago without any revisions. At the same time it shows how important the pedagogical and exemplary aspect can still be in Arab national historiography.

These Muslim and Christian critics of Zaidan, the historian, completely miss the mark. Zaidan was not interested in writing "Christian history" or a "Christian critique" of Islamic history. He was committed to a secularist approach, believing in modern science and scholarship. Zaidan remained consistent throughout his historical work: the reasons he offered, the models he used, and the laws he applied for the analysis of history were all down-to-earth, pragmatic, and free of metaphysical explanations. No metaphysical teleology had a place in this approach. The religious worldview had lost the authority to interpret history. On the contrary, the changes in religion now also became a subject of historical analysis.

This was one of his major contributions as an intellectual to the Nahda Movement: the secularized interpretation of Arab history based on scientific information and scholarly insight and on the systematic application of the laws of nature—especially the evolutionary theory—to this history. Central to this application was his concept of the community of benefit and usefulness. According to Zaidan, the benefit or usefulness of any human association or community to its members was to society, what the survival of the fittest was to evolution in nature. Formation, longevity, or disintegration of societies depended on their usefulness.

The New Triptych

There is no doubt that in Zaidan's considerable work on history we will find contradictions, the inconsistent use of historical models and their mixture, and different periodization attempts. At some points, he considered the Islamic civilization the "modern period of the East." This was preceded by the Middle Ages initiated by the Conquest of Persia by Alexander and an antiquity reaching back to Hammurabi. At other points he linked the history of Islamic civilization with European history and considered it the history of the world, while Europe was sinking into its Middle Ages. How can one explain his claims that the Nahda is "borrowed from the civilization of the West," when he says at the same time that "Islam has had a long life, and in fact it is in the middle of a reformist revival which will help it to flourish for even longer"?[250]

A close reading and comparison of his texts permits several observations. Zaidan never tries to discuss the history of the Islamic faith or theology. He always dealt with the "history of Islamic civilization," a much more inclusive concept, which left space for other people and religions.[251] In the end he reconstructed a new triptych that brought together the first development of urban civilization, *tamaddun*, as expressed in the Code of Hammurabi; the Islamic civilization, guided by a religious worldview; and the Nahda, based strictly on modern sciences. The value of investigating the first two phases, popularizing their findings and publishing scholarly research about them for the national historian, was that they testified to the "civilizational" abilities of the Arabs, who would and could, therefore, also fully participate in the new third phase, which was just beginning.

Zaidan gave much more space and attention to Islamic civilization and to the Nahda than to "Arab antiquity." This had to do with the simple fact that the Code of Hammurabi was found and deciphered rather late in the lifetime of Zaidan and general knowledge about Babylon was sparse. But he was fascinated by the new findings and began immediately to incorporate the Babylonian civilization into Arab history, as his discussions in several articles show.

The link between Arab antiquity and Islamic civilization was a somewhat tenuous one. After all, more than two thousand years lay between them. The cultural link to Babylon could only be constructed via a philological argument of shared Semitic language roots. And a thousand years separated them, if we follow Zaidan's argument that "Eastern antiquity" came to an end with Alexander's conquest of Persia.

The situation is very different when we consider the relationship of Islamic civilization to the Nahda. As we saw earlier, Zaidan seemed to take sometimes contradictory positions and it is not always clear whether he saw one phase evolving from the other; understood them as co-existing and overlapping; or perceived the Nahda as part of Islamic civilization. Here a careful analysis of the texts provides greater clarity. Two points become clear very quickly: The first point is that modern civilization, with its origins in the West and based on modern sciences, made it, in his opinion, qualitatively different from and far superior to all the preceding ones.

The second point is that Ibn Khaldun's theory held true only as long as physical power was decisive in achieving political control. This could no longer happen because independence was gained within a national framework based on political and social rights, which had become powerful because of education and science. Scientific knowledge of a specific subject, Zaidan claimed, was not enough; a general scientific attitude in society as a whole was necessary to obtain rights and independence. The character of modern civilization therefore also broke through the eternally repeated cyclical movement of history as Ibn Khaldun described it. What is noticeably lacking in Zaidan's analysis is any acknowledgment of the violence and force the imperialist powers of Europe applied—at the very moment he was writing this—to subject whole continents to their control. Like many of his contemporaries Zaidan focused on European modernity, the strength of natural sciences, and the promise of progress. Only on the eve of World War I did they become aware that European Imperialism was threatening the existence of the Ottoman Empire.

In this three-stage model of world history, Zaidan considered the most recent stage, modern civilization, as far superior to all other stages, based as it was on "true" science. He answered a reader's question in *al-Hilal* thus:

> Q: Will this civilization come to an end as did those of the Greeks, the Romans, and the Arabs, or will it survive because it is not based on the ways of its predecessors? Indeed some scholars predict its end, others claim its stability.
>
> A: There is no doubt about the end of this civilization or its transformation, *inqilāb*, as the earlier civilizations were transformed. But it is

> firmer and will last longer because it is built on the true sciences. It also benefits from the causes of the downfall of those civilizations. It learned a lesson [from them], became alerted, and made great efforts to remove [these causes]. The attention to health extends the lifespan but does not prevent death.[252]

Only three years earlier he had argued, even more assertively, that modern civilization transcended all earlier civilizations, from Japan to the Ottoman Empire, and almost literally stated that modern civilization would stay "until Hell freezes over."[253] There was no doubt in his mind that this civilization was qualitatively different from (and superior to) all other civilizations.

He spoke of the Nahda as "borrowed" from Western civilization. Did this mean it had replaced Islamic civilization, dominated by a religious worldview? In 1914 he had finished publishing his *History of Arabic Culture and Literature*. Its fourth volume constitutes in fact the first history of the Arab Nahda. He delved into the distinguishing characteristics of the movement, and it is well worth quoting him at some length, particularly because this passage turned out to be his final major statement on the matter:

> [Regarding the] distinguishing characteristics of this Nahda: This age differs from other ages of Arabic culture and literature just as its social and political conditions differ. The most important [difference] is the impact of European civilization, *madaniyya*, on it because since the rise of Islam, Arabic culture, *al-ādāb al-ʿarabiyya*, did not cease to revolve around Islamic civilization. If it adapted to the different phases of this civilization it never left, though its sphere passed through an internal growth, enjoying the fruits of the talents of its own members, according to what the law of growth demanded in terms of expansion and ramification. But to this Nahda all the factors of modern civilization were transferred and they are in form and style different from the civilization of the Muslims. Its adherents are moved from phase to phase as they were at the beginning of Abbasid rule at the time of translations from the sciences of antiquity into Arabic. Arab rule found itself then in its stage of formation and greatest vigor. It assimilated the sciences imported from other nations and gave them an Arabo-Islamic coloring. But in this Nahda the trends of modern civilization are overwhelming and its adherents are

> forced to follow its path, though they are perplexed by it upon the first contact with it, deem it preposterous and reject it because it differs so much from what they are accustomed to.[254]

The somewhat radical character of this statement is heightened by accompanying quotes from Volney, describing the decay and disintegration of culture and society in the Middle East at the end of the eighteenth century. The emphasis on the decay of the preceding times—be it the eighteenth century, or the length of the Ottoman rule over the Arabs, or ever since the fall of Baghdad—had become already a common theme in the discourse of the Nahdawis. But the statement reflects—more than anything else—how far Zaidan had gone in his lifetime's work to disengage Arab from Islamic history. For him it confirmed the ability of the Arab people to participate fully in a civilization (modern civilization) that was distinct from the Islamic one.

Using modern sciences as ancillaries for historical research provided the methods and the knowledge for Zaidan's research. Relying on evolutionary theory and the laws of nature invested his interpretations of history with authority. A radical and systematic application of evolutionary theory would have necessarily led to its bitter conclusion, the total randomness in history and its meaninglessness—intellectual suicide for the historian. But then again, history is never written—and at the same time interpreted—in a neutral space, a sterilized bubble, to which no other factors, preconceived ideas, and worldviews have access.[255] Zaidan wrote history in the general context of an all-pervasive nationalism and in the particular context of the Arab nation. The second half of the nineteenth century was a period of renewal and an intellectual awakening that provided the Nahda Movement with a firm belief in progress. His lifelong preoccupation with the history of the Arabs convinced Zaidan of their ability to participate fully in modern civilization. In this way the knowledge of the past gave meaning to contemporary events and the future of Arab society.

VI

◆ ◆ ◆

Society and Its Educator

Three concepts to describe the structure of society were used by Zaidan. Though partially contradictory he used them all, often simultaneously. The first was the static division of society into the elite, *al-khāṣṣa,* and the masses, al-*'āmma,* as typically found in traditional Arabic Muslim literature. Zaidan used both terms frequently but changed their meaning, as we shall see.

The second concept was the model of social Darwinism that at first sight seemed very different from the traditional static model. It introduced social mobility. For Zaidan survival of the fittest in society meant, as it did for the social Darwinists, that any individual, regardless of his origins, could rise in the social hierarchy by hard work, self-discipline, and perseverance. The theme recurs in his letters to his son; and a number of the biographies he wrote about famous men of the East in the nineteenth century read like model descriptions for such social mobility of the individual.[256] As far as the hierarchy of society was concerned, however, there were points of similarity with the traditional model. The ruling elites were still the ruling elites, only in the case of social Darwinism they were in this position not by the grace of God or the sanctity of any dynasty, but because of the survival of the fittest or the rule of the strong (in social Darwinism often, but erroneously, considered synonymous).

The attempt to apply the laws of evolution to society encountered the inherent difficulty of determining exactly what constitutes the basic unit that is fighting for survival. On different occasions Zaidan considered either the individual or the whole society as that basic unit struggling against other similar units. He emphatically denied that such struggle could take place between different social classes within one society. Any kind of socialist or communist concept of a class struggle with an egalitarian society as the final result contradicted what Zaidan believed to be the "natural," that is, hierarchical, order of human society and provoked his sharpest criticism.[257]

A third model of society contradicted the one of social Darwinism in that it relied on a more egalitarian, socially inclusive approach, providing guidance and education to the masses. In truly enlightened fashion Zaidan assumed that all human behavior was guided by rationality when based on information, that is, education. He was convinced that the spreading of education and of scientific knowledge among all members of society would guarantee the progress of society and the improvement of conditions for all its members; in due time all could be educated. But both Darwinism and the Enlightened approach based on education for all were determined by a secularized view of the world.

The three models do not signify consecutive stages in Zaidan's thought. They were, rather, applied to different contexts. Generally one can observe that the hierarchical structure of society played a much larger role in his political thought, while an egalitarian, socially inclusive approach can be regularly found in his educational activities. Only after the Young Turk Revolution did his Enlightenment concept of the rational, informed, and responsible human being play an important but not decisive role in his political thought.[258]

Zaidan saw himself first and foremost in the role of the educator of society, that is, the nation—a role we shall dwell on here. He considered education to be the most important factor in the progress and development of society, which could only be reached by internal reform, relying on education and knowledge. He was critical of political activists such as Mustafa Kamil, and the best that he could say about them was that their actions and programs were premature. What was needed at this stage was not the political activist but the educator of society. Although Zaidan saw himself very much in the role of an educator he spent surprisingly little time as an actual teacher in a school. When he accepted a position teaching Arabic to high school students, it was for financial reasons. If we consider the many projects Zaidan undertook as a journalist, scholar, and writer, he must have felt that teaching a few students was not the best use of his time.

He rather saw his role as *kātib 'āmm,* a public educator, of whom he said: "He is the servant of the nation, *umma,* and he is in charge of its guidance. It is his duty to exert himself for its welfare. He should have no question about three stipulations for his writing: 1) He should choose a subject for which he discerns a need for the nation; 2) he should write in an easily comprehensible style; 3) he should display truth and frankness without taking sides."[259]

Relevance, comprehensibility, and objectivity were demanded from the educator in his writings. He also addressed himself to society as a whole and not to any particular social stratum: "The teaching of the elite alone, which is the situation with most nations, is not enough. The aim is the instruction, education, and training of the common people, *al-'āmma,* because they constitute the public of the nation. No nation will succeed with its plans as long as its common people are ignorant."[260]

According to Zaidan the whole project of his historical novels was guided by the idea of familiarizing the common people with their own past in an easily comprehensible and entertaining manner and by the hope of leading them in this fashion to more serious scholarly readings. Even in his first book[261] he emphasized that it was written for the benefit of the general public, *maṣlaḥat al-'āmma.* He justified writing his book on Egyptian history by pointing to the absence of any history of Egypt that was "close to the understanding of common people and yet pleasing to the elite."[262] We must, however, be careful with the term *al-'āmma,* the "common people" or the "general public," which Zaidan used frequently and somewhat loosely. The enlightened belief in the universality of education, reason, and knowledge remained a strong feature in his thinking. Yet it is worth differentiating between his declared educational intentions toward the common people and the social group he actually addressed.

At the time he was writing only 10.5 percent of men and 0.3 percent of women in Egypt knew how to read and write.[263] Even taking into account that a literate person would read aloud in a café to those of his family or friends who were illiterate, the number of people coming into direct contact with Zaidan's work could have constituted only a very small part of society. The use of the term *'āmma* would certainly be misleading if we think of the large number of illiterate masses. Zaidan realized that people had different educational levels and that it was necessary to spread "knowledge among the people in accordance with the difference in their comprehension and the diversity of knowledge."[264] Whom he really meant by *'āmma* were literate people whose reading habits had to be strengthened. By writing in a simple, comprehensible style on "pleasing" topics, he hoped to make reading more popular: "We intended to prepare the mind of the readers—in accordance with the different levels, variety of knowledge and perception—to read such history with the help of the Islamic historical novels, which we published in serialized form in *al-Hilal,* since the reading of sheer history is difficult for the literate public, *jumhūr al-qurrā',* especially in our country where learning is still in its infancy."[265]

His target was the literate public rather than the specialist in religious studies: the newly developing, secular bourgeoisie in Arab society. Its own past and Western contemporary civilization were the two sources from which this new class tried to forge its own identity and norms. A different light is shed on Zaidan's use of the terms "elite" and "common people" when we relate them to a dimension of time of which Zaidan himself was conscious. He realized that the Arab Nahda was only at its beginning and that the new literature was still in its infancy. He did not publish the historical novels to entertain the masses. They were written to arouse in the uneducated reader an interest in his own history and to enable and encourage him to follow up with more serious readings on history. When Zaidan began to publish scholarly studies on history and language, he did so because he believed that the audience he had always addressed, the new Arab bourgeoisie, had improved with regard to education and intellectual perception and would be more receptive to scholarly works.

He ascribed to himself—and to the Nahda Movement—the role of the Enlightened educator, preparing society for membership in the community of modern nations. But "education" was a flexible concept. What were the criteria for successful education? When were new values and responsibilities sufficiently well understood and internalized to justify independence and self-government of a nation? The Nahda Movement had certainly created the public space needed for venting and debating new ideas with their use of the printed word and the press.[266] But when could the intellectual trust the masses to be enlightened and responsible enough to participate in politics? Zaidan's answers to these questions were rather conservative and ambivalent. The time needed for the educational process and for the masses to reach social and political maturity was uncertain. Only then could the claim for independence be justified. At the beginning of the Young Turk Revolution he believed for a while that this moment might have come for the Ottoman Empire, but his mistrust toward the masses grew again as the dissent among the Ottoman people grew. This ambivalence determined also his relationship to Europe. He admired Europe for his belief in the irreversible and continuing progress it had brought. But he saw clearly the danger to Arab society of losing its authenticity in the process, and he feared the European expansionism he observed during his lifetime. Imperialism lurked in the background and the nation was not yet ready to resist. The presence of the Ottoman Empire was the best defense against imperialism. But his faith in progress permitted him also to believe that over time and with maturity national independence would be obtained.

Was he successful in his educational endeavor? The question can only be answered in the narrower framework of what he set out to achieve with his literary, scholarly, and journalistic work. There is no quantitative answer to this question, because we have no indications on the number of copies sold of his novels or the volume of the circulation of *al-Hilal*. But there is some circumstantial evidence. The novels were found to be educational, entertaining, and informative. No other than Taha Husayn testified to this experience:

> I shall not forget that in the days of my youth, when I started reading one of the historical novels of Zaidan, as soon as I began reading it I would hardly have proceeded with the reading when I was so enthralled by it that it would keep me from my al-Azhar lessons until I had finished it. The critics may say what they want, but about one thing there is no doubt: the historical novels that Zaidan published had the most important impact which enabled this Nahda to bear the novelistic fruits still enjoyed by the readers of today.[267]

One might add that even today Arabs often refer to these novels as their first introduction to history. The readers were, to use a neologism, "interactive" with the author. When Zaidan gave the novel *The Caliph's Sister: Harun al-Rashid and Fall of the Persians* (*al-'Abbasa ukht al-Rashid*) a dramatic ending with the killing of Harun's sister, 'Abbāsa, and her husband and sons, his readers reacted strongly and protested. They even sent telegrams from Syria immediately after the last installment of the novel in *al-Hilal*. His response was that, unfortunately, he had no choice in the matter—he had to be true in the novel to the events of history.[268] A more objective criterion for the popularity of the novels is the fact that by the time of his death several of his novels had already been translated into Persian, Turkish, and Azeri. Urdu and Indonesian translations followed, and today the most numerous translations are published in Uighur. Reprints in Persian appeared after the Islamic revolution in Iran.[269] New editions of the whole series of novels have appeared in Arabic repeatedly to this day.

The novels, however, were in their original, serialized form only a part of Zaidan's main endeavor, *al-Hilal*. The magazine offered much more than pleasant reading. Much of his scholarly work was first published as articles in the magazine. Topics from Arab history and literature were balanced with reports on modern sciences and theories, combined with almost encyclopedic information on any contemporary topic such as health issues, constitutional government, the role of women, and archaeological discoveries. Through the many letters that Zaidan received on average from his readers every month he had a clear sense of what moved them, what their interests were, and what information they were seeking. He was always responsive to their questions and requests, and often felt the need to follow up his answer to a question with a whole article on the issue. A fine journalistic sense guided him to always find the right mix of topics, and also to change the combination of themes whenever conditions changed.

Again, quantitative information on the development and success of *al-Hilal* are hard to come by. In the seventh year Zaidan had to reprint the first volume because demand was so high. Reprints of other volumes were also made later on.[270] In 1897 *al-Hilal* could be found in Syria, Iraq, Persia, India, Japan, the Maghreb, West Africa, the Transvaal, Australia, New Zealand, the West Indies, and North and South America.[271] In the same year another source estimates the number of readers at 10,000.[272] In 1902, in the tenth year of the magazine, Zaidan claimed that "of all the Arabic journals it was the most widely spread in the civilized countries and tens of thousands of people read it."[273] In 1912 he observed that the readership had doubled every year.[274] Clearly the magazine must have expanded rapidly in numerical and geographical terms. But neither of the two above observations tells us the basis for such estimates. The number of readers did not equal the number of copies sold. Sometimes letters to the editor would arrive that referred to an article published a year or even more earlier. In other words, each copy went through many hands. Geographically, its spread followed the destinations of Syro-Lebanese emigrants to wherever they went in the world. In many cases local emigrant clubs subscribed to one copy, read by many.

If imitation is the greatest compliment, then certainly *al-Hilal* must have been very successful. In 1898 Rashid Rida founded his *al-Manar* in Cairo and Louis Cheikho, a Jesuit, started *al-Mashriq* in Beirut. In appearance and format the two magazines were very similar to *al-Hilal*. While the former had a Muslim modernist orientation, the latter declared explicitly in the introduction that the Catholic reader was the major target for such a magazine. If one counts how often Cheikho attacked Zaidan's writings in *al-Mashriq*, especially on religious and philosophical issues, one can feel the threat the Jesuit saw in the impact of such a secular magazine.

VII

◆ ◆ ◆

Arab Nationalism

The end of the nineteenth century abounded with ideologies claiming to offer a coherent explanation of the path of mankind throughout history and into the future. Zaidan disdained any socialist, not to mention Marxist, interpretation of history; throughout his life he opposed political revolution, and class struggle held no attraction for him. The influence of Smiles's book *Self-Help* and his own career as a self-made man had been too strong. The ideal of the persevering, self-disciplined, strong-willed individual—so popular in Victorian England and so smoothly integrated into Spencer's social Darwinism and survival of the fittest—was a notion Zaidan held onto firmly all his life. But the most revolutionary and powerful ideology of the time in Europe, as well as in the Middle East, was nationalism. It was used to legitimize political power and action and to justify wars. Even in the age of imperialism, individual European nations were identified as the creators of imperialist political structures abroad. Imperialist politicians did not hesitate to establish nation-states, such as Panama or Lebanon, if they believed that the creation of collaborative, local (i.e., "national") elites could serve their imperialist interests more effectively and cheaply than direct political or military interference.[275]

In the early nineteenth century Greece had demonstrated what awesome political energy nationalism could unleash in the Ottoman Empire. In his own time Zaidan witnessed the political force Egyptian nationalism was developing under Mustafa Kamil's leadership. Although he was very critical of Mustafa Kamil and his political program, he was nevertheless inspired like him by the idea of the nation—only it was the Arab, not the Egyptian, nation that he had in mind. The reasons for doing so, apart from the ubiquity of the idea of nationalism in his time, were strong and, partially, very personal ones. But before we discuss them, let us trace how the Arab nation and Zaidan's nationalism manifested itself in his writings.

In his works on the Arabic language and literature we can observe from early on his intimate knowledge of Arabic and the connection he makes between language, especially the written language, and society. Language was for him not only the means of communication in society; it also reflected the state of that society and its development, whether frozen in time or active and progressive. He attacked linguistic conservatism or philological classicism, which upheld an ideal from the past, defying any change as a corruption of the ideal. On the contrary, he believed language *had* to change, to adapt to new situations and stages of civilization. When language was alive and moving forward, so was society. Language was at the same time a symbol and an instrument of the strength for the nation; it reflected its intrinsic essence and was also malleable.

In Zaidan's historical writings the nationalist aspect is not to be traced so easily, and it comes to the fore much later than in his works on the Arabic language. He started out writing or compiling histories on all sorts of subjects: a history of the Freemasons, a general history, a history of the Greeks and Romans, a modern history of Egypt, and a history of England. But it is his first magnum opus, the *History of Islamic Civilization*, published between 1902 and 1906, that is here of particular interest to us. The title of this four-volume work would suggest that the author dealt with Islamic civilization in its various phases, dominated by the Arabs, Persians, and Turks, respectively. In fact, he only dealt with the early period of Islam, when the Arabs were the dominant element. The Mamluk, Safavid, and Ottoman contributions, as well as those of a number of others, were not mentioned. The book would be better described as the "History of the Islamic civilization in its predominant Arab period." His second multivolume work, published a few years later, concerned Arabic topics even more specifically, and said so explicitly.[276] Even more significant is that, rather than continuing with his project on "Islamic civilization," he immediately turned back in time and wrote a book on the history of the Arabs before Islam.[277] It was not just a return to the more distant past but a work of perception and interpretation of history. As can be traced in *al-Hilal*, this shift was quite a while in the making. In 1895 Zaidan published a short article, actually under the same title, "The Arabs before Islam," about how Muslim historians had dealt negligently with the period, accepting the wildest stories and the most unreasonable claims. The article was a complaint about how little was known about this period, and observed that the Arabs of the period had not written about themselves.[278] This was followed two years later with an essay on the origins and kinship relations of the Arabs. He referred to the Torah for some Arab tribal names, regretting that the Bible did not speak about their origins. He divided the tribes into *'arab al-bādiya, al-muta'arribīn*, and *al-musta'ribīn*. Among the first, the nomadic Arabs, he counted the Amalek, a super-tribe mentioned in the Bible, but he claimed that they had not been Hebraic but Arab Bedouin. The second, the Arabized elements, were those who belonged to al-Qahtan and had acquired Arabic from their settled neighbors. The third, the assimilated Arabs, were the descendants of Ishmael.[279] In 1899 another article followed about women during the *Jahiliyya*. The essay described the *Jahiliyya* in bleak terms: "In *Jahiliyya* times the people lived under the shadows of superstition, venerating idols, and sacrificing to stones and trees. People were drowning in a sea of ignorance, having no other preoccupation in life than with food and shelter. Their only craving was to lay their hands on the possessions of others by raid and plunder."[280] Hypothesizing that the status of women within society reflected the overall status of that society on the evolutionary scale,[281] he observed that the birth of a daughter was considered a blow from fate, and burying her alive was acceptable. Incest existed, and in contrast to all other nations in ancient or modern times the Arabs had no rules for divorce. "[The woman] was the willing tool or the slave of the man with no right to self-determination."[282]

Until then Zaidan had relied on biblical stories and on the Muslim historians, reporting the traditional image of the *Jahiliyya* as a barbarian age of ignorance, though the term "ignorance" had referred specifically to ignorance about divine revelation; the early converts to Islam would hardly have considered themselves or their ancestors as "primitive" and "barbarian." Some six years later two seminal articles changed this image completely. For them he relied on the works of European scholars on the ancient Near East, but at the same time he was highly critical of what some European authors had to say.

In January 1905 he published an article on Hammurabi.[283] Zaidan argued that the eleven names of the dynasty, of which Hammurabi was the sixth, were not Babylonian but Arabic. Chaldean and Assyrian, as Semitic languages, were, according to Zaidan, very similar to Syriac, which itself was close to Arabic.[284] He pointed out that the Babylonian civilization was one of the oldest in the world; it introduced astronomy and medicine to the world, and produced the oldest written legal code for mankind. Almost as an answer to his own article six years earlier, he remarked that "as in the most advanced civilizations" Hammurabi's legal code mandated marriage contracts and the equal division of inheritance between men and women. Zaidan also explained in some detail that it was European archaeologists who had discovered this civilization and had gathered information about it. Both the Akkadian of Hammurabi and the Arabic that was used extensively for the first writing of the Koran belonged to the Semitic languages. Whether this made Hammurabi's Code part of Arab culture might be debatable. But what Zaidan achieved with his argument was momentous: he appropriated an ancient civilization[285] for Arab history. He later emphasized its achievements and at the same time secularized its history, that is, separated it from an Islamic history.

In March 1906 a lengthy article by Zaidan appeared, this time severely criticizing a British Orientalist.[286] The object of his wrath was the book by Robert Smith, *Kinship and Marriage in Early Arabia*.[287] The article differed from most other articles, partly by its length: twenty-four pages, when Zaidan usually took a page and a half to discuss a book. He began by establishing his own academic credentials by mentioning his good friend the British Orientalist Margoliouth, who had pointed out this book to him and who, incidentally, was just then translating a part of Zaidan's *History of Islamic Civilization* into English. At several points during the article he supplied the history of ideas that led to the concepts of totemism and the matriarchate as typical structures of primitive societies. He mentioned scholars (mainly British) who promoted and opposed the idea. He traced, for instance, the sources of the ideas presented by Smith[288] and mentioned an extensive critique of Smith's book.[289] He had no particular position on the veracity of these hypotheses, but rejected the association of the early Arabs with such "primitive" concepts. Clearly the issue was important to him and he wanted to give full scholarly weight to his criticism and to his rejection of the idea that early Arab society indulged in totemism and had a matriarchal structure.

Zaidan was at the time working on his book *The Arabs before Islam,*[290] a complete reevaluation of the negative image of the period in Islamic history. It irked him to read that the Arab tribes "related themselves to forefathers who were animals or plants which they venerated and sanctified and whose names they took and that they were exactly comparable with the savage tribes of Australia, America and Africa."[291] By this time he saw nothing barbaric or primitive in the Arabs of the *Jahiliyya* period, and sensed that this was a derogatory statement about the early Arabs. He argued lengthily and not unreasonably as to the dearth of evidence for the claim of totemism among the Arabs. He accused Smith of having taken a model that McLennan had applied to the Aborigines of Australia and the Native Americans and transferred it with little knowledge and shaky evidence to the Arabs,[292] while all the evidence spoke for " the rootedness of the Arabs in civilization for thousands of years. The evolution of their language in its complexity and expressions proves the mental evolution of its speakers from the earliest times of history and even in pre-history. Is it likely that they would claim as fathers plants and animals, like the most barbarian people of today?"[293]

In his book *The Arabs before Islam*[294] Zaidan systematized his new concept of the *Jahiliyya*, though it has to be pointed out he, too, suffered from the same dearth of reliable information on the Arabs before Islam.[295] He subdivided it and expanded it over a time span longer than Muslim historiography ever had, or ever could have, conceived of. He spoke of a first phase of Arab history before Islam that he called "Nomadic Arabs" or "the Northern Arabs in the first phase." These were the Amalekites, the very first Arab people in Mesopotamia and Egypt. They were part of the civilization of Babylon from 2500 B.C., and included the dynasty of Hammurabi. Zaidan insisted that he had supplied the linguistic, historical, and social proof that they were Arab.

Muslim historians had talked about the Arabs immediately preceding the appearance of the Prophet. Emphasizing the negative aspects of that period made the impact of the revelation much more pronounced.

Zaidan took an opposing stance. He expanded the history of the *Jahiliyya* by more than two thousand years and included ancient high civilizations in the history of the Arabs before Islam. With one stroke he had established a glorious history of the Arab nation long before the rise of Islam, the impact of which he was keenly aware of. As his two most voluminous works show, Zaidan also recognized a period of advanced Arab civilization during the early history of Islam. But he now understood it as the expression of Arab civilization in Islamic garb, not as an Arab component of Islamic world history. As a theist and evolutionist he had no difficulty in observing that the "adherence to a religion is a natural phenomenon in mankind."[296] Just as evolution would continue, so would religion in various forms. But Zaidan was neither a theologian nor a historian of religion or faith. His interest was the history of civilizations. He introduced a distinction between the history of the Arabs and the history of Islamic civilization, informed and formed predominantly by the tenets of a specific faith and religion. He not only interpreted Arab history in a secular, cultural fashion, but envisioned also a past earlier than and a future beyond Islamic civilization. Zaidan had made it abundantly clear that during the European Middle Ages the history of Islamic civilization had taken on the role of universal history.[297] He had written volumes to demonstrate what height the early, predominantly Arab phase of that civilization had reached and was highly appreciative of its heritage. But he was also convinced that, with the secularism of the new age, civilization would henceforth be driven by a far more prominent role for modern science and natural law.[298] By identifying the Arabs as founders of various civilizations before Islam as well as of Islamic civilization, he saw the way open for the Arabs as well as for other Eastern nations to participate in this modern civilization and actively contribute to it.

Zaidan was not alone but shared with the other Nahdawis, and many intellectuals of other Eastern nations in the period before World War I, a profound belief in the progress of human society, whether by evolution, by the application of human reason, or both. In contrast to European society the members of the Nahda had not witnessed the socially devastating consequences of industrialization, and certainly showed no "civilization fatigue." There was no talk of a "conservative revolution," an ideological attack on modernity, and no sign of a "romantic nationalism" or the "politics of cultural despair," which "sought to destroy the despised present in order to recapture an idealized past in an imaginary future,"[299] trends already very visible in Europe at the time. The followers of the Nahda observed instead the stagnation of their own society—which they believed could be corrected by education, societal evolution, and general progress, leading directly to modern civilization.

One cannot help but observe the negatively symmetric contrast between Zaidan and Sayyid Qutb, who half a century later also introduced a radically new view of the world by reinterpreting the *Jahiliyya*: both of them enhanced its role much beyond that which traditional Muslim historiography had attributed to it. Sayyid Qutb expanded it by two thousand years into the present, and elaborated its negative character. He made it a key experience of Islam, not bound to any particular historical period or place. The threat of *Jahiliyya* was ever-present, and even people who claimed to be Muslims could be part of it. Hence, a complete break with the present and total rejection of modernity was necessary, and only a return to an imagined golden age could constitute the (utopian) future of the community of the faithful. Zaidan, on the other hand, expanded the period of the *Jahiliyya* by two thousand years into the past; he disconnected it from Islamic history and elaborated on its achievements, attributing to the Arabs a capacity to build advanced civilizations in the past as well as in the present. Again, the point is not how much solid scholarship went into the details of his analysis of pre-Islamic history, but what this reconstruction of Arab civilizational history meant in terms of a secular national history for the Arabs.

The highly modern and political conclusion, drawn by nationalist ideologues, that the apparent existence of national groupings gives them a right to self-determination and independence, finds itself, historically speaking, on the shakiest of grounds. Nationalist ideology always attempts to find legitimization for its present-day political programs in history. This search can only be successful if a vague ethnic awareness—basically the "us-versus-them" variation—is deliberately confused with the political aspect of today's nationalism. The ancient Greeks were always aware that they were Greeks and—as importantly—that they were better than others. Rightly or wrongly, they called all others "barbarian"—Greek for "babblers," that is to say, people who could not talk intelligibly, that is, speaking Greek. Yet this awareness of difference and even superiority never induced the ancient Greeks to unite politically on the grounds of being a Greek nation. Early on the Greeks acted politically as tribes, then as city states, and later as part of multiethnic empires. The case of the Arabs under Ottoman rule is similar until the second half of the nineteenth century. There occurred public protests and even occasionally riots against the governors Istanbul sent to Arab cities. The usual causes were taxes, oppression, suspicion of unorthodox Islam, or a too-public licentious lifestyle of the governor. In the eighteenth century we actually can observe separatist movements on the Arab periphery of the Ottoman Empire. However, the argument is never made that in itself it was intolerable that Arabs should be ruled by Turks. There did not exist a political Turk–Arab dichotomy because political loyalties went to religion, the Ottoman dynasty, and possibly to the local city.

The historical weakness of the nationalist argument and the lack of historical evidence, however, should not lead us to underestimate its enormous power for the political mobilization of society and as a source of legitimacy for political rule in modern history.[300] Any society needs a certain amount of homogeneity and consensus in order to function. As a concept of political order, as a source for identity and mobilization of society, and as legitimization for political action, nationalism dominated the politics of the nineteenth and twentieth centuries and remains a strong force in the early twenty-first. Much of the debate over definitions of nationalism in the past has been rather sterile, because more often than not it reflected the ideological standpoint of the discussant and the historical particularity of the nationalism he was identifying with. In recent decades the nationalism debate has turned much more to the question of the circumstances under which nationalist ideologies developed and what constituted their usefulness.

At the time Arab nationalism developed in the Middle East, the idea of nationalism was already widespread in the region and had proven its political power in the case of Greece and Egypt and, to a certain degree, with the Armenian national movement, not to mention contemporary nationalist movements in the Balkans. Nationalism as a legitimization for a political order was, so to speak, in the air. The efficiency of the political organization of society that nationalism could provide was such that "in effect, by the second decade of the nineteenth century, if not earlier, a 'model' of the independent national state was available for pirating."[301] The idea of the "imported" or "pirated" character of nationalism is convincing, especially as its superiority in mobilizing and organizing society seemed obvious in the nineteenth century. Another author observes: "When nationalism started to spread in the eighteenth century, the emergence of new national identities was no longer the result of original creation but rather of the importation of an already existing idea."[302] But she qualifies that statement in an important way: "The adoption of national identity must have been, in one way or another, in the interest of the group that imported it."[303] This seems to be a central aspect of the analysis of nationalism. Zaidan had already remarked, as a youngster, that a new class was rising in Beirut:

> During this period, i.e. after the unrest of the sixties, there developed a third class [in addition to the masses, al-*'āmma,* and the elite, al-*khāṣṣa]* amongst the people of Beirut educated in the Christian missionary schools, especially the American, English and German ones. . . . They founded schools in order to spread the knowledge and culture of modern, civilized Europe. . . . This third social group was determined to change the social norms from what they were to what they became, so that the contemporary morals of Beirut became comparable with the most advanced habits and customs of the Europeans. . . . Yet this group grew gradually. When it first appeared, the common people of Beirut considered it a sinful breach with tradition, manifesting effeminateness and licentiousness. Especially after these students began to dress in Western clothes, they faced the contempt of many. I myself regarded these students with contempt.[304]

The rise of this new educated class—a modern intelligentsia, which seemed to have nothing to offer but Western education and outlandish fashions, and which could not claim authority by social standing, wealth, genealogical exclusiveness, or religious sanction—progressed by leaps and bounds. Jurji Zaidan, despite his youthful contempt for them, became an outstanding figure in this new educated class, which first came into its own with the Arab Nahda Movement. For this new intelligentsia, nationalism served as a legitimization—that is to say, by speaking "in the name of the nation," having the "interest of the people" at heart, or claiming to know the "will of the people," the intelligentsia acquired the legitimacy to implement their ideas and to guide the nation toward "progress and modernity." In other words, it gave the newly educated class the legitimacy to claim first cultural authority and, later, political power. The territorial nation-state became the political framework in which the intelligentsia could legitimately exercise such power. The task of the intellectuals was then twofold. Since the idea of nationalism was an import of an "already existing idea," they did not have to invent it; but they had to convince themselves—and even more so society—that, together, they constituted a nation, and that that nation was a source of pride with which one could identify and that superseded all other group affiliations. Based on the recognition of constituting such a nation, a national political program was to be developed, which always included the demand for independence, that is, for territorial sovereignty, and, albeit less frequently and not as clearly, the idea that all members of the nation share political power, whether in an institutionalized form of representation or by a self-appointed elite that claimed to speak "in the name of the people."[305] Logically the two tasks—establishing the existence of the nation and developing a program of political action for it—should follow one another. Frequently, however, this intelligentsia would carry out both tasks simultaneously, or even agitate for independence while still preoccupied with establishing a visible and defined national identity. In the case of Zaidan and his Syrian contemporaries in Egypt, neither a pan-Arab nor a Syrian state existed. The foremost need was to establish the national identity of the Arabs in order to demand such a state for themselves.

Zaidan, as should be evident by now, saw it as his personal mission to establish the identity of the Arabs as a nation. In his prolific output of scholarly works and popular novels he constructed an Arab national history. His preoccupation with the Arabic language and literature was an attempt to make Arab society aware of its cultural heritage and make it fit for the modern world. With his journal *al-Hilal* he hoped to reach an ever-increasing Arab reading public and to introduce it to the natural sciences and every other possible aspect of modern civilization—in itself a nationalist project of progress for society.

From Fichte to Zaidan and from Elie Kedourie to Benedict Anderson, the nationalists and the scholars of nationalism have pointed to the enormous role that language plays in creating a national identity and a homogeneous society. Ideologues of almost every strand of nationalism used language, its maintenance, and its development as a focus for national identity. Yet this connection is not as simple and straightforward as it seems at first sight. Even a casual look at contemporary mankind shows that not every language or dialect (the distinction between them can be very fluid!) has become a national language. Neither is it true that each nation possesses an exclusive and singular national language. From Hanover, where by common consensus the spoken German is closest to its printed version (referring to Luther's translation of the Bible), the Upper Bavarian dialect, Schweizer Deutsch, and Dutch seem equidistant. But why one continued as a dialect without a written language, while the other remained a dialect using *Schriftdeutsch*[306] as a print language, and the third made its dialect also the print language cannot be explained by the characteristics of the language or the dialect but only by an analysis of the particular political and cultural circumstances and the state of the elites at a given moment in history. In many instances several nation-states share the same national language, as is most obvious in the case of Arabic, English, and Spanish. Then again, there are cases where two or three languages or an imported language (e.g., English) may become the official language(s) of a state. In other words, as powerful as the attraction of languages as a focus of national identity may be, they rarely coincide with the territorial borders of one nation-state. Other factors, such as the aims of the cultural and political elites, the economics of print capitalism, the prior administrative conditions created by colonial rule, or, in Europe, by Enlightened Absolutism, to mention just a few, will play a role in determining the identity of each nation-state.

One of the most helpful concepts for the analysis of contemporary nationalism is Anderson's "print capitalism." It helps analyze the pan-Arab character of the nationalism promoted by the Nahda Movement in general, and Zaidan in particular. Anderson sees language as a major contributor to the development of the homogenous, chronologically forward-moving, "imagined" national community.[307] At this point he introduces his concept of print capitalism. The art of printing was the world's first introduction to mechanical mass production. As Anderson argued, a larger market for printed items meant lower per-unit costs and higher profits for the print entrepreneur.[308] This particular market could be widened by increasing literacy in the population and the creation of a written language accessible to more sections of society than just the *Schriftgelehrte*, that is, a specialist in the classical, holy, and therefore unchangeable language of the religious books and rites. "Nothing served to 'assemble' related vernaculars more than capitalism, which, within limits imposed by grammars and syntaxes, created mechanically, reproduced print-language, capable of dissemination through the market."[309] According to Anderson, the printed language had to maintain a balance between being close to the understanding of the people and being sufficiently standardized to reach the largest possible market. While the accidental character of historical circumstances may determine which language or dialect becomes a print language, the important point Anderson makes here is that only print languages will serve as national languages.

As helpful and as convincing as Anderson's advocacy for print capitalism is, his argument that print languages adopt a vernacular or combine several vernaculars into a standard printed language becomes muddled and questionable when applied to Arabic. He establishes first a dichotomy between the sacred and profane languages in pre-print societies. The former is the language in which the holy texts are transmitted. For all purposes it remains the only written language, used by small, learned bilingual elites. The latter are the vernaculars, that is to say, the spoken—unwritten—languages of society at large.

What remains unclear is whether the vernaculars are different, mutually unintelligible languages or variations of one language. He writes:

> These print languages laid the basis for national consciousness in three different ways. First and foremost they created unified fields of exchange and communication below Latin and above the spoken vernaculars.

> Speakers of the huge varieties of Frenches, Englishes, or Spanishes, who might find it difficult to or even impossible to understand one another in conversation, became capable of comprehending one another via print and paper.[310]

Each print language seems then to "assemble" dialectical varieties of one vernacular language. But what is the relationship between French, Spanish, and Italian to Latin? Are they spoken dialectical varieties of Latin? At one point they become more than that when there develops a "slow, geographically uneven, spread of particular vernaculars as instruments of administrative centralization by certain well-positioned, would-be absolutist monarchs."[311] The decisive difference is the existence of a written form of some vernaculars before a print language is developed. Written vernaculars can then "assemble related vernaculars . . . within the limits imposed by grammars and syntaxes" with the help of the print language for a large, popular market.[312] Vernacular dialectical variations that are close enough to the print language for their speakers to understand the latter will typically fail to develop a print form. Vernaculars that cannot be assimilated to a print language—Anderson mentions as an example Bohemian spoken Czech with regard to High German—either disappear altogether or establish their own print form. In Anderson's analysis the sacred language, which was in any case only spoken by a small, educated class, and thereby became bilingual, disappears almost completely with modernity and nationalism.

At first sight the histories of Arabic and Latin as sacred languages have much in common. Both were the language of Holy Scriptures—although the New Testament in Latin was never claimed to be the actual word of God, it was nonetheless often treated as such. The theologies and their ancillary sciences, too, were expressed in their respective scriptural languages. Arabic and Latin were also both used initially for the secular purposes of rudimentary administration of the communities of the believers. Finally, both languages became entrenched in their written form, but over the centuries they experienced the development of local or regional spoken dialects, which diverged increasingly from the written version and from each other. Around 1500 the spoken Arabic of the

Maghreb, Egypt, and Mesopotamia most probably differed as much from each other and from the written version as did the contemporary French, Spanish, and Italian languages. By 1800 the latter languages differed from each other even more because they had by then been standardized and cast in their print form.

Here lies the great difference in the development of the two sacred languages. Spoken variations of written Arabic, regardless of how great their linguistic distance from the written form might be, never developed into written languages of their own, as had been the case with spoken dialects of Latin. There is a variety of reasons that can help to explain this, such as the differences between Europe and the Middle Eastern world in the development of the territorial state since the Middle Ages: the fundamental economic importance of long-distance trade in the Arab world, and beyond, made it more of a necessity for the merchants in Oman, Aleppo, and Fez to communicate in some mutually comprehensible form of Arabic than to develop a locally written form of the local dialect that could not be understood elsewhere. There is no need to analyze the reasons in detail here. Only one aspect seems relevant to mention in this context. After the initial development and expansion of Arabic into the secular aspects of life, such as in administration, taxation, the military, and trade, two other languages began to flourish with Abbasid rule in the ninth century. Persian and Turkish played an important role in the Arabo-Islamic civilization. Persian became the language of administration, but also somewhat of a court language and the language of poetry. Already an important language of the military, Turkish became with the Seljuks and the Ottomans also the language of administration. Arabic remained the language of theology, of science, and of knowledge, considered ancillary to it, such as history, philosophy, and parts of literature. Nothing in this division of functions between those languages was exclusionary or absolute. But in sum it meant a reduction of the role of Arabic in the secular aspects of society—without, however, disappearing altogether from the scene, as was the case for Latin. When print language became an issue for the Arab Nahda in the second half of the nineteenth century, there were no written vernacular languages derived from the sacred language.

Those were the issues the members of the Nahda had to tackle in the Arabic-speaking and writing societies. They belonged to the new, educated elite we have discussed above—and the emphasis here is on "new"—and they saw great benefit in adopting nationalism as their own. To begin with, hardly any of them was a *Schriftgelehrter*, a learned man of the Scriptures. Many were complete autodidacts; others had a smattering of formal education or had studied in the schools of foreign missionaries. These circumstances denied them the legitimacy of the traditional "educated classes" in religion or administration. But at the same time their lack of formal education freed them to look at the role of language and knowledge in a wholly new way. The members of the Nahda were not only open to the modern sciences and methodologies; they became firm believers in them, trusting that they would lead to progress within their society. They therefore felt strongly that the traditional written Arabic could not reflect the new ideas, concepts, and terminologies with which they intended to familiarize their society, unless the classicist premise of the immutability of the sacred language was dropped and innovation of words and expressions accepted as standard. The ideas of the Enlightenment and the French Revolution suggested that the education of all members of society would produce rational, informed citizens. This could only be done with a print language that was comprehensible to all.

In 1891 Zaidan became, together with Najib Mitri, owner of a small printing press that they called *Matba'at al-ta'lif*. But the joint enterprise came to an end one year later. Zaidan kept the *Matba'at al-ta'lif*, which he renamed *Matba'at al-Hilal* in 1896.[313] Later, his brothers Mitri and Ibrahim would help him manage it. Ibrahim, who was the eldest, only worked for a few years at *Matba'at al-Hilal* and then opened a nearby bookshop called *Maktabat al-Hilal*. Mitri was in charge of the printing press and continued to do so well after Zaidan's death under his two sons, Emile and Choucri. Beginning in the fall of 1892 Zaidan edited (and mainly wrote) the monthly magazine *al-Hilal* for the next twenty-two years. In addition, he continuously wrote scholarly books and novels.

This work was not just a hobby for him but, as for many other Nahdawis, his livelihood depended on it. Five years into his own journalistic enterprise Zaidan wrote a long series of articles dealing with all aspects of writing, printing, publishing, and reading in Arabic.[314] Much of it is of a very technical nature, but the last two sections, written in 1897 and 1899, deal particularly with the success and failure of the printing and publishing business. They were written in the style of a man who clearly felt that he knew what he was doing and was successful at it. In the first article he dealt with newspapers and journals. He declared that this literary genre had been imported from the West but in Arabic it had developed on its own, "in the way of general evolution, *irtiqā'*, and especially in its variety and specialization." He warned that one of the laws of evolution was the survival of the fittest and that not all newspapers and journals would survive.[315] In answer to a letter from a reader, some months later, he wrote that to be successful, a scientific journal must be constantly up-to-date and at the forefront of scientific developments and discoveries. In general, journals had to choose topics that entertain and interest the reader and develop his desire to know more about them.

In the last part of the series he tackled the issue of the market for publications. Optimistically he wrote that the market for print products does not only consist of Arabs but also of all Muslims who know Arabic: "There are millions of those in Iran and India and then there are several hundred thousand Syrian emigrants in North and South America," of which many were regular readers of *al-Hilal*.[316] He believed "there were more readers than books." The impression that the market was stagnant had arisen because some books did not sell well. But that had to do with a bad choice of topics and an unreadable style.[317] He discussed the problem of marketability, *rawaj*, of Arab authors. He admonished them to keep the interests and the character of the readers in mind; observed that books on history and literature generate sales only if they concern their own language and history, in this case Arabic; and hoped that with the increase of educational facilities the readership would increase. His own experience told him that "the most marketable are the novels, because they are read by the elites as well as by the common people."[318] The use of the terms here is somewhat curious considering the low literacy rate in Egypt. But it is true that within this educational elite he had always differentiated between "serious" and "recreational" readers. The latter had to be enticed by lighter fare, such as the historical novels, to read more serious material as well. How Zaidan meant to reach the illiterate masses became clear in a dispute with the journal *al-Mu'ayyad*. When one of the editors of *al-Mu'ayyad*, Ahmad Effendi Hafiz, proposed that what would be most useful for Egypt would be many more primary schools in villages,[319] a policy the British pursued, Zaidan felt challenged. He had argued for the need for an academic institution of higher education for many years. Summarizing his argument for the establishment of a university once more he stated that good, qualified teachers, who also personally set an example for the students, were needed more than anything else; good teaching was more important than school buildings.[320]

He seems to be in agreement here with Anderson that the establishment of a print language and the enlarging of the market is a top-down process. But the print language is not only the result of the profit motive of capitalist authors and publishers or of the educational ambitions of the enlightened reformer. Both Zaidan and Anderson completely ignored the fact that there is also a bottom-up process, carried by groups of illiterate people entering the modern age. Those were people who began to realize that their own unwritten, printed vernacular was an obstacle to their personal progress and improvement. They wanted, just like Zaidan himself, to participate in the new print language, which appeared as the key to new opportunities. Frédéric Pichon has recently analyzed the attitudes peasants of *Ma'lula* had to their spoken and unwritten dialect of Aramaic—the disappearance of which was continuously lamented by Western Orientalists. With improved infrastructure and greater security, these peasants, contemporaries of Zaidan, began after 1861 to migrate in numbers to Damascus. They made every effort to learn the city Arabic and to send their children to school so that they could have better lives. The Aramaic dialect was considered a sign of backwardness.[321] The same sentiments could still be observed in the 1930s in Brittany concerning the Breton language: "The French language was for her [the grandmother] as for so many rural people the language of social mobility, the one that opened the doors to teaching, the post office, city hall and to jobs and places where life was less hard; the exclusive use of the Breton language in turn was synonymous with contempt and misery."[322]

We have seen how intensely Zaidan cared about the issue of language and what role he assigned to it. Not surprisingly, he fiercely opposed any suggestion of elevating the Egyptian Arabic dialect into a written language. But his assertion that the introduction of various vernacular versions of Arabic (in this specific case the Egyptian dialect) as written languages would lead to the division of the nation, and the separation of Arabs from each other, was not only a nationalist concern but also that of the professional writer and publisher: "This would mean that what was written in Egypt would be inaccessible to the reader in Syria or Morocco!"[323] No doubt a legitimate concern for the market of his major print product, *al-Hilal*, can be discerned here. He launched the magazine in the fall of 1892, explaining in his opening statement that it would be the main task of the journal to always please the readers and cater to their wishes.[324] This goal would lead in the following years, among other things, to the introduction of new sections. Some of the most interesting sections for the historian are those introduced very early: Letters to the Editor, *Bāb al-murāsalāt,* and Questions and Suggestions, *Bāb al-su'āl wa-'l-iqitirāḥ*. These were the instruments through which Zaidan stayed in touch with his readers and their interests, worries, and tastes. The thoughts and questions published there often led him to compose more general articles on specific topics and occasionally moved him to introduce a whole new section. There was undeniably a pedagogical purpose to this dialogue with the reader, but clearly it was also meant to maintain and enhance the attractiveness of *al-Hilal*—in other words, its marketability. In that sense the Arab Nahda was a perfect example of how print capitalism contributed to nationalism.

The creation of what is commonly known today as Modern Standard Arabic is certainly one of the greatest and most enduring achievements of the Arab Nahda. It also offered a solution very different from Anderson's vernacular origins of print language. The sacred language did not disappear, replaced by some "already written" or printed vernacular. Self-consciously Arab nationalists and perhaps unselfconsciously practical entrepreneurs, the members of the Nahda, with Zaidan in the forefront, changed the paradigm of the language from a classicist idealization and unalterable sacred standard to a secular and evolutionary one, in which change was not only good but necessary as a proof that the language, and with it society, still possessed its vital powers of growth and development. The language became symbol and program at the same time: symbol for the existence of an Arab nation, consisting of all Arabic-speaking people; and program for establishing practical communication between all Arabs. It became the basis for a pan-Arab national identity. With a modernized version of written Arabic established as the vernacular language, another simple—but not negligible—factor contributed to Zaidan's role as a pioneer of Arab nationalism, and once again it was a factor that concerned the marketing aspect of his work. He had reached the conclusion that people preferred to read about subjects that concerned them directly. Serious writing and scholarly studies would only be read when they dealt with the readers' own society—and for Zaidan that meant Arab society, its culture, and its history.[325]

But in addition to a secular approach to language and history, the availability of "an already existing idea," the economic aspects of print product and market, and the role of language as a symbol of national identification and a means for the education of the nation, another factor has to be added that further helps to explain why an Arab nationalism—or, more precisely, a pan-Arab nationalism—was developed by the Syrian Nahda Movement in Egypt and not, for instance, Syrian, Lebanese, or Egyptian nationalisms. The key concept here, I believe, is "nationalism as caused by migration." It is common knowledge that nationalist movements have often had their beginnings in emigration, such as the Greeks in Odessa or Antun Saadeh in South America. Most of the members of the Arab Nahda Movement were Syro-Lebanese emigrants to Egypt. But this situation was not comparable to the usual understanding of emigration. For one thing, it was not legally an emigration, but a sort of labor migration within the all-encompassing Ottoman Empire. In fact, until almost the end of the nineteenth century there existed no legal means in Egypt to differentiate between an Egyptian and any other inhabitant of the Ottoman Empire.[326] Second, Egyptians were Arabic speakers, even though the term "Arab" was at the time still used typically to designate Bedouins, while Egyptians called themselves *miṣriyyūn*. Third, the regions were not only geographically adjacent to each other but, historically speaking, there had often existed strong economic and political ties between the two. These factors should all have helped to achieve a smooth integration of the most recent wave of immigrants.[327] But it occurred during the rise of the new Egyptian intelligentsia, which considered the Syrian immigrant intellectuals as competitors for government jobs and feared their domination of the press (for a time quite rightly, when considering the proportions of Syrians active in both fields). In addition, Egyptian nationalism was already more articulate and established than the nationalism of any other Arabic-speaking region. Thanks to the colonial state established by Muhammad 'Ali, its political identity and program was more territorially defined than in any other Arabic-speaking region of the time. The representative of the radical edge of this nationalism was Mustafa Kamil. He had coined the expression "the intruders," *al-dukhalā'*,[328] by whom he did not mean so much the British occupiers, who prevented Egypt from obtaining her independence, as the Syro-Lebanese immigrants. It did not help that these immigrants were frequently pro-British, not only because some found employment in the British-run administration of Egypt but also because they preferred British occupation to Ottoman oppression.

In a time of pronounced Egyptian nationalism, Jurji Zaidan felt defensive about his own origins. On various occasion he took the trouble to answer the accusation that the Syrians were not *dukhalā'*. He argued that Syria and Egypt were really one country because there were no natural barriers between them; the Europeans called them one people—Arabs; and the two regions often had been politically or economically integrated into one unit.[329] He asserted that emigration had been a typical characteristic of Syrians since the time of the Phoenicians, always playing the role of transmitters of knowledge and learning; they were the link between one culture and another. If emigration was a characteristic of the Syrians, immigration was the distinguishing characteristic of Egyptian society. In order to prove his argument he provided examples from Egyptian history starting with the Pharaohs. Wave after wave of immigrants reached Egypt in antiquity, and it had always been only a question of time before they were considered Egyptians.[330] One cannot help but note how neatly Zaidan and his Syrian compatriots in Egypt would, according to this definition, fill the characteristics of both societies, in particular the intellectuals among them as "transmitters of knowledge and learning." In spite of this apparently flawless fit of Syrians in Egypt, Zaidan felt a certain uneasiness: "In modern times there are some people who consider immigrants as Egyptians if they belong to the state religion, but not if they are Christians or Jews. This conclusion is strange and does not fit the principles of civilisation, since it is clear that nationality and religion are two different things."[331]

We can observe here an odd tension in the argument. He acknowledged the existence of two different regions; yet their respective national characteristics complement each other to the point that in reality they constitute one country, *al-quṭrān quṭr wāhid yuqsamu ila shaṭrayn*.[332] The term *quṭr*, region, quarter, or district, later used again in the terminology of the United Arab Republic, reflects the uncertainty of the argument. Here we have to differentiate between the use of two other terms, *waṭan* and *umma*, fatherland and nation, a territorial and an ethnic definition as the basis of nationalism. When referring to Egypt and Syria he used term *waṭan* rather than *quṭr*. He spoke frequently about the Syrian *waṭan* and clearly was emotionally attached to the place of his youth. He never, however, thought that love for one's fatherland made it an obligation to stay there forever. Emigration was as old as mankind, and happened mostly in search of livelihood. In fact, to emigrate was part of the evolution and development of mankind.[333] Rather touchingly and naively he once stated that Syrian emigrants actually have a stronger longing for their homeland than other emigrants, and he pondered the greatness Syria could obtain if all its emigrants would return.[334] But he was also very sober in his estimate of keeping alive a Syrian Arab identity in a non-Arab environment. He predicted that Syrians in America would eventually acquire an American identity, while losing their Syrian-Arab one. This was not reprehensible or a crime; it only meant the interests and orientations of immigrants changed. This would probably be a faster process in the case of the Syrian immigrants than other groups, because of their small size and because "the strong eats the weak."[335]

For Syrian immigrants in Egypt, neither Pharaonism nor Phoenicianism would do. The limited fatherland, in the narrow sense of Egypt, Syria, or Lebanon, bore no strong attraction, at least not for the emigrant/immigrant who could not claim an innate identity with either *waṭan*. For Zaidan the *waṭan* was the place where one grew up. The love for this place was based on familiarity and habit. But "we do not think that his love is natural in the sense, that man loves the place he was born in even if he does not live there . . . if one was taken away as a little baby . . . that in reality is not one's fatherland."[336] The *waṭan* was for him a sentimental attachment, an emotion-laden location. He almost never associated with it a political order or obligation. The one force that could create a common identity between the Muslim and Christian, the Syrian and Egyptian was the Arabic language. As we have seen, Zaidan hardly missed an opportunity to point out the importance of language as the most important criterion to define a society and as the most decisive factor for a common identity and a community of usefulness. This identity was not formed by a territory but by the people who spoke Arabic, the Arab nation, *al-umma al-'arabiyya.* For Zaidan the existence of the Arabic language—he of course meant the written language—as a functioning means of communication and information for society was proof that the Arab nation existed. Language was the symbol and the means for proving the existence of a national identity. Only this entity had historical, linguistic, and cultural characteristics that were also politically relevant. Zaidan's conviction originated from his personal experience as a Syrian immigrant in Egypt. But as part of his principal argument about Arab nationalism, the Arabic-speaking community, at least in theory, reached much further than Egypt and Syria as he also included the Arabian Peninsula, Iraq, Syria, Sudan, and the Maghreb.[337] It remains remarkable that for Zaidan Egypt and, marginally, the Maghreb constituted part of the Arab entity and identity, when even for the pan-Arabists of the next generation it was not at all certain that Egypt was part of the Arab nation.[338]

The factor of migration was to contribute to the strengthening of pan-Arabism after World War I, precisely at a time when the Arab world was split into a number of states-in-process, *aqṭār*. The pan-Arab ideologue Sati' al-Husri is a perfect example of migration making pan-Arabism the perfect political order. By the time he shifted his allegiance from Ottomanism to Arabism in 1919 he had lived in many places. Both his parents were Arabs from Aleppo. His father worked in the Ottoman administration, which had sent him to Yemen, where Sati' was born in 1880. Between 1880 and

1893 the family moved six times: from Yemen to Adana, Ankara, Tripoli, back to Yemen, and finally to Konya. Sati' attended the Mülkiye Mektebi in Istanbul from 1893 to 1900; he worked as a teacher and an administrator in the Balkans from 1900 to 1908; and he then returned to Istanbul and stayed there until 1919.[339] Dawn stated that "Arabism won its first success . . . when the failure of the Ottoman Empire in World War I left the dominant faction of the Arab elite with no alternative to Arabism."[340] The explanation is not quite convincing in this case, considering that al-Husri's language of education had been Turkish and that he had spent all his adult life in non-Arab parts of the Ottoman Empire. He had lived a total of eighteen years in Istanbul. His Arabic could not have been as strong as his Turkish. Having had close associations with the Young Turks, he could have just as well chosen a Turkish identity. Cleveland claims that actually much spoke for al-Husri's remaining in Istanbul, even though he had very good offers for a position in Syria. He adds that al-Husri probably could not perceive a future for the Ottoman Empire and could not imagine the rise of a Turkish nation state and therefore turned to Syria and to Arabism.[341] But if it had to be an Arab identity it could only be a pan-Arab one. The career path of his father had not permitted Sati' to have a *waṭan*. He was precisely the "baby taken away" of which Zaidan spoke. He could not even claim Aleppo, home of his parents, as his own, since he never lived there. We have seen earlier how much he valued the role of the Arabic language as the decisive factor in constructing the nation. Without that language there could be no pan Arabism. The division of the Arab nation into political subdivisions, *aqṭar,* was unfortunate and had to be overcome.

The same holds true for Muhammad Kurd 'Ali, who became an "intellectual migrant" when he rejected his Kurdish vernacular in favor of Arabic, which made him by necessity a pan-Arabist and later the founder and head of the Arabic Academy in Damascus.

When Sati' al-Husri arrived in Syria in 1919, he joined the Hejazi emigrant King Faisal, only to accompany him, after the French arrival in Syria, in a further (labor and political) migration to Iraq: two strangers in a strange country. In the age of nationalism only the appeal to pan-Arabism could give them some legitimacy for their educational and political authority in Iraq. The same holds true, of course, also for Amir

'Abdullah, the brother of Faisal, in Transjordan. Migration did not influence the concept of nationalism per se, but influenced the choice of which variation of pan-Arab or regional nationalism was to be employed most advantageously in a given situation.

Regarding Arab nationalism in the thinking of Jurji Zaidan, one final point has to be addressed. Through a secular approach to history and language, Zaidan had firmly established an independent Arab identity and the existence of a living nation—a nation whose fate was independent from that of Islam and which was completely able to participate in the modern world. But he did not carry this nationalist thought to its logical conclusion: he did not clamor for the political independence of the Arab nation.

Part of the reason was surely Zaidan's own character and thought. Though described as friendly and at ease in the company of friends, he was extremely shy in public and reluctant to become a public figure. As we saw, he belonged to few formal associations or political organizations, and was never very active in any one of them. He gave no public speeches and did not participate in demonstrations, as he did not believe in the benefit of violent revolutions. His temperament was much more that of the private scholar. As an intellectual he also kept a certain critical distance from adopting any concept or thought as exclusive and superior to all others. Perhaps one could claim that his concept of *jāmi'at al-manfa'a*, the community of usefulness, was such a foundational concept, but it served him to perceive even nationalism as only one of many options of human communities and associations. He had warned that even the community of language could disintegrate if the common language ceased to be of benefit; in this context he mentioned Arabic explicitly. This sort of relativity of values and cultural phenomena must have been anathema to nationalists who attached a metaphysical, absolute value to the Arabic language in particular.

For Zaidan, the Young Turk Revolution was a great divide: he was fascinated by it and saw in the resurrected Ottoman constitution and the reopened parliament the instruments for holding this multiethnic and multifaith empire together. In a letter dated 3 November 1908 to his son Emile, who was at this time studying in Beirut, he suggested that his son learn Turkish—as he was doing at the time—since "it is the language of the government and will become of great importance for all subjects."[342] In the following letter he added, "You [Emile] are an Ottoman by nature, *bi-l-ṭabī'a,* because your parents are Ottomans and because the Egyptians are Ottomans. Even if not all Ottomans are Egyptian, you are also a Syrian Ottoman."[343] He implicitly acknowledged that the option of separation existed, but even when he became critical of the Young Turk regime he preferred other solutions. In April 1909 he published an article discussing the relations of the Arabs with the Young Turks and the Ottoman Empire.[344] After a typical historical introduction he acknowledged that the Turks and even the members of the Committee for Progress and Union had exercised tyranny over the other people of the empire. But he argued the case of the "community of mutual benefit or usefulness"[345] and insisted that "that community is today the Ottoman community."[346] In another letter to Emile, dated 10 November 1911, he expressed his admiration for the Ottoman army defending Libya and described with approval the enthusiasm of his younger son for the Ottoman cause.[347]

Zaidan was not an exception, but rather the rule, in supporting and accepting the Ottoman government. Before World War I we hear practically no Arab voice demanding Arab independence.[348] In 1909 a small group of Syro-Lebanese emigrants in Cairo and Alexandria founded *al-Ittiḥād al-Lubnānī,* the Lebanese Union. Their aim was to preserve the *Mutaṣarrifiyya* and eventually to achieve full Lebanese independence.[349] The group consisted almost exclusively of Maronites, plus a few Greek Catholics. The group counted Jibra'il Taqla, son of the founder of the newspaper *al-Ahram,* and Dawud Barakat, its manager, as members.[350] Jurji Zaidan, like the overwhelming majority of the Greek Orthodox, was not a member.

Of more substance was the *Ḥizb al-Lāmarkaziyya al-'Uthmāniyya,*[351] which was founded in December 1912 in Cairo. The party's program focused, as the name indicated, on reducing the power of the central government by devolving authority over financial, educational, and even, partially, military affairs to provincial governments. The use of local languages in administrative and educational institutions was a major point in the program. Ottoman sovereignty was, however, to be maintained. Theoretically the party was open to all ethnic groups, but in fact it consisted of

Arabs only; or, to be more precise, exclusively Syrians.[352] Zaidan did not become a member. The most remarkable feature of this party was that it was the first political organization joined by both Christian and Muslim Syrians. The fact that Rafiq al-'Azm (a Muslim) was president and Iskandar 'Amun (a Christian) was vice president had an almost programmatic character.[353] Although founded in Cairo, the party's interest was in practice concentrated on geographical Syria. This also meant separating itself from Egyptian nationalism, and giving up the idea that Egypt could be integrated into an Arab identity. For the Syro-Lebanese immigrants it also meant forgoing the hope of integrating into Egyptian society.

To illustrate this atmosphere, where a cultural Arabism had crystallized but its political consequences—Arab separation from the Ottoman Empire—could still not be imagined, let us look at a revealing poll Rashid Rida carried out in March 1914.[354] He had asked a variety of established intellectuals, ideologues, and politicians to comment briefly about the best means to revive and strengthen the sultanate.[355] General education was most often mentioned (Sabri, Abu Shadi, Shumayyil, Zaidan, Mutran, Qusayri, Antun, Khanki, Lutfi al-Sayyid); next was the demand for decentralization and federation of the empire (Zaghlul, Sabri, Abu Shadi, Rida, Barakat, Khanki, 'Amun, N. Bustani). Some asked for a stronger government; one demanded that all should be taught Arabic, since this was the language of the religion of the empire; others demanded more railways and development of infrastructure, such as telegraph and telephone; firmer legal institutions was another demand. Zaidan probably expressed one of the more pessimistic views when he predicted that it would take forty years before such measures would show results. Admittedly, the question was weighted in favor of "revive" and "strengthen"; nevertheless, it remains striking that no answer suggested that such effort was not worth it because the empire was doomed in any case. Zaidan, though pessimistic, reflected the typical national thinking of his time when he hesitated to demand complete independence from the Ottoman Empire. In March 1914 nobody could predict—or, more importantly, imagine—the collapse of a political order that had lasted, for better or worse, for some four hundred years.[356]

But Zaidan also realized that the Ottoman Empire was in danger and, along with it, the Arabs. In 1913 he discussed once more the constitutional state. He wrote in a detached and even pessimistic tone. Considerable change and progress in society was needed before a constitutional system could be established. Lucky were those nations who had reached this state of affairs step by step in a slow process. Others had tried to do so in one stroke, but the result was that it took much longer before true constitutionalism could take hold. Some states tore up their constitutions and in the end were ruled by other states, as was the case in Iran and *"as we fear—might happen to the Ottoman Empire"* (emphasis mine).[357] The maintenance of a reformed Ottoman Empire was, in his opinion, the best guarantee against a direct colonization of the Arab territories by the European powers.

When Sharif Husayn declared independence in the summer of 1916 in defense of Islam and Arabs, Rashid Rida broached the issue only a year later in an article on the "Arab question."[358] He firmly rejected all suggestions that Arabs wanted independence, not because they were weaker than the Greeks, but because they knew that Europeans would carve up the weakened and divided empire among themselves and rule it. Still somewhat on the defensive, Rida finally came to the conclusion that the Ottoman Empire could not be saved and that a political order of nation-states should take its place. At the same time *al-Hilal*, now under the editorship of Emile Zaidan, son of Jurji, had already shifted in a completely different direction, reacting to the Arab Revolt by publishing a long article that presented the full catalogue of arguments about the "evil and barbarian Turk who for four hundred years had held Arabs in servitude and misery," a narrative that would dominate Arab nationalist mythology for the next three generations.[359] The collapse of the Ottoman Empire meant, as Dawn observed, that the Arabs no longer had any choice in the matter.

Zaidan was fully immersed in the Arab Nahda Movement and was one of its major driving forces. As such he took on three major roles that were essential components of the Nahda and were played out in various ways by all its participants: the educator, the popularizer-entrepreneur, and the nationalist thinker. As an educator, Zaidan's aim was to spread knowledge, science, and moral education and his target was, in principle, the whole of society. His means were the simplification and development of the language, adapting it to modern needs, and the provision of information. As a popularizer and entrepreneur, he aimed to promote education and enlarge the market for print products, with the growing secular bourgeoisie in mind, the choice of topics and form of their delivery was of greatest importance to him. He always claimed that topics should be close to a reader's life and interests and the presentation should be entertaining and attuned to a specific audience. As a nationalist thinker, his major aim was to create a national identity, which he achieved through the secularization of Arab history and language. In theory, his audience included all those who spoke Arabic; in practice, he also addressed the new secular bourgeoisie and educated classes.

It is easy to see how all these different aims, and the means to attain them, overlapped and fused. More than most other intellectuals of the Nahda, Zaidan emphasized history and modern science, in particular the theory of evolution, in order to interpret for his audience conditions in the contemporary world and the possibilities for Arab society to participate in it. His understanding of himself as a scholar and educator, combined with his keen sense for the tastes and interests of his readers, made him a major thinker on Arab nationalism before World War I.

Notes

1. *Al-Hilāl.*

2. For details, see the *General Bibliography on Jurji Zaidan and His Works.*

3. George Antonius, *The Arab Awakening* (1938; 2nd ed., New York: Capricorn Books, 1965).

4. Sylvia Haim, "The Arab Awakening: A Source for the Historian," *Welt des Islams* n.s. 2 (1954): 237–50, 237.

5. ʿAbd al-Raḥmān al-Kawākibī (1849–1903) was from Aleppo and of Kurdish origins; he moved to Cairo 1898 and wrote two books on politics: *Ṭabāʾiʿ al-istibdād* and *Umm al-qūrā.*

6. Antonius, *Arab Awakening,* 94–95.

7. Sylvia Haim, ed., *Arab Nationalism: An Anthology* (1962; 2nd ed., Los Angeles: Univ. of California Press, 1976).

8. Haim, "Arab Awakening."

9. Albert Hourani, *Arabic Thought in the Liberal Age 1798–1939* (1962; 2nd ed., London: Oxford Univ. Press, 1986): 246, 277. Basically Hourani's book was a continuation of Arabic *Ṭabaqāt* literature, i.e., collected biographies of people who share the same profession, place of residence, historical period, or other common denominators; in the case of Hourani the shared trait was liberal and national thought.

10. Qusṭanṭīn Zurayq, *al-Wa'y al-qawmī, naẓarāt fī 'l-ḥayāt al-qawmiyya al-mutafattiḥa fī 'l-sharq al-'arabī* (Beirut: Dār al-Makshūf, 1938).

11. 'Alī Nāṣir al-Dīn, *Qaḍiyat al-'arab* (Beirut: Manshūrāt 'Uwaydāt, 1946).

12. William L. Cleveland, *The Making of an Arab Nationalist: Ottomanism and Arabism in the Life and Thought of Sati' al-Husri* (Princeton: Princeton Univ. Press, 1971), 89n 14.

13. Zākī al-Arsūzī (1900–1968) led the Arab nationalists in Antakya in a struggle against the takeover of the province by the Turks; later he became a philosopher and ideologue of Arab nationalism. See Dalal Arsuzi-Elamir, *Arabischer Nationalismus in Syrien: Zaki al-Arsuzi und die arabisch-nationale Bewegung an der Peripherie Alexandretta/Antakya 1930–1938* (Hamburg: Lit Verlag, 2003).

14. Antun Sa'adeh (1904–1949); see Christoph Schumann, *Radikalnationalismus in Syrien und Libanon: Politische Sozialisierung und Elitebildung 1930–1958* (Hamburg: Deutsches Orientinstitut, 2001): 250–310 and passim.

15. Michel 'Aflaq (1910–1989); see also Patrick Seale, *The Struggle for Syria* (London: Yale Univ. Press, 1986).

16. But see Thomas Philipp, *Ǧurǧī Zaidān: His Life and Thought* (Beirut: in Kommission bei Franz Steiner Verlag, Wiesbaden, 1979). It was published much later than the Ph.D. thesis from which it emanated. Also see Bassam Tibi's *Nationalismus in der Dritten Welt am arabischen Beispiel* (Frankfurt: Europäische Verlagsanstalt, 1971), which in spite of its title is a monograph on Sati' al-Husri.

17. C. Ernest Dawn, *From Ottomanism to Arabism: Essays on the Origins of Arab Nationalism* (Urbana: Univ. of Illinois Press, 1973).

18. Rashid Khalidi et al., eds., *The Origins of Arab Nationalism* (New York: Columbia Univ. Press, 1991).

19. Yasir Suleiman, *The Arabic Language and National Identity* (Washington, DC: Georgetown Univ. Press, 2003).

20. For more on al-Yaziji, see p. 121n40.

21. Suleiman, *Arabic Language*, 126. To his credit it should be said that he also analyzes Zaki al-Arsuzi's work on language; he is an important nationalist ideologue, linguist and philosopher, who has received hardly any attention in Western scholarship.

22. *al-Jāhiliyya* (lit., the time of ignorance), i.e., the time without the revelation/before the Prophet Muhammad.

23. Suleiman, *Arabic Language*, 147, makes the same observation: "despite their abiding interest in the language and their common belief that the Arab nation is defined by it, al-Husri and al-Arsuzi do not refer to each other. . . . If one reads al-Husri on his own, one would be excused for thinking that al-Arsuzi does not exist, and vice versa."

24. In Arabic, *al-Nahḍa* refers to the Arab intellectual movement from the 1830s to 1914, which was to have a profound impact on all aspects of social life, education, knowledge, and political order. For a detailed discussion, see pp. 11–15.

25. Elie Kedourie, *Nationalism* (London: Hutchinson, 1960), 9.

26. Muḥammad ʻAlī Pasha (r. 1805–1848), semi-independent ruler of Egypt, and founder of a dynasty that lasted until 1952; he was a radical modernizer of the Egyptian state and economy.

27. Roughly the area described in European languages as the Levant.

28. E. W. Lane, *Arabic Language Dictionary*, 2 vols. (London: Williams & Norgate, 1863).

29. Buṭrus al-Bustānī, *Muḥīṭ al-Muḥīṭ* (Beirut: s.n., 1867–1870), 2:2137.

30. "Tanabbahū wa-'stafāqū ayyuhā al-ʻArab!" Quoted, p. 118n3, as the title of Antonius's book.

31. "Nahḍat al-ṭibb fī miṣr," *al-Muqtaṭaf* 12 (Sept. 1888): 735–39, 753.

32. *Al-Hilāl* 1, 123.

33. See N. Tomiche, "Naḥda," *Encyclopedia of Islam*, 2nd ed. (Leiden: 1970–2007); quoted as *EI2*.

34. Dagmar Glaß, *Der Muqṭataf und Seine Öffentlichkeit* (Würzburg: Ergon Verlag, 2004), 1, sec. 1.

35. Salma Khadra al-Jayyusi, *Trends and Movements in Modern Arabic Poetry* (Leiden: Brill, 1977), 12ff., quoting H. A. R. Gibb and H. Bowen, *Islamic Society and the West* (London: Oxford Univ. Press, 1962): 2, 154–60. For the antecedents see also Thomas Philipp, "Class, Community and Arab Historiography in the Early 19th Century," *International Journal of Middle Eastern Studies* 16 (1984): 161–75.

36. Al-Jayyusi, *Trends and Movements*, 14.

37. Stephen Sheehi, *Foundations of Modern Arab Identity* (Gainesville: Univ. Press of Florida, 2004), 16.

38. Buṭrus al-Bustānī (1819–1883), Maronite, born in Lebanon. Family was professionally closely connected to Maronite Church; Butrus studied first in the Maronite seminary. He was a scholar of Arabic language and literature, collaborated with the American missionaries in the translation of the Bible into Arabic, and after the unrest in 1860 founded *al-Madrasa al-Waṭaniyya*, one of the first attempts to establish a school providing secular, national education. He wrote the first modern Arabic dictionary, *Muḥīṭ al-Muḥīṭ*, began an encyclopedia, *Dā'irat al-Maʻārif*, and founded several magazines: Yūsif Dāghir, *Maṣādir al-dirāsa al-adabiyya*, 2nd ed. (Beirut: Maktabat Lubnān, 2000), 665; Carl Brockelmann, *Geschichte der Arabischen Literatur, 5 vols.* (Leiden: Brill, 1937–1949), *GAL* 2, 495; Supp. 2, 767; Supp. 3, 390; quoted as Brockelmann *GAL* vols. 1–2, or Supp. 1–3.

39. Aḥmad Fāris al-Shidyāq (1804–1887), Maronite, later Muslim; studied at Maronite Seminary in ʻAyn Waraka; generation of the early Nahda; taught Arabic for missionaries, wrote a simplified Arabic grammar; he was also involved with the Bible translation project; wrote a history of Mt. Lebanon; most known for his autobiographical *al-Sāq ʻalā 'l-sāq fī mā huwa 'l-faryāq*; early support of women's emancipation: Dāghir, *Maṣādir al-dirāsa al-adabiyya*, 409–13.

40. Nāṣīf al-Yāzijī (1800–1871), Greek Catholic; 1840 Arabic tutor for missionaries; participant in Bible translation project; founded in 1847 with Buṭrus al-Bustānī and Mikhā'īl Mishāqa *al-Majma' al-sūrī li-'l-'ulūm wa-'l-adab*; he also published *Kitāb majmā' al-baḥrayn*, a collection of essays in rhymed prose, in the style of al-Ḥarīrī's (1045–1122 A.D.) *Maqāmāt*.

41. 'Abdallah al-Nadīm (1845–1896), Muslim b. in Alexandria; essayist, journalist; friend of Salīm Naqqāsh and Adīb 'Isḥāq; in the circle of Muhammad 'Abduh and later participant in the 'Urabi rebellion; after several false starts he published, starting in 1892, *al-Ustādh*, the magazine which Zaidan alludes to: Dāghir, *Maṣādir al-dirāsa al-adabiyya*, 905.

42. Al-Jayyusi, *Trends and Movements*, 12 ff., considers this group in addition to Niqūlā Turk (1763–1828), a Greek Catholic, and Buṭrus Karāma (1774–1851) as the second generation. To them the poet Mikhā'īl al-Baḥrī from Homs should be added.

43. The first was initiated by the American missionaries, particularly Eli Smith, who translated the New Testament into simple Arabic, understood also by people with little education; Butrus al-Bustani and Ahmad Faris al-Shidyak participated in this project. The second was a translation of the Old Testament, initiated by the Jesuits, which Ibrahim al-Yaziji supervised.

44. Jurjī Zaydān, *Tārīkh ādāb al-lugha al-'arabiyya*, 4 vols., new edition by Shawqī Ḍayf (Cairo: Dār al-Hilāl, 1957–1958), 4, 236

45. Ibrāhīm al-Yāzijī (1847–1906), son of Nāṣīf al-Yāzijī, was the author of *Lughat al-Jarā'id: The Language of Arabic Newspapers* (Cairo: 'Ali Maḥmūd al-Ḥaṭṭāb, 1910). Like his father he was a scholar of Arab history and language, published and wrote in various magazines, and supervised the Arabic translation of the Old Testament for the Jesuits: Dāghir, *Maṣādir al-dirāsa al-adabiyya*, 540.

46. I am indebted to Prof. Jens Hanssen for sharing with me his thoughts on the early Nahda Movement as a precursor to the later Nahda. He is preparing a major study on the topic.

47. Philipp, *Zaidān*, 149.

48. See Anne-Laure Dupont, *Ǧurǧī Zaydān 1861–1914: Écrivain réformiste et témoin de la Renaissance arabe* (Damascus: s.n., 2006), 490). The fourth volume of Zaidan's *Tārīkh ādāb* is the closest he came to a monograph on the Nahda. Several biographies in his *Tarājim mashāhīr al-sharq*, 2 vols., 3rd reprint (Cairo: Maṭba'at al-Hilāl, 1922), relate to the Nahda. He continued to come back to the topic in many articles, appearing over the years in *al-Hilāl*.

49. Rifā't Rāfi' al-Ṭahṭāwī (1216–1290/1801–1873); Egyptian *'ālim*, who spent five years (1827–1832) with an Egyptian student group in Paris. After his return from France he provided in a long report on Paris and the French the first in-depth analysis of European society by a Muslim scholar in Arabic. In Cairo he was involved in establishing the School for Languages and, in general, in the construction of a government-run educational system: Zaydān, *Tarājim*, 2, 22–26.

50. Harvey Cox, *The Secular City* (New York: Macmillan, 1965), 17.

51. Ibid., 2.

52. Rotraud Wielandt, "Zeitgenössische ägyptische Stimmen zur Säkularisierungsproblematik," *Welt des Islams* 22 (1984): 117. The article shows how far that process had gone in Egypt in the 1980s.

53. Asad, *The Formation*, 27.

54. Here and in the subsequent section (57–59) he follows closely an article by Magret Canovan, "On Being Economical with the Truth: Some Liberal Reflections," *Political Studies* 38 (1990): 5–19.

55. Asad, *The Formation*, 57.

56. Ibid.

57. Ibid., 58–59.

58. Fritz Stern, *The Politics of Cultural Despair*, reprint (Los Angeles: Univ. of California Press, 1974). For the secularization of Protestantism see Reiner Schulz's essay "Islam und Judentum im Angesicht der Protestantisierung der Religionen im 19. Jahrhundert," in *Judaism, Christianity, and Islam in the Course of History: Exchange and Conflicts*, edited by L. Gall and D. Willoweit, *Schriften des Historischen Kollegs, Kolloquien 82* (München: Oldenburg Verlag, 2011), 139–66.

59. Asad, *The Formation*, 60.

60. Charles Kurzman, *Democracy Denied: 1905–1915: Intellectuals and the Fate of Democracy* (Cambridge MA: Harvard Univ. Press, 2008), 32.

61. Asad, *The Formation*, 185.

62. An extensive discussion of the origins and form of the autobiography goes beyond the scope of this paper. For a general discussion and analysis of Zaidan's autobiography see: Abdallah Cheikh Moussa, "L'Écriture de soi dans les Mudhakkirāt de Ğurğī Zaydan," *Bulletin d'Études Orientales* 37–38 (1985–1986): 23–50; Anne Laure Dupont, "Transformations sociales et culture arabe réformiste dans les Mudhakkirāt de Jūrji Zaydān," in *al-Ṣiyar al-dhātiyya fī Bilād al-Shām*, ed. Maher Cherif and Kais Ezzerelli, 145–68 (Damascus: IFPO, 2009); Thomas Philipp, "The Autobiography in Modern Arab Literature and Culture," *Poetics Today* 14, no. 3 (Fall 1993): 573–604. Cheikh Moussa offers a structural analysis that leads him to the convincing conclusion that the first part of the manuscript is indeed autobiographical while the second one belongs to the genre of memoirs. He then, however, turns around and argues—not as convincingly—that in spite of its structure the second part is also autobiographical. His concern seems to be to show that the manuscript—never published during Zaidan's lifetime—is a fully integrated and complete work. He tries to explain the unfinished character of the manuscript with the observation that no autobiography can be "complete" since we are unable to describe our own end. But surely there is a difference between a well-composed and published, albeit "unfinished" autobiography, and using heterogeneous parts which lingered for unknown reasons in some drawer to craft an autobiography. Dupont recognizes some patterns of the classical biography that

Zaidan integrated into his own autobiography. The third article traces mainly the literary and cultural history that makes the genre of the autobiography at all possible and demonstrates the strong link that exists between the modern vision of man and the autobiography.

63. 'Alī Pasha Mubārak (1823–1893) Egyptian statesman, engineer, educator, author of *al-Khiṭaṭ al-tawfīqiyya al-jadīda* (Cairo: Bulaq Press, 1886–1889) 9, 37–61. This is, however, a report with a great deal about his youth which is very personal and not at all "normative." Another example is 'Abd al-Raḥmān al-Jabartī (d. 1825), historian and author of *'Ajā'ib al-āthār fī tarājim wa-'l-akhbār* (Cairo: Boulaq Press, 1879–1880) 1, 385, where most of his autobiographical information appears in his father's necrology but parts are also dispersed over the whole work.

64. "Bewusstsein eines Eigenwertes des einmalig Persönlichen"; see Franz Rosenthal, "Die Arabische Autobiographie," *Analecta Orientalia* 14 (1937): 34.

65. G. Gusdorf, "Conditions and Limits of Autobiography," in *Autobiography: Essays Theoretical and Critical*, edited by J. Olney (Princeton: Princeton Univ. Press, 1980), 31.

66. See also Philipp, "Autobiography," passim.

67. Mikhā'īl Mishāqa (1800–1888) studied medicine, worked as an administrator for Emir Bashir II, and later became vice consul in Damascus for the United States; he joined together with Butrus al- Bustani and Nasif al-Yaziji in *al-Majma' al-sūrī li-'l-'ulūm wa-'l-adab* in 1847. He is best known for his *Muntakhabāt al-jawāb 'ala 'qtirāḥ al-aḥbāb* (Beirut: al-Maṭba' al-Kathūlikiyya, 1955), quotes are from the English edition; see also Zaydān, *Tarājim*, 2, 156–59. Selections from Mishaqa's *Muntakhabāt* were published in Cairo by Milḥim Khalīl 'Abduh and Ḥanā Shakhāshīrī, *Kitāb mashhad 'iyān bi-hawādith: Sūriyya wa-Lubnān* (Cairo: n.p., 1908). The translation by Wheeler Thackston, *Murder, Mayhem, Pillage and Plunder* (Albany: SUNY Univ. Press, 1988), has the advantage of including those parts of the manuscript that were considered politically inexpedient for the Arabic editions. Though a contemporary of Butrus al-Bustani, Nasif al-Yaziji, and Ahmad Faris al-Shidyaq, Mikha'il Mishaqa cannot be counted among the neoclassical precursors of the Nahda mentioned above. His educational background and career was more similar to that of the next generation of Nahdawis.

68. *Al-Hilāl* 62 (Feb.–May 1954): 14–20, 14–20, 56–61, 20–25; the section about the student rebellion "al-Madrasa al-kulliyya" appeared first in *al-Abḥāth* 20 (Dec. 1967): 323–55.

69. Ṭāhā Ḥusayn, *al-Ayyām* (Cairo: Maṭba' Amīn 'Abd al-Raḥmān, 1926).

70. Renamed in 1920 as American University of Beirut (AUB).

71. Ya'qūb Ṣarrūf (1852–1927), born in Lebanon. In 1870 he belonged to the first batch of graduates from the Syrian Protestant College (SPC); from 1873–1884 instructor at the SPC; close ties to Fāris Nimr and Shāhīn Makāriyūs. They all joined the Freemasons; Ṣarrūf and Nimr began publishing their journal *al-Muqtaṭaf*. Inspired by van Dyck, their teacher and patron, they were drawn to science and became fervent proponents of the Evolutionary Theory. They were eventually forced to resign from the SPC and transferred their journal

to Cairo; see Dāghir, Maṣādir, 441–46; Filīb dī Ṭirrāzī, *Tārīkh al-ṣaḥāfa al-'arabiyya*, 4 vols. (Beirut: al-Maṭba'a al-'Arabiyya, 1913–1934), 4:124–29.

72. Glaß, *Der Muqtaṭaf*, 1; 182, 192, 195.

73. Leila Tarazi Fawaz, *An Occasion for War* (Los Angeles: Univ. of California Press, 1994), 75.

74. Jens Hanssen, *Fin de siècle Beirut* (Oxford: Oxford Univ. Press, 2005), 4.

75. *The Autobiography of Jurji Zaidan, including Four Letters to His Son*, trans., ed., and introd. Thomas Philipp. (Washington, DC: Three Continents Press, 1990), 25; quoted as Zaidan, *Autobiography*.

76. Zaidan, *Autobiography*, 33.

77. Al-Mutannabī (905–965). His *dīwān* (collected works) was first printed in Beirut in 1860; before that it had appeared in print several times in India from 1814: Brockelmann, *GAL*, 1, 86 ff., Supp. 1, 138 ff. Ibn al-Fārid (1182–1235). His *dīwān* was lithographed in 1872 in Aleppo, first printed in Beirut 1882: Brockelmann, Supp. 1, 463.

78. Nāṣīf al-Yāzijī, *Kitāb majma' al-baḥrayn* (Beirut: Maṭba' al-Ābā' al-Yassū'iyyīn, 1856), a collection of essays in rhymed prose. Asa'd Ibrāhīm al-Shudūdī, *Kitāb al-'arūs al-badī'a fī 'ilm al-ṭabī'a* (Beirut: Maṭba' al-amīrikānī, 1873), a book on the philosophy of nature.

79. *Lisān al-Ḥāl*.

80. *Self-Help*, first published in London in 1856, went through innumerable editions over the next hundred years. The Arabic version *Sirr al-najāḥ*, *The Secret of Success*, trans. Ya'qūb Ṣarrūf, was published in Beirut 1880; later editions 1913, 1922.

81. A. M. Rihbani, *A Far Journey* (New York: Houghton Mifflin, 1914), shows marked parallels to Zaidan's youth: both came from a Greek Orthodox background and the parents of both were illiterate, Rihbani's father being a stone mason. Both mothers tried to encourage their sons to get some education. Primary education was haphazard and provided by the lower clergy. In Rihbani's case the priest did not fall asleep while the pupils recited their psalms, but he was, while teaching, working on a weaving frame to add to his income. Both were unhappy with their situation and restless. In both cases the missionary school was a key experience; see Rihbani, *A Far Journey*, 57–69, 104–45.

82. Zaidan, *Autobiography*, 44.

83. *A quoi tient la supériorité des Anglo-Saxons?* (Paris: Firmin Didot, 1897).

84. "al-Shābb al-sharqī," *Al-Hilāl* 6 (Jan. 1898): 333–40, 339. In *Al-Hilāl* 6 (Nov. 97): 183, in answer to a letter to the editor "Kayf a'milu li'unjiḥau" (What should I do to succeed?), he suggested: *al-thabāt* (reliability), *al-ṣabr* (patience), *al-istiqāma* (probity), al-iqtiṣāḍ (thriftiness), and *al-muwāẓaba* (perseverance).

85. For the reference and full English text see *Anthology*, "Salim Saydnawi: Proprietor of the Largest Store in Cairo."

86. For a discussion and a lengthy description see Philipp, *Zaidān*, 18–24, 179–206.

87. Cornelius van Dyck (1818–1895). born in the United States, came to Beirut in 1840 after finishing his medical studies. He was the only nontheologian among the American

missionaries. Besides working as a physician, he helped establish a village school, collaborated on the Bible translation project, and wrote textbooks for Arab students. In 1867 he joined the faculty of the SPC as a professor of medicine.

88. Glaß, *Der Muqtaṭaf*, 1, 183, 193.

89. Philipp, *Zaidān*, 180. Lewis gave the speech in July 1882 under the title "al-Ḥikma, al-ma'rifa wa-'l-'ilm" ("Wisdom, Knowledge and Science"); text in the *President's Annual Reports to the Board of Managers 1866–1922 Syrian Protestant College Beirut*, s.n., 1961–1965, 251 ff. The Arabic text appeared one month after the speech was held in *al-Muqtaṭaf* 7 (1882): 158–67.

90. For more about this relationship between religion and science in Zaidan's thinking, see pp. 35–52, 153–55.

91. Philipp, *Zaidān*, 180.

92. Hourani, *Arabic Thought*, 250.

93. Philipp, *Zaidān*, 182.

94. *Al-Maḥfil al-Thabāt*; see Anne-Laure Dupont, "Usages et Acculturation de la Franc-maçonnerie dans le milieu intellectuel Arabe à la fin du XIXe siècle à travers l'exemple de Jurji Zaydan," *Cahiers de La Méditerranée* 72 (June 2006): 331–52.

95. Dupont, "Usages," 351.

96. See the *General Bibliography on Jurji Zaidan and His Works*.

97. See Dupont, "What Is a Kātib al-'āmm? The Status of Men of Letters and the Conception of Language according to Jurji Zaydan," *Middle Eastern Literature* 13 (Aug. 2010): 171–81.

98. *Al-Zamān*.

99. At sixteen he found a person to teach him English for several months. Then he tried to compose an Arab-English dictionary, but quickly gave up the idea. Zaidan, *Autobiography*, 36. He must have learned more English from his teachers in the Syrian Protestant College. Later he improved his English in London, but he never had any formal instruction.

100. Jabr ibn Mikhā'īl Dūmiṭ (1859–1930) went to Egypt in 1884; edited *al-Maḥrūsa*; and participated in the Wolseley expedition as a translator. He was Professor of Arabic at the Syrian Protestant College (1889–1923). He wrote among several books on language also *Falsafat al-lugha al-'arabiyya wa-taṭawwuruhā*.

101. Dāghir, Maṣādir, 396–400.

102. The Eastern Scientific Society.

103. Salīm al-Bustānī (1848–1884), born in Lebanon; collaborated with his father in the journals *al-Jinān*, *al-Janna'*, *al-Junayna*; author of the first historical novel *Zaynūbiyā malikat tadmur*, published in 1871 in *al-Jinān*; author and translator of many novels and historical works. Dāghir, Maṣādir, 284.

104. The Syrian Scientific Association.

105. Zaydān, *Tārīkh ādāb*, 4, 73. *Al-Majma'* disintegrated after Butrus and Salim al-Bustani died in 1883 and 1884 and Sarruf and Nimr left for Cairo in 1886. For a full list of members, see ibid.

106. *Letters*, Zaidan to his Father (Beirut, 2 August 1887).

107. Najīb Miṭrī (b. 1865) came to Egypt from Lebanon in 1884 and worked there in various printing presses. Khalīl Sābāt, *Tārīkh al-ṭibā'a fī 'l-sharq al-'arabī* (Cairo: Dār al-Ma'ārif, 1966), 248; the same source, 237, gives also 1889 as the founding year of *Maṭba'at al-ta'līf*, which seems less likely.

108. *Al-Mamlūk al-shārid.*

109. For a detailed description of Zaidan's engagement and marriage, see Lewis Ware, "The Role of Popular History in the Formation of a New Arab World-View" (Ph.D. diss., Princeton Univ., 1974), 68–77. He quotes various letters of Habib Zaidan to his son and from the latter to his father from the years 1887 and 1888 until consent is finally given.

110. Information supplied by Hada Zaidan, grand-daughter of Jabr Dumit, May 2010.

111. *Jihād al-muḥibbīn* (Cairo: n.p., 1893).

112. He wrote in his memoirs about one of his teachers preparing him for the entry exam to the medical school: "I learned from him to be conscientious about time, *muḥāfaẓa al-waqt*. I observed that he was most conscientious about putting his time to good use. The high esteem in which I held him made him an example for me. . . . We would study some lesson and if he left me to do some experimental work by myself, taking two minutes, he would turn to the book he was in the process of translating and would busy himself with it. He would translate two lines or three or a page rather than sit idly while I was finishing my work. I acquired this virtue from him and it was of great use to me." Philipp, *Zaidān*, 168.

113. Salama Musa, *The Education of Salama Musa*, trans. L. O. Schuman, (Leiden: Brill, 1961), 154.

114. His brothers, though, and sons became active members, thereby asserting the separate identity of the Arabic-speaking Greek Orthodox community from the Hellenic Greek Orthodox community in Egypt; Dupont, *Zaydān*, 67–70, 290–91; and Thomas Philipp, *The Syrians in Egypt 1725–1975: Berliner Islamstudien 3.* (Wiesbaden: Franz Steiner Verlag, 1985), 128 ff.

115. *Letters*, Zaidan to Emile, Cairo, Dec. 23, 1908.

116. About the issue of Muslim response to his work, see pp. 77–79.

117. Musa, *Education*, 154.

118. For full reference and excerpts from it see the *Anthology*, "Ottoman Egypt: Preliminary Remarks."

119. Philipp, *Zaidān*, 173.

120. Dupont, *Zaydān*, 55.

121. Shiblī Shumayyil (1860–1917), born in Lebanon; studied medicine at SPC; outspoken protagonist of Darwinism in the Arab world; settled 1885 in Egypt; worked as a physician and writer.

122. See the *Anthology*, "The Sensitive Matter of Religion. "

123. For more on this, see discussion on pp. 76–79.

124. Philipp, *Zaidān*, 179–80.

125. "Arkān al-'ulūm al-ṭabī'iyya aw khulāṣat abḥāth al-'ulamā' al-ṭabī'iyyīn," *Al-Hilāl* 3 (April–July 1895): 605–13, 647–54, 729–38, 764–72, 810–15, 846–52.

126. "Qidam al-arḍ," *Al-Hilāl* 16 (June 1908): 554–59. But see also *Al-Hilāl* 3 (May 1895): 654, where he estimates the age of the earth to be two billion years.

127. "Ithbāt wujūd Allah." *Al-Hilāl* 1 (Dec. 1892): 114–23; "Hal fī 'l-wujūd 'ālam ākhar?" *Al-Hilāl* 17 (May 1909): 470–76, 476. For both articles see the *Anthology*, "The Proof of the Existence of God" and "Is There Another World in the Universe?"

128. Zaydān, "Ithbāt wujūd Allah," 123.

129. Zaydān, "Hal fī 'l-wujūd, " 476.

130. Zaydān, "Hal fī 'l-wujūd?" a subsequent exchange between Shibli Shumayyil and Jurji Zaydan about the first essay, *Al-Hilāl* 17 (June–July 1909): 537–42, 600–13.

131. For a detailed discussion of this controversy see Dupont, *Zaydān*, 482.

132. "al-Ṭabī'a wa-'l-ṭabī'īyyūn wa-'l-kutub al-muqaddasa." *Al-Hilāl* 4 (Oct. 1895): 139–42, 141.

133. See also *Anthology*, "The Proof of the Existence of God" and "Is There Another World in the Universe?"

134. George C. Zaidan, son of Choucri, reported that his father told him that Jurji Zaidan "firmly believed in and never betrayed any doubts about the Hereafter." conversations of the author with Jurji Zaidan's grandson, 2010.

135. "Sharī'at Hamùrābī malik bābil: aqdam shāri' al-'ālam," *Al-Hilāl* 13 (Jan. –Feb. 1905): 195–216.

136. "Adyān al-umam," *Al-Hilāl* 7 (Nov. 1898–May 1899): 71–74, 100–105, 137–43, 209–11, 232–35, 275–78, 297–304, 329–33, 484–88.

137. "Diyānat al-būdhiyya," *Al-Hilāl* 8 (Feb. 1900): 290–95; "Diyānāt ahl al-sīn," *Al-Hilāl* 7 (May 1899): 484–88; "Kutub al-dīn 'inda 'l-ṣīn," *Al-Hilāl* 7 (May 1899): 538–42.

138. "al-Dīn wa-'l-'ilm," *Al-Hilāl* 8 (March 1900): 329.

139. "al-Dīn, al-'ilm wa-'l-tamaddun," *Al-Hilāl* 8 (Aug. 1900): pp. 676–77.

140. "al-Dīn wa-'l-'umrān," *Al-Hilāl* 16 (Feb. 1908): 310.

141. See the *Anthology*, "The Sensitive Matter of Religion and How the Elites Monopolize It at the Expense of the Masses."

142. "Falsafat al-nushū' wa-'l-irtiqā' li-'l-duktūr Shiblī Shumayyil," *Al-Hilāl* 18 (June 1910): 565–67.

143. This paragraph is indebted heavily to Glaß, Der Muqtaṭaf, 2, 415–22.

144. The full German title is L. Büchner, *Sechs Vorlesungen über die Darwin'sche Theorie von der Verwandlung der Arten und die Entstehung der Organismenwelt, sowie die Anwendung der Umwandlungstheorie auf den Menschen, das Verhältnis dieser Theorie zur Lehre vom Fortschritt und den Zusammenhang derselben mit der materialistischen Philosophie der Vergangenheit und Gegenwart* (Leipzig: s.n.,1868). Shumayyil translated it into Arabic from the French version of this book.

145. Glaß, Der Muqtaṭaf, 2, 423.

146. In German "Das Überleben des Stärksten [the strongest]" was the most widely used phrase. Even such a perspicacious observer as the repeatedly quoted Dagmar Glaß

uses the term "Überleben des Tüchtigsten," "survival of the most competently productive one"; Glaß, Der Muqtaṭaf, 2, 426.

147. Jacques Barzun, *Darwin, Marx, Wagner* (New York: Doubleday, 1958), 10.

148. From the same root as *taraqqin*.

149. Thomas Philipp, "Progress and Liberal Thought in *Al-Hilāl, al-Manār* and *al-Muqtaṭaf* before World War I," in *Nationalism and Liberal Thought in the Arab East*, ed. Ch. Schumann, 132–44 (London: Routledge, 2010), 135.

150. Marwa Elshakry, "Knowledge in Motion: The Cultural Politics of Modern Science" (translation into Arabic), *Isis* 99 (2008): 701–30, 715.

151. Elshakry, ibid.

152. Glaß, Der Muqtaṭaf, 2, 426.

153. During the same period in Persian the term *takāmul* was introduced for evolution. It comes from the Arabic root *k-m-l* meaning complete, whole, perfect and is associated with the Shi'ite concept of *al-insān al-kāmil*, the perfect human being. I am indebted to my wife, Mangol Bayat, for pointing this out to me. See also her *Mysticism and Dissent* (New York: Syracuse Univ. Press, 1982), 28–31.

154. As far as we know he never tackled the question of the completely accidental character of the process of evolution, i.e., some genetic mutations fitting a given environment better than others.

155. Ilham Khuri-Makdisi, *The Eastern Mediterranean and the Making of Global Radicalism, 1860–1914* (Los Angeles: Univ. of California Press, 2010), 48.

156. Barzun, Darwin, Marx and Wagner, 65.

157. In a letter to Emile, written 12 October, 1910, Zaidan describes his dismissal from the teaching position he had been offered by the new university, *which he read about in the al-Mu'ayyad newspaper before being informed about it by the university administration* [emphasis mine]. *Al- Mu'ayyad* apparently triggered the change of opinion of the university administration. In a letter dated 28 March 1912, he complains bitterly about Muslim criticism of his work. For a translation of both letters see Philipp, *Zaidān*, 210–14 and 216–19.

158. "Madrasa kulliyya miṣriyya hiya ḥājatunā 'l-kubrā," *Al-Hilāl* 8 (Feb. 1900): 264–67.

159. "al-Katātīb aw madrasa kulliyya," *Al-Hilāl* 14 (Oct. 1905): 18–22.

160. "al-Jāmi'a al-miṣriyya," *Al-Hilāl* 15 (Nov. 1906): 810–88.

161. "Iḥtifāl al-miṣriyyīn bi-'l-jāmi'a al-miṣriyya," *Al-Hilāl* 17 (June 1909): 242–43.

162. "al-Jāmi'a al-miṣriyya wa-'l-ta'līm al-lāzim li-'l-bilād," *Al-Hilāl* 17 (Feb. 1909): 272–79, 273.

163. Letter from Zaidan to his son Emile, 12 October 1910, trans. in Philipp, *Zaidān*, 210–14. See also "Naḥna wa-'l-jāmi'a wa'l-tārīkh al-islāmī." Al-Hilāl 19 (Dec. 1910): 177–81.

164. Shiblī Nu'mānī, "Naqd tārīkh al-tamaddun al-islāmī," *al-Manār* 15 (Jan. 1912): 58–67; (April 1912): 270–80; (May 1912): 343–52; (June 1912): 415–27. For more detail see Philipp, *Zaidān*, 63 ff. and chapter IV

165. "Watar al-dīn ḥassās," *Al-Hilāl* 19 (Jan. 1911): 241–44. See *Anthology*, "The Sensitive Matter of Religion."

166. "al-Ta'aṣṣub al-dīnī wa-'l-ta'aṣṣub al-siyāsī," *Al-Hilāl* 19 (Oct. 1910): 54–55.

167. "Jāmi'at al-manfa'a." *Al-Hilāl* 19 (Feb. 1911): 280–85. For the full translation of the essay see the *Anthology*, "Community of Interest: The Source of All Other Communities and the Primary Motivation for Undertaking Great Deeds."

168. *"Limā yatawassamūhu min al-naf' bi-wasīṭatihā."*

169. Zaydān, "Jāmi'at al-manfa'a," 280.

170. Ibid.

171. "If the people of Syria, Iraq and Egypt had been forced at the time of Ottoman rule to adopt Turkish they would today consider themselves Turks—defend the Turkish race": "Ajyāl al-duwal aw i'māraha qadīman wa-jadīdan—al-dawla wa-'l-umma" *Al-Hilāl* 21 (May 1913): 451–66, 459.

172. Zaydān, *al-Lugha al-'arabiyya bi-i'tbārihā kā'in ḥayy khādi' li-nāmūs al-irtiqā'*, (n.p., s.n., 1904). New ed. by Murād Kāmil (Cairo: Dār Al-Hilāl, 1960); quoted as Zaydān, *al-Lugha kā'in ḥayy*.

173. The preceding is heavily indebted to Elshahkry, "Knowledge in Motion," 712.

174. Zaydān, "al-Lugha al-'arabiyya al-fuṣḥā wa-'l-lugha al-'āmma," *Al-Hilāl* 1 (Jan. 1893): 200–204, 203; see the *Anthology*, "Literary and Colloquial Arabic" for full text. Zaidan came frequently back to the issue that the print-language had to be clear, readable, and enjoyable.

175. *al-Alfāẓ al-'arabiyya wa-'l-falsafa al-lughawiyya* (Beirut: Maṭba'at al-Qiddīs Jāwiriyūs, 1886). The book was republished with the title *al-Falsafa al-lughawiyya wa-'l-alfāẓ al-'arabiyya* (Cairo: s.n., 1904), which explains the variations in the title. For excerpts from the book see the *Anthology*, "The Philosophy of Language and the Arabic Vocabulary."

176. Zaydān, *al-Alfāẓ al-'arabiyya*, see the *Anthology*, "The Philosophy of Language and the Arabic Vocabulary." *Ṣīn* is Arabic for China, *kīm* or *kīmī* is the Coptic word for "Egyptian."

177. For the relation between the Arabic language and Arab nationalism, see chapter VII.

178. Zaydān, "Jāmi'at al-manfa'a," see the *Anthology*, "Community of Interest: The Source of All Other Communities and the Primary Motivation for Undertaking Great Deeds."

179. Zaydān, *al-Alfāẓ al-'arabiyya*.

180. Zaydān, *al-Alfāẓ al-'arabiyya;* Zaydān, *al-Lugha kā'in ḥayy*.

181. See the *Anthology*, "The Arabic Language as a Living Being."

182. Ibid.

183. Ibid.

184. Zākī al-Arsūzī, *al-Mu'allifāt al-Kāmila* (Damascus: Maṭābi' al-idāra al-siyāsiyya li-'l-jaysh, 1972), vol. 1, esp. "Ḥawla 'l-'abqariyya wa-'l-ibdā'," 191–214, and "Risālat al-lugha," 233–40. See also Arsuzi-Elamir, *Arabischer Nationalismus in Syrien*.

185. Cleveland, *The Making of an Arab Nationalist*, 99, 103.

186. Ibid.

187. Haim, *Arab Nationalism*, 44.

188. Zaydān, "Ajyāl al-duwal," 459.

189. He touched on the issue repeatedly in *Al-Hilāl*. But one article presents the most explicit and tight reasoning: Zaydān, "al-Lugha al-fuṣḥa," 373; see the *Anthology*, "Literary and Colloquial Arabic." When he published a letter from Iskandar Ma'luf in defense of the spoken language, for instance, he introduced it with the observation that this was a position very rarely taken. The issue is still occasionally debated, for example in a book written, not surprisingly, by an anthropologist: Niloofar Haeri, *Sacred Language, Ordinary People*, (New York: Palgrave, 2003), where she calls for spoken Egyptian to be made the written language. However, she does not point out *which* Egyptian dialect (e.g., Cairene or Saidi) should take on this function; for a Western throwback to the traditional theological view of Arabic as unchangeable see Dan Diner, *Versiegelte Zeit* (Berlin: n.p., 2005); see the review article by Thomas Philipp, "Creating the Enemy." *Welt des Islams* 48 (2008): 50–57.

190. Fritz Steppat, "Nationalismus und Islam bei Mustafa Kamil." *Welt des Islams* 4, no. 4 (1955): 241–341, 252.

191. William Willcocks (1856–1932), a high-ranking irrigation engineer in the British administration in Egypt.

192. For the text of the article see the *Anthology*, "Literary and Colloquial Arabic."

193. For a discussion of this concept in connection to nationalism, see chapter VII.

194. The last item is part of his concept of the education of society; see chapter VI.

195. Zaydān, *Tārīkh ādāb*, 1, 8.

196. The principal limitation of human knowledge to facts that can be experienced and tested assuming that only such scientific approach would make knowledge applicable to the world, in other words, the belief that rationality and modern sciences could make our universe explainable.

197. Charles Seignobos (1854–1942), French historian, wrote on European and French history and historical method (*histoire méthodique*). He was a positivist, in the sense that he believed that the only known things are phenomena. We do not know their essence, their meaning, or how they develop. He connected them in linear fashion through cause and consequence.

198. "La critique de sincérité et d'éxactitude, l'établissement des faits particuliers," quoted by R. Marical, "La Critique de Textes," in *L'Histoire et ses méthodes*, ed. C. Samaran, *Encyclopédie de la Pleiade*, vol. 11 (Paris: Gallimard, 1961), 11:1247–1360, 1341.

199. However, he was inclined to exaggerate the absence of precursors to his enterprise of writing "new" history. For a good critique see Muḥammad Ḥarb's introduction to the *Tārīkh miṣr al-'uthmāniyya* (Cairo: Dār āfāq al-'arabiyya, 2002), 16 ff.

200. Jurjī Zaydān, *Tārīkh al-tamaddun al-islāmī*, 5 vols. (Cairo: Maṭba'at Al-Hilāl, 1902–1906), 3, 109 ff.

201. Chains of transmitters of the sayings, *ḥadīth*. of the Prophet; the veracity of such sayings was determined exclusively by the trustworthiness of the transmitters and not by historical context, etc.

202. Zaydān, "Tārīkh al-'arab qabla 'l-islām: wa-mā fīhi min al-ashkāl wa-'l-ibhām," *Al-Hilāl* 3 (March 1895): 534–41. See the *Anthology,* "The History of the Arabs before Islam: Its Difficulty and Complexity."

203. Zaydān, "Ibn Khaldūn wa-'l-ṭabābi'a." *Al-Hilāl* 10 (May 1902): 504. See the *Anthology,* "The Himyarite Kings and Ibn Khaldun."

204. Walī al-Dīn 'Abd al-Raḥmān Ibn Khaldūn (1332–1382), most famous for his attempt to develop a secular theory of historical developments, based on the concept of *'aṣabiyya,* translated as identity, group loyalty or *esprit de corps,* which serves as the motor for historical movement. He discusses this and his concept of *'ilm al-'umrān* in his famous work *Kitāb al-'ibar;* see especially the translation of the Introduction by F. Rosenthal, *The Muqaddima,* ed. and trans. F. Rosenthal, 3 vols. (Princeton: Princeton Univ. Press, 1958).

205. See Ibn Khaldūn, *The Muqaddima,* 1958, vol. 1, 22ff.

206. A mythical, unidentified people, often associated with the Himyarites or Sabaeans.

207. Also see pp. 239–53, 275–90.

208. Cf. M. J. de Goeje, "Review of Zaidan's Tārīkh al-tamaddun al-islāmī," *Journal Asiatique* 10, no. 3 (1904):357.

209. Zaydān, *al-Tārīkh al-'āmm* (Beirut: s.n., 1890).

210. Ibid., 20.

211. *Al-Hilāl* 16 (Feb. 1908): 306.

212. *Al-Hilāl* 19 (Oct. 1910): introduction, where he also speaks of the evolutionary process observed in the readership of the magazine.

213. Zaydān, *al-Alfāẓ al-'arabiyya.*

214. See the *Anthology,* "Community of Interest: The Source of All Other Communities and the Primary Motivation for Undertaking Great Deeds."

215. Jurjī Zaydān, *Tārīkh al-māsūniyya al-'āmm* (Cairo: Maṭba'at al-Hilāl, 1889).

216. A very sober, frequently reprinted and translated book by Eugen Lennhoff, *The Freemasons,* (1934: reprint, London: A. Lewis, 1978), 22, starts with a clear statement: "Freemasonry made its first appearance as a society, i.e. as a distinct organization in the year 1717. Four lodges then existed in London."

217. See the translation of the introduction of *The Surest Path* by Khayr al-Dīn al-Tunisī in L. C. Brown, *The Surest Path: The Political Treatise of a Nineteenth-Century Muslim Statesman,* Harvard Middle Eastern Monograph Series 16 (Cambridge, MA: Harvard Univ. Press, 1967): 99–123 and passim; see also Nikki Keddie, *Sayyid Jamāl al-Dīn al-Afghānī* (Los Angeles: Univ. of California Press, 1972),192.

218. Answer to a letter to the editor, *Al-Hilāl* 19 (Nov. 1910): 110.

219. "al-Tārīkh al-islāmī bi-naẓar ilā sā'ir al-tawārīkh," *Al-Hilāl* 19 (Dec. 1910): 154–61, 158; see also Zaydān, *Tārīkh al-tamaddun,* 4, 247: "it is worth observing that Islam exercised a special power on the people of the East and drew them gradually towards civilization."

220. For this affair, see p. 46.

221. Zaydān, "al-Tārīkh al-islāmī," 154–61. Later he integrated it into his manuscript *Tārīkh miṣr al-'uthmāniyya*, published posthumously as *Miṣr al-'uthmāniyya*, researched and edited by Muḥammad Ḥarb (Madīnat Naṣr, Cairo: Dār al-Āfāq al-'Arabiyya, 2002), 44 ff. See also the *Anthology*, "Ottoman Egypt: Preliminary Remarks, Islamic History Compared with Other Histories, and General History."

222. For a discussion of these issues see the beginning of the next chapter and in the *Anthology* the articles "Kinship among the Ancient Arabs" and "The Pre-Islamic Arabs."

223. Jūrjī Zaydān, *al-Ḥajjāj ibn Yūsuf* (Cairo: Maṭba'at al-Hilāl, 1902).

224. See the *Anthology*, "Ottoman Egypt: Preliminary Remarks, Islamic History Compared with Other Histories, and General History."

225. See the *Anthology*, "Ottoman Egypt: Preliminary Remarks, Islamic History Compared with Other Histories, and General History."

226. Zaydān, *Miṣr al-'uthmāniyya*, 51. See also Dupont, *Zaydān*, 489–96. She suggests that Zaidan actually contributed to establishing this divide in Egyptian history.

227. See pp. 88, 115–17, 395–408. Though one should differentiate here between the Ottoman Empire after the Young Turk Revolution and the "old" Ottoman Empire of which Zaidan was most certainly critical: see for instance, Zaydān, *Miṣr al-'uthmāniyya*, 122.

228. *Muḥaddithūn*. It should be noted that much of the criticism was restricted to grammatical mistakes and wrong use of terms in Arabic, implying that Zaidan did not have the basic qualifications of a scholar. Letter from Rafīq al-'Aẓm to the editor and reply by Zaidan, *Al-Hilāl* 14 (Oct. 1905): 104–11.

229. Collection of pre-Islamic epic oral literature about battles and heroes and some historical personalities.

230. "Ilmāma [sic] bi-kitāb tārīkh al-'arab qabla 'l-islām li-khadrita al-fāḍil Jurjī Effendi Zaydān," *al-Manār* 11 (Oct. –Nov. 1908): 681–87, 780–87.

231. Such criticism resurfaced at the end of the twentieth century. See pp. 77–79.

232. See Shiblī Nu'mānī, "Naqd tārīkh al-tamaddun al-islāmī," al-Manār 15 (Jan. 1912): 58–67; (Apr.) 270–80; (May): 343–52; (June): 415–27.

233. The collection was called *Kitāb Intiqāḍ tārīkh al-tammadun al-islāmī*, intro. Rashīd Riḍā (Cairo: Maṭba'at al-Manār, 1912). For more detail see Philipp, *Zaidān*, 63 ff.

234. "Le problème soulevé par le père Shaykhū était surtout d'ordre religieux. Entre lui et Zaydān, deux conceptions de l'origine du monde et des rapports entre foi et science s'affrontaient. Le père Shaykhū reprochait à Zaydān de dire que les enseignements de la religion ne s'accordaient pas avec les découvertes des savants, en particulier celles de Darwin et de ses disciples. Il l'accusait d'ignorer toute intervention divine, dans sa présentation des origines de l'humanité." Dupont, *Zaydān*, 649.

235. Zaydān, *Tārīkh al-tamaddun*, 4, 124.

236. Amīn ibn Ḥasan al-Ḥulwānī, *Nabsh al-hadhayān min tārīkh Jūrjī Zaydān*, ed. and anno. Māzan Mutabakkānī (Medina: Maktabat ibn Qayyim, 1989), 6.

237. He may mean here the community of the Egyptians, the faithful, or both.

238. al-Ḥulwānī, *Nabsh al-hadhayān,* 34–35.

239. The accusation that Zaidan as a Christian writer was belittling Islamic history reappeared twenty years later in Shiblī al-Nu'mānī's essay, see p. 76.

240. Shawqī Abū Khalīl *Jūrjī Zaydān fī 'l-mīzān* (Damascus: Dār al-Fikr, 1983); 'Abd al-Raḥmān al-Ashmāwī, *Waqfa ma'a Jūrjī Zaydān* (Riyadh: Maktabat al-'Ubaykān, 1993); 'Abd al-Jawād Muḥammad al-Muḥs, *Riwāyāt Jūrjī Zaydān* (Cairo: Maṭba' al-Nahḍa al-Miṣriyya, 2004).

241. Ashmāwī, *Waqfa,* 48.

242. "Huwa kataba 'an al-tārīkh al-islāmī bi-qalam naṣrānī."

243. Abū Khalīl, *Jūrjī Zaydān,* 7.

244. al-Muḥs, *Riwāyāt,* 44–45.

245. Ibid., 49.

246. Ibid., 69.

247. Ibid., 148.

248. Ma'mūn Fāris Jarār, *Khaṣā'iṣ al-qiṣṣa al-islāmiyya* (Jidda: Dār al-Manāra, 1988).

249. al-Muḥs, *Riwāyāt,* 180.

250. For both quotes see the *Anthology,* "Ottoman Egypt: Preliminary Remarks."

251. Though at times he talked about "Islamic history" as, for instance, in the above division of it into five phases.

252. Query to the editor, *Al-Hilāl* 21 (1913): 236.

253. Actually, he said it would stay in place "unless a new Ice Age would develop": "Maṣīr al-tamaddun al-ḥadīth," *Al-Hilāl* 19 (April 1911): 419–22.

254. Zaydān, *Tārīkh ādāb,* 4, 14–15.

255. See the article by W. Granara, "The Historical Poetics of Jurji Zaidan's Andalusian Fictional Cosmos," in George C. Zaidan and Thomas Philipp, eds., *Jurji Zaidan's Contributions to Modern Arab Thought and Literature: Proceedings of a Symposium Held in June 2012 at the Library of Congress* (Washington, DC: Zaidan Foundation, 2013).

256. See Zaydān, *Tarājim.* See as an example from this book in the Anthology "Selim Saydnawi."

257. "al-Ishtirākiyyūn," Answer to a letter, *Al-Hilāl* 9 (Oct. 1900): 20; "al-Ijtimā'iyyūn wa-'l-ishtirākiyyūn," *Al-Hilāl* 16 (Feb. 1908): 265–82, 276; "Tolstoi," *Al-Hilāl* 19 (Jan. 1911): 195–210, 205, where he criticized Tolstoi's philosophy for not taking human nature into account.

258. By itself a topic worth a lengthy analysis, but which would go beyond the frame of the present study.

259. Zaydān, *Tārīkh ādāb,* 2, 5.

260. "'Allamuhum wa-'trukuhum," *Al-Hilāl* 7 (Oct. 1898): 9–14, 10.

261. Zaydān, *al-Alfāẓ al-'arabiyya.*

262. Zaydān, *Kitāb tārīkh miṣr al-ḥadīth min al-fatḥ al-īslāmī ilā hādhā 'l-'aṣr: ma'a fadhlaka tārīkhiyya fī tārīkh Miṣr al-qadīm* (1889; 3rd reprint, Cairo: Maṭba'at al-Hilāl, 1925). See the introduction.

263. Afaf Lutfi al-Sayyid, *Egypt and Cromer* (London: Murray, 1968), 159.

264. "al-Riwāyāt al-islāmiyya." *Al-Hilāl* 7 (May 1899): 489–93, 491.

265. Zaydān, *Tārīkh al-tamaddun*, 1, 12.

266. See the discussion of this issue in chapter I.

267. Taha Husayn, "Athār *al-Hilāl* wa-munshi'hi," in *al-Kitāb al-Dhahabī* (Cairo: Dār al-Hilāl, 1942), 133.

268. Because his main purpose in writing historical novels was to educate the public and teach them history in an enjoyable manner, he sought to be true to history. In that he differed from many Western historical novelists whose emphasis was more on entertainment than education. A different situation arose with the ending of the novel *al-Mamlūk al-Shārid* published in 1891 where a devoted servant meets a cruel end when he is killed by his old master who does not recognize him. Zaidan was severely criticized by his readers. He defended himself in a letter to the editors of *al-Muqtaṭaf*, and gave in: "if the distinguished readers prefer his resurrection, then I will resurrect [the servant] for them in the second edition, so God will"; *al-Muqtaṭaf* 16 (March 1892): 404–7, 405. Indeed, in the next edition a chapter was added that showed the servant in good health. He had the latitude to change the ending in this case because these events were imaginary, not based on any historical facts. But both examples illustrate how close he was to his readers.

269. For details see the General Bibliography on Jurji Zaidan and His Works.

270. *Al-Hilāl* 7 (May 1899): 512.

271. Ṭāhir al-Tanāḥī, "al-Hilāl fī niṣf qarn," in *al-Kitāb al-Dhahabī*, published by Dār al-Hilāl (Cairo: Dār al-Hilāl, 1942), 148.

272. Ilyās Zakhūrā, *Mir'at al-'aṣr fī tārīkh wa-rusūm akābir al-rijāl bi-maṣr* (Cairo: Maṭba'at Ilyās Zakhūrā, 1897), 457.

273. *Al-Hilāl* 10 (Oct. 1901): 8.

274. "Khātimat al-sana al-'ishrīn." *Al-Hilāl* 20 (July 1912): 600.

275. For the role of local collaborative elites see Ronald Robinson, "The Eccentric Idea of Imperialism with or without Empire," in *Imperialism and After*, ed. Wolfgang Mommsen and Jürgen Osterhammel, 269–89 (London: Allen & Unwin, 1986).

276. Zaydān, *Tārīkh ādāb*, passim.

277. Jurjī Zaydān, *Tārīkh al-'arab qabla 'l-islām* (Cairo: Maṭba'at al-Hilāl, 1907).

278. "al-'Arab qabla 'l-islām." *Al-Hilāl* 3 (March 1895): 534–41.

279. "Nasab al-'arab qabla 'l-islām." *Al-Hilāl* 5 (June 1897): 768–78.

280. "al-Mar'a fī 'l-jāhiliyya." *Al-Hilāl* 7 (July 1899): 585–91, 585.

281. Qasim Amin's book *Taḥrīr al-mar'a* (Cairo: Maktabat al-Taraqin, 1899) made its appearance in the same year.

282. Zaydān, "al-Mar'a fī 'l-jāhiliyya," 591.

283. Zaydān, "Sharī'at Ḥāmūrābī," 195–216, 283–95. The code had been discovered in Khusistan in 1901. It was deciphered in 1903; one English and two German translations appeared at the beginning of 1904: see R. F. Harper, *The Code of Hammurabi, King of Babylon* (Chicago: Univ. of Chicago Press, 1904), preface.

284. Zaydān, "Sharī'at Ḥāmūrābī," 197.

285. He would later call it *al-jāhiliyya al-ūlā*, the first *jāhiliyya* period: "al-Mar'a qabla 'l-ḥijāb wa-ba'dahu," *Al-Hilāl* 22 (Dec. 1913): 163–76, 166.

286. "Ansāb al-'arab al-qudamā': radd 'alā 'l-qā'ilīn bi-'l-umūma wa-'l-ṭutamiyya 'inda 'arab al-jāhiliyya," *Al-Hilāl* 15 (March, 1906) 337–43. (Apr.) 393–401; (May) 473–82.

287. First published in Cambridge 1885, republished in 1903.

288. John Ferguson McLennan, *Primitive Marriage* (Edinburgh: A & C Black, 1865). McLennan (1827–1881) was a Scottish ethnologist, who also wrote a series of articles on totemism and linked totemism to religion.

289. Zaidan refers in the text to Herbert Spencer and mentions the Arabic title of a work by the latter: *Uṣūl al-'umrān wa-uṣūl al-tamaddun*. It is not clear which English book Zaidan was referring to. Perhaps he meant *First Principles* (New York: Appleton, 1860). Perhaps he referred to Spencer's *Education: Intellectual, Moral, Physical* (New York: Appleton, 1860). The only book for which an Arabic translation could be identified is Najīb Shukrī, *Afyad al-kitāb fī 'l-tarbiyya* (Cairo: s.n., 1903).

290. Zaydān, *Tārīkh al-'arab*.

291. See the *Anthology*, "Kinship among the Ancient Arabs: A Response to Those Who Argue in Favor of Matriarchy and Totemism among the Pre-Islamic Arabs."

292. Zaydān, "Ansāb al-'arab," 398.

293. Ibid., 401.

294. See the *Anthology*, "The Pre-Islamic Arabs."

295. With respect to the uncertainty about historical facts for the period see G. R. Hawting, *The Idea of Idolatry and the Emergence of Islam* (Cambridge: Cambridge Univ. Press, 1999), chap. 4, "Names, Tribes, and Places." I am indebted to Reader 1 for this reference.

296. See the *Anthology*, "The Sensitive Matter of Religion," and chapter III of this essay for the discussion of the relation between science and religion.

297. See the *Anthology*, "Ottoman Egypt: Preliminary Remarks: Islamic History Compared with Other Histories and General History."

298. See the *Anthology*, "The Future of Modern Civilization and How the East May Advance." But also see the introduction to the fourth volume of his *Tārīk ādāb* and chapter V of this essay.

299. Stern, *Politics of Cultural Despair*, xvi.

300. What Benedict Anderson calls the paradox of nationalism: "the political power of nationalisms vs. their philosophical poverty" (Anderson, *Imagined Communities: Reflections on the Origin and Spread of Nationalism*, 2nd ed. [London: Verso, 1991], 5).

301. Ibid., 81.

302. Liah Greenfeld, *Nationalism: Five Roads to Modernity* (Cambridge, MA: Harvard Univ. Press, 1993), 14.

303. Ibid.

304. Zaidan, *Autobiography*, 32–33.

305. Today the concept of the sovereignty of the people, whose will is the only source of legitimization for the exercise of political power, is so widespread that, in addition to democracies, every sort of political system, regardless of its form—patrimonial, monarchical, dictatorial, totalitarian, dynastic republic, etc.—has officially adopted it.

306. Or *Schriftdütsch* as the Swiss say. It literally means "written German." This may be confusing as Anderson's argument below differentiates between "written languages" existing obviously long before "printed languages." But only the latter, according to Anderson, became "national languages." By his definition the Swiss *Schriftdütsch* refers actually to the printed German!

307. By which Anderson means that each member of this community knows only a fraction of all members personally, but can "imagine" the others as sharing an identity with himself.

308. It should be remembered that Zaidan, among other activities, also owned a printing press.

309. Anderson, *Imagined Communities*, 44.

310. Ibid.

311. Ibid., 40.

312. Ibid., 44.

313. See Dupont, *Zaydān*, 276. At some point between 1939 and 1942 the name was changed to *Dār al-Hilāl*.

314. Zaydān, "Kuttāb al-'arabiyya wa-qurrā'uhā," *Al-Hilāl* 5 (Feb.–May 1897): 448–59, 489–99, 529–37, 731–36; 6 (Oct. 1897): 126–32; 7 (April 1899): 393–400.

315. Ibid., 6, 126, 128.

316. Ibid., 7, 393.

317. Ibid., 7, 396.

318. Ibid., 7, 398.

319. "Ay anfa' li-maṣlaḥat al-quṭr al-miṣrī al-ḥāḍira: al-katātīb wa-hiya 'l-madāris tunshi'a fī 'l-qurrā am madrasat kulliyya 'āliyya." Zaidan does not give the precise quote or name of the article in *al-Mu'ayyad* (1905) that he takes issue with. It was not possible to verify the source.

320. Zaydān, "al-Katātīb," 2.

321. Frédéric Pichon, "Du vieux avec du neuf: histoire et identité d'un village chrétien de Syrie: Ma'lula (XIXe–XXI siècles)," Ph.D. diss., Sorbonne, Paris, 2009.

322. "Le Français, pour elle [la grand-mère] comme pour tant de ruraux était la langue de la promotion sociale, celle qui ouvrait la porte de l'enseignement, de la poste, de la

ville, de métiers et de lieux où la vie est moins lourde; la pratique exclusive du Breton, en revanche, était synonyme de méprise et de misère." Mona Ozouf, *Composition Française: retour sur une enfance bretonne* (Paris: Gallimard, 2009), 68.

323. Zaydān, "al-Lugha al-fuṣḥa," 201. See the *Anthology*, "Literary and Colloquial Arabic."

324. *Al-Hilāl* 1 (Sept. 1892): 1–2.

325. Zaydān, "Kuttāb"; and the *Anthology*, "The Writers and Readers of Arabic."

326. See Thomas Philipp, "Copts and Other Minorities in the Development of the Egyptian Nation-State." in *Egypt: From Monarchy to Republic*, ed. Shimon Shamir, 131–50 (Boulder, CO: Westview Press, 1995), 134.

327. For an in-depth analysis of this immigration see Philipp, *The Syrians*.

328. Steppat, "Nationalismus und Islam," 258.

329. Zaydān, "Miṣr wa-'l-Shām," *Al-Hilāl* 16 (Oct. 1907): 15–26, 17.

330. Zaydān, "al-Suriyyūn wa-tajannusuhum bi-'l-jinsiyya al-amirīkiyya," *Al-Hilāl* 13 (Oct. 1904): 14–20, 16; "al-Waṭaniyya al-miṣriyya," *Al-Hilāl* 13 (March 1905): 349; Zaydān, "Miṣr wa-'l-Shām," 15–16.

331. Zaydān, "al-Waṭaniyya," 351.

332. Zaydān, "Miṣr wa-'l-Shām," 17.

333. Zaydān, "al-Sūriyyūn . . . ," 17.

334. Ibid., 15.

335. Ibid., 20.

336. *Al-Hilāl 3* (March 1895): 504, in answer to a reader's letter.

337. Zaydān, *Tārīkh al-'arab*, 38.

338. Haim, *Arab Nationalism*, 45–47.

339. Cleveland, *The Making of an Arab Nationalist*, 14–15.

340. C. E. Dawn, "The Rise of Arabism in Syria," *Middle East Journal* 16 (1962): 164.

341. Cleveland, *The Making of an Arab Nationalist*, 42–45.

342. It should be noted, though, that at the same time Zaidan took great pains in his letters to correct Emile's Arabic!

343. *Letters, Zaidan to Emile*, Cairo, 10 Nov. 1908. See also Dupont, *Zaydān*, 581–82.

344. "al-'Arab wa-'l-turk qabla al-dustūr wa-ba'dahu," *Al-Hilāl* 17 (April 1909): 408–17.

345. Zaydān's "Jāmi'at al-manfa'a" was published two years later: *Al-Hilāl* 19 (Feb. 1911): 280–85.

346. Zaydān, "al-'Arab wa-'l-turk," 416.

347. Philipp, *Zaidān*, 214–15.

348. The only one who explicitly called for separation from the Ottoman Empire was Najib Azouri, in his book *Le réveil de la nation Arab* (Paris: Plon Nourrit, 1905); Haim, "Awakening, " 241n2 calls him "a man of dubious connections and questionable integrity."

349. The special-status province of Mount Lebanon, established in response to the unrest of 1861.

350. Yūsuf Sūdā, *Fī sabīl al-istiqlāl* (Beirut, Dār al-Riḥānī, 1967), 24. The author, a major protagonist of this group, only came to Egypt in 1906 and was a great admirer of Mustafa Kamil. The latter's territorial nationalism was an example for his own Lebanese nationalism.

351. Ottoman Decentralization Party.

352. "Bayān ḥizb al-lāmarkaziyya al-idāriyya al-'uthmāniyya," *al-Manār* 16 (1913): 226–31.

353. Tawfīq 'Alī Barrū, *al-'Arab wa-'l-turk fī 'l-ahd al-dustūrī al-'uthmānī* (Cairo: Jāmi'at al-Duwal al-'Arabiyya, Ma'had al-Dirāsāt al-'arabiyya al-'ālamiyya,1960), 434. For a complete list see Philipp, *The Syrians*, 116.

354. Rashīd Riḍā (1865–1935), born in Syria, he went to Egypt to attach himself to the Muslim reformer Muḥammad 'Abduh. He followed the latter in his modernist approach to Islam. Beginning in 1898 he published the journal *al-Manār*, which remained until his death the major platform for the Muslim modernist debate. He also wrote an extensive biography of 'Abduh: Dāghir, Maṣādir al-dirāsa al-adabiyya, 373–76.

355. "Afḍal al-waṣā'il li-'nhāḍ al-salṭana," *al-Manār* 12 (1914): 303–12. Eighteen answers were published from: an "anonymous politician"; Fatḥī Zaghlūl, Egyptian lawyer and writer; Fāris al-Nimr, editor and owner of *al-Muqaṭṭam*; Ismā'īl Ṣabrī, poet and writer; Shiblī Shumayyil, writer, intellectual, promoter of the evolutionary theory; Abū Shādī, editor of *al-Mu'ayyad*; Rashīd Riḍā, founder of *al-Manār*; Dāwūd Barakāt, editor of *al-Ahrām*; Jurjī Zaydān, owner of *Al-Hilāl*; Khalīl Muṭrān, poet; Muḥammad Mas'ūd, writer; Sāmī Quṣayrī, editor of *al-Muqaṭṭam*; Farāḥ Anṭūn, writer and intellectual; 'Azīz Khankī, lawyer; Iskandar 'Amūn, writer, politician; Najīb al-Bustānī, writer; Amīn al-Bustānī, writer; Aḥmad Luṭfī al-Sayyid, intellectual, politician.

356. This mind-frame is somewhat comparable with the second half of the eighteenth century in Syria and Egypt. The Ottoman center had been weakened considerably, and the centrifugal forces in the Arab provinces became dominant: 'Alī Bey al-Kabīr was practically independent in his policy, concluding agreements and entering into an alliance with a foreign power; Ẓāhir al-'Umar and Aḥmad Pasha al-Jazzār did whatever they pleased; and the mighty al-'Aẓm clan in Damascus had all the makings of a local dynasty. But they all officially recognized the sultan as the sovereign and pledged allegiance to him. This was not only due to an inability to imagine an Eastern Mediterranean world without the Ottoman political order, but also to a lack of alternate sources—such as nationalism, which emerged later—for the legitimization of their own power.

357. Zaydān, "Ājyāl al-duwal," 523.

358. "Innanī 'arabī muslim [*sic*] aw muslim 'arabī?": "al-Mas'ala al-'arabiyya." *al-Manār* 20 (July 1917): 33–47, 33.

359. al-Mas'ūdī (pseudonym), "al-Dawla al-'uthmāniyya fī lubnān wa-sūriyya," *Al-Hilāl* 25 (Dec. 1916): 183–92; (Jan. 1917): 292–301; (Feb.): 385–93); (March): 461–69; (April): 573–81); (May): 643–50; (June): 747–53; (July): 807–12. The author's name is a pseudonym. He

is more interested in the history of Lebanon than all the rest of Bilad al-Sham. He might be Lebanese or he could be of British origin and Oxford-Cambridge education. This article appeared after the beginning of the Arab revolt in the Hejaz and after meetings between members of the Ottoman Decentralization Party with Husayn and Ibn Saud.

PART TWO

◆ ◆ ◆

Anthology of Essays by Jurji Zaidan

The headings and subheadings of the translated essays follow as closely as possible Jurji Zaidan's own arrangement of each essay. Square brackets in Zaidan's texts indicate additions by Thomas Philipp and the translators; round brackets indicate those inserted by Zaidan. His own infrequent footnotes are mentioned in our own footnotes. The footnotes were prepared by Thomas Philipp unless indicated otherwise in the respective footnotes. For the full reference for each article, see the Bibliography of Sources Quoted in this Book under "Zaidan."

The Proof of the Existence of God

Translated by Paul Starkey

Acknowledging the existence of God has been an accepted matter in the eyes of the vast majority of researchers and philosophers, in both ancient and modern times, to such an extent that it has been said that it is self-evident and that it does not require any proof.[1] However, we have certainly seen a number of people who have rushed to judgment and stated the opposite. Their denial of this truth has made it necessary to bring forward proofs and prompted researchers since ancient times to seek to prove the existence of God through logical evidence, based on intellectual and philosophical reasoning. People who have denied the existence of God in recent times, however, have based their rejection purely on natural phenomena and said that they do not accept any proposition so long as it is not supported by natural laws, and can be clarified by evidence of the senses. It is for people like these that we have written this article, to prove the existence of God, may He be honored and exalted, by natural evidence and the evidence of the senses, to the extent that our knowledge allows, hoping that it may have the effect of supporting the facts and clarifying the truth. It is for the reader to examine carefully the preliminary matters that we bring to his attention, in the hope that he may find in what follows some clarification of what he believes to be obscure or thinks false. God alone guides to the truth.

1. We have no knowledge that we do not arrive at through the senses.

It is an accepted fact that, were it not for sight, we would have no knowledge of the existence of any visible thing, and if it were not for hearing, we would not be conscious of anything audible. The same may be said of things perceived by smell, or touch, or taste. In short, were it not for our senses, we would know nothing of this universe. The man who lacks senses also lacks imagination. For the intelligence of man cannot comprehend or imagine anything except through the senses, and if he loses them, he also loses his imagination. A blind man cannot imagine colors or dimensions, and a deaf man cannot imagine musical or other sounds, because sounds, even if they are imaginary, have no form, but only imaginary forms in the minds of those who hear them; otherwise, they would be unable to distinguish between the pitch and volume of sounds in terms of high, low, and so forth. The person without a sense of touch has no concept of rough and smooth, nor can he distinguish between hard and soft, or between solid and liquid. The person without a sense of smell cannot distinguish between good and bad smells, and cannot picture them in his mind. The same may be said about taste and other senses, for we can only have knowledge of things through our senses, and the man without senses is deprived of his imagination.

2. The senses vary from one person to another, and differ according to the medium.

We said that a man cannot apprehend anything except through the senses. However, these senses vary in mankind with variations in bodily health, age, physical constitution, and lifestyle. Desert dwellers have longer sight and sharper hearing than city dwellers; manual craftsmen are more sensitive to touch than other people; and so on. In a single city—indeed, in a single family—we can see variations in the power of the senses between different individuals. Some people can see shapes at distances unimaginable to others. If two people stand on a hill looking at the horizon and one of them says "I can see a bird on that tree," or "I can see a man coming from that direction," his companion may see nothing of all that, but may not dare to call him a liar, because he is aware that people vary in the strength of their vision, and he knows that one person may not be able to see what another person can. The most that he can say, if he is asked, is that he cannot see anything. If he is presumptuous enough to accuse his companion of lying, we reckon him an arrogant and stubborn man. The same is true if two people disagree about hearing a sound, so that one says he has heard a gunshot that his companion has not heard because it is too far away. And so on and so forth with the other senses. The variations in perception are increased by the use of instruments such as the telescope and microscope to magnify objects or bring them closer, as well as hearing aids and other such devices. These have enabled us to perceive celestial bodies and microscopic creatures that our ancestors were unaware of, but which have astonished and dazzled our own intelligence.

3. Some creatures have senses that men do not possess.

We have often heard or read how certain types of animals can perceive things that we cannot imagine. The most striking example is the dog, which can distinguish between people in a remarkable way, in a way that humans themselves cannot. It will know its master, for example, even if—and no matter how much—his clothes and appearance change. Some people attribute this to the sense of smell, while others say that the dog knows it through a different sense that we do not possess. In either case, it is a matter for wonder, either that a dog should possess a special sense or that its sense of smell should be developed beyond that of man. Of a similar sort is the sense of direction in bees. If you let a bee out of its hive, put it in a box, and take it somewhere far away, and then release it, it will set out, seeking the direction of the hive and returning to it of its own accord, which is something a man cannot do; so, too, with the actions of other animals.

4. Perception varies in human beings.

Just as different people vary in their senses, so too they may vary in perception. This variation may occur between regions, tribes, or between families, and even between individuals within a single family. There may be many reasons for this, related to different circumstances and lifestyles. It is apparent in the shape and structure of the brain. In primitive tribes, there are people who cannot count beyond five, and you may not find in their language terms for expressing a higher number than two when counting. For example, an Australian tribe has the word *natat* for "one," and *nais* for "two"; if they want to express "three," they will put them together and say *nais natat*; for "four" they say *nais nais*, for "five" *nais nais natat*, and for "six" *nais nais nais*. When it comes to seven and above, they are baffled, however, since their powers of conception do not extend that far. They simply express larger numbers by saying "many." Similarly with peoples who are unable to comprehend some other obvious phenomena. Differences have also arisen between inhabitants in a single city, where you will find people unable to comprehend a geometrical problem. If you tried to make them understand, for example, that the three points of a triangle were equivalent to two right angles, and produced your evidence, going to the most enormous lengths to adduce intellectual comparisons and logical proofs, your efforts would be totally wasted. This is despite the fact that, for some people, the question does not require proof, for they regard it as being self-evident. Among these people, however, there may be some who are unable to understand a question of the "second degree," however much trouble you take to clarify it, because their senses are incapable of imagining it. And among those who comprehend this sort of question, there may be people who cannot comprehend questions of the "third degree."[2] And among those who comprehend these sorts of questions, there are people who cannot understand anything more complicated, until you reach some geniuses who can understand the most complex questions, which are understood by only a few people whose mental powers have attained the highest levels of comprehension.

It is said of the famous mathematician Maxwell[3] that when he was studying geometry, he found geometrical problems to be self-evident truths. He could understand them just by looking at them, and could expound the proof of his own accord. A similar thing is said about the famous philosopher Isaac Newton, who had one of mankind's most developed intellects. He expounded astronomical and mathematical problems that no one else had yet managed to understand, and that some people had reckoned as insoluble because they themselves had been unable to comprehend or solve them. All of this demonstrates how people vary in their intelligence, and it needs no further clarification.

5. Zayd should not call 'Amr a liar in relation to a question he himself does not understand.

As suggested, someone who has not seen a shape in the distance when his companion has seen it should not accuse him of lying. In the light of what we know about the variation in men's understanding, this also applies to someone who does not understand a question that his companion has grasped. If this were not the case, groups would not be guided by particular individuals in their opinions and beliefs, unless they themselves had fully grasped their truth. There would then be no room for political parties, and schools of thought and sects would disappear, since it is impossible for every individual to comprehend every issue, when people, as you are aware, differ greatly in comprehension and intelligence.

6. We should not accuse the prophets or their followers of lying.

The prophets told us what they had seen or heard, and we were amazed by it, since it was beyond our imagination, and far from the experience of our senses. Different groups disagreed amongst themselves: one group said: "We have heard and obeyed," while others said: "No, those are distortions without foundation, myths that do not accord with natural phenomena." One group said that they had been invented for personal motives, while others said different things—too many to be counted. But the prophets told us their stories, and stressed to us the truthfulness of what they related. They said they had only told us what they had seen or heard and that it was in no way right for us to accuse them of lying, or to think ill of them. Perhaps the reason we thought their statements strange was some deficiency in our perceptions, because, as we have already stated, people vary in their intelligence, and perhaps these people had grasped what we had not. All we can say is that "We have not grasped what you have grasped," or, as one companion said to the other: "You saw, but I did not see."

We have no basis for accusing them of fraud, for it appears from the biography of each one of them that they believed what they were saying so completely that they would expose themselves to the danger of death and torture, in order to stand firm by their beliefs and to support what they believed was right. If they had not really believed what they were saying, they would not have stood firm by it or defended it to the point where some of them spent many years enduring the harshest forms of torture; some preferred to be crucified rather than renounce their views; while others exposed themselves to the hostility of their tribes and relatives, abandoning their homelands in order to give their words additional support. There is no doubt at all that they firmly believed in the truth of what they preached.

A similar statement may be made about the philosophers and wise men who have followed the path of the prophets since antiquity. How many of them exposed themselves to danger, and suffered by sword and fire, to defend their assertion of the existence of an almighty creator. It is not right that we should accuse them of lying when they believed what they were saying.

7. When a number of people agree on a story, it is more likely to be true.

We have said that the prophets, and those who followed in their path, asserted the existence of the supreme creator. If they had differed in their accounts or contradicted each others' views, their message would have been in vain. However, they agreed completely in the essentials. Take the statements by the ancient Egyptian and Greek philosophers and so on, and look carefully at how they describe the supreme creator. You will not see any difference between them, for they agree that the power that brought the universe into being (and which each people has called by a different name) is omnipotent and omnipresent, and beyond the reach of the senses. The agreement of the prophets and a group of wise men and philosophers on an account or assertion of a truth makes it more likely and indeed confirms its veracity.

8. The views closest to the truth are those that provide the easiest explanation of events.

Events are the natural phenomena that we observe every day, such as the rising and setting of the sun, the blowing of the wind, the falling of rain, the combining and dissolution of the elements, and similar things such as the actions of attraction and repulsion, dissolution and combination, birth and death, sickness and health, and so forth. We see these events every day, and are naturally inclined to investigate their causes, formulate a theory, and apply those events to it. If the theory is applicable, and we can explain their occurrence on the basis of it, the theory will be correct, or at least close to it. Otherwise, we will adopt another theory. If we can explain events on the basis of two theories, we will adopt the simpler one as being closer to the truth, for there is nothing more straightforward than the truth.

There are many such theories in the natural sciences, such as atomic theory, as well as theories about the rotation and roundness of the earth, the eclipses of the sun and moon, and so on. You will find some of these theories, such as those about the eclipses of the sun and moon, simple and easy to explain. Even the least advanced student can understand them without great difficulty. They are followed in complexity by the rotation of the earth, which is more complex, then by atomic theory.

People observed the rising and setting of the sun, the movement of the stars, and the different positions of the sun and moon, and concluded that all this arose from the movement of the sun and the sky as a whole and that the earth was fixed in its position. They built a whole science on this theory, and manufactured a variety of instruments on that basis. Astronomers acted on it for a long time, without being troubled by doubts, until an innovative philosopher appeared, who took the view that the theory that the earth was fixed and that the sun and heavens rotated was completely at odds with natural phenomena. He put forward a theory that the earth rotated, and that the sun and heavens were fixed. He was persecuted at first, until people examined his theory slowly and carefully, and saw that it accorded better with the facts, being more straightforward than the former theory, and did not contradict any natural phenomena. So they chose this theory over the former one, and will continue to hold to it, until something simpler becomes available to them and more in accordance with the facts.

Natural scientists, *al-'ulamā' al-ṭabī'iyyīn,* take the view that bodies are combined and dissolved in a single way. Elements combine with each other in known proportions which do not allow change, and which are defined by basic weights and balance. They have seen a relationship between the density of the elements, and their specific and atomic weights, and have developed other theories that there is no space to discuss here. They have started to search for a theory that would explain those chemical phenomena, and have espoused various views, culminating in the "atomic theory," and stated that all substances perceptible by the senses—whether solid, liquid, or gas—are made up of particles that the senses cannot apprehend because they are so small. They call these "atomic" particles. Their view is that these particles are equal in volume but different in weight, and incapable of division or erosion, being constantly in motion in an extremely fine fluid, which they call "the ether." They have posited this as a fact, although they have never seen any of that "essence" or apprehended any of its dimensions or movements; on the contrary, they have simply been inclined to accept it because they saw in it an explanation for natural phenomena. They said that the reason for chemical elements to be combined in a fixed proportion was because the combination occurred between elements of fixed weight that were indivisible. They took the view that the causes of heat, light, and electricity depended on the movement of those elements, and that the movement would manifest itself as heat if it was vibrating, and as light if it was oscillating, and as electricity if it was neither of the two. And so on and so forth for an explanation of other natural phenomena. They were satisfied with this view and accepted its validity as a near certainty, despite the fact that they had not apprehended the truth of the matter with any of their senses. A similar observation may be made about other natural theories. But their inadequacy should not stand in the way of an acknowledgement of their correctness.

9. The theories needed to explain natural facts or intellectual and moral truths.

What may be said about natural phenomena may also be said about intellectual or moral phenomena. Dividing intellectual powers into memory, perception, judgment, and so on was only a theory by which people have sought to explain various intellectual acts. The same applies to moral phenomena which we do not have space to expound on at length.

10. The truest theories are those that provide the most general explanations of events.

The theory that explains two phenomena must be nearer to the truth than one that explains a single event. Even nearer to the truth is one that explains three events, and so on. The more phenomena can be accommodated under that theory, the nearer to the truth does it approximate, in proportion to the facts that are explained thereby. If we adopt one theory to explain meteorological phenomena, another theory to explain chemical phenomena, and another for natural phenomena, and we then see a theory that will explain all these facts together, we can judge that this theory is nearer to the truth than the previous theories. And if we formulate a theory to explain all these phenomena, as well as intellectual and moral phenomena, it will become clear to us that the latter theory must be nearer to the truth than the others.

11. There are many natural phenomena hitherto unexplained.

We have so far discussed phenomena that we can explain by theories or hypotheses. However, many current phenomena in the natural world are unexplained by science or philosophy. In particular, we may mention biological phenomena, for scientists (*al-'ulamā'*) have so far been unable to understand how life arose, or how diseases were generated, and they are completely in the dark about organic structures. They know that starch, sugar, fibers, resin, and so on are made up of elements in a common proportion, but they are unable to comprehend the reason for the different appearances of these compounds. The same goes for organic compounds in their various forms. Do not ask about the inability of the chemists to reproduce those compounds with the chemical means presently at their disposal.

This is in addition to the innumerable mysteries of nature, especially the origins of existence, and the boundaries of the universe, how it has developed into such a form, and what will become of it in the future. The scientists' philosophy is totally incapable of comprehending the essence of such questions, nor do we consider that they will comprehend it in the days to come.

12. An acknowledgment of the existence of God with all His attributes will explain natural, intellectual, and moral phenomena, however obscure.

Acknowledging the existence of an omnipresent and omnipotent supreme creator can explain all the phenomena of this world, self-evident or obscure. It is a straightforward fact in conformity with intelligence and its judgments, even if our senses are incapable of comprehending it and our minds unable to imagine or contemplate it intelligently. This is because it provides the most straightforward and most widely applicable explanation for events. Moreover, it is among the oldest theories adopted by philosophers down the ages, for all their differences of intellectual approach.

In short, this is the conclusion we have reached on the basis both of our own intellect and of tradition. But above everyone is the All-Knowing.

Notes

1. Zaydān, "Ithbāt wujūd Allah."

2. What is meant here are probably polynomes, i.e., equations with unknowns. The degree of an equation depends on the power of the unknowns. The degree of an algebraic term is equivalent to the exponent of the unknown. Thus, the term 3x is a first-degree term, 3x squared is a second-degree term, and 3x cubed is a third-degree term.

3. James Clerk Maxwell (1831–79), English physicist.

◆ ◆ ◆

Religion, Science, and Civilization

Translated by Paul Starkey

Question from Nasim Efendi Fahmi, station assistant, Nile Barrages [work of dams, north of Cairo], al-Qanatir al-Khayriyya:

Do manners and politeness come from science or from religion? We see people crowned with the garlands of good behavior and wearing the suits of good manners, and yet they lack religion.[1]

al-Hilāl: A full answer to your question would require a long and detailed reply for which we do not have enough space. In general, however, we can say that it is religion, despite the differences in its types and manifestations, that have taught men good behavior, softened their temperaments, and restrained the strong from the weak, the naked, and oppressed. There is no social, moral, or legal principle in the civilized world that does not have its basis and origin in religion, even though this may not be apparent at first. No individual or group undertakes a charitable or praiseworthy act unless spurred on and led by religion. Modern European civilization sprang from the Christian religion, just as Islamic civilization had its origins in the Islamic religion and Jewish civilization in the Jewish religion. Similarly, if you tried to look for the source of civilization among other peoples, you would see that religion was their guide in drawing up laws, in curbing wicked impulses, and in restraining the strong from the weak through a mixture of threats and promises.

In short, you will see that religion is the source of all good behavior and righteousness, and that it is absolutely indispensable. The thing that has persuaded some Europeans to say that religion can be dispensed with, and that we can be satisfied with science, is that they have looked at the state of their society and seen some individuals progress to the extent that they have imagined themselves to be in no need of any restraint and that science alone can be guaranteed to regulate society. Some of them have gone so far as to discredit religion and declare that it has had no influence on people, and that it is of no use among civilized people. But they have taken a short-sighted view and made a grave error, for no intelligent, right-minded individual could deny the benefits of religion for society.

We do not deny that there is a group of civilized men of learning who, despite having detached themselves from religion, act in an exemplary way in their dealings with regard to the giving of charity, upright behavior, service to mankind, and support of the truth. But we do not think they would deny that those qualities are the fruit of a seed planted by religion in the hearts of their forefathers—a fruit that has been passed down to them through several generations, having matured to its present extent. Even granted that those men of learning have stated that they could dispense with religion themselves, they would not maintain that their workers or partners could dispense with it. Nor do we imagine that, if one of them required an agent for his storeroom, or a custodian for his possessions, he would not seek out a man who believed in God, who hoped for His forgiveness, and who feared His retribution.

We know a number of these people who do not see any need for prayer or worship themselves but who impose the duty of prayer on their children and actually lead them by the hand to church. Do you suppose after this there can be any doubt about the dependence of modern civilization on religion or that it is in any way dispensable? The possibility of dispensing with the restraint that we observe in some individuals is surely no objection, for they have arrived at that point through religion, as I have observed. Even if they themselves have the intelligence and sensitivity to guide them to the good and restrain them from evil, who can guarantee that their sons and grandsons will grow up virtuously like themselves, since science alone cannot guarantee that?

What the enemies of religion argue, and use as evidence of the damage it can cause, is that it has often been a cause of civil dissent, instigating wars, and destroying people. We do not deny that, but we do not believe that the cause of such unrest has been religion in itself. The real reason, as we see it, lies in people's struggle for power. Some kings have used religion as a means of gaining the popular vote because they know that the people are so attached to it. If they had seen that the people could be led on by something other than religion, they would have used that to win them over. Some commanders have used their kings as a pretext for stirring up the passions of the people and goading them to war; others have summoned their people to war in the name of the homeland; and others have used wealth or something different. The real agent of civil discord is not religion but selfishness and greed, which religion forbids. And even if we allow that religion might be the cause of this evil, should that be reckoned as a proof of the harm of religion in general? Should rain be called damaging if it is accompanied by lightning or followed by a storm?

Notes

1. Zaydān, "al-Dīn, al-'ilm wa-l-'umrān."

◆ ◆ ◆

Jinn, Spiritism, and the Talking Table

Translated by Paul Starkey

(Cairo) 'Ali Ahmad al-Shahidi, Ministry of War:

I am busy writing a book about man's most important discoveries since the day he was created to this day.[1] From time to time it refers to discoveries about spirits and jinn, and whenever I hear a story of this sort, I seize on it eagerly, hoping to find something to illuminate my path in these researches. I was getting absolutely nowhere when I happened to meet in a friend's house a group of upper-class young Egyptians, among them the grandson of Latif Pasha Salim. He told us that he had visited France with his father and the lawyer Hilbawi Bey, investigated its institutions, and visited many of the sites there. Among the things they had seen there was a Frenchman who was famous for summoning spirits. He had taken them into a room, in the middle of which they saw a table with feet. The man sat down and some tapping began, like telegraph tapping. Then one of those present came forward with some secret information about his mother, who had died recently. He told him her name, identified her as his mother, and [gave] the date of her death, but the [Frenchman] couldn't summon her because she had died so recently. The strange thing was that at the time of her death she had been suffering from ophthalmia, so her eyes were bandaged, and he saw her like that. Then two other people came forward and the man told them something similar about things they were harboring in their hearts.

Then the gentleman (the grandson of Latif Pasha) turned to the subject of the jinn and said he had read in a European newspaper that the Europeans had managed to summon the jinn and see them with their own eyes. They had bodies that moved and talked as if they were people. When I heard that, I was even more astonished, and whenever I related it to my colleagues, they denied it or dismissed it as idle talk. So I would ask you to give a judgment on this matter, which is an important issue in terms of its relationship with the human species.

al-Hilāl: We have received many questions on this topic. We have not replied to them because we have written on this subject more than once—quite apart from the fact that the natural sciences are widely taught in schools, and our minds have been enlightened through them, so that we have considered it unnecessary to return to this investigation. However, now that the questions on this topic have multiplied, we have decided to reply to them.

Among the beliefs widespread among us is that the Europeans are an educated and serious people who never do anything unless guided by reality. This is a correct belief in many respects, but it does not prevent the circulation of myths among the common people there. Moreover, some unscrupulous people have taken advantage of the simplicity and ignorance of the common people to rob them of their wealth, just as our swindlers do. Indeed, the Europeans are even better at devising tricks and dressing up the truth, because they are more advanced in the methods of industry and better able to perfect them.

Judging an individual incident and clarifying its truth or falsity can only be done by seeing firsthand what has happened, examining the means used, and ascertaining the intentions of the person carrying it out. Was he sincere in what he was doing? Did he, indeed, use sleight of hand or devise some trick before undertaking the action, either conspiring with someone else or using other secret means to deceive those present? This is quite apart from any differences that the spectators may have in terms of recounting a single incident or the exaggerations that each of them may make when relating the incident to other people. In so doing his intention may not be to deceive, but simply to please the audience by strengthening the weak points in fashioning his account. But if someone else retells that story with additions and exaggerations, he will end up believing that it is true and forget the things that he actually made up himself. If you were to ask the two companions who witnessed these events with the narrator, you would find considerable differences in their account as compared to his. Indeed, they would probably contradict it in many respects. Merely relying on an eyewitness account in incidents like this is not sufficient for delivering a final judgment on it; rather, it is necessary to refer to established scientific principles that have so far not been contradicted. And they do not make it easy for us to accept assertions like these.

The question of spirits and their appearance is a matter that has exercised the minds of learned men for a long time. They have set up societies and written books, newspapers, and magazines in which they have recorded thousands of accounts on the basis of reliable informants in support of the assertion that there exists a world of the spirits. Among these we may mention a society established in England in 1882 called the Society for Psychical Research, whose aim it was to collect evidence of specific times and places, some of which were published in the English *Review of Reviews* at the beginning of 1892. The founder of the magazine, the famous author William Thomas Stead,[2] appended some long chapters [to these accounts] from which he extracted results based on proving the existence of spirits, and he even drew a spirit that was said to have appeared to some people.

In their researches, those investigators took the view that some people had two spirits and others three. They laid down laws and rules for them and specified their natures and morals. They described the world of the spirits like a tourist who has visited a city and comes back with descriptions of the places and behavior he has seen. They backed this up with extensive evidence supported by actual accounts. If you were to examine the accounts they published, you would recall the stories of the jinn related by the Arabs and recorded in their books, or [accounts of] what is called a "spirit."[3] People today, however, have dressed up these accounts as research so that they appear like the truth, while stories of the jinn have continued to be regarded as fables. Serious researchers have attacked adherents of this view and refuted it with scientific proofs, so that it has gone out of fashion. But they have not been able to uproot that belief from the minds of the masses. A group of writers still asserts the existence of spirits, including W. T. Stead, the founder of the *Review of Reviews*.

To date, science does not support belief in these accounts. On the other hand, we cannot deny the testimony of all those who have seen them and related their experience to us. There must have been reasons that drew them to believe their accounts — generally some sort of trickery, or simply the fact that fantasy is not totally devoid of truth. In the case of the moving table, you did not say how it spoke or how it indicated the names or ages of those concerned. The thing that is usually said about it is that it indicates the letters by tapping on the ground, with one of its legs, after the questioners have put their hands on it. Usually, it taps every letter of the alphabet until it reaches the first letter of the name, or the thing being inquired about; then it stops and goes back again, starting its taps from the first letter of the alphabet, just like the first time; then, when it reaches the second letter of the name being inquired about, it stops, and so on until the end. If the name being asked about is *'Umar*, for example, it carries on tapping from the letter *alif* to the letter *zā'*, then stops when it reaches the letter *'ayn*. Those present write the letter *'ayn*, after which it resumes its taps from the beginning of the alphabet until it reaches the letter *mim*. After a silence, it then resumes its tapping from the beginning, starting with the first letter of the alphabet until it reaches the letter *rā'*, which is the last letter of the word *'Umar*, after which it is completely silent.

The movements of this table are not without a basis in reality or something like it. Things published in *al-Hilal* about mind reading are relevant here, for some people have the ability to read the thoughts of others or the power to influence them and reveal what is hidden in their breast. For that, the tapping of the senses of the investigator may be enough. If you were sitting with friends and one of them said to you, "Keep your thoughts concentrated on one of those present and I will reveal to you who it is," you might at first think it impossible for him to do so, because you know that he is not a mind reader. But it won't be long before he is reading what is in your mind in full view of people, and you will be helping him without knowing it. You stand ahead of him, while he stands behind you with his eyes blindfolded and his hands on your shoulders. He then asks you to walk slowly in front of him between those present and then to concentrate on the person you have in your mind and not stop thinking about them. You and the mind reader then walk on, one of you leading the other, and he continues to bring you close first to one person, then to another. Meanwhile, his hands are registering the direction your senses are moving in, until he realizes which way you are directing your thoughts and knows the person you have in mind, although you yourself are not conscious of having shown the least movement to indicate what is in your mind. Only rarely will he be disappointed, unless you have not directed your thoughts well. We have tried this ourselves on more than one occasion and have established that it works with more than one of our friends.

If members of a group sits around a table with three legs, put their hands on it, and all direct their thoughts together to the same thing, it is not unlikely that the table will move in a way that they know indicates that thing. But it will not go beyond this simple indication, and it may not even reach that far. However, we have quoted it as an explanation of what may happen in this sort of situation.

As for those who use tables to summon spirits, speak to them, and reveal people's secrets, this represents a sort of fraud based on trickery. It can be done either by collusion with another person, by connecting the table leg via an electric current with another place (where one of the conspirators moves the table however he wishes), or through some other means of deception.

Spirits are not seen except by those who believe in the power of the trickster to summon them. Such a man will see an image produced by his imagination, as hallucinations are produced in a darkened room in which the supplicant sits, expecting to see a phantom whose form is engraved on his mind. People usually ask to see people they know. If they wait a long time expecting the spirit to come, the picture that is in their mind will take on a substance, which is usually the last form to have been etched in it after some disturbing incident. In this way, the correspondent saw his mother with a bandage over her eyes, because it was the last state in which he saw her and he was affected by the sight.

The trickster will often show the client a faint image thrown onto a stage or wall by means of a magic lantern. The person will be dressed in a white shroud, as if emerging from the dead. Then he will use the lantern to make the client imagine that the phantom is walking toward him, and he will shake all over and imagine that he is seeing the person he was asking for. Some of them actually bring in real people, whom they dress in a similar fashion to the person being asked for (if they know him), or else dress him in a long, shawl-like robe that covers him from head to foot. Professor Tindall, the English expert, wrote an article in which he described a visit to a place whose owners asserted that they could summon spirits. In it, he described the various methods of trickery and deception that they committed against people by dressing up fantasy in the garb of truth. Another scientist related how he had visited a place whose owners declared that they could summon for you the sprit of someone you knew, and if you spoke to it and heard its reply, you would not doubt that it was precisely the person you asked for. He said:

> I went into a spacious room, where someone wanted to see the spirit of one of his friends or relatives. The room was bare and windowless, with no door except for the one I had entered by, and nothing in it except for some chairs. I sat down on a chair, and they shut the door and left me alone. The place was dark; I had prepared a phosphorus candle to light as soon as I heard any movement. As I was sitting there, I heard a movement, so I lit the candle, and lo and behold there was a phantom in a white wrap, just like the spirits they claim to see, about to descend to the hall from an opening between the ceiling and the wall. As soon as he saw the light, he hurried back and disappeared. Then the superintendent of the place came up to me and reprimanded me for what I had done because it was contrary to their regulations. If he hadn't known who I was, he would have gone even further in reprimanding me. But he soon became embarrassed and suggested to me that I should simply draw a veil over what I had seen.

The same thing may be said about the jinn as about spirits, for they are the same thing. For the reasons we have already given, therefore, no notice should be taken of the gentleman's account of what was published in the newspapers about summoning the jinn and seeing them moving and talking with one's own eyes.

Notes

1. Zaydān, "al-Jinn wa-'stiḍār al-arwāḥ." The terms "jinn" and "genie" are derived from the Arabic word "jinn" and they all mean the same thing: a demon. "Spiritism" and

"spiritualism" refer here to the belief that communication with the dead is possible and also to any action related to this belief; e.g., mention in this article of the table as a means of communication.

2. W. T. Stead (1849-1912) was a popular British journalist who took up many humanitarian causes. He was very interested in parapsychology. He died on the *Titanic*.

3. The term *al-hātif* means somebody who can be heard but not be seen, a voice without a body. In today's Arabic it signifies "telephone."

◆ ◆ ◆

Is There Another World in the Universe?

Translated by Paul Starkey

It is no secret that the search for the world to come represents one of mankind's oldest investigations, for there is not a single advanced nation, *umma*, that has not thought about its fate after death.[1] Most people have taken the view that there exists another world to which the inhabitants of this world will be transported for punishment or reward. They base their judgments on well-known knowledge available to them. For this reason, the books of the ancients were full of proofs based on their philosophy and sciences (*'ulūm*), which we cannot understand because their technical terms differ so much from ours and the principles of their sciences are so far removed from our own. In proving the world to come, the ancients used argumentative proofs similar to those of scholastic theology and largely relied on words. Today, however, our sciences are based on tangible evidence and rely on the natural sciences backed up by experiments that leave no room for doubt. One cannot prove this reality by means of these sciences. It is a tedious undertaking, not easy to achieve, but we shall investigate it by way of intellectual deduction, though without expecting to attain an unambiguous proof.

Investigating this matter differs from investigating the problem of spirits. We do not consider proving the existence of spirits to be necessary in order to complete the order of things, whereas our very existence demonstrates nature's need for eternity and the hereafter, for we cannot imagine this world becoming extinct. If we have come into this world to spend our days here and then disappear, our existence would be a joke, and the whole of creation would be a meaningless game of no value.

If we investigate eternity and the hereafter in the light of natural science, we do not find them to be contrary to the laws of nature, for eternity is one of the properties of the matter of this universe. It has been proven by chemistry and the natural sciences that matter and force—which are the basis of everything in existence—do not perish, but rather change from one form to another, with changes in composition and dissolution in varying proportions. All things in existence, despite their different states in terms of animal, vegetable, and mineral, are simply manifestations of that changeability. The quantity of matter and force in this universe has been constant from the day of Creation until today, and will remain so forever, with not a single grain being added or subtracted. If eternity is one of the characteristics of the original matter from which all things are made up, is it impossible that it should apply to us in some of its forms?

It remains for us to consider whether there is another world in which punishment or mercy is dispensed. A consideration of the order of things proves that the world in which we live is not complete or intelligible unless we suppose that there is another world connected to it and complementary to it. Here is the proof:

If we consider natural phenomena, we see that they take place according to fixed principles within specific limits. The planets revolve in their orbits at times and distances that are completely fixed, so that we can predict the path of each one of them; specify the place that it will have reached in a hundred or a thousand years, or more; know the times of the eclipses of the sun and moon to the minute and the second, and beyond; and see the four seasons following each other in succession in a temporal pattern that we can understand. Similarly, if we consider other natural phenomena, we also have explanations that satisfy the mind and enlighten our understanding. If rain falls, we know that it is water vapor that has been drawn up from the surface of the sea by the heat of the sun, which then becomes denser because of the cold air, turns back into water, and falls as rain. It then flows as streams and rivers that empty into the seas, so that it returns to the place it came from. Then the sun evaporates it once again, so that the vapor rises up into the air, to be turned to liquid by the cold and fall again as rain, and so on through the ages.

If we burn a candle until it is all consumed, we know that it has not disappeared but rather has turned into invisible gaseous matter. If we capture a ray of sunlight with a mirror and it breaks up into the seven colors of light, we know that the light is composed of these colors, and if we combine them the light will return to its former state.

If we pour sulfuric acid on sodium carbonate, we have no doubt at all that the resultant compound will be sodium sulfate, the carbonic acid having evaporated into the air. The same applies to other chemical reactions, for the laws governing compounds and reactions are among the most precise and strictest of laws. The proof of that is when you can predict the consequences of an action before it happens, or if you see an event you can explain in an intellectually convincing way with no room left over for doubt or confusion on your part.

I consider this to be a marvel or wonder of life. If we plant an olive pit in the ground, we know for certain that it will produce only olives, and a lemon pip only lemons, and so on with all other varieties of plants. We also know for certain that plants cannot produce animals, or animals plants. Every type of plant or animal has a lifespan that it cannot extend. In matters of life there are laws that operate extremely strictly. An animal is born from a fetus, and the fetus comes from an egg, all in accordance with clear laws that satisfy the intellect. If we wanted to give all the possible examples, there would not be enough space.

Order embraces all creatures, which are bound to one another by chains of cause and effect that the intellect has to rely on and accept. If a wall falls on a passerby and kills him, for a moment we may think that it happened by chance. But chance is a meaningless term, for the wall will only have fallen because it has been affected for years by factors such as the wind, temperature, and rain, and the wind will only have passed over it because it is driven by well-understood natural forces in accordance with the established laws of aerodynamics. The man, for his part, will only have passed by the wall for reasons that demanded he walk there, and if you look for those reasons you will see that they are based on permanent natural laws to which there are no exceptions. If someone dies suddenly we think that his death is by chance or has no reason, but if we dissected the corpse we would find in one of the principal organs a disease that had taken hold of him for reasons based on natural laws.

To sum up, we see natural processes connected with matter and force occurring with great precision and order, despite their different manifestations. They all adhere to laws, principles, and explanations in which the mind can have confidence, admiring the precision of their structure and the correctness of both their antecedents and their results.

We still see that same order preserved when we move from material works to spiritual, mental, or moral events that appear to depend on natural events. If we see some deficiency or flaw in them we are perplexed, not knowing what sort of wisdom or justice there can be in their occurrence.

If someone is struck down by a disease, which gains such a hold over him that he dies, we have no lack of explanations for the cause of his disease or the manner of his passing. We have recourse to the well-established laws of nature. If someone is afflicted by poverty or hardship, we have no difficulty in attributing that to its origins or causes and providing an explanation that is intellectually satisfying. All of that relies on natural laws connected with matter and force. But if we looked at the sum of these events from a moral viewpoint, or measured them by the yardstick of justice or tried to apply intellectual judgments to them, we might see in them some defect or deficiency that has only increased our ignorance so that our investigation becomes more complicated, making us confused and doubtful.

To clarify what I have in mind, we can divide the events of this universe into the material and the spiritual. By material events, we mean things that happen through the interplay of matter and force, such as astronomical events, meteorological phenomena, chemical reactions, the laws of growth in plants and animals, and other similar natural events. By spiritual events, we mean the actions of the spirit, in accordance with the judgments of the intellect on the sum of events in the universe and their relation to the wisdom that we are conscious of or at least anticipate in creation. As examples of the actions of the spirit referred to above, we may base our judgments on certain events as conforming or failing to conform to justice, mercy, or compassion. For example, if we hear or read that a man intentionally killed his son, we feel depressed and want to take vengeance on the killer, even if we do not know him or have no connection with the murdered man. By contrast, if we hear that a man has come to the aid of an injured man and helped him and saved him from the hand of an oppressor, we feel satisfaction with this action and find ourselves siding with the man who has done it with a desire to praise and reward him. That shows that in our nature there is a force by which we measure moral or spiritual events and judge their rightness or wrongness, without any instruction or training. The existence of this instinctive force within us requires its application to other forces.

If we consider the operations of this universe, we see that the material ones conform to rational principles, and we find ourselves satisfied with them because they take place in conformity with established laws that relate to one another in an intelligible system in a unified way. As a consequence, if we know their first stages, we can predict their results, because we know that a single cause always has a single result.

Spiritual or mental events, however, are different, for we seldom see in them anything that complies with logical laws or satisfies the spirit. Take, for example, a man who has spent his life doing good works, giving charity to the poor, helping the afflicted, and living a life of piety and abstinence. But despite that, we see him continually beset by setbacks, and surrounded by hardship, so that he hardly has time to forget one disaster before he is afflicted with another. Indeed, his whole life is spent in sadness and regret, and he may even die of grief. Another man may continually be committing sins and doing all sorts of reprehensible things. He may never stop injuring and abusing others, but we may still see blessings heaped upon him, so that he spends his life happily, enjoying the pleasures and bounty of this world!

Then there is the young man in the prime of youth, with every advantage he could want, intelligent and sharp-witted, so that people expect good deeds from him, and he wants to serve mankind. He begins to prepare himself, with high hopes and an open heart. His parents dote on him, counting the hours till they can reap the harvest of the learning and manners they have sown in him and enjoy the fruits of their exertions. But he has scarcely begun his labors before he is overtaken by death and passes away. His death puts an end to their hopes, and his labors and preparations are scattered to the winds!

Another young man, however, may grow up hated and despised by his family and acquaintances, so that people long for his death, but he flourishes for a long time, enjoying the fruits of his labors, and perhaps the labors of others!

Then there is the infant who was born sick with an illness inherited from his father, so that he spends his short life suffering in agony, before dying without having done anything wrong. It may happen that the father, who has passed on the disease with its suffering, has never himself suffered any pain at all as a consequence of the disease. Another person may have inherited great wealth and good health from his father, and lived in comfort and prosperity, enjoying a life of luxury and constantly indulging in amusements. But he may be a wicked man, using his wealth and influence to harm others. Another man may have been born into poverty, or his father may have died in debt, so that he has to spend his whole life working tirelessly to repay his debts until he dies from an excess of toil and overwork!

Then there is the widow who has chosen to remain so for the sake of her only child, bringing him up single-handedly with tears in her eyes from birth to youth. When he walks, her eyes watch him; when he speaks, her heart beats for him; when he smiles, her whole body feels reinvigorated; and when he goes away, she follows him in her thoughts. Then, when it is nearly time for him to return, she starts to lean out of the window, her eyes searching everywhere, and whenever she sees a shadow she thinks it is her son. If he is a little late, her strength fails her and she kneels down in prayer, beseeching God to preserve him from the vicissitudes of time. When he returns, she forgets all her worries and serves him, praising God for His grace. And when he grows up, she has no care but to attend to his marriage, so that whenever she sees a girl she looks at her from the point of view of the compatibility between the two of them, imagining that there is not a girl in the world suitable for her son. This continues until both he and his mother choose a virgin whose qualities conform to their requirements. So she seeks the girl's hand in marriage for him and begins to make preparations for the wedding. She summons attendants and carpenters, and purchases the best furniture, as she counts the days and hours to the wedding day. In the meantime, the bridegroom is struck down by an illness that does not let him survive a single night, so he dies, leaving his mother in a state that you can only imagine!

And here is Christopher Columbus, the discoverer of America who performed an unparalleled service to the world, but who spent a troubled and dangerous life and died sad and desperate. How many inventors and explorers have ruined their brains and exhausted their bodies to invent a machine or discover a hidden place, before dying from exhaustion without having tasted the fruits of their labors!

These are just a few examples, which may prompt the reader to recall even stranger events that he has heard of or seen. They all demonstrate the disorderly nature of moral events and their lack of adherence to intellectual principles and spiritual feelings. These and similar examples do not demonstrate any rational system, and we cannot see in them any wisdom or logical connections as we can in material events, because our rational or moral principles require that those who do good be rewarded or the converse in the case of evildoers. We have learned mercy toward the afflicted and the sad, and we have learned to assist the wronged and take vengeance on evildoers, but we do not see this principle operating here.

The order of the universe proves that there is a superior wisdom that has designed it. We see the effects of this wisdom in every material action, but we seldom see any wisdom in nonmaterial events. So it seems that this system is deficient in an obvious respect, namely, with regard to spiritual or nonmaterial events. It is unintelligible that the creator of this perfect universe should have intended there to be any deficiency, injustice, or disorder in it without having created a supplement to the universe to correct such a deficiency. But that could only happen in another world that complements the present one. And insofar as this deficiency is basically concerned with mankind, it cannot be remedied unless man is present in that world. But he cannot be there unless he is resurrected. And that is the world to come.

Do any natural events contradict this statement? Does it depend on a view of the world to come that contradicts the universe that we know? No, because we have not yet been able to comprehend the limits of this universe or of the time frame in which it exists. So how can we make a definitive judgment on what lies behind it, or on the part of it that our senses cannot perceive? In this respect, we are like the man who was taken to a garden with his eyes blindfolded. When the blindfold was removed, he walked about the garden and found it surrounded by a high wall that he could not cross or see beyond. If someone had come and told him that behind this wall there was sea, land, a valley, a mountain, or a city, he would not have been able to call him a liar, nor would he have been obliged to believe him unless he could produce some rational proof.

So the existence of another world does not contradict the way this world is organized; rather, it complements it, as has been explained.

Notes

1. Zaydān, "Hal fī 'l-wujūd 'ālam ākhir?"

◆ ◆ ◆

The Sensitive Matter of Religion and How the Elites Monopolize It at the Expense of the Masses

Translated by Paul Starkey

There are many aspects of a man's life that he is keen to protect, and for which he can be roused to anger, including religion, honor, ancestry, and the like.[1] But religious fury has the widest scope and the strongest effect, because it may be shared by thousands of people of one religion against thousands of another religion. Adherence to a religion is a natural phenomenon in mankind, for you will not find a people without a religion, despite the wide differences in its nature and in the nature of man's adherence to it. If you were to make a tour of cities and villages, you might see among them cities without walls, countries with no rulers, markets with no money or cash, or places with no schools or theaters, but you would never find a town without a place of worship. You might see peoples without politics or laws, without cities or industry, but you will not find a people or tribe without religion; it is as though it is a natural emotional instinct. It is no wonder, then, that religion touches a sensitive nerve, for people have held it to be a fundamental pillar of society from the earliest historical times.

Man is a social animal by nature—that is, he is disposed to exchange benefits through helping and seeking help. The reason for this is perhaps that he has so many needs and cannot fulfill them all independently. This has led him to adopt social institutions, which are no fewer [in number] than the reasons for his weakness. The oldest social institutions are those based on relationships, which may involve group loyalties based on ancestry, then on homeland, *waṭan*, religion, and language, then on customs, habits, trades, and professions, and even on sex, color, marriage, celibacy, youth and middle age, tallness and shortness, or other innumerable things. A man may share a link of ancestry with someone, a link of homeland with someone else, and a link of religion with yet another person.

Social ties are numerous and available to everyone. A man will lean toward a particular tie in case of need, according to his perceived advantage from the link. If a people or tribe linked in solidarity is afraid of an enemy attacking them, they will unite against the enemy using the link of ancestry, as one family or set of relations. And if that does not help them, they will make use of the ties of homeland. If that does not enable them to prevail, they will seize on the link of religion or language, which may vary in different ages and circumstances.

If you examine these group ties, *'aṣabiyya*, you will see that religion is the most extensive of them all, because it brings together black and white, near and far. Unlike the ties of kinship, descent from a single ancestor is not one of its preconditions; nor is living in a single country, as with the ties of homeland; nor is speaking a common language, as with linguistic ties. It is enough to believe in a single object of worship. The tie of religion is a stronger bond between people than any other bond, because people share similar natures and virtues through having grown up in accordance with a single set of customs and practiced similar rituals that have cast them in a single mold. English and African, Arab and Indian, rich and poor are all alike, because religion has no homeland, although you will not find a homeland with no religion.

People may unite to defend their country, *waṭan*, just as they may unite to defend their religion. But they will defend their country only when forced to by considerations of advantage and the guidance of reason, because through preserving their country they will preserve their wealth, their family, and the other appurtenances of this mortal life. It is for this reason that they will unite to defend it. They will defend their religion, however, not for rational reasons but rather because they are driven by emotion. For this reason, they will be roused to anger, and be stirred up for revenge, and if their agitation bears no fruit in this world then it will have better and more lasting effects in the world to come. Above all, it is the comfort of the poor and the hope of the weak. For this reason, religion touches a more sensitive nerve with the masses than it does with the elite, because the latter are more concerned with the pleasures and goals of this world.

The elite are aware that the common people are attached to religion, and they take advantage of that sensitivity to achieve their aims. The elite seek the help of the common people against their enemies and use them in the name of religion for their own interests and advantage. They gather them together to fight, and they call fighting in the name of religion "holy war." Holy wars go back a very long way. The Torah is full of stories of such wars between the Jews and others or between other peoples from various homelands and religions. The reasons for all these confrontations were religious, involving a people supporting the victory of their god or taking revenge for some insult that had been directed at him. But were their leaders really always applying themselves to this goal, or were they often using it as a pretext for mastery and superiority? That is a question on which there is more than one view.

Let us consider the matter in relation to holy wars among pagan peoples, of which there were indeed many. In Greek history many struggles broke out between tribes or cities to restore the honor of a god, to defend his pilgrims, or to recover sacred wealth plundered from temples. The last and best known of these was when the Phocaeans (a Greek people) trespassed on the land of the temple of Delphi in the time of Philipp of Macedon, the father of Alexander. They cultivated part of the land, so Philipp punished them; they then attacked the temple and looted it, so Philipp declared war on them and cleared the land of them in 346 B.C. .

Compare the foregoing examples with wars involving the Christians, the first being the war of Constantine the Great,[2] the defender of Christianity. Historians have doubts, even in the case of this hero, about the genuineness of his intentions in his conversion to Christianity. Some of them say that he made a show of being a Christian so as to gain the help of the Christians against his enemies. He called on them in the name of religion, and they came to his aid.

If Peter the Hermit[3] had called on the people of Europe to make war on the East for political reasons, they would not have responded to his call. But he played the religious card and called on them to save Christ's tomb from the hands of the Muslims. So they left their homes and attacked the East on horseback and on foot. Troops of soldiers were formed in the name of religion, such as the Knights Templar and others. Compare that with the wars of the Muslims and other nations, which are so well known we do not need to mention them.

During every period, kings have exploited the religious sensibilities of the masses and spurred them on through men of religion. For this reason, the elite in ancient times—consisting of two groups, rulers and priests—would cooperate to exploit the masses and enslave them in the name of religion. Such was the case during the period of the Pharaohs in Egypt, the Phoenicians in Syria, the Chaldeans in Babylon, and other pagan kingdoms of both East and West. It was like this too during the Christian period, for the kings could not dispense with the priests if their authority was to be established over the masses.

The Muslims behaved in the same way following the establishment of the caliphate, for religious scholars provided the means of religious domination between the caliph and the common people, just as emirs and commanders were the means of perpetuating temporal power. Religious scholars might dispense with these intermediaries completely because ordinary Muslims followed their scholars and submitted to them, just as ordinary Christians followed their priests. The Abbasid caliphs would cultivate religious scholars and seek their help in subduing the masses and winning their hearts. The sultans and emirs would do the same thing, for this same reason and for others. It was to the mutual advantage of both parties, because the scholars gained wealth and influence from being close to the caliphs, but what the caliphs gained from them was more important and lasting. Respect for the caliphs became ingrained in the hearts of the masses, so that they adhered to them and revered them in the name of religion.

The caliphs were also in submission to the common people in the name of religion. They were often forced to go along with sections of the populace in some of their religious beliefs, even though those beliefs might be contrary to their own or in opposition to the facts. For example, when a man brought the Caliph al-Mahdi[4] a sandal that he claimed was the Prophet's sandal, the caliph took it from him and accepted it even though he believed that he was lying. He was afraid that if he declared the man a liar, the common people would attribute his statement to a lukewarm attitude toward religion.

The caliphs had no choice but to exhibit piety and undertake religious duties so that the common people would not find fault with them or come to despise their authority, even though the caliphs themselves might not have believed in these rituals. It is related how the Umayyad al-Walid ibn Yazid,[5] despite his reputation for licentiousness and lack of piety, would throw off his dyed, perfumed clothes and carefully perform the ritual washing at prayer time before being brought clean white clothes as befitted a caliph. He would then pray in these clothes, meticulously performing all the rituals—recitation, silence, stillness, bending, and prostration—before returning to his original clothes when he had finished.

At every period, the common people have followed and supported any Tom, Dick, and Harry who could win them over in the name of religion. That might be done by preachers with a genuine faith, or it might be done by people who made a show of their religion for their own purposes, like political tricksters in every state. These people might also seduce the common people with food, setting up tables for them in the streets. The pilgrimage superintendent would set up a thousand tables every day during Ramadan, and on other days five hundred tables, with ten types of food at each table as well as freshly grilled fish and rice with sugar. Then he himself would go around the tables to inspect them. His [servants] would carry him around in a sedan chair from table to table, and if he saw some rice with no sugar on it he would order the baker to bring sugar. Then, if the baker was so slow that the rice was eaten with no sugar, he would order him to be given two hundred lashes. The pilgrim superintendents did the same thing in the other cities. Some of them would set up tables twice a day, for lunch and dinner. Yusuf ibn 'Umar, the agent of Hisham ibn 'Abd al-Malik, would set up five hundred tables to feed people, and Yazid ibn Hubayra would set up a thousand tables. But most shrewd politicians would seduce the common people through religion.

The sensitive matter of religion can, however, just as often be used for good as it is used for evil. Most of the charity performed in this world is done in the name of religion in order to seek a reward from God. Especially in past times, there would have been no charitable organizations in any nation had it not been for religion. These mosques, churches, chapels, monasteries, schools, hospitals, and the like are all the fruits of religious feeling, of the sensitive sinew of religion.

This is not to speak of the Christian religious missions of our own day or the charitable institutions that they have founded. It is enough to mention their schools and their role in the Nahda of the East in general, and of Syria in particular. The American College[6] would not have been with us had it not been for religious pride, for the people who paid to establish it and support it acted out of fervor for their religion. There are many similar examples in Syria, Egypt, and the other countries of the East, quite apart from the effect that such fervor has had in Europe and America.

In short, mankind, and in particular the common people, will respond to a religious propagandist before any other, for the reasons stated. The results of such preaching may be good or bad according to the aims of the preacher. If he calls them to war, revolution, hostility, revenge, and the like, then the result of such religious sensitivity may be evil. But if he preaches charity or benevolence, the call will be beneficial. So may God multiply the preachers of good!

Notes

1. Zaydān, "Watar al-dīn ḥassās." This article was published a few months after Zaidan's dismissal from Cairo University before he had actually started teaching. The reason for his dismissal was Muslim pressure to keep him from teaching Islamic history.

2. Constantine I (r. 306–337), founder of Byzantium (Constantinople), recognized and tolerated Christianity.

3. Peter of Amiens (1050–1115) was an ambulant eschatological preacher who called for popular participation in the First Crusade in 1096.

4. Al-Mahdī, third Abbasid Caliph (r. 775–785).

5. Al-Walīd ibn Yazīd II, eleventh Umayyad Caliph (r. 743–744).

6. What is probably meant here is the Syrian Protestant College, renamed in 1920 as the American University Beirut.

The Philosophy of Language and the Arabic Vocabulary

Translated by Hilary Kilpatrick

The Origin of Languages

The division of languages according to their origin corresponds to the division of the peoples who speak them.[1] When we say that the languages are divided into Turanian, Aryan, and Semitic ones, this means that the peoples who speak the Turanian languages have a single origin, those who speak the Aryan ones also have a single origin, and other peoples likewise. Some of the peoples who speak Aryan languages live in Europe, others in India and Persia. And however great the distance between them and however much their manners and customs differ today, in most ancient historical times they were undoubtedly one people or family, living in one place. Then circumstances forced them to separate into two groups, one in the south and the other in the north. The southern group settled in the middle of Asia, while the northern one migrated to Europe. Then each of these groups divided further after varying periods. The same holds for the Semitic languages. In earliest times their speakers lived in Mesopotamia; they were the Assyrians or their ancestors, and they spoke a single language that may have been Assyrian. Then circumstances forced some of them to migrate to the Arabian Peninsula either in search of food or fleeing from war, and there they settled. In the course of time their original language diversified in accordance with the law of evolution, and the Arabic language and Arab people emerged. Another group emigrated and settled to the north of the Arabian Peninsula. Its language, too, evolved into an independent language, becoming known as the Hebrew language. Perhaps Abraham the Friend of God[2] was the first to emigrate. While these different branches were diversifying, the original language in Mesopotamia was doing likewise because they were all subject to the same law.

The evolution of the branches of each of these languages was analogous. After Hebrew became independent, its most ancient form being Phoenician, a group of its speakers migrated west and settled in Carthage. Their language evolved into an independent language known as Carthaginian. The same thing goes for the other branches. The Carthaginian language is closer in vocabulary and structure to its Phoenician sister than to its Hebrew aunt or its Assyrian grandmother. But it is closer to all of them than it is to the Aryan languages, though it is closer to the Aryan than to the Turanian languages, and closer to all the preceding languages than to the Chinese languages. Thus the greater the distance in space between people and the distance in time from their branching off from one another, the more their languages will differ.

Now if we consider the stages through which a language has grown and relate those stages to the languages in use today, the manner and periods in which languages diversify into separate languages will become clear to us. It is well known that the first men appeared on the banks of the Euphrates and Tigris, between Iraq and Armenia. They grew and multiplied, and from their descendants sprang the different peoples on earth. But they did not separate all at once. Each time that region became unable to provide their livelihood a group migrated in one direction or another. The Pentateuch mentions the greatest migration that caused the number of languages to multiply and calls it the story of the confusion of tongues (the Tower of Babel). It refers elsewhere to the dispersion of peoples over the world, but it only speaks of the peoples, descendants of Noah, who separated after the Flood and ignores the peoples who appeared before the time of the Flood. Where were Cain's descendants and their various descendants? Where were the other peoples who existed before the Flood, apart from those who lived in Mesopotamia and were engulfed by it? The period between the appearance of the first man and the Flood certainly lasted a long time during which different peoples emerged, separating, diversifying, and migrating so as to settle large parts of the earth.

It is clear that the speakers of languages that are not highly developed were the oldest emigrants from Mesopotamia, like the Chinese and the original Egyptians; one group went east and the other went west. Because these two peoples are among the most ancient on earth, if not the most ancient, their languages are the simplest. They broke away before the time of the Flood, when language was still in its earliest stage, before the appearance of particles and the distinction between verbs, nouns, and prepositions. The Chinese may be descended from Cain, for the Pentateuch describes his descendants as skilled in handicrafts and music, and the Chinese are the oldest masters of the different crafts and the most skilled in working in them.

We can see a similarity between the words *sīn*, China, and *qain*, Cain; indeed it is true to say that they are the same, for the [letters] *qāf* and *ṣād* often replace each other, and the letter *c* in European languages is sometimes pronounced as *q*, the Arabic *qāf*, or *k* and sometimes *s*, the Arabic *ṣād* or *sīn*. Similar differences exist in the pronunciation of the Arabic *jīm* between Egypt and Syria[3] and the letter *kaf* among some Arab tribes; this last is pronounced by some as *k*, by others as *sh*, and by yet others as *s*. A resemblance can also be seen between the word *qain* and the name of Egypt, because the country used to be called *Kīm* or *Kīmī*. The substitution of *m* for *n* or the reverse is well known, and the vowels are of no consequence. But this is not the place to delve into that subject. What concerns us is that the peoples who speak languages that are not highly evolved settled the world before the Flood. Then the ancestors of the speakers of the Turanian languages migrated and came to live in the northern part of Asia; they include the Mongols, Tatars, and others. Subsequently the Aryans migrated, staying together for some time and then dispersing, moving to India, Persia, Kurdistan, and Europe; and finally [there are] the Semites with their various branches, as we have mentioned. When a language split from its mother, it began to develop by itself, while the mother language continued to develop as well, each one following the course determined by the conditions of its speakers and their surroundings, and so before long they had distanced themselves from each other. But comparison and careful examination reveal the similarities between these distant languages, indicating their common origin. This similarity between languages varies according to the time when they split from one another. The similarity between Arabic and Hebrew words, constructions, and etymology is perfectly obvious. The same is true of the European languages derived from Latin, because all of them split from their mother tongue after their constructions and etymology had evolved, and so the resemblance between them is evident. Arabic and Latin are only remotely similar because they broke away before that development was complete, and so they developed separately and in different ways. For the same reason, Arabic and Chinese have an even fainter resemblance; the Chinese broke away from the original population many centuries before the Semites did, when language was still in its simplest stage.

Despite all this, we do not exclude that there are similarities in certain respects between distant languages if we look for such evidence where we may hope to find it. It is not appropriate for us to look for similarities in verb derivation between the Aryan and Semitic languages, or the construction of sentences between Chinese and Arabic. But let us look for the most ancient elements in each of these languages' sources and seek similarities between them; then we shall most likely come across what we are looking for. [. . .]

What Is the Arabic Language?

Arabic is one of the Semitic languages, and it is the most developed in form, concepts, etymology, and phraseology. Indeed it is one of the most highly developed languages in the world. It has already been mentioned that the various kinds of languages can be divided into highly developed and undeveloped, and the former into inflected and noninflected. The inflected languages fall into three main groups: (1) Aryan; (2) Turanian; and (3) Semitic, including Arabic, Syriac, Hebrew, Phoenician, Carthaginian, Assyrian, and Babylonian. The most developed Semitic language is Arabic.

The Semitic languages are those languages that the descendants of Shem, the son of Noah, speak. Specialists in linguistics disagree about how they separated from each other. But it is clear that the main living Semitic languages today are Syriac, Hebrew, and Arabic, and they are not derived from one another but have branched out from a common root that time has destroyed, namely the language of the ancient Semites who lived in Mesopotamia. Philologists call it Aramaic, referring to Aram, one of Shem's sons. It was spoken by the inhabitants of Mesopotamia, who are perhaps referred to in the Pentateuch as the dwellers in the land of Shinnar, the people who settled in Mesopotamia after the Flood.

It appears that when the population of the land of Shinnar was forced by circumstances to scatter and migrate to various parts of Asia, their languages gradually diversified after their wanderings according to the environment and way of life of each people. Some settled on the Syrian coast, and their language acquired distinct traits, becoming known as Phoenician, from which Hebrew developed. Others settled in Arab Iraq, and the diversification of their language produced Assyrian, from which came Chaldean and Syriac. Yet others moved to the Arabian Peninsula, their language evolving to produce Arabic and its various branches, including Ethiopian, South Arabian, and North Arabian. One of them is the language of Quraysh, in which the Koran was written and which speakers of Arabic write to this day.

The diversification of the above-mentioned Semitic languages did not occur all at once but gradually, according to the laws of evolution in nature. In the earliest period of the Semitic peoples' dispersion, the languages continued to resemble each other very closely. This is also the case with the speakers of Arabic after the spread of Islam. The Arab peoples of today in Egypt, Syria, the North African countries, and so on speak Arabic, but the degree to which one language differs from the other depends on the distance between them and differences in their circumstances. Were it not for the Koran, these differences would have become such that the various groups [of Arabs] would not have been able to understand each other's languages, as happened with the languages derived from Latin (French, Spanish, Italian, and so on). But Arabic speakers' preserving the language of the Koran and reverting to it in their writings and speeches gave their various modern dialects a point of reference, linking them to a single origin, as is evident.

In the distant past, when Shem's descendants scattered throughout the world, they took with them no recorded language or anything to link them to each other and to their roots in the age of paganism. Thus natural factors influenced the diversification of their languages far more than it does today, and over generations they became entirely independent languages.[4] But anyone who studies their origins has the means to trace them all back to one origin because of the resemblance between their rudiments and rules. Arabic and Syriac are very similar in their etymology, inflections, and the meanings of their words, which leaves no doubt as to their single origin.

From what we read in the books of the Old Testament, the conclusion can be drawn that those languages were very similar in the earliest times until the Israelites' exodus from Egypt and thereafter. The Israelites spent forty years in the Sinai desert and the Arabian Peninsula; their language was Hebrew, but they lived side by side with Arabs and mingled with them, each people understanding the other without an interpreter. There are many events mentioned in the Old Testament that indicate that Arabs and Hebrews understood each other, among them the visit of the Queen of Sheba—who was an Arab ruler—to Solomon the son of David, King of the Jews, in the tenth century B.C., that is, five centuries after the time of Moses. She visited King Solomon and they understood each other without needing translators. Another example, one of several, is Ishmael's migration and his settling in Arab lands and living among the Arabs. They all indicate that the various branches of the Semitic languages were very similar up till then, because not enough time had passed for them to become entirely independent from one another. After that time, each variant came to have its own separate vocabulary and constructions, growing away from the others until it became an independent language, following the course of evolution of everything in this world.

The Arabic language, then, is one of the Semitic languages, derived from the original Semitic language that is now lost, which some call the Aramaic language, as we have explained. For our part, we believe that the language of Assyria and Babylon, traces of which have been found in cuneiform inscriptions in the ruins of the kingdom of Assyria, is the closest to the original Semitic language, if not its remnant. If those ruins continue to be studied over time and new excavations and research are undertaken, the results may support this conviction. [. . .]

The Investigation of Some Aspects of Foreign Languages and Relating Them to Our Language According to Analogy and Comparison

The Arabic language was collected not long after the rise of Islam. The oldest written Arabic document we have is the Koran. Some poems composed shortly before that time have come down to us, and there is no difference worth mentioning between them and the recorded language. In short, when Arabic was recorded it was already highly developed and refined. Its speakers were obliged to preserve its order completely, so that the written language today is almost the same as the language of the Arabs before Islam. But if we had not preserved those dictionaries and if each generation had added its own technical terms, the literary language would now be a foreign language we do not understand. The written languages would have become more and more diverse and varied, as is the case with the spoken languages. Syrians would be unable to understand the Egyptians' language, Egyptians the North Africans' language, and vice versa. In other words, the Arabic language would have diversified, with each variety differing from the others no less than do the languages derived from Latin (French, Italian, Spanish, Swedish [*sic*], and so on). We would be forced to study the ancient Arabic language and its modern varieties in order to understand the writings of our forebears and our contemporaries, as is the case with the Romance languages. In view of what has been said, we do not have materials to help us follow the origins of the words in our language as we would have liked. Perhaps looking at other languages will clarify the matter.

It is well known that languages, when they first appear and are in the simplest stage of development, are composed of a small number of words, enough to enable the speakers to understand each other with respect to their plain needs. As their circumstances develop and they require new words to express novel concepts, they construct words that meet their needs from the vocabulary they have. [. . .]

A large proportion of Arabic verbs are known to come from defective nouns, perhaps foreign words that have been Arabized. Most of them have four radicals, like *f-l-s-f*; *"tafalsafa 'l-rajul"*, that is, "the man philosophized," is equivalent to saying that he "passed judgment," *taḥakkama*, derived from *ḥikma*, wisdom, and "exercised perspicacity," *taḥadhdhaqa*, about a matter. The origin of *tafalsafa* is the Greek word *philosofia* [*sic*], "philosophy," which is a combination of two words *philia*, "love," and *sofia*, "wisdom." There are many such borrowed words in Arabic, most of them taken from Persian, Greek, or Latin. The language is continuously borrowing always and everywhere. Common people use *sattif*, meaning "to stack up"; it is a word they use a great deal, but we find no mention of it in the dictionaries. It is evidently Arabized from stow," which has the same origin as "stuff,"[5] and probably our people took this verb over from the English. If that had happened before the language had been recorded, it would be counted now as an Arabic word and we could say that it had been taken from a foreign language. What was to prevent such things occurring in the language before it was recorded? For at that time it was more receptive to such borrowings, given its need for vocabulary and the fact that it had not yet been recorded when limits were set and its speakers were forbidden to use foreign words.

There are words in Arabic that are considered among the most deeply rooted in Arab identity, and yet they do not belong to the language. One is *nabiyy*, meaning "prophet" and related concepts. The author of the *Qamus*[6] derived it from *naba'a*, "to be elevated," but there is nothing in the meaning of this word that indicates prophethood except for what is discernible in its derived forms, such as *tanabba'a*, "to predict, to pose as a prophet," *nabba'a*, "to inform, to announce," and *nāba'a*, "to give someone news," all of which contain the idea of informing. It seems to us that this idea is obtained from the word "prophet," that is, the words are derived from *nabiyy*. As for *nabiyy* itself, we believe that it is most likely ancient Egyptian, a compound of the two words *n-b* and *y-*, meaning together "master of the house" or "head of the family."[7] Apparently the Jews borrowed this word from the ancient Egyptians when they were living in Egypt and used it first in this sense to designate the earliest forefathers before applying it to prophets in general.[8] The Arabs took it over from them in this sense, just as they took over other religious customs before Islam.[9] The Jews had previously called a prophet or seer *rā'ī*, meaning "one who can foresee the future."

Another word believed to be authentically Arabic is *al-sarāb*, the mirage, an apparition of water close to the ground seen at midday, which is caused by extreme heat. The author of the *Qamus* derived it from *sariba (al-mā'u)*, "the water flowed," explaining "It is called thus because it travels along the ground." But it is a Persian word, a compound of *sīr*, full, and *āb*, water, that is, "full of water," which is what a mirage is.

Another example is *malak*, "angel" (pl. *malā'ika*). It is a Hebrew word in origin, a passive participle from *hālak*, to send, meaning "messenger," and that is what *malak* means in Arabic. The author of the *Qamus* derived it from Arabic *ālaka*, "to convey a message." These are many such words of foreign provenance that have become Arabicized and their origin forgotten.

To sum up: from the fact that a large group of trilateral roots can be reduced to bilateral ones, imitating sounds of nature, and that the words of any language are bound to change and diversify in form and meaning, we can infer that the uninflected words conveying a meaning in themselves mostly go back to bilateral monosyllabic roots that imitate the sounds of nature.[10]

Results

Our language is composed essentially of a few monosyllabic elements mostly derived from imitating sounds from the world outside, some of which are natural sounds that a human being pronounces instinctively. On the basis of what has previously been demonstrated, namely, that words related in pronunciation and meaning are variant forms arising from a single origin; that invariable words signifying a meaning outside themselves are remnants of words with an inherent meaning; that invariable words signifying an inherent meaning mostly go back by induction to bilateral roots that imitate natural sounds; that exclamations can by induction be traced back to a single word or a few words; and that words used to convey abstract concepts were originally coined to express perceptible phenomena and then turned into metaphors because of similarities in mental images.

I consider it extremely likely that our language is composed essentially of a few monosyllabic elements mostly derived from imitating sounds of the outside world, some of which are natural sounds pronounced by a human being instinctively. It grew and developed from these origins until it attained its present state of structure and diversity, including neologisms, metathesis, and borrowings, to meet people's needs and follow the general law of progress. To clarify the subject I shall approach the question according to induction, as follows: Is language innate and something mankind has been endowed with, or is it acquired and dependent on convention?

If it is innate, that implies it occurs without being acquired and without reflection, and if mankind is endowed with it, that implies it has a fixed structure and meaning and cannot be altered or influenced, like everything which Almighty God has endowed man with.

The reality, however, contradicts that. We only reproduce the sounds we hear from those around us. We only speak Arabic because we grew up among people who speak it. If we had been brought up among the Greeks, [Greek] would have been our language; if among Indians, it would be Hindi. On the other hand, if we had been destined to grow up among dumb animals, we too would be without language. Language is known to be subject to change and influence through the coining of new words, substitution, metathesis, and borrowings, so that the language with which we communicate now differs in meaning and vocabulary from the language with which our forefathers communicated and the one with which our children will communicate. Languages that did not exist in the past have appeared, such as those derived from Latin and Sanskrit. But if language were something fixed mankind had been endowed with, it would remain unchanged. It cannot be affirmed that these derived languages appeared as unchanging natural gifts because historically they can be traced back by induction to when they first appeared or, rather, branched off from their parent language. This all happened according to general laws that order everything around us: structures, life and its activities.

In sum, language is acquired and dependent on convention; that is absolutely evident. To make it clearer, I mention what the great scholar Ibn Khaldun wrote in the course of his discussion commenting on taste:

> When acquired characteristics become firmly established in their appropriate places, they appear to be inborn, which is why many ignorant people who do not understand this fact think that the correct inflexions and proper eloquence in the Arabs' language are something natural and maintain that the Arabs used to speak in that way naturally. Not so. They are a linguistic characteristic of ordered speech which has established itself firmly, so that on first sight it appears original and natural. But as has been mentioned, it is only acquired by practice in the Arabs' speech, hearing it repeated and grasping the special characteristics of its constructions.[11]

The great scholar Abu Ishaq al-Isfara'i,[12] when speaking about the origin of language, observed: "Language started when people agreed on usage; when it will end is in God's hand." And al-Suyuti stated: "The proof that it is possible to agree on language usage is that an individual or group undertakes to create words for concepts which they then convey to others by gestures, as mothers do with their babies."[13] [. . .]

Understanding one another: Let us imagine man in the earliest stage of his development, walking through the fields and forests, naked or half-naked, gathering the fruits and plants. When night fell, out of fear he took refuge in a cave or cavern or climbed a tree to escape the attacks of wild animals. In the morning he came out to search for food, which he had to exert himself to find. Such efforts involved searching for a tree whose fruit he could eat or an animal that he could strike with a stone and kill to eat its flesh; in that he was no different from dumb animals. But he was soon forced to adopt a life in a community, which is a trait proper to human beings. The reason for his inclination to live in a community was his inability to resist natural disasters or defend himself alone from wild animals. People therefore applied themselves to helping and supporting each other, that is, they lived in a community. When they came together, they were forced to exchange thoughts and discuss aims, which is the goal of communal life, and that led them to understand each other. Gradually they advanced from gestures to sounds and then to words and sentences, as you will see.

From what we have said it appears that man's weakness was what led him to speak. Many an objector will say: "Is weakness an exclusively human quality, forcing humans alone to live in society, the situation which was the prerequisite for language and civilization to emerge?" Our answer is that among animals there are species weaker than man, and they may have been forced to live in groups more than once. But they were not able to speak because by nature they lack the gifts that nature has conferred on man in mind and body, such that he is able to articulate, combine words, and explain thoughts. We do not believe that the other species of animals cannot understand each other; on the contrary, comprehension occurs between members of one species and between different species in ways and by means that we do not entirely understand. Comprehension does not necessarily have to occur through speech; one species of animal may be led to find a method by which to communicate that is different from [the method] of another, depending on the capacity of each to understand the other through movements of the skin, ears, tail, and so on. Various animal species have languages with which they communicate, but they are inevitably inferior to the language of man, just as their intellectual powers are less than his.

The necessity to form social groups exists among all animal species, but only man has achieved what he wanted from this because of his ability to invent methods of communication by way of voice. What helped him to communicate from early on were his skill in moving his hands and his highly developed vocal cords, because he had spent ages making himself understood through signs and imitating sounds.

If you consider the history of language, you will see that the start of its growth and evolution goes back to a talent the Creator gave man, namely that of imitation. Imitation is the basis of language, the origin of its growth, and the crucial factor for its evolution. Comprehension, whether by gestures or by sounds, goes back to imitation, because gestures imitate the shapes or ideas of things, and sounds imitate the noises of the outside world coming from various sources which people hear. Imitation is a faculty that has reached a degree in man beyond anything it has reached in any animal species. It consists of the imitator replicating an image that his mind acquired from outside either directly or implicitly. When imitating it, he must have formed a clear picture of it in his mind as well as possessing the means necessary to convey it to others. Forming a clear picture of something is the work of the intellect, while representing it is the work of the hands or whatever takes their place. Man has the most powerful intellect of all the animal species and [one that is] the most appropriately structured, which is the reason why he alone has such extensive possibilities of communication and so many ways of doing so. This supported the society he was living in, and then civilization and culture developed, as we know. Man founded cities, established kingdoms and nations, explored the universe, and invented philosophy. People held different opinions about the nature of creation and its Creator, and so separate schools, religions, communities, and sects emerged. Wars broke out, increasing the need for arms and other resources to help achieve victory and reinforce power, which led to many inventions and other developments that cannot be dealt with here. What concerns us here is that because he was weak, man was obliged to come together in society, and so he needed to exchange thoughts and aims, which involves communication. Thanks to his talent for imitation he was able to establish the foundations of language. [. . .]

The first step a language takes from simple imitation to articulation is when the exact imitation of a sound is altered into reflecting something that resembles it closely. Thus simple words with simple meanings appear, lacking particles, conjunctions, or derived forms and without any distinction made between nouns, verbs, and prepositions. Their grammatical function is indicated by the context, so the same word may sometimes be a noun, sometimes a verb, and sometimes an adjective or particle. Chinese, for instance, with their term *tuwān* convey many meanings that all go back to one origin; they use it to convey the meanings "to roll up," "to encompass or to contain," "round," "ball," the preposition "around," and other related meanings. Because the language has such a limited vocabulary at this stage, they use the same word to express other meanings close to its original one, as is the case in Acadian. There a word of one syllable has fifteen meanings, while the origin is the same; the word is *gn* or *cn*, which they use to signify "mouth," "face," "eye," "ear," "form," "foot," "leg," "look,, "city," or "to speak".[14] The origin is "the outside of the city."

Then language moves into another stage where distinctions between nouns and verbs emerge, although it still lacks prepositions, conjunctions, and other particles and derived forms, as is the case in Chinese. The

Chinese express the preposition "in" with the word for "middle," so they say, for instance, *kūsh-n-g*, which means literally "kingdom—middle," to signify what in our language is "in the kingdom. ." They have a strange way of expressing causative constructions, for they say "*shāj-n ay t-n-gh*" which is, translated literally, "man killed he used stick" to mean "the man killed with the stick." Among the inhabitants of Central Africa are tribes called the Mandingo. When they want to express the concept "on" they say *kang*, that is, "neck," and for "in" they say *kono*, "belly." For the phrase in our language "Put the book on the table," they say "Put the book table neck," and similarly for "in." In the Chinese languages the particles to express plural, feminine, masculine, adjectives, and so on are generally verbs or nouns with independent meanings.

Some languages of the islands of the Pacific Ocean do not have particles to distinguish gender, state or number, tense, or person. The best known of these is Polynesian. By analogy with other languages, it will certainly not be long before making out the origin of these words becomes impossible, and so people will believe that they were revealed in that form. Then the language evolves a stage further and some particles and prepositions appear in it, their emergence resulting simply from the diversification of its vocabulary through new coinages over time. Nouns or verbs, which have an intrinsic meaning, become prepositions or acquire an extrinsic meaning in innumerable ways and manners. But they still remain without the markers of number or gender in their verbs, as is true of the Ancient Egyptian language (hieroglyphics), which is supplied with enough particles and adverbs but shares with the languages mentioned earlier the absence of markers of time or person in its verbs. The markers that are considered necessary in the Aryan and Semitic groups of languages to construct tenses and derived forms are completely absent from Egyptian; the conjugation of verbs in Egyptian consists simply of adding the pronoun to the root expressing the action without the root being changed or the speaker's intention being indicated. Specification is supplied by the context. Egyptian has none of what we call derived stems of verbs, because the root stands for all the various meanings in speech. It also shares with the languages mentioned earlier the use of a single word as noun, verb, or particle. For example, the equivalent of our word "great" has a meaning in Egyptian, but that varies depending on its position; it may mean "very," "great," or "a great man."

After that the language evolves yet further, to the stage where gender, number, and derived forms are distinguished, as you can see in the Semitic languages (except Arabic). They have derivation and gender markers in nouns, adjectives, and the like, but we notice certain deficiencies common to them and Ancient Egyptian, like the absence of an elative form.[15] In those languages the positive form of the adjective serves for the three kinds of comparison. So they say, for instance, using the positive form, "This is good", and in the comparative, "This is good than that," meaning "This is better than that." If they want to convey the superiority of someone over all his fellows, they use the equivalent of our expression "king of kings," meaning by it, as we would say, "the greatest king" or "the greatest of kings."

A further stage in the evolution of language is reached when all these characteristics are present but declension is still absent. This is the situation in the modern Aryan languages, including most of the modern European languages, which do not distinguish between the nominative, accusative, and genitive. These case endings are replaced by special particles, most of which are prepositions, or else by placing words before or after each other. The French, for instance, say "*Le lion tue le tigre*," that is, "The lion kills the tiger," but if they mean the opposite they reverse the word order in the phrase, which gives: "*Le tigre tue le lion*." The English equivalents are "The lion kills the tiger" and "The tiger kills the lion."[16] Likewise, in possessive constructions, word order is crucial too. It is known that the language of the common people falls into this category because of its ignoring the final vowels marking case endings.

Finally, language evolves still further and reaches the highest stage that languages have attained at the present time when the markers of declension appear. This is the case for classical Arabic and the Greek, Latin, and German languages. Putting words before or after one another has little influence on the meaning of a phrase if the vowels marking inflection are present. In classical Arabic one can say, "*Qatala al-asadu al-nimra*" (The lion killed the tiger) or "*Qatala al-nimra al-asadu*" or "*al-asadu qatala al-nimra*" or "*al-asadu al-nimra qatala*" or "*al-nimru al-asadu qatala*" [better: *qatalahu]* or *"al-nimra qatala al-asadu,"* and they all mean that the lion was the killer and the tiger was killed. If we want to say the opposite, we have only to change the vowels marking the case ending, as is clear.

This is a brief account of the stages language may pass through in evolving from the imitative stage to the stage of articulation in its most developed state.

Notes

1. Excerpts from Zaydān, *al-Alfāẓ al-'arabiyya.*

2. 'Khalīl Allah' Abraham's epithet in Arabic.

3. In Egyptian dialect *"j"* is pronounced as a hard *"g"*; translator's note.

4. I.e., distances in space and time.

5. "Stow" and "stuff" are in Latin letters in the text; translator's note. Actually, "stuff" is derived from Middle English *stuffen,* Frankish *stopfon* meaning to furnish, to equip. "Stow" derives from Middle English *stowen* and *stow,* place.

6. Abu 'l-Ṭāhir Muḥammad al-Fīrūzabādī (1329–1415), author of a famous dictionary, *al-Qāmūs al-muḥīṭ wa-'l-qābūs al-waṣīṭ al-jāmi' limā dhahaba min al-'arab shamaṭīṭ*: *EI2.*

7. The foreign words Zaidan transliterated in Arabic script do not have the short vowels marked. Where it has been impossible to determine them, the consonants that are given in the text are separated by a hyphen; translator's note.

8. Genesis 20:7 or perhaps 20:1. Samuel 9:9 is meant.

9. Read *ka-mā,* just as, for *kullamā,* "whenever," in the text; translator's note.

10. This hypothesis—that the typical Semitic word root consisting of three root consonants (triradicalism) can be derived from earlier words consisting of two root consonants (biradicalism) and that all words sharing these two radicals share a common basic meaning—has been debated ever since by linguists in general and Semitists in particular. A recent, exhaustive discussion of the issue appears in Rainer Maria Voigt, *Die infirmen Verbaltypen des Arabischen und das Biradikalismusproblem,* Veröffentlichungen der Orientalischen Kommission 39 (Stuttgart: Steiner Verlag, 1988). Voigt in the end dismisses the hypothesis on the grounds that the history of languages shows most often a reduction of words to shorter and simpler forms; that weak consonants cannot be taken as a proof for biradicalism, rather it has to be assumed that they were originally strong consonants; that there do exist rare aboriginal words with two radicals and they have not changed. The assumptions that the two consonants of the biradical word are also changing, as letters do—e.g., from *s* to *sh* and *k* to *q,* equaling *q* to *s* which can also appear as k-sh—means that everything can be derived from anything and the hypothesis becomes meaningless.

11. Compare Ibn Khaldūn, 3, 342, ff.

12. Probably meant is Abū Isḥāq al-Isfarayīnī (d. 1027), an 'Ashar'ī theologian.

13. Jalāl al-Dīn al-Suyūṭī (1445–1505), who as the most prolific author in Islamic literature, also a juristconsult, scholar of *ḥadīth*, biographer, and historian. The above quote probably comes from his *Muzhir fī 'ulūm al-lugha wa-anwā'ihā.*

14. In Latin letters in the text; translator's note.

15. This form expresses the comparative and superlative in Arabic; translator's note.

16. These phrases are in Latin letters in the text; translator's note.

◆ ◆ ◆

Literary and Colloquial Arabic

Translated by Paul Starkey

We have read an address given by Mr. William Willcocks at the Ezbekiyya Club and reported by the *al-Azhar* newspaper in its latest edition last month.[1] The subject of the talk was "Why is the creative faculty not to be found among the Egyptians of today?" The learned speaker spoke at length about the reasons hindering the creative faculty, then went on to mention the cure and a number of ways to revive it. It is not our intention to discuss at length any of the content of his speech, except insofar as it relates to the Arabic language.

The gentleman said that among the factors in the loss of the creative faculty by the Egyptians was their retention of the literary Arabic language. He suggested that they should abandon it in exchange for the colloquial language, as other nations had done, and he mentioned in particular the English-speaking people. He said that they had derived great benefit from abandoning Latin, which they had used for writing, and exchanging it for the present English language. It is our opinion that Mr. Willcocks was not correct in his view on this topic, because what was true for English does not hold true for our language. There are several reasons for this, of which we may mention the following:

1. When the English exchanged Latin for English, they exchanged a foreign language for a native language. That is not the case with Arabic, for the difference between our written language and our spoken language is not very great, possibly no more than the difference between the language of English writers and the language of the common people who do not know how to read.

2. If changing from literary Arabic to spoken Arabic saves us from one evil, it will plunge us into another greater evil, for the spoken language of native Arabic speakers varies from country to country (*bayna 'l-aṣqā'a*). The difference between the languages of Egypt and Syria is no less than the difference between literary and spoken Arabic, and similarly the difference between the language of one of these two areas (*al-birrayn*) and the language of Morocco or the Hejaz or any other Arab country (*bilād*). We cannot gloss over the literary, civil, and political links that exist among these Arab countries. Exchanging literary Arabic for the Egyptian colloquial, for example, would deprive the Syrians or Moroccans of the benefit of what we wrote in that dialect, and there would be a similar effect if we exchanged it for the Syrian, Moroccan, or Hejazi dialect. Even if the only thing we lost thereby was the sense of Arab unity, that would be loss enough.

3. In every time and place, a language follows the mentality of its speakers in terms of its higher or lower registers. The colloquial language is lower, in terms of register, in accordance with the mentality of its speakers, and it cannot take the place of the literary language. This is particularly the case with Arabic, because it is the most sublime language in the world, with means of expression that the colloquial language is incapable of. If we wanted to record the various branches of the sciences in colloquial Arabic, as the learned speaker suggests, I do not think that colloquial Arabic could convey the written meanings properly. Where would it get the words or phrases with which to express technical terms, especially modern ones—terms that even literary Arabic is almost incapable of rendering? If the speaker is saying that we should introduce those terms into it, we say that the terms in question are no small matter and are actually a large portion of the language, especially scientific language, for most of them are scientific (*'ilmiyya*) terms. Teaching the common people the vocabulary of literary Arabic as it exists is easier than teaching them scientific terminology and introducing this vocabulary into their language. This is the case in other areas of the world also. Mr. Willcocks knows that specialized scientific books written in English now cannot be understood by ordinary English people, however much effort is put into explaining and clarifying them. That is proof that there is a sort of veil between

ordinary people and the educated elite; and if we tried to lift the veil, nature would simply let it down again.

4. Arab collective identity depends on preserving the literary language. If it had not been for the Holy Koran, its preservation since the dawn of Islam, and our continued reference to it to correct those features of our language that have become naturally corrupted—if it had not been for all this, the Arab people would have split apart, and each Arab country (*qaṭar*) would have become independent of all the others, with its own incomprehensible language, whether written or spoken. This is what has happened to those peoples who used to speak Latin, for each one has acquired an independent language that is not understood by any other nation. Examples are France, Spain, Italy, and so on. The main credit for preserving the Arab collective identity until today rests with the Holy Koran and our continued attention to it.

5. Abandoning literary Arabic would entail abandoning all the varied sciences written in it for 1,300 years. This would be an irreplaceable loss, whatever might be said about the advantages of writing in colloquial Arabic.

From what has been said above, it will be clear that exchanging literary for colloquial Arabic is an idea that we would do better to ignore, not merely because it would be unproductive but also because it would actually harm the language and its speakers as far as science, religion, and culture are concerned.

However, we should not conclude our discussion of this topic without referring to something we have often complained about, namely the propensity of some writers to choose outdated or rejected expressions, either to show their skill in remembering vocabulary or to revive expressions that time has rendered obsolete because of the demands of civilization and the varied needs of mankind. If Mr. Willcocks was saying that he simply wished to abandon this sort of language, then we could support him and agree with his view. For using outdated expressions hinders the achievement of the aim of this writing, especially on general topics such as historical works or literary tales. As for specialized scientific subjects, necessity permits people to use technical expressions applicable to the field without simplification, especially since those topics are read by specialists who are required to know such terminology.

As for stories, novels, history, and other general literary topics, the writer is required to select expressions that will be understood by the ordinary reader while respecting the formal aspects of language. If a writer is expounding on an idea for which there are two expressions, one obsolete and the other well known, he is required to ignore the obsolete and use the well-known expression. That is one of the principles of correct composition, well known to writers, for instead of expressing the idea "and he sat down facing him" by saying *"wa-jalasa sijāh wajhihi,"* we say *"wa-jalasa tujāh wajhihi,"* for *sijāh* and *tujāh* both convey an identical intended meaning in terms of both pattern and sense. We also think that to go further and use two or three well-known expressions to convey the desired meaning is better than using a single obsolete word to convey that meaning. It may be that we are slightly contradicting one of the principles of eloquence by doing so, but on the other hand, it allows us to make the reader (whether he be one of the common people or not) understand what we want him to understand rather than making him bored with reading or reluctant to study. What we require is his perseverance in order to derive the intended benefit from our writing. We have to understand the exact purpose of writing literary books for the masses as being for them to acquire the fundamental concepts of literature and history but [not][2] to teach them vocabulary and grammar, because they do not need that; they are all busy working to earn a livelihood and they do not need to know the inner workings of language. And for those who want to study the grammar and vocabulary of the language, there are books specializing in that, so let them rely on those.

To sum up, the writer on specialized scientific subjects must rely on the conventions and expressions, devised for every particular science, and use them whether or not they are understood by the ordinary reader; for the ordinary reader has no need whatever for these subjects, which are so far removed from his faculties and needs.

As for general literary and historical topics and other topics of that sort, the writer is required to avoid anything that may impede understanding on the part of either the specialist or the common reader. His expression should be simple, clear, fluent, and free of any complication so that the meanings may be entirely transparent to the reader, who should not need to stop for a moment or consult dictionaries in order to understand them. If the writer fails to do that, it may be counted a deficiency in the practice of his craft.

We are in the position of having to find an excuse for Mr. Willcocks for putting forward his viewpoint. We think he has judged it preferable to exchange literary Arabic for colloquial Arabic only because he has seen in some books a confusion of the sort referred to above.

However if we continue to write in the style indicated, making it easy and lucid, while at the same time respecting the formal elements of the language, we shall not give the gentleman or others like him any opportunity to object or any scope for putting forward views of this sort. Indeed, God—may He be praised and exalted—knows best.

Notes

1. Zaydān, "al-Lugha al-fuṣḥa."
2. In the text a negation is missing to give the sentence meaning; translators' note.

◆ ◆ ◆

The Writers and Readers of Arabic

Translated by Hilary Kilpatrick

(1) Writers; (2) Authors

By literary composition we mean the assembling of information about the natural world, culture, and other fields from different books into a single work organized in a particular manner to suit a particular purpose.[1] As a result the subject of the book takes on an integrated form in which the conclusions follow from the premises.

Writing books in Arabic has a long history, but in this age it has taken a different course, just as knowledge has changed from what it was in the past. For the sciences suffered a decline and almost died out after they had flourished among the speakers of our language in the age of Islamic civilization when writers abounded. Then, when we began our recent renaissance, we conveyed our knowledge from modern sources, imitating the European writers from whom we translated it.

Since we have only recently started to translate these sciences, our composing books is still in its infancy. Most of what we write is limited to translations or summaries, especially in the natural sciences, for reasons that we mentioned earlier when speaking of translators and abridgers. As for the branches of literature, we compose our texts as European writers do, and we refer in our writings to European sources, except for the Islamic sciences or related subjects. Otherwise our authors derive their information from European books.

We observe a strange phenomenon in this respect—namely that some people rely on those sources even when what they write is connected with the sciences of the Arabs themselves or their history. Perhaps they do so because of their confidence in the Europeans' accuracy. But this leads them to commit errors that mar their works. We read a book on Islamic history in which we found letters written by some Muslim generals to their caliphs in the early Islamic period. In the original they are splendid examples of rhetoric and clear exposition. But the book's author translated them from a European language and they sounded foreign, stripped of Arabic rhetoric, although they could have been quoted in the original in both form and content.

It is well known that science came to us initially from the French and Italians in the time of Muhammad 'Ali Pasha; we then acquired knowledge in certain sciences from the English and the Americans, especially in Syria. When the British occupied Egypt, they sought to spread their language among us. Thus the sources that we use for what we write are in French, Italian, or English. Italian, however, has not continued to play a part because of Italy's limited influence in our region, and so our sources are now limited to French and English.

It is self-evident that a person who acquires scientific knowledge from a nation whose language and culture he has studied grows to love that nation and strives to follow its customs and imitate its leading personalities. Our writers have thus formed two parties, one French-oriented and the other English-oriented, and there are few who belong to both. Our tastes differ according to differences in their principles and moral standards. This affects what we write in both style and content. You will rarely read a book written by a contemporary author on a modern scientific subject without also reading the convictions of either the English or the French between the lines. Perhaps this explains why the common people take sides with one or the other of the two, because a nation follows in the steps of its writers where principles and morals are concerned, and each party follows a school of writers emulating them in word and deed.

Our imitation of European writers is not confined to the content of what they write, but also concerns styles of expression. You can see the European idiom clearly in some of our writers' locutions, however authentically Arabic the words are, because each language has its own mode of expression. So anyone who reads and refers to French books learns to express himself in that language, especially if he neglects to read Arabic books, and the same can be said for those who consult English books.

Anyone who intends to write books should preserve the character of the Arabic language and avoid European expressions. He will only succeed in that if he reads Arabic books free of any foreign flaws; indeed he must read the books produced by the Arabs on the subject he wants to write on or on related subjects, so as to pick up the specific locutions in that field. Every branch of knowledge has its own terms and expressions that should not be used in other branches. The language of the natural sciences, for instance, is different from that of cultural subjects, and [the language] of history is not that of medicine. The language of expository writing differs from that of oratory. So the phrases embellished with figures of speech that are admired in an educational and literary context will be considered ugly on scientific or mathematical topics. Abu 'l-Fadl al-Hamadhani's[2] style in his *Rasa'il* (Letters) is not appropriate to expounding a problem in geometry or reporting facts in physics. If educative themes are expressed in the language of geometry they will not have the same effect on the readers' minds as if they used a style that is embellished with metaphors and various kinds of imagery. Besides, scientific facts require simplicity, while literary subjects call for exaggeration and prolixity, employing threats, disparagement, intimidation, and incitement. In view of this, prose writing falls into two main categories, scientific and literary, with subdivisions for specific subjects. If you read a book on any topic, you will see that it consists of two different elements, each with its own rules and ramifications: the subject matter and the style. We will discuss each of them separately.

The Subjects

For our purposes, subjects can be divided into two categories, scientific and literary.

(1) Scientific Subjects

We have few works on scientific subjects except for some doctors' writings on certain areas of medicine and the like. Our books on these subjects are all, or almost all, translated from European works because they are the product of modern civilization, and European scholars deserve the credit for developing or inventing the ideas in them. We do not blame our authors for refraining for a while from plunging into these subjects; they may perhaps be excused because they can expect little success with them, for reasons we set out earlier. The main cause is the failure of the schools to teach these subjects extensively using Arabic textbooks. But we find it inexcusable that our authors refrain from writing on them in a style appropriate to readers' tastes and their ability to understand. They could write readable works on branches of science illustrated with explanatory drawings and examples such as lithographers provide. For if the common people learn about the basic principles of these sciences their minds will be broadened, the scope of their opinions extended, the veils of ignorance lifted from their eyes, and the shame of the superstitions that dominate their minds exposed. They will cease to fear lunar or solar eclipses, tempests, and hurricanes, and instead of beating copper vessels to frighten the great fish that tries to swallow the moon, as they imagine, they will praise the Creator for the rules which he has established that explain all these phenomena.

Among the books on the sciences which are needed are compendia on some branches of medicine, for instance, dissection, physiology, and the like, such as Dr. Wortabet's book on principles of physiology[3] and Dr. Post's *Principles of Dissection,*[4] which were both published in Beirut; Dr. Ibrahim Effendi Mansur's manual of household medicine;[5] and Dr. Farid Effendi 'Abdallah's *Brilliant Pearls concerning the Physiology of Animals.*[6] But that is little compared with what the common people require. They are in the greatest need of books about family hygiene, to teach parents to guard against accidents and protect themselves and their children from the calamity of epidemics and malignant diseases, such as Dr. Wortabet's work *Hygiene and Disease Control,*[7] Dr. Ahmad al-Shafi'i's *The Fulfilling of Wishes in the Arts of Good Health,*[8] and 'Abd al-'Aziz Effendi Nazmi's *'Abbas' Garden: on the Canon of Medicine.*[9] Similar works are Dr. 'Abd al-Rahman Effendi Isma'il's[10] *Quack Medicine,* which examines the use of folk remedies and charms among the common people in Egypt; *The Medical Properties of Household Remedies*[11] by 'Abidin Effendi Khayr Allah, Inspector at the

Ministry of Education; *Thousand and One Remedies* by Najib Bey Yusuf;[12] and *Pediatrics*[13] by Dr. Salim Jalkh[14] of Beirut. Books written on such subjects should include only the simplest remedies, because complicated prescriptions, if mistakes are made in them, may be extremely dangerous and lead to chronic diseases.

Other much-needed works on health matters include a book exposing the harmful habits common among young men and women, who do not understand their consequences although they may lead to hard-to-cure diseases. Besides, their least fearful consequence is corruption of manners and immorality. We know of a book on this subject written by Dr. Shakir al-Khuri,[15] a Beiruti doctor, titled [*The Object of Desire for*] *the Married Man's Health and the Marriage of Bachelors*, and we are sure it has been an invaluable help to young people. But the first edition of it is sold out. Hopefully it will be reprinted and widely circulated. We also request our respected doctors to write on related subjects. In this connection we draw attention to some ladies' current habits that are harmful to their health, such as the use of stays.

Other works on medical subjects that are needed include short surveys of particular diseases, like the work on venereal diseases by Dr. Ibrahim Matar[16] of Beirut, in which he details their causes and symptoms and warns against their fatal consequences. We ask our honored doctors to write similar books on, for instance, gastric diseases, their causes and consequences, and how to avoid them; on the prevention of different kinds of eye diseases; on chest diseases and their prevention; on liver diseases and their causes; on heart disease and on the harm done by intoxicating substances and their consequences. Dr. 'Id,[17] the editor of the magazine *The Doctor of a [Healthy] Family*, has promised us to write on these topics. We also ask doctors to write works on epidemics and their prevention, like Dr. Shibli Shumayyil's treatise on the plague, Dr. Salim Sham'un's book on preventing contagion,[18] and other medical works that ordinary people cannot do without. And we beg them to offer few prescriptions and to focus on prevention, leaving the treatment of the diseases to practitioners. And let them aim for an easy and simple style, replacing technical medical terms with everyday words wherever they can.

(2) Literary Subjects

These are more numerous, and closer to the understanding of the common people, not to mention the elite. Therefore those well versed in literature and culture have no excuse for not writing on these subjects. We will treat the different branches one by one.

Language. We cannot deny that many works on linguistics exist in our language; inflexion, grammar, rhetoric, and tropes are all treated both at length and concisely, and there is no space here to mention the works concerned. But most of them belong to the past and are unsuited to the tastes of people today, whether because they are too long or too short, or for some other reason. We draw the attention of scholars of language to the importance of writing on their subject in an accessible style as do books the late Sheikh Nasif al-Yaziji produced on inflexion, grammar, and rhetoric; the textbooks with lessons on rhetoric for government school pupils written by Sultan Effendi Muhammad,[19] Hifni Bey Nasif,[20] Muhammad Effendi Diyab, and Mustafa Effendi Tammum;[21] or the books the Jesuit fathers in Beirut prepared to teach these subjects in their schools. But we still need many books of this kind, including philosophical approaches that are pleasing to the intellect and easily remembered, such as *Good Thoughts*[22] by Jabr Effendi Dumit, professor of Arabic language at the Syrian Protestant College, which we have referred to in *al-Hilal* more than once. We do not deny that many Egyptian and Syrian men of letters have been active in writing in this style, but we ask them to do more, and may God increase their reward.

Among the books on language that we need is a dictionary of both Arabic-derived terms, which Arab writers used after the coming of Islam but that are not mentioned in the handbooks of the language, neologisms coined for the terms that modern civilization demands as a result of scientific discoveries unknown to the Arabs in pre-Islamic times or early Islam, like the terminology current in the natural sciences and literature. Here attention needs to be paid to the conditions of word borrowing, which determine if a term should be translated into Arabic or else retained in its foreign form. Some years ago a select group of meritorious Egyptians turned their attention to this and set up a language academy presided over by Tawfiq Effendi al-Bakri, head of the sheikhs of the Sufi orders, but it only met a few times and made no contribution to the language. Perhaps, it will begin to meet again and continue its work. We have mentioned more than once that Sheikh Ibrahim al-Yaziji, one of the founders of the magazine *al-Bayan*, has embarked on compiling a dictionary on the topic; may he complete it.

Likewise, we need a thesaurus in which the words are arranged thematically, like al- Tha'alibi's *Principles of Language*.[23] But it should be longer and more comprehensive. That is a demanding task, and we believe one scholar began it but did not complete it. Lest the benefit of it be lost, we draw philologists' attention to a long work on the subject titled "Summary of Language," compiled by Ibn Sida,[24] a manuscript of which we have seen in the Khedivial Library. It is in a poor North African hand and runs to sixteen large volumes, but we reckon that if it were published it would be about three thousand pages long in the page size and typeface used by *al-Hilal*. A book like that would achieve the above-mentioned aim, if an appendix were added including new words such as modern scientific terms. We have heard that Najib Effendi al-Bustani, the son of the late Teacher Butrus al-Bustani, tried to print *al-Mukhattat* [*sic*] several years ago but did not pursue the matter.

We also need an analytical dictionary tracing words back to their biradical roots, as we mentioned in our book *The Philosophy of Language*, and tracing the source of foreign words back to their original language, indicating their root meanings in those languages in the most comprehensive manner seen in famous dictionaries. It is very difficult to do, and we do not know that anyone has tried, because it requires knowledge of many ancient languages such as the Syriac, Hebrew, Persian, Greek, Latin, Ancient Egyptian, Ethiopic, and Indian languages.

Our language also stands in need of a book recording the colloquial, including new words and expressions and the forms of nouns and verbs, with an indication of parallel or similar features in the literary language. We are not aware of any Arabic speaker having embarked on this project but we know that the late lamented Khalil al-Yaziji compiled a dictionary of colloquial words with their equivalents in the literary language in a book he titled *Verity in Terms Colloquial and Literary,*[25] but death overtook him before he could publish it.

Another requirement are books on the philosophy of language based on the state of the language today, like Jabr Effendi Dumit's *Thoughts on Language,*[26] *Remarques sur les mots français derivés de l'arabe* by Father Lammens[27] of Beirut, Hifni Bey Nasif's *Mumayyizat lughat al-'arab,* and our own work on the philosophy of language.

These are some examples of the kind of works on linguistics which our language needs. Furthermore, one can mention, among others, books on composition, books setting out the use of verbs with particles, conjunctions, and other such topics, and books on the theory of metaphor and imagery.

History. This is a vast and unfathomable subject. However many books are written on it, they will always be considered few compared with what is needed—how much more so, when there are in fact few history books and the ones with the widest circulation are old! We do not deny the revival of historiography that today's writers have achieved, but they are still at the beginning. For our scholars' concern at the beginning of the cultural revival to translate the modern sciences into our language distracted them from producing historical works. They were satisfied with the writings they had of authors of the past, and few took the trouble to write histories. This is especially true of Egypt. We may say that when we came to Egypt, some ten years ago, we wanted to learn about its history but we found no book that satisfied our needs. We felt that the language lacked a book which met the purpose, and so we collected what we could find from old and modern histories in Arabic and other languages and, despite our limitations, we compiled our book *The Modern History of Egypt* in two large volumes. It was the first book in Arabic covering the history of Egypt from the beginning of Islam till today. Then it was suggested we write a history of Freemasonry, so we did, appending it to the general history. The interest that readers showed in history encouraged us to concentrate on it. We decided to write historical novels, which in our view is the best method to spread knowledge of history among the common people as well as the elite. Our books were well received, and we realized the need to publish a history of Islam in a style that would not bore the reader. So we started a series of novels beginning with the emergence of Islam and ending in our time. We had already published *Armanusa the Egyptian* on the conquest of Egypt in the early days of Islam, but we went back earlier and started on *The Ghassanide Damsel,* which we are publishing in *al-Hilal* in installments.

We have only mentioned this to show how fond the public is of history, especially where it concerns their country and people. Our writers rarely pay attention to this, being satisfied with the old histories that the publishers produce, such as the works of Ibn Khaldun, Ibn al-Athir,[28] Abu 'l-Fida',[29] al-Maqrizi, al-Mas'udi,[30] and the like. These are magnificent books and publishing them is a great service, but we would like to draw their publishers' attention to an observation. We see that when they print a book, most (or all) of them publish it just as they found it in its manuscript version, as far as divisions into chapters and sections are concerned. If only they would imitate the European publishers of such texts, who append to them alphabetical indices of names of persons and places, which make them infinitely more valuable. We have in front of us a copy of Ibn al-Athir's *The Complete Book on History* printed in Egypt without indices, and another printed in Europe with indices arranged alphabetically of everything mentioned in that valuable history. We have found out by experience that the European edition is a hundred times superior to the Egyptian one, although the two books are identical. If we want to consult what Ibn al-Athir says on a given subject, it is difficult to find in the Egyptian edition. By contrast, in the European edition there is nothing easier than to find the subject in the index and the numbers of the pages where it occurs, even in passing. The same is true of the other old histories and chronologies. We are dismayed to see that some valuable books on these subjects written nowadays suffer from the same defect. Thus *Tawfiq's Topography,*[31] which the late 'Ali Pasha Mubarak compiled in twenty volumes, contains important facts about the geography and monuments of Egypt and the biographies of its famous sons, but because it lacks a general alphabetical index it is hard to use; you may search for a given subject for hours and not come across everything that is written about it.

Some of our publishers, however, have become conscious of this defect and seek to repair it; foremost among them is the Jesuit Fathers' press in Beirut. It does not publish any book on such subjects without incorporating extensive indices to it, as in Abu 'l-Faraj al-Malati's[32] *Concise Account of Dynasties* and al-Maydani's[33] *Collected Proverbs* with the commentary by the late Sheikh Ibrahim al-Ahdab, which his sons published. We see that the Wahbiyya Press in Cairo has done likewise for *Quintessential Information about the Generations of Physicians*[34] and other books. Let us hope that writers and publishers will follow this laudable plan, for publishing old histories with indices attached may be more useful than composing new ones.

But all this does not meet the need we have both for new histories—which is dictated by the passage of centuries—and for a new way of writing about the present and earlier times, avoiding the repetitive chains of authorities[35] that often lead to older works being unnecessarily voluminous. Moreover, tastes vary from age to age. We now need different kinds of books on history and geography, to which we direct writers' attention.

1. For example, we need a historical and geographical dictionary including the biographies of famous people and descriptions of places past and present. It is a project that Salim Effendi Shahada[36] and the late Salim Effendi al-Khuri[37] started in Beirut twenty years ago, with a book to be published in successive parts that they called *Traces of the Ages*.[38] But one of them died an untimely death, so the work stopped while it was still at an early stage. A somewhat similar fate befell the *Da'irat al-ma'arif*, the Encyclopedia, started by the late Teacher Butrus al-Bustani, who undertook many scholarly useful projects. During his lifetime seven volumes appeared, and when he died his son, the late Salim al-Bustani, published the eighth volume. When he, too, met his Lord, the ninth volume was brought out by his brother Najib Effendi together with his nephew Sulayman Effendi al-Bustani,[39] author of the verse translation of the *Iliad*. Then work on the project stopped for a while and we almost despaired of it ever being completed, until we discovered that the said Sulayman Effendi had recently come to Cairo, intending to complete the project soon. May God reward him for his efforts! It has to be said that the *Da'irat al-ma'arif* includes all the different branches of knowledge, historical and otherwise,

and its size may be an obstacle to it circulating among the different classes of people. So we need something like a shortened version of it, running to not more than two or three volumes.

2. Another requirement is for separate books on the history of individual peoples and countries, like our work on the modern history of Egypt, Muhammad Bey Farid's work on the history of the Ottoman Empire,[40] Jurji Effendi Yanni's *History of Syria,*[41] Nakhla Effendi Qalfat's *History of Russia,*[42] and so on. We therefore suggest that our esteemed authors write works on the histories of the countries of Europe and the ancient and modern Near East. The most important subjects are the history of Islam, the history of the pre-Islamic Arabs, and the history of the Arabs in our times. As for the last-named, after lengthy research and study during his travels through the Arab lands Sulayman Effendi al-Bustani has collected the information and showed some of it to us. The book is unique, and it is to be hoped that he will not deprive Arab readers of it. A similar kind of book is a detailed history of the Sudan which Na'um Bey Shuqayr,[43] a member of the Egyptian Intelligence Service, has embarked on. Na'um Bey was involved in Sudanese affairs for some ten years, visiting the Sudan several times, witnessing many of the Sudanese wars, and meeting the country's prominent figures. We urge him to publish it soon.

3. We also need books recounting the lives of famous contemporaries in the East, especially those who have distinguished themselves by their diligence and independence of mind, tracing the path they have taken to reach their achievements in spheres such as learning, politics, or the acquisition of wealth. Thus they may serve as an example to others. Our language now lacks a comprehensive book on this subject; there are only scattered articles published in various books like *The Guide to Egypt and the Lives of Famous Men of Our Times* by Yusuf Bey Asaf,[44] the editor of *al-Muhakim*, The Prosecutor, and the lawyer Qaysar Effendi Nasr,[45] and what we publish under the heading "The Most Famous Events and Greatest Men" in *al-Hilal.*[46] But that is by no means enough. An esteemed friend told us that the late Sheikh Ahmad Faris al-Shidyaq wrote a book on the famous men of this century but did not publish it. We urge his son, Salīm Effendi, to have it printed. Another need is for a detailed history of the noble Khedivial family.

4. We also lack detailed histories on topics such as the following: the history of Arab literature, along the lines of what we have published in *al-Hilal*; a history of Islamic civilization, how it arose and established itself, and the vicissitudes it has undergone; the history of the situation today in all its details; the history of interstate relations such as *The History of the Eastern Question* by the Cairene lawyer Amin Effendi Shumayyil,[47] of which only two parts have appeared; a work on the philosophy of history; a work on the history of systems of government; a history of civilization in antiquity and today.

5. There is a need for detailed works on general history from the beginning of the Caliphate until the present, including illustrations and maps for each period, so that anyone who reads them will feel that he has been a contemporary of all the different generations, mingled with every people, and witnessed every event.

6. Among the most important works of history are historical novels. At first glance, they may seem to be the lowest form of historical works because of the entertaining elements they contain. But assuming they conform to the conditions of the genre, they are superior to other historical works and more useful than them, because while they too investigate history, they present historical facts in a more attractive manner. They express them in a pleasant style that encourages reading, so that the reader learns about historical facts while he thinks he is reading an entertaining story. This is a course European writers have followed before us, and they have produced many such books. People say that but for Alexandre Dumas' historical novels and other similar works the French would know little about the history of their country and their nation.

7. Related to history is the science of geography. We have few books on the subject, so we need an extensive general geography with a detailed atlas and also specialized geographical works, like a lengthy one on Egypt, another one on Syria, a third on Arabia, and one on the rest of the Middle East and North Africa. Several books on geography have appeared in Arabic, the largest being by the Tunisian Muhammad Bayram al-Khamis',[48] *The Best Considerations on Cities and Regions*, which he wrote as a travel account in five parts, covering eighty-seven independent countries. It may well be the most comprehensive book on world geography. Then there

is *The Clear Mirror of the Terrestrial Globe*[49] by our teacher Dr. Van Dyke, *The Pure Essence of Geographical Knowledge* by the late Razuq al-Barbari,[50] Khayr al-Din Pasha of Tunis's *The Straightest Means to Know the State of Domains*,[51] and *Adequate Replies to Geographical Queries* by the late Ibrahim Sarkis[52] of Lebanon. 'Ali Pasha Mubarak's *Tawfiq's Topography*,[53] which has already been mentioned, belongs to this category. As for the geography of specific countries, the most extensive geographical work on Egypt and the Sudan is by Amin Pasha Fikri,[54] inspector in the administration of the royal domains. The geography of Syria by Fadl Allah Effendi Abu Halqa[55] of Beirut is concise but unique of its kind. There are also short works on the geography of Egypt, but they are unsatisfactory. Moreover, the changes and reorganizations in the country's administrative divisions require geographical texts and maps to be revised from time to time. And there is a lack of extensive geographical works dealing with each country separately with detailed maps.

Notes

1. This is a continuation of the essay by Zaydān, "Kuttāb," 489–99. For the other parts of this long, serialized essay see the Bibliography of Sources Quoted in this Book. The first part of this series was titled "I: Writers, 1) the writers of books." Concerning the latter Zaidan differentiates here between three kinds: *mutarjimūn*, translators; *mu'allifūn*, authors; and *muṣannifūn*, compilers/writers (*Al-Hilāl*, 5, 451). However, he does not follow strictly his own categorization and while with *mu'allifūn* he means authors of original books, he did not return to the category of the *muṣannifūn*; translator's note.

2. Ṣāliḥ ibn Aḥmad Abū 'l-Faḍl al-Hamadhānī (d. 994), scholar of *ḥadīth*: Khayr al-Dīn al-A'lām Ziriklī, *Qāmūs tarājim ashhar al-rijāl wa-'l-nisā' min al-'arab wa-'l-muta'arrabīn wa-'l-mustashriqīn*, 5 vols. (Cairo: Maṭba'at Kūstātsūmās, 1954–1959), 2, 424.

3. Yūḥanā Wartabāt *al-Fisiyūlūjiyya*: Zaydān, *Tārīkh ādāb*, 4, 220. J. Wortabet (1827–1908), Armenian born in Beirut; studied medicine in Edinburgh; 1866 joined faculty of Medical School SPC; resigned 1890. Zaydān, *Tarājim* 2, 232–37.

4. Jūrj Būsṭ, *Mabādī' al-tashrīḥ wa-'l-hījīn wa-'l-fisiyūlūjiyya*; Zaydān, *Tārīkh ādāb*, 4, 220. George Post (1838–1909) arrived 1863 in Beirut as missionary-physician; 1867 professor of medicine in SPC; Zaydān, *Tarājim*, 2, 238–42.

5. Ibrāhīm Manṣūr, *al-Maṭālib al-Ṭibbiyya*; Zaydān, *Tārīkh ādāb*, 4, 222.

6. *al-Farā'id al-saniyya fī 'l-fīsiyūlūjiyya al-ḥayawāniyya*. Rhyme and assonance are traditional features of Arabic titles from the tenth century until the modern period, occurring in many titles mentioned in this article; translator's note.

7. *Ḥifẓ al-ṣiḥḥa wa-tadbīr al-maraḍ*: Zaydān, *Tārīkh ādāb*, 4, 220, has *Ḥifẓ al-ṣiḥḥa asamahu kifāyat al-'awām*.

8. Aḥmad Muḥammad al-Shāfi'ī, *Balāgh al-amniyya bi-'l-funūn al-ṣiḥḥiyya* (Cairo: n.p., 1887); 'Ā'īda Ibrāhīm Nuṣayr, editor, *al-Kutub al-'arabiyya allatī nushirat fī Miṣr fī 'l-qarn al-tāsi' 'ashar* (Cairo: Qism al-Nashr bi-l-Jāmi'a al-Amrīkiyya, 1990), 178.

9. 'Abd al-'Azīz ibn 'Abd al-Razzāq Naẓmī' (1878–1945) studied in Cairo and France; specialist for pediatrics; wrote nine books on medicine; edited the journal *al-Ḥikma*; was also parliamentarian: Ziriklī, 4, 144. *al-Riyāḍ al-'Abbāsī fī qānūn al-ṣiḥḥa al-asāsī*, the 'al-'Abbāsī' in the title is the Khedive 'Abbās, to whom the book was dedicated; translator's note.

10. 'Abd al-Raḥmān ibn Ismā'īl (ca. 1865–1897), *Ṭibb al-rukka*; studied in Cairo, ophthalmist; attached to the army; wrote several books on medicine and a novel *Ghādat al-Andalūs* (Cairo: n.p., 1893); Brockelmann, Supp. 3, 728; Zirikli 4, 70.

11. 'Ābidīn Khayr Allah (d. after 1894), *al-Fawā'id al-ṣiḥḥiyya fī'l-fawā'id al-manziliyya*; the title is given correctly as *al-Fawā'id al-ṣiḥḥiyya fī 'l-'aqāqīr al-manziliyya*; 'Umar Riḍā Kaḥḥāla, *Mu'jam al-mu'allifīn* (Beirut: Mu'assasat al-Risāla,1993), 5, 49.

12. Najīb Yūsuf (d. after 1896), inspector of administration of the commission for royal lands; *Alf waṣfa wa-waṣfa fī-waṣfāt al-ḥukmiyya wa-ghayr ḥukmiyya* (Cairo: s.n., 1896), Kaḥḥāla, *Mu'jam al-mu'allifīn*, 13, 82.

13. *Tarbiyyat al-aṭfāl*. Zaydān, *Tārīkh ādāb*, 4, 222, has *Murshid al-'ayyil li-tarbiyyat al-aṭfāl*.

14. Salīm al-Jalkh, Maronite from Dayr al-Qamar; graduated from Medical School SPC in 1873. Shafik Jeha, *Darwin and the Crisis of 1882 in the Medical Department* (Beirut: Univ. Press of the American University of Beirut, 2004), 157; Ṭarrāzī, 2, 123, 178.

15. *Tuḥfat al-rāghib fī ṣiḥḥat al-mutazawwij wa-ziwāj al-'āzib*. Shākir ibn Yūsuf al-Khūrī (1847–1913); Lebanese, studied in SPC and Cairo; lived in Damascus, wrote several books on medicine: Ziriklī, 3, 224.

16. Ibrāhim Maṭar; Lebanese; brother of Ilyās Maṭar; father Dīb was a rich merchant: Tarrāzī, 2, 228.

17. Alfred 'Īd, studied in London and Paris, where he got his medical doctor certificate in 1895. He published in Egypt the magazines *Ṭabīb al-'ā'ila [al-siḥḥiyya]* and *al-Ṭibb al-ḥadīth li'l-aṭibbā'*; he introduced the use of X-rays in Egypt. He also was an economist and entrepreneur with various publications: Zakhūrā, 2, 201–3.

18. Salām Sham'ūn, *Risāla fī 'l-wiqāya min al-'adwā'* (Alexandria: n.p., 1896); Nuṣayr, 181.

19. Sulṭān Muḥammad (d. after 1911). Taught at the law school in Cairo; the book referred to is *Durūs al-balāgha li-talāmidha 'l-madāris al tajhīziyya* (Lessons in Rhetoric for Students of the Preparatory Schools); Kaḥḥāla, 4, 238.

20. Ḥifnī Bey Nāsif (1857–1919), Egyptian; scholar of Arab language and literature, poet; taught at al-Azhar, then Dār al-'Ulūm and later the Egyptian university, which he helped to found; specialist on rhetoric and logic; major work *Mumayyizāt lughāt al-'arab* (The Characteristics of the Arabic Dialects); Dāghir, 722.

21. Muḥammad Diyāb and Muṣṭafā Ṭammum collaborated with Nāṣīf Hifnī on a school book *al-Durūs al-naḥwiyya*, published 1893: Brockelmann, Supp. 2, 728.

22. *Al-Khawāṭir al-ḥisān fī 'l-ma'ānī wa-'l-biyān* (Cairo: s.n., 1896).

23. Abū Manṣūr 'Abd al-Malik ibn Muḥammad al-Tha'ālibī (961–1038), b. in Nishapur, lived mainly in Baghdad; prolific writer in literature; the work mentioned here is *Fiqh al-lugha wa-'l-shi'r al-'arabiyya:* Brockelmann, *GAL* 2, 284.

24. Abū 'l-Ḥasan Ibn Sīda (1007–1066); Zaidan has *al-Mukhaṣṣaṣ*, but correctly *Mulakhkhaṣ al-lugha*, 17 vols.; Brockelmann, *GAL* 1, 309.

25. *al-Ṣaḥīḥ bayn al-'āmma wa-'l-faṣīḥ*, Khalīl al-Yāzijzī (1857–1889) son of Nāṣīf; author of novels and theater pieces; Dāghir, 1163.

26. *Khawāṭir fī 'l-lugha* (Beirut: s.n., 1886).

27. Henri Lammens (1862–1937), S.J. Belgian; lived in Beirut; knowledgeable Orientalist with a clear Christian point of view; his book *La Syrie: précis historique* (Beirut: Imprimerie Catholique, 1921), in which he argues a separateness of Syria from the Arab world, had a great impact on French colonial policies in the Mandate.

28. 'Izz al-Dīn Abū 'l-Ḥasan 'Alī Ibn al-Athīr (1160–1233) accompanied Salāḥ al-Dīn in his fight against the Crusaders; best known for his work *al-Kāmil fī 'l-tārīkh, The Complete Book on History*, which traces the history of the world from its beginning to 1231 and constitutes the height of Muslim annalistic historiography.

29. Ismā'īl b. 'Alī Abū 'l-Fidā (1273–1331), Syrian historian and geographer; most noteworthy works: his *Mukhtaṣar tārīkh al-bashar*, which basically continues the universal history by Ibn Athir by a hundred years; and *Takwīn al-buldān*, a descriptive geography with added physical and mathematical data in tabular form: *EI2*.

30. Abu 'l-Ḥasan al-Mas'ūdī (d. 956), author of a huge historical, geographical work of Islamic history and beyond: *Murūj al-dhahab wa-ma'ādin al-jawhar*: *EI2*.

31. 'Alī Mubārak, *al-Khiṭaṭ al-tawfīqiyya al-jadīda*, 20 vols. (Cairo: Boulaq Press, 1886–1889).

32. Yūḥannā Abū Farāj Barhebraeus (1226–1289); born in Malatia; 1252 bishop of Aleppo; *Mukhtaṣar al-duwal*; Brockelmann, *GAL* 1, 349.

33. Abū 'l-Faḍl al-Maydānī (d. 1124) his *Farā'id al-la'āl fī majma' al-amthāl* is the most comprehensive collection of classical Arab proverbs: Brockelmann, *GAL* 2, 697. *Majma' al-amthāl* (Cairo: s.n., 1867); Nuṣayr, 201.

34. Aḥmad ibn Qāsim Ibn Abī Uṣaybi'a (1200–1270), Damascene; *'Uyūn al-anbā'fī ṭabaqāt al-aṭibbā'* (Cairo: Wahbiyya, 1881–1882); Nuṣayr, 178; Ziriklī, 1, 188.

35. The term used here is the *'isnād'*.

36. Salīm Shaḥāda (1848–1907) studied in the college Three Moons of the Greek Orthodox Patriarchate; learned French and English; he and his father Mikhā'īl were deeply involved in founding and managing the G. O. welfare society, whose head he was for twenty-seven years; managed the college for several years; 1868 he reestablished the Syrian

Scientific Society; reorganized it 1880 under the name Eastern Scientific Society; 1870 he added to the journal *Ḥadīqat al-Akhbār* a section in French together with the brother of the owner, Salīm al-Khūrī; together they started *Āthār al-Adhār;* after the death of his partner he continued this geographic, historical encyclopedia for another five volumes, reaching the entry "Belgium"; published in 1878 with almost a thousand pages; Salīm Shaḥāda was many years the official translator for the Russian consulate: dī Tarrāzī 1, 133–35.

37. Salīm al-Khūrī (1843–1875) Lebanese; studied with Nāṣīf al-Yāzijī; studied music; began to write a history of Syria in verse form; assisted his brother Khalīl for fifteen years to publish *Ḥadīqat al-Akhbār;* author of a historical novel The *Catastrophe of the Barmakids* (see also Zaidan's *'Abbāsa Ukht al-Rashīd*); 1873 he started with Salīm Shaḥāda the project *Āthār al-adhār,* a geographical, historical encyclopedia, the first to be arranged alphabetically, which served Buṭrus al-Bustānī as a model; the first vol. appeared early 1875; Salīm al-Khūrī died a few month later: dī Tarrāzī 1, 131–32.

38. Salīm al-Khūrī and Salīm Shaḥāda, *Āthār al-adhār* (Beirut: al-Maṭba'a al-sūriyya, 1875–1876).

39. Sulaymān Effendi al-Bustānī (1856–1925), b. in Lebanon; writer, journalist, poet; representative of Beirut in the Ottoman parliament; translator of the Iliad into Arabic; prepared volumes 10 and 11 of his father *Dā'irat al-ma'ārif*; Dāhir, 286.

40. Muḥammad Farīd *Tārīkh al-dawla al-'aliya al-'uthmāniyya* (Cairo: s.n., 1896); Nuṣayr, 257.

41. Jurjī Yannī (1856–1941), journalist; author and translator of historical works; known for his *Tārīkh Sūriyā,* published 1881; Dāghir, 1169–1170.

42. Nakhla Qalfāṭ (1851–1905), b. in Beirut; author, of novels and stories, translator of novels from Turkish and Persian, scholar of history; in addition to the above-mentioned *Tārīkh rūsiyā,* he wrote a *Tārīkh mulūk al-muslimīn* and *Ḥuqūq al-duwwal*: Zaydān, *Tārīkh al-ādāb,* 4, 293.

43. Na'ūm Bishāra Shuqayr (1863–1922), b. in Lebanon, BA from SPC 1884; joined—like Zaidan—the Wolseley expedition of the British to Sudan; worked later as a historian for the British-Egyptian government in Sudan; most important work *Tārīkh al-Sūdān al-qadīm wa-'l-ḥadīth wa-jughrāfiyyatayhumā,* published 1916; Dāghir, 850–51.

44. Yūsuf Humām Aṣaf (1859–1939), b. in Lebanon; worked in Egypt; author, lawyer, journalist, translator, editor; the mentioned work is *Dalīl Maṣr wa-tarājim mashāhīr al-'aṣr;* many works on law, a history of Egypt and a history of the Ottoman Sultans; Dāghir, 599.

45. Qayṣar Naṣr (d. after 1889): *Dalīl Miṣr,* 2 vols. (Cairo: s.n., 1889); Kaḥḥāla, 8, 136.

46. *Ashhar al-ḥawādith wa-a'ẓam al-rijāl.* See also Zaydān's *Tarājim,* in which he collected many of the biographies, published previously in *Al-Hilal.*

47. Amīn Shumayyil (1828–1897), b. in Lebanon; brother of Shiblī Shumayyil, poet, author, journalist. He studied in American missionary schools, studied *fiqh* with al-Sayyid Muḥyi' Dīn al-Yāfī; in England as a merchant he made a fortune; in Egypt he published a

journal *al-Ḥuqūq* and with his relative Rashīd the newspaper *al-Baṣīr*; wrote political, legal, and historical essays; the mentioned book is *Tārīkh al-mas'ala al-sharqiyya*; Dāghir, 420–22.

48. Muḥammad Bayram al-Khamīs(?), *Ṣafwat al-i'tibār bi-mustawda' al-amṣār wa-'l-aqṭār*; possibly meant is Muḥammad Bayram al-Thālith who published a book in 1888 in Tunis; Brockelmann, Supp. 1, 843.

49. *al-Mir'ā al-waqīyya fī 'l-kurra al-arḍiyya.*

50. Razūq al-Barbarī (d. after 1884), *al-Khulāṣa al-ṣafiyya fī 'ilm al-jughrāfiyya*: Kaḥḥāla, 4, 155.

51. Khayr al-Dīn al-al-Tūnisī (1810–1890) of Circassian origins; administrative career at the court of Ahmed Bey of Tunis; long stays in France; reformer and constitutionalist; his work *Aqwam al-masālik fī ma'rifat al-mamālik* (Tunis: n.p., 1867) discusses his proposals for reforms: Zaydān, *Tārīkh ādāb*, 4, 290. For the translation see Brown.

52. Ibrāhīm Sarkīs (1834–1885), Lebanese; studied in a village school directed by van Dyck; helped edit the translation of the Bible into Arabic; became director of the American missionary press and editor. He published articles in the journals *al-Nashra al-Shahriyya, al-Nashra al-Usbu'iyyam* and *al-Ṣabaḥ al-Munīr*; author of books on calculus, astronomy, and also geography: *al-Ajwiba al-shāfiyya fī 'ilm al-jughrāfiyya*; Tarrāzī 2, 122–24.

53. 'Alī Mubārak, *al-Khiṭaṭ al-tawfīqiyya al-jadīda*, 16 vols. (Cairo: Boulaq Press, 1886–1889).

54. Amīn Fikrī (1856–1899), studied law in Aix-en-Provence, lawyer, geographer; *Jughrāfiyya maṣr wa-'l-sūdān*; Kaḥḥāla, 3, 9.

55. Faḍl Allah Fāris al-Dimishqī (Abū Ḥalqa) (d. after 1890), *al-Mukhtaṣar fī 'l-jūghrāfiyya* (Beirut: n.p., 1890).

◆ ◆ ◆

The Writers and Readers of Arabic

Translated by Hilary Kilpatrick

In some issues of the fifth year of *al-Hilal* we published a series of articles titled "The Writers and Readers of Arabic."[1] There we set out the substance of what can be said about the first part of the subject, the writers. But for various reasons we could not go into the second part, the readers, at that time, although we meant to return to it when the occasion arose. We have decided to devote our article in this issue of *al-Hilal* to this series.

By "readers of Arabic" we mean the reading section of the public, whether their native language is Arabic or they know Arabic without being Arabs. This latter category is widespread throughout the Muslim world, from the furthest parts of India and Persia in the east to the most distant regions of Tunis and Morocco in the west, and from the shores of the Mediterranean in the north to the furthest part of the continents of Asia and Africa in the south, together with the nearby islands. As you can see, this covers vast regions whose inhabitants number hundreds of millions, in addition to the Syrian community's hundreds of thousands of emigrants to the Americas, Australia and adjacent islands such as Tasmania and New Zealand, and the islands of the Caribbean.

Do not be surprised that we include the Indians and Persians among the readers of Arabic. For the great majority of the Muslims among them, even if their language is Hindi or Persian, know literary Arabic well. Indeed they are obliged to do so for religious reasons—to read the Koran, the *ḥadīth* collections, and the Koran commentaries. This is particularly true of the Persians because Arabic is a compulsory subject in all their schools. The educated class reads Arabic even if they do not write it.

Moreover, in various regions of the Muslim world we now observe a general renaissance of the Arabic language such as we have not known before. Perhaps the reason for this is what Muslims in Asia and Africa perceive to be European designs on these continents. So they have sought to unite and speak with one voice in self-defense, and they have seen no better unifying factor than this noble language.

We in Egypt who are at the heart of the Arab world, and have imams and masters of the language as neighbors, observe the government schools trying to quench its spark. At the same time our brothers in India and Persia seek to turn this language into an ever-brighter beacon and to strengthen its base, establishing schools and instilling into their children the desire to learn it. We did not realize the importance of this until last year, when we received many letters from different parts of India with a request for advice about the best Arabic books to be taught in their schools. One of the largest Muslim associations there wrote to ask us about the conditions of admission to Dar al-'Ulum in Cairo. Their aim was to send a contingent of young men for advanced study of subjects relating to the Arabic language and also of educational methods; they would then return home to teach in the association's schools. In addition there are many articles that Indian Muslims publish in their newspapers and speeches that orators deliver at public meetings, urging their fellow believers to strengthen ties with their brothers in Egypt and Syria. The Indian newspaper *Wakil* even suggested building a railway between El-Arish and the Indian frontier, and the Egyptian papers took up the idea, discussing it at length. However difficult that project may be to carry out in practice, it clearly shows that the Nahda is now alive in the hearts of Indian Muslims, and they see no better way to stimulate it than by making good use of the Arabic language as a common link.

We have said enough about the spread of the Arabic language in general! Turning to the particular case of Egypt, the country today has innumerably more readers than it did some ten years ago. You can see that from the enthusiasm its inhabitants show in reading newspapers of different tendencies and their desire to peruse books on a variety of subjects. They devote time and money to reading; in fact they are no less keen in this respect than the other inhabitants of civilized countries, especially if we bear in mind the number of educated people among them as given in the population statistics. If you walk through the Cairo markets, you will see the greengrocer, the perfume vendor, and other tradesmen competing with each other to buy newspapers and books that meet their needs or that they find pleasant and amusing. You will see that even more clearly when some event occurs that causes people to take sides and challenges their ideas. Then you see the coachman, the muleteer, and the doorkeeper all looking for a paper to read or to listen to someone read aloud to them. That happened in the recent Greek War, as we saw with our own eyes. We noticed the carriage-drivers and others with lowly occupations clustering together in dozens to read a paper or listen to it being read. What a difference from the Arabic-reading public in Egypt some twenty years ago, when newspapers were put on sale like soap! There were only two or three of them, yet they had too few readers. Today not a week passes without a new newspaper or magazine being published, in addition to books published on different subjects. They all find buyers, although their circulation varies depending on how much they correspond to readers' tastes or needs.

Then there are the printing presses. Some ten years ago a handful of them existed, and they used to complain of lying idle. Now they number in the dozens, producing scores of books and newspapers that all sell and are read, with people asking for more.

This situation is not contradicted by the fact that some authors complain that there is a lack of demand for their works. The reason for the lack of interest may be that what they write is far removed from what readers want, or the latter are satisfied with other books. We do not regard this as something those authors should be ashamed of but as being in the nature of the process of civilization. For when a people begins its revival, it harbors contradictory inclinations and draws on different sources. This is particularly true in our case, since our tastes and points of reference vary according to the different kinds of education and social contacts that have influenced our character. Our tastes differ as a result of our mixing with members of many Western nations, each preferring his own people's customs and seeking to further their aims and spread their education in accordance with their own material interests.

If we examine our readers' tastes, we can see that they are evolving in the same direction as those of other nations. French readers, for instance, like to read what is written in their language about their country, nation, history, and the rest of their affairs. Likewise the English general public reads novels, in the first place, followed by history and poetry. Among readers of Arabic, too, novels and stories are the most popular books, followed by history and poetry. The books with the greatest circulation are on subjects connected with the Arabs, Islam, or the East. Any book on these subjects will inevitably be popular, so long as it fulfills the criteria of good writing. Given this, we are more in need of writers than of readers. Readers are simply the creation of writers. To put it differently, when a writer becomes an expert in different styles, such as to make his texts a pleasure to read, he awakens in people a desire to read and accustoms them to reading, so that it becomes a habit. In this writers are like fashion designers in Europe today. Each day they present the world with a new model that people eagerly buy. The wearers of these clothes are not expected to buy them before seeing them and making sure they are different from previous models. When such models exist, people will be found to wear them.

Some may think that the market for culture in Egypt is sluggish because they observe a lack of interest in books and journals on scientific subjects. But if they studied the country's situation, they would know that this failure is mostly due to the poor choice of subjects, bad sales management, or other reasons connected with writers, not readers.

You may find that some Arab authors who speak of the circulation of the works of their European colleagues, and how much more the latter earn than they do, are full of rancor against readers of Arabic. They claim our readers are ignorant, knowing neither the value of science nor the meaning of culture. If they write books and sell only a few copies, compared with the hundreds of thousands sold of some European titles, they accuse our readers of ignorance and tightfistedness. But we merely consider them overhasty in their judgment, for reasons that will be clear to any thoughtful person. I will now give some of them.

First, a European writer writes for a category of readers who all have similar tastes and morals. In European nations the children have a standard education and grow up with similar moral values that the writer knows well. If he writes a book or an article, he understands clearly how to please his readers, although the degree of his skill and his style and the subjects of his texts may vary.

By contrast, we write for groups with different leanings and moral standards. Their tastes may differ with or even contradict each other. What Zayd likes, 'Amr dislikes, and what pleases Bakr may anger Khalid. That is due to the well-known multiplicity of beliefs and variety of tastes inherent in the people of the East since earliest times—and apart from the recent cultural Nahda, which has led to some of us taking sides with one European nation and others with another. This is because we received our education in schools, each of which was established with different goals. As a result, someone who has gone through the French schools does not like the moral standards of the English, a graduate of the English schools has an aversion to French customs, and so on through all the countless other schools. Nor should we forget the conflicting opinions that the Nahda is bound to produce in its early stage, because people possess varying degrees of knowledge and culture not to mention the presumptuousness of claims that goes with it. All this may well be truer of Egypt than other Eastern countries, because of its people's mixing with all the world's nations with their different creeds and [. . .].[2]

The Arab writer, then, writes for a public in disarray, one without a single or coherent cultural frame of reference. If he satisfies the Egyptian, he may not satisfy the Syrian, and if he pleases both of them, he may anger the Persian or Indian. If the Muslims are content, the Christians may be annoyed—not to speak of each country, each people, and each community being divided into God Almighty alone knows how many parties and factions. This is a huge obstacle impeding the path of writers in Arabic, and only a few surmount it, whereas the European writer may satisfy his readers with only a hundredth of the pain and effort his Arab colleague needs.

One thing standing in the way of a higher circulation of Arabic books is the different styles Arab writers adopt in the face of the heterogeneous and chaotic character of their readership. When someone sets out to write a book, he has difficulty in following a particular style as his pen is curbed by the knowledge that what will please one reader may anger another. In that respect, he finds himself in the situation of journalists subjected to strict censorship. In addition, we have only recently become acquainted with the craft of authorship and are still in its initial stages. Some even turn to writing when their only incentive is to make a name for themselves.

Something worth reflection is that most of the material that our writers publish is taken from European authors. When one of them reads a book in a European language (and rarely does he read any but the books written in the language in which he was taught in school), likes its subject, and enjoys it, he imagines it will make the same impression on all readers of Arabic. So he undertakes to translate and publish it, expecting it to be popular and sell well. But he soon hears criticism from the groups with other cultural affiliations, quite apart from the difficulty of translating and finding the right Arabic mold into which to pour European concepts. Assuming the translation is polished, it may not suit the taste of Arab readers because of the text's origin, and so it may not be successful. The readers are not to blame, for they are under no obligation to read texts that do not suit their taste. The writer, too, is not to blame, for he meant well when he performed this service and he took much trouble to produce good work. But he did not make a good choice.

Some writers choose their subjects well and have an excellent style, but they do not know how to manage the marketing of their books. In Europe that is the task of the printers, publishers, or booksellers. The efforts they make to distribute books are unheard of here. In our part of the world the author is the printer, publisher, and bookseller; indeed he may even have the books bound and packed and take them to the readers' houses, inviting them to buy them. It is rare for an author to distinguish himself in all these activities as well as being an outstanding writer.

With respect to the readers, books are of two kinds, either useful or entertaining or both. Anyone who writes a work meant to be useful, who composes it carefully and well and succeeds in achieving the intended purpose, can be certain it will have a good reception and circulation, assuming people need it. But if he writes a book on a learned subject that only a few people have a need of, for business or study, and it is not entertaining enough for people to read in their spare time, how can he hope to attract readers? If someone produces a work on architecture, trigonometry, or some other subject that only a small number of people require, or for instance on Hindi or Chinese, he will not find buyers and yet he is not entitled to complain of poor sales.

If, however, someone prepares a complete manual of commercial accounting, an Arabic dictionary, or textbooks on European languages that Easterners need in their new business relations, or if he writes on hygiene or disease management or other such topics that people need for their work and physical well-being, and he succeeds in producing books appropriate for their needs, they will sell. That has been the course followed by most writers who have made profits and profited others with their books. For instance, the late revered Teacher Butrus al-Bustani in Syria saw that the language needed an accessible dictionary, and so he compiled his *Comprehensive Dictionary*,[3] which sold well. He also wrote on arithmetic and geography, and last but not least he published his *Encyclopedia*.[4] All of them have done well and become famous. The late philologist Shaykh Nasif al-Yaziji had a similar success with his books on language. And the same can be said of all those who have written textbooks to meet the needs of schools. There are many of them in common use now.

Diverting subjects, which include history, combining entertainment with usefulness, have a larger number of readers and so they have a wider circulation. They reflect people's goals and habits. Those with the widest circulation are novels, because they are read by both the common people and the elite, and their authors take account of readers' special interests and values. Rarely has someone produced a novel of this kind without having some success; how much depends on the novel's subject and how closely it caters to people's tastes.

Historical subjects only sell well if they have an affinity with the speakers of Arabic. If a book is written on the history of any country in the world, it will not have the same success as what is written on the history of Egypt, the Ottoman Empire, Islam, the Arabs, or the East. The same holds true for studies on literature, civilization, or customs; you will see in reality that the books written on these subjects are among those that have the widest circulation.

An author of a history on a specialized subject such as France, America, or Russia cannot expect much success. But publishers in Europe, too, print tens of thousands of copies of the history of their own country and only a few hundred of histories of other countries.

The press offers the easiest way to discover readers' likes and writers' choices. In this country hundreds of newspapers and journals have sprung up, but only a few of them have survived. Most of them have closed down with their owners complaining about the decline of the East and attacking readers for not appreciating writers at their true value. If they reflected a little, they would blame no one but themselves, because if readers felt satisfied with what they wrote they would read their articles attentively and enthusiastically.

That is shown by the situation of the newspapers and magazines that are now in demand or that were in demand but closed down for particular reasons. Take the magazine published by the late Mr. 'Abdallah al-Nadim.[5] Hardly had it come out before it had crowds of readers; and only after a few months it had a wider circulation than any other magazine had reached after many years. If circumstances had not forced it to disappear, it would be a model of successful circulation and sales. Its author was an Arab and its readers were Arabs—the very people whom others reproach for their aversion to reading.

Dozens of patriotic political newspapers have been founded in Egypt, but only a few survive because they print what readers need to know or else voice their feelings and are in tune with their desires. Many newspapers were founded by Egyptians without any of them achieving *al-Mu'ayyad*'s popularity with its readers or its readers' admiration for its editor. He won his readers' hearts by simply printing on the pages of his newspaper articles that expressed their feelings and chimed with their tastes.

A journal's lack of success, however, is not always a sign of its contributors' incompetence. Some of our newspapers are very well written—yet they have few readers, because circulation does not only depend on an excellent style but also demands a choice of subjects that readers need or enjoy reading about. The same is true of all the printed books in circulation with their various subjects; they are only successful to the extent that their readers derive enjoyment or benefit from the subjects they cover.

In general, the sluggishness of the market for literature in Egypt (to the extent this is true) cannot be blamed on readers. The fault (or most of it) lies with the writers, and we have already explained why their excuses are not valid. In our view, however, literature—thanks be to God—is in demand. The Arabic reading public is increasing day by day and will continue to do so , and the time will come when tastes will become less diverse and clearly differentiated, since education will improve, becoming universal and more standardized. People will then be more inclined to read and they will have developed more constant and uniform interests. As a result it will become easier for writers to satisfy them adequately, and no one will complain of a lack of demand.

Some writers may compare their situation with that of European authors who receive encouragement from their rulers and financial rewards for their writing. But it has escaped their notice how much support Egyptian princes have provided in this respect. The late Isma'il Pasha, the former khedive,[6] used to hand out purses of money to every author, poet, or orator.

When the late Teacher Butrus al-Bustani began to compile his encyclopedia, Isma'il Pasha was of the greatest help to him in publishing this weighty work. He paid him a large sum and allowed him to use the valuable books he needed from the Khedival Library, in addition to the copies of manuscripts that the Egyptian government contributed. He often acted in this manner with anyone whose works he sensed were useful; indeed he went too far, rewarding any poet who dedicated a poem to him with a position, decoration, or money. And that is in addition to the efforts his courtiers made in those days to urge people to subscribe to newspapers, sometimes going so far as to give them financial incentives. Until today the government has spent money encouraging those scholars whose books it selects for use in school. And if it had not placed an obstacle in the path of the Arabic language, that would have remained a certain source of income for our writers. But this income has been threatened because of recent laws that cause us to fear for this noble language, so long as no one among its speakers rescues it and raises its status. And that will only happen when writers strive to develop the art of literary composition and produce good work, responding to readers' tastes and developing their interest in reading. Only then will readers become interested in buying books and enable writers to do without government assistance.

Notes

1. Zaydān, "Kuttāb al-'arabiyya wa-qurrā'uhā," *al-Hilāl* 7 (April 1899): 393–400. For the earlier parts of this serialized essay see the *Bibliography of Sources Quoted in This Book.*

2. There is an elision here for a word, *wa-za'ātihim*, the meaning of which is not clear (translator's note).

3. See al-Bustānī, *Muḥīṭ*.

4. See Buṭrus al-Bustānī, *Dā'irat al-ma'ārif*, 11 vols. (Beirut: s. n., 1867–1870).

5. *Al-Ustādh*, founded 1893 in Cairo.

6. Ruler of Egypt 1862–1879.

◆ ◆ ◆

The Arabic Language

A Living Being Subject to the Laws of Evolution

Translated by Hilary Kilpatrick

Preface

This is a small book on a new subject.[1] Our attention was drawn to it when we were publishing the second edition of our book *Philosophy of Language and the Arabic Vocabulary*,[2] because it belongs to that topic. Or rather it represents a second step in the history of language, with respect to its origin, formation, and development. The philosophy of language examines how the first man came to speak, how language developed, and how words were produced by imitating sounds exterior to man, like thunderclaps, the blowing of the wind, cutting or breaking objects, spitting, blowing, whistling, and so on. There are also the natural syllables that man pronounces instinctively, such as when yawning and sighing. It also traces how sounds came to be differentiated, both in enunciation and in meaning, through creative combinations, phonetic changes, and transposition until they became independent words. Then verbs, nouns, and particles were formed, and language became what it is.

The history of language looks at words and constructions after a language, in this case the Arabic language, has become fully developed, examining the changes that they undergo through renewal or obsolescence. It shows which of them have fallen into disuse and which new words and constructions have replaced them, whether they have originated in the language itself or been borrowed from elsewhere. It also explains the conditions that led to the old elements becoming obsolete and the new ones being produced, giving examples of what is obsolete or rarely used, neologisms, and borrowings. This is a subject with linguistic, historical, and philosophical aspects, and we have divided our treatment of it into eight chapters, corresponding to the stages that the language has gone through:

1. The Pre-Islamic period: This treats the history of the language from earliest times up to the appearance of Islam. We have included examples of the foreign words that became part of it, such as Ethiopic, Persian, Sanskrit, Hieroglyphic, and Greek ones, relating the borrowings to historical causes and articulating the principles for determining the origins of those words. We have also given examples of the new words produced in the language itself, comparing Arabic with its sister languages or looking at the Arabic words themselves to support our argument.

2. The Islamic period: We have in mind here the new Islamic terms required by law, jurisprudence, the science of languages, and so on after the rise of Islam.

3. Administrative terms in the Arab empire: This covers the administrative terms that entered Arabic; they were required by Muslim civilization when the Arab empire was established. They are either borrowings or coined according to foreign models, and the chapter includes a study of how the meaning of words evolved over time.

4. Scientific terms in the Arab empire: This treats the words and constructions demanded by the translation of science and philosophy from Greek and other languages into Arabic in the Abbasid period.

5. Terms of general vocabulary in the Arab empire: These are words coined in the language or borrowed from elsewhere but not according to the method used for law or science, like words denoting social phenomena.

6. Christian and Jewish terms: These are the words and constructions that entered the language from Syriac or Hebrew with the translation of Christian books into Arabic.

7. Borrowings under the non-Arab dynasties: This deals with the words the Arabic language acquired after the end of the Arab empire and the establishment of Turkish, Kurdish, and other states.

8. The modern renaissance: This covers modern civilization's need for coining new words and adopting European words to convey new concepts in science, industry, commerce, administration, and so on.

We have begun the book with a foreword on the laws of life and language's subordination to them. And we have ended it with a chapter on chancery jargon and a conclusion summarizing what has been said. We believe that our writings on this new subject contain good ideas, with which we have opened the way for leading essayists and scholars of language to follow. We suggest that they accord the subject the attention it deserves and expand it further for us, because it needs much investigation and lengthy study. Now that this Nahda in science, literature, and poetry has taken place, the language is in dire need of such studies and investigations, so that writers may know that language is a living and growing being subjected to the laws of evolution, continually renewing its vocabulary and constructions. Writers should not be afraid to use new words that the ancient Arabs did not employ. Their fear impedes the full use of their talents. If they let their pens roam freely, the greatest benefits may result, enhancing the literature of the Arabic language. The general principles and fundamental connections must be taken into consideration, as we have pointed out in the appropriate place. And knowing the origin and history of a word may further the understanding of its true meaning.—J. Z.

Introduction

The Laws of Life

Growth and renewal are laws of life; they involve tissues being destroyed and new ones being created to replace them. A living organism is composed of cells, each of which has an independent life, and according to this law when the cell's life ends and the cell dies, its components disintegrate and are dispersed, and a new cell is created in its place from nutritive fluids such as blood. A living organism, then, is perpetually disintegrating and being recreated. It has even been said that the human body is entirely renewed every few years. In other words, at the end of the process it contains none of the materials it had at its beginning. Without such renewal, a body is not alive. If something occurs in an animal's body to prevent its tissues being renewed, it will quickly die. For renewal is necessary for life.

A nation's life is like an individual's life. Indeed the processes of life are more obvious in the nation than in the individual. For nations live only through the disappearance of the old and through the generation of the new. It is as though the nation's individual members were cells forming that nation's body, which renews itself in a century as a human body is renewed in each decade. If we follow the growth of a nation over generations, we can see that it divides and branches out, a single nation becoming many nations, with the distance between them varying according to periods and circumstances. Each of these nations in turn divides into further nations in the course of centuries, and so on and so forth. This is what is meant by the general law of progressive evolution.

Language Is a Living Being

Biological and other phenomena depending on life are subject to this law [of evolution] just like living beings. This is especially true of everything connected with human intellectual activity, such as language, customs, religions, legal systems, sciences, literature, and so on. They are considered manifestations of a nation's life, subject to the laws both of growth and renewal and of evolution. Each of them has a long history with a philosophical dimension, which we call the history of the nation's civilization, or the history of its literature, its sciences, its government, its religion, and the like. These are exciting subjects that involve reflection and insight. The history of a language and its literature belong in this category.

In general terms, the study of the history of a language has three parts:

1. The study of its growth since its formation, including the stages it went through in prehistoric times, such as the emergence of verbs, nouns, and particles, the production of derived forms, modes of expression, and so forth. All this is part of the philosophy of language, which we discussed in detail in our book *The Philosophy of Language [and the Arabic Vocabulary]*.

2. The study of outside influences to which the language has been subjected to, after its speakers mixed with other nations. It acquired words and new expressions from their languages, just as its speakers adopted elements of their customs, manners, and culture. And all this is accompanied by the differentiation of words according to different situations, together with the creation of new forms and words.

3. The study of the history of the sciences and literature expressed in the given language in the course of the centuries. This is what is called

"the history of the literature of the language." This division is approximate, since there is no clear demarcation between these three parts.

When you consider the history of each aspect of a nation, its culture, its language, its laws, or anything else, taking into consideration the circumstances it has passed through during its rise, development, and diversification, you can see that its growth is a process so gradual as to be almost hidden and only perceptible after much time has passed. That slow movement is interspersed with powerful and sudden leaps forward, bringing about visible change. This is what people mean by a Nahda. Such surges are usually caused by the exchange of ideas when nations come into contact with each other. Such situations may follow migrations imposed by nature and caused by famine or fear. They may result from the advent of a prophet, lawgiver, or great philosopher, or the emergence of an ambitious leader who induces people to undertake conquests and raids. Or there may be other reasons for these contacts. Then ideas interact, characters and dispositions mingle with each other, and customs, manners, religions, and culture take on different forms. Language is subordinate to those changes, or rather it retains the traces of those changes, preserving them for centuries after these customs, cultures, or laws have ceased to exist. And if any of those change, it preserves the traces of that change.

We will confine ourselves in this study to the history of the Arabic language in its second phase, that is, the history of its words and constructions after its creation.

The Pre-Islamic Period

What is meant here is the period of the Arabic language before the rise of Islam. Its beginning cannot be determined because it is lost in the mists of the ages preceding the historical era. But we believe that the Arabic language appeared and developed, that is, its nouns, verbs, and particles became distinct and most of its derived forms and compounds were created, while it was still in its mother's arms, that is, before it was separated from its sisters, Chaldean, Hebrew, Phoenician, and the other Semitic languages. In other words, the mother of all these languages, which is called the original Semitic language or Aramaic language,[3] was fully developed, with verbs, nouns, particles, and various derived and augmented forms, before its speakers separated, moving to Phoenicia, the Arabian Peninsula, and Mesopotamia. There, after these migrations, their languages became distinct, corresponding to the differences in their circumstances, and so the well-known Semitic languages were born. The language of the Semites who settled in the Arabian Peninsula varied according to the conditions of their environment or the peoples who were their neighbors. It differed from its sister languages in particular ways that became the specific characteristics of the Arabic language. This language developed in the meantime into different branches, varying according to region; they are the languages of the Hejaz, Yemen, and Ethiopia. The language of each of those regions also split up into variants or dialects, according to the innumerable tribes and clans. That all happened in prehistoric times.

Here we need only to study the language of the Hejaz, the Arabic language that has come down to us. Before it was set down in writing, that is, before Islam, it consisted of many dialects, known as tribal dialects, which differed in their pronunciation and construction. There were the dialects of Tamim, Rabi'a, Mudar, Qays, Hudhayl, Quda'a, and others, as is well known. The one that most closely resembled the original Semitic language was the one that had undergone the least amount of admixture. The contrary was true of the tribes that mixed with other peoples, like the Hejazis who neighbor Syria, especially the Meccans and above all the Quraysh, who were merchants trading and traveling north to Syria, Iraq and Egypt, south to Yemen, east to the Persian Gulf and beyond, and west to Ethiopia.

In addition, different peoples gathered around the Ka'aba, among them Indians, Persians, Nabateans, Yemenis, Ethiopians, and Egyptians, apart from the Jewish and Christian communities who used to travel to it. All that led to the Hejazi dialect developing, thanks to the derived words and constructions that were generated or incorporated through borrowing, which the other dialects had no equivalent for.

These acquisitions increased especially following the cultural upsurge that occurred in the two centuries preceding Islam, with the arrival of the Ethiopians and Persians in Yemen and the Hejaz, following the autocratic rule of Dhu Nuwas, the king of Yemen. He was Jewish, and he oppressed the Christians of Yemen in the fifth century A.D., especially the people of

Najran, demanding they embrace Judaism. When they refused, he burned and butchered them. But some took refuge in Ethiopia, and consequently the Ethiopians attacked Yemen, conquering it and colonizing it for a time and subjugating its kings for many years. One of its kings, Dhu Yazan, turned to the Persians for help in the days of Chosroes Anushirwan[4] and he responded, hoping to conquer the country. He expelled the Ethiopians from Yemen after they had ruled there for seventy-two years, during which time they made regular expeditions to the Hejaz. In the mid-sixth century they tried to conquer it, bringing elephants and men to Mecca, but they did not succeed. The Hejazis were so impressed by the Ethiopians' march on Mecca that they used it as a marking date, the Year of the Elephant. When the Persians conquered Yemen, they spent time there and mixed with the population, establishing ties of allegiance and intermarriage and settling down. They used to travel to Mecca, while the Hejazis visited them frequently.

The Islamic Period

Islamic Terms

In the context of the Arabic language, we understand the Islamic period as the period from the appearance of Islam until the recording in writing of the Islamic sciences such as exegesis of the Koran, *ḥadīth*, and the other sciences of jurisprudence, language, and so on, and the burgeoning of culture in the Abbasid age. It is indisputable that Islam had a great influence on the language, consequent to its influence on customs, manners, and beliefs. Part of this influence is reflected in the religious, legal, linguistic, and literary technical terms that were coined in Arabic, as well as the administrative terms that entered it with the establishment of the government and its various spheres of administrative activity. Another part is reflected in the scientific and philosophical vocabulary developed by the translation of Greek, Persian, and Indian books into Arabic.

We have therefore divided our treatment of the Islamic period into three chapters. In this one we confine ourselves to the changes introduced because of the Islamic sciences; this is what we mean by the "Islamic terms." We will devote separate chapters to the changes connected with administration and translation.[5] The Islamic sciences' influence on the language is almost entirely confined to the diversification of Arabic words and the modification of their meanings to express the new concepts created by Islam. It is rare for non-Arabic vocabulary to be introduced.

1. *Terms of law and jurisprudence:* The best-known modifications of Arabic words in the Islamic period are the religious, legal, jurisprudential, and linguistic technical terms. These words existed before Islam, but they had other meanings. They evolved to denote new concepts that were related to the older ones. For instance, the word *mu'min* existed in the pre-Islamic period referring to *amān*, security, or *īmān*, placing one's trust, that is, believing. After Islam it came to denote the believer, as opposed to the unbeliever. Islamic law lays down certain conditions for being a believer that did not exist before. The terms for "believer," *muslim*, "unbeliever," *kāfir*, "dissolute," and "godless," *fāsiq*, underwent similar changes, as did the technical legal terms such as for the ritual prayer, *ṣalāt*, which originally meant "prayer," "supplication," and, for "bending," *rukū'*, and "prostration," *sujūd*, "pilgrimage," *ḥajj*, "almsgiving," *zakāt*, and for "marriage," *nikāḥ*. All these words and others like them had meanings that changed and diversified in Islam.

The same holds true for terms of jurisprudence, such as *īlā'* for annulment of a marriage, *ẓihār* for repudiation, *'idda* for the waiting period before a widow or divorcée can marry again, *ḥaḍāna* for the right to custody of a child, *nafaqa* for adequate support of a wife, *i'tāq* for manumission of a slave, *istīlā'* for seizure of property, *ta'zīr* for the discretionary corporal punishment decided by a judge, *laqīṭa* for a foundling, *ābiq* for a runaway slave, *wadī'a* for the contract regulating the deposit of an object, *'āriyya* for a loan, *shuf'a* for the right of preemption, *munāsakha* for the transfer of inheritance shares, *farā'iḍ* for the fixed shares of inheritance, and *'iṣāma* for ompurgation.

2. *Linguistic technical terms*: What has been said above also applies to the technical terms required by the sciences of language, like "grammar," *naḥw*, "metrics," *'arūḍ*, "poetry," *shi'r*, "grammatical flexion," *i'rāb*, "assimilation of phonemes," *idghām*, "anomalous elision," *i'lāl*, "literal meaning," *ḥaqīqa*, "figurative meaning," *majāz*, "diminution of a poetic foot," *naqḍ*, "indeclinable quality of a noun," *man'*, "metathesis," *qalb*, "nominative

case," *raf'*, "accusative case," "subjunctive mode," *naṣb*, "genitive case," *khafḍ*, and the "long" and "extended" poetical meters, *ṭawīl* and *madīd*.

There are very many such terms, with branches and derivations. So a single word may have one specialized meaning for jurisprudence, another for linguistics, another for prosody, and another for religion; such specialized senses are countless. We shall mention other cases when we come to speak of the technical terms used in logic and Islamic theology.[6] Islam made great changes in modes of expression, like the formula "May God grant you a long life"; the first to use it was 'Umar ibn al-Khattab,[7] speaking to 'Ali ibn Abi Talib.

3. *Abandoned words*: Just as Islam created new words to convey new concepts required by the new law and science, it eradicated from the language old words, which disappeared together with some beliefs and customs of the pre-Islamic period. One example is *al-mirbā'*, that is, the "quarter of the booty" that the tribal chief took in pre-Islamic times, and another is *al-nashīta*, the booty that the chief took before he arrived at the enemy tribe's main concentration or what raiders seized on their way before arriving at their destination. Then there are *al-maks*,[8] money taken from sellers of wares in the markets of pre-Islamic Arabia, *al-itāwa*, tribute, and *al-hulwān*, a father's appropriating part of his daughter's bride-price. Other expressions that became obsolete are: *"In'im sabāḥan wa-in'im zulāman,"* "May you have a pleasant morning and a pleasant night"; the use of ab'ada 'l-la'n, meaning "Far be it from you that men should curse you," to address kings; the slave's calling his master *rabbī*, "My lord," and the denoting of those who have never performed the pilgrimage as *ṣarūra*. We see that some of these words are used in the language today, but either they are used in a different sense than the original one, or else they were reintroduced in the language after being abandoned.

We do not doubt that many Arabic words were abandoned in the first two centuries of the Islamic calendar for no other reason than the renewal and decay demanded by growth. To verify that, it is enough to consult the dictionaries and look at the words they contain. You will see hundreds and thousands of words which are not in use, and we cannot imagine that the compilers collected them in early Islamic times for any reason other than that they were widely employed in speech. It may be objected that those words were abandoned in later times, and we do not deny that some of them have been abandoned recently, but many became obsolete in the early period. Furthermore, certain words were rarely used even before Islam, so a person listening to a Bedouin using obsolete words may not have understood them, even if he was a specialist in the language.

The Recent Scientific Nahda

The Arabic language has known no period that has influenced its words and constructions as much as the recent Nahda in the middle of the last century. This Nahda's influence was unexpected and sudden. The sciences flourished, including medicine, the natural sciences, mathematics, and the different branches of the rational sciences, and there was time neither to search for the technical terms that were needed, such as the Arabs had invented in their earlier renaissance, nor to coin new words. The reason was that those working in the different fields of the new sciences when they first entered Egypt and Syria in the middle of the last century did not have an extensive knowledge of the language. When they translated those sciences into Arabic, they only discovered some of the old technical terms, if any. For the rest, they coined words that conveyed only approximately the intended meanings. But as the years passed, these terms were refined so that they now convey what is meant in a process similar to that in the Abbasid renaissance and other similar periods.

When the sudden influx of the sciences had subsided, and when many schools had been opened and writers and specialists of the language had emerged, they started to review the new scientific or administrative terms that had entered the language. They were seldom able to alter any of them, because their widespread use in books, newspapers, associations, and so on firmly established them in the language. But these writers were not without means to reform literary composition and reverted in their expressions to the style of the early Arab empire. They vied with the outstanding writers of those centuries for keeping good taste and a smooth style. Writers have emerged among us who are in no way inferior to Ibn al-Muqaf'a,[9] Ibn Khaldun, or other noteworthy writers and masters of composition. They have abandoned artificial rhymed prose, are seldom prolix, and eschew the use of synonyms. They are engaged in purifying the language of the chaff and rubbish which entered it and the weakness from which it suffered during the Age of Decline. If you consider the language of the writers and journalists at the beginning of this renaissance and compare it to the language of our writers today, you will see a great difference, and you can expect it to return to the summits of perfection it reached in the age of its splendor and youth. We do not believe, however, that these writers are capable of purifying the language from the foreign words and expressions that have entered it or the Arabic neologisms that have been coined in response to the new customs, literature, and sciences required by modern civilization. Many old terms have been dropped from the language and replaced by new ones—as is the case with any living being subject to the laws of development.

The change that has affected the Arabic language in the recent renaissance, then, concerns its words and expressions. Some of them were adopted from foreign languages; others were created by modifications and ramifications. To cover the subject we have divided our treatment of it into two parts, one discussing the imported elements, and the other the neologisms. [. . .]

Conclusion

From our review of the state of the Arabic language in the various periods and stages during its emergence and development from the pre-Islamic period to today, the reader will have realized that it has followed the course of living beings, with cells dying and being renewed in what is called "living growth." Words and expressions were created in the Islamic period that had not existed before Islam, and in the following period terms, not known earlier, appeared. In our recent cultural Nahda too, new terms and expressions have been coined. To stand still during such a process of growth is contrary to the course of the laws of nature, quite apart from being useless. For language is a living, growing being subject to the laws of evolution—and disintegration and generation are inevitable whether people like that or not. New words appear and old ones disappear, as circumstances require, according to a rationale common to all existing beings.

Now is the time for us to free our pens from the chains of the pre-Islamic Age of Ignorance and bring them out of the prison of nomadic life. Otherwise we shall not be able to survive on this new level [of civilization]. We should not despise every word the Bedouin did not pronounce some ten centuries ago, because the language of deserts and tents is inappropriate to cities and palaces—unless we dress it in the garb of cities. There is no harm in using a neologism that no pre-Islamic word can replace because its meaning was unknown at that time, or else the term that existed for it has become obsolete. The use of neologisms is better than reviving dead words; keeping a newborn alive is preferable to bringing someone who has been long dead back to life. And if a foreign expression for which the Arabs had no equivalent occurs to us, there is nothing wrong in adopting it. We believe that giving pens free rein in this way will enable us to discover a host of gifted people, held back from embarking on writing by their fear of committing a fault of language or style for which they can be blamed. These potential writers lack the literary courage to enable them to disregard criticism, if what they write is worthwhile. Faults of language in no way reduce a writer's value, because it is only given to a few to know all its rules, forms, and exceptions.

We do not have the same understanding of this freedom, however, as the Europeans have with respect to their languages. For our concern with Arabic is not the same as theirs. Together with freedom to develop the language, we must also go back to the general rules and fundamental linguistic bonds. We shall not corrupt the language with words and expressions of the common people, or introduce an excessive amount of foreign words so that our language becomes like Ottoman Turkish. Because of the quantity of Arabic, Persian, and European words that have entered it, it has become unique. The only other language in the world it resembles is Hindustani (Urdu), which the Indians use in their newspapers and books. If the Ottoman language's vocabulary is analyzed with regard to the languages from which it is drawn, 70 percent of the words are Arabic, 15 percent Persian, and 5 percent from European languages. Only 10 percent are authentic Turkish words. Something similar is said about Urdu and Maltese.

The Arabic language's health must be preserved and retaining its rhetorical power and eloquence must be our concern, especially now that it has begun to rise to the heights attained in its youth. Excessive assimilation of foreign words and coining of new ones cannot be approved of, but they should be resorted to when necessary; we consider such borrowings as a form of growth and progress, not corruption and decline.

We regard what we have written on this subject as ideas that we have expressed to open the discussion. But an exhaustive treatment of the history of the language, its words, and its expressions can only be undertaken in large tomes. We ask the leading exponents, writers, and scholars of the language to write more on it, as a service to the present renaissance.

Notes

1. Excerpts from Zaidān, *al-Lugha kā'in ḥayy*. The excerpts were not so much chosen for his philological insights and scholarly conclusions but, rather, for illustrating Zaidan's use of the theory of evolution to analyze the history of the Arab language and to argue for the legitimacy of change within the language.

2. Zaydān, *al-Alfāẓ al-'arabiyya*.

3. It appears that Zaidan equals here, incorrectly, "Ur-Semitisch" with Aramaic.

4. Chosroes (r. 531–572), Sassanian emperor; reformed and reorganized the empire; made peace with the Romans and conquered Yemen.

5. Not included in this selection.

6. Not included in this selection.

7. 'Umar ibn al-Khattāb, second caliph (r. 634–644).

8. Today common for sales tax, custom duty, toll.

9. Abū 'Amr 'Abdallah ibn al-Muqaffa' (d. 757), author of *Kalīla wa-dimna*, fables based on a collection in Pahlavi Persian with origins in India: Brockelmann *GAL*, 1, 151, *Supp.* 1, 234.

HISTORY

The History of the Arabs before Islam

Its Difficulty and Complexity

Translated by Paul Starkey

In the last issue of *al-Hilal*, in the course of replying to some people's suggestions, we promised to discuss the obstacles and difficulties that stand in the way of writing a history of the pre-Islamic Arabs.[1] I am now fulfilling that promise. Our purpose is to prepare a justification for the work on this subject that we are now embarking on, with God's help, in response to requests by a number of worthy people, a reply to whose suggestions we regard as a duty incumbent upon us.

It seems to us, from a perusal of what has been written on the pre-Islamic Arabs by Muslims, that the Arabs did not record any of their history before the Islamic period, or if they did write it, none of it has reached us. People of other nations such as the Egyptians and Babylonians have left us inscriptions that give an indication of their civilizations and provide us with some historical evidence, even though they did not record history. In the case of the Arabs, however, the first book to mention their history is the Koran, which gives only a brief and tangential account, on which commentators have taken different views with various levels of support. However, the Prophet's Companions and other contemporaries circulated some stories about the Arabs by word of mouth. They were passed down to the next generation and the following one, until they came to the attention of historians during the early period of Islam. These historians recorded the stories they heard with all their shortcomings. They explained some of them on the basis of the poems and proverbs that had reached them in contradictory, imperfect, and summary form—rarely congruent with the judgment of reason.

The non-Muslims [*sic*][2] who were contemporaries of the pre-Islamic Arabs seldom took any interest in their affairs, and only recorded information about them haphazardly. This amounts to a very small quantity, which may indeed only make the researcher more confused. The oldest of such sources is the Torah, which only mentions a few names of cities and persons in the oldest historical periods. We can only make the names correspond to their names now by intuition and guesswork. The oldest of the Greek historians is Herodotus, the traveler. The purpose of his history was to give an account of the wars of the Persians, Greeks, and Egyptians, so he did not mention the Arabs except in passing. The same goes for the Greek and Roman historians who wrote after him, although some geographers, such as Strabo, the contemporary of Christ, and Ptolemy al-Fuladhi the Alexandrian who lived about two centuries later, wrote about the Arabian Peninsula. These writings were not entirely clear because of the differences between the names of the cities and tribes as they mention them, and those reported by Muslim historians. In short, almost everything that has come down to us concerning the history of the Arabs in pre-Islamic times has its origins in what the Muslim historians wrote, which is contradictory and inconsistent because of the exaggeration, guesswork, and deficiencies contained within. So it is difficult to extract the truth without much effort, involving an indulgent approach and the application of intellectual judgment. This is why the history of the Arabs in pre-Islamic times is notorious for its difficulty and complexity. Historians, therefore, have been reluctant to plunge into its torrent and explore it. This is what prompted the Swedish King Oscar II some years ago to encourage learned men to write about it, by instituting a named prize for the best such historian. I have heard that someone won the prize, but I have not seen the book, nor do I know who wrote it.

However, a group of friends who hold me in high esteem invited me to plunge into these waters and to write a book bringing together the scattered fragments of this history, after investigating the facts. So we have responded to this invitation, while acknowledging the impossibility of undertaking this adequately—our reason for this being, as we have already explained, the weakness of the historical sources, which are muddled and contradictory, as we shall explain further on.

We said that the basis of the historical sources that we have relating to the pre-Islamic Arabs are the books written in the ancient period by Muslims such as Ibn Ishaq,[3] Ibn Hisham,[4] al-Tabari,[5] al-Masu'di, al-Isfahani,[6] Ibn al-Athir, Ibn Khaldun, Abu al-Fida',[7] and others. By referring to their books and stories, and comparing them to each other, we have found contradictions, differences, and weaknesses in them that reinforce our determination and redouble our resolve [to tackle the issue]. Here are some examples:

1. Determining the Dates of Births, Deaths and Events

One of the biggest causes of confusion in constructing an accurate history of the pre-Islamic Arabs is that historians do not record years of birth, death, or reign, but rather mention the names of kings and rulers one after the other without specifying any particular time or period. So they say, for example, that the ancestor of the kings of the Yemen was Qahtan, that is, Qahtan ibn 'Abir ibn Shalih ibn Arfkashad ibn Sam ibn Nuh, that is, there are five generations between him and Nuh.[8] That must mean that Qahtan lived in the twenty-fourth century B.C. at least. This is what Arab historians indeed maintain, for al-Mas'udi, for example, after mentioning the names of the kings of the Yemen descended from Qahtan, thirty-seven kings in all, says that they ruled for 3,190 years. The calculation of the period between Qahtan and the last king of his lineage is more or less correct, for the last of these kings ruled just before the *Hijra*. But that requires that the average rule of one king should be just over eighty-six years. However, this is far longer than the average human lifespan, quite apart from the lengths of their reigns—unless that was by some divine miracle. For the average human lifespan did not usually exceed thirty to thirty-three years. I suppose that the historians must have realized this fact and were thereby forced to apply those years to the number of the kings of Himyar referred to; so they increased the lifespans of those kings, saying, for example, that Ibra Dhu al-Manar, one of their kings, ruled for 180 years, that his son Afrish ruled for 160 years, that Tabban As'ad Abu Karab ruled for 320 years, and so on for the others, to a greater or lesser degree, thereby moving further away from the generally recognized calculation. Abu al-Fida', however, says that the length of the reign of the kings of Himyar was 2,020 years. Although he differs from al-Mas'udi in this, it does not conform to the facts, for the average is still a long way from reality. As another example, Abu al-Fida agrees with the other historians of Islam concerning Queen Bilqis,[9] who was also one of the rulers of Himyar. He says that she was a contemporary of King Solomon, son of David, meaning that she was the Queen of Sheba mentioned in the Torah. Between her and the Yahtan or Qahtan already mentioned, however, there were thirteen generations. As for Solomon, he lived in the tenth century B.C., and there were fourteen centuries between him and Yahtan. This must mean that between the birth of one of these descendants and his son there were a hundred and some years, which would be even stranger than the previous calculation.

Al-Tabari says that the Tabban As'ad Abu Karab already mentioned was a contemporary of Azdeshir Bahman,[10] one of the kings of the Persians, and Abu al-Fida' says that Azdeshir Bahman was the Koresh mentioned in the Bible.[11] This Cyrus ruled in 538 B.C., which would mean that there were eighteen centuries between the aforementioned Tabban As'ad and Yahtan, whereas there were actually seventeen generations, despite the differences and contradictions in these peoples' genealogies.

Genealogists are agreed that the Banu 'Adnan, including Quraysh, can be traced back to Isma'il, son of Abraham—al-Khalil, as he is known—but they are not agreed on the number or names of his descendants until we reach Adnan himself. They hold that from 'Adnan to 'Abdallah, the father of the lawgiver of Islam, there were thirty-one generations, and they are agreed on that; but they disagree about the generations from 'Adnan to Isma'il as to whether it was seven or forty generations. It is agreed that Isma'il lived in the nineteenth century B.C., and that between him and 'Abdallah, the father of the Prophet, there were thirty-five centuries. [As we mentioned], they agreed also that the descendants between 'Adnan and 'Abd Allah amount to thirty-one. If we take the average length of a generation, that is, the time between the birth of a father and the birth of his son, as thirty-three years, then there would be 613 years between the birth of 'Adnan and the birth of the giver of the Holy Law. That would put the birth of 'Adnan at 132 B.C. However, the Islamic historians all agree that Mu'id ibn 'Adnan was a contemporary of Nebuchadnezzar, king of Babylon, and give an account of his wars with him. But this Nebuchadnezzar lived in the seventh century B.C.

As for the interval between 'Adnan and Isma'il, according to our reckoning it was eighteen centuries, which would mean that the number of generations between them was at least fifty-four. But most of the historians say that it was seven, while others make it forty.

Even odder than all of this is the account given by al-Mas'udi and others of the lineage of Jadhima al-Abrash, who was killed by al-Zabba. He described him as Jadhima ibn Malik ibn Fahm ibn Dawas ibn al-Azad ibn Anfuth ibn Malik ibn Zayd ibn Kilan ibn Saba ibn Yathjab ibn Ya'rub ibn Qahtan. That means that there were thirteen generations between him and Qahtan. There is no doubt that this Jadhima lived more than two centuries after Christ, but Ibn Khaldun says that he lived thirty years before Christ. If we accepted his statement, then there would be at least thirty-three centuries between Jadhima and Qahtan, whereas we have seen that in the view of al-Mas'udi there were thirteen generations between them, which would mean that there must be two hundred years between father and son!

2. Names of People and Places

Among the things that deserve attention in the history of the pre-Islamic Arabs are the frequent differences in the pronunciation of names. The reason generally is the absence of dots and vowels from written Arabic at first. Arabic letters were deficient, so that they made no distinction between *bā'*, *tā'*, and *thā'*, or between *jim*, ḥā', and *khā'*, or *sīn* and *shīn*. They would write a word without dots, so that it could be read as *bilqis*, *nilqis*, *yilqis*, *tilqis*, *bilqish*, *nilqish*, *yilqish*, or *tilqish*. A word might also be pronounced differently by moving the dots and changing their positions, so there was confusion in the reading of names, the results of which became apparent in the differences between historians and genealogists in relation to the names of people, places, and tribes. By way of example, Ibn Khaldun calls one of the kings of Himyar Afriqash, while al-Mas'udi and Abu al-Fida' call him Afriqas. Ibn Khaldun says al-Maltat, and al-Mas'udi al-Malzaz. Ibn

Khaldun says Nashir al-Na'am, while al-Tabari calls him Yasir An'am or Yasir Yan'am, and al-Mas'udi Nafis al-Ni'am, while Ibn al-Athir calls him Yasir ibn 'Amr and In'am al-An'ama. Ibn Khaldun says Kakikarb, while al-Tabari and Ibn al-Athir call him Malikikarb, and al-Mas'udi and Ibn al-Fida' call him Kalikarb. Ibn Khaldun calls Bilqis's father Alishrah, while al-Tabari calls him Yalishrah, and Ibn al-Athir Ilashrah. Some writers call Bilqis Balqama. Some call one of the inhabitants of Himyar Wa'il, while others call him Wanil, and so on. Non-Arab names include many, indeed innumerable, variations.

It is self-evident that this phenomenon may extend to verbs and derived nouns and change the sense and meaning. It seems that al-Tabari's *Summary of the History* printed in Europe was transcribed from a manuscript copy that was either wholly or partly lacking diacritical points, for the publisher filled the book with footnotes to clarify the variations in reading.

3. Differences in the Succession of Kings

Scarcely any two historians can agree on the order of the succession of the kings in a single kingdom. This is particularly common in the case of the kings of Himyar and other ancient dynasties. The following table will illustrate the differences between three historians of the kings of Yemen, from Himyar to Dhu al-Adh'ar only, to avoid excessive length (see the table [below]).

It will be clear from this table that, quite apart from the differences in names and persons, they differed in number, so that al-Mas'udi made them seven, and Abu al-Fida' fifteen, which is an enormous, fundamental difference. When they compare the succession of the kings of Hira, Ghassan, and Kinda, we will see a similar sort of variation.

Abu al-Fida'	Ibn Khaldun	al-Mas'udi
Ardeshir Bahman	Ardeshir Bahman	Ardeshir Bahman
Himyar	Himyar	Himyar
Wa'il	Wa'il	Kahlan
al-Kisk	al-Kisk	Abu Malik
Ya'far	Ya'far	Jabbar ibn Ghalib
Dhu Rayyash	al-Mu'afir	al-Ra'ish ibn Shaddad

al-N'uman
Ashmakh
Shaddad
Luqman
Dhu Sadad
al-Harith
al-Sa'ab
Dhu al-Manar
Afriqash
Dhu al-Adh'ar

Dhu Rayyash
al-Ra'ish
Dhu al-Manar
Afriqash
Dhu al-Adh'ar

Dhu al-Manar
Dhu al-Adhar

4. Differences in Lineages

These [differences] appear frequently in the books [of scholars]. The genealogists only infrequently agree on the lineages of the kings and princes, and indeed they usually only agree on the Quraysh lineage. On the lineages of the other kings, they differ a great deal. Ibn Khaldun and Ibn Ishaq describe the lineage of Tubba' As'ad Abu Karab as being As'ad ibn 'Adi ibn Sayfi, while al-Tabari has Ibn al-Kalbi and Ibn Hazm, and Ibn al-Athir describe him as As'ad ibn Kalikarb ibn Zayd al-Aqran ibn 'Amr ibn Dhu al-Adh'ar ibn Abraha Dhu al-Manar al-Ra'ish ibn Qays ibn Sayfi. There is a great difference between these two statements. They also differ about the lineage of Zayd, between whether it should be Ibn Salma ibn Mazin ibn Munabbih ibn Sa'ab ibn Sa'ad, or Ibn Munabbih ibn Sa'ab ibn Sa'ad, or Ibn Sa'ab ibn Sa'ad. Ibn Khaldun and others say it is Yashjib ibn Ya'rub, while Ibn Ishaq says that it is Ya'rub ibn Yashjib.

Jewish genealogists say that the Arabs of Yemen are descendants of Ham, while the Arabs say that they are descendants of Shem. Even odder is that they disagree about the genealogy of Qahtan. Some of them call him Ibn 'Abir ibn Shalih ibn Arfakshad ibn Sam, while others describe him as Ibn Yaman ibn Qaydar; others have claimed that Qahtan was descended from Isma'il, while the majority says that he preceded Isma'il by several generations. Ibn Khaldun explained that the Arabs take liberties with non-Arab names, changing and varying the letters, which supports this interpretation. A similar phenomenon may be seen in the way they differ about Dhu al-Qarnayn, as to whether he is al-Sa'ab ibn

Mudathir, one of the kings of Yemen, or Alexander of Macedon, son of Philipp, or someone else.

Genealogists also disagree about the lineage of al-Harith al-Ra'ish, the first of the Tubba' kings. Ibn Ishaq said that he was Ibn 'Adi ibn Sayfi, while Ibn al-Kalbi said Ibn Qays ibn Sayfi, and al-Suhayli says that he was ibn Humal ibn Dhu Sadad ibn al-Maltat ibn 'Umar ibn Dhu Yaqdim ibn al-Suwar ibn 'Abd Shams ibn Wa'il, while al-Mas'udi says that he was Ibn Shaddad ibn al-Maltat ibn 'Umar. Odder than this is that one person may make two different statements concerning the lineage of a single person. Al-Tabari says in one place that al-Harith al-Ra'ish was a descendant of Saba the younger, and in another place he says something different. Historians also disagreed about the lineage of Afriqash, one of the Tubba' kings. Ibn Khaldun said that he was the son of Abraha ibn al-Harith al-Ra'ish, whereas Ibn Hazm said that he was the brother of al-Harith al-Ra'ish. Afriqash was either the brother of Harith al-Ra'ish or the son of Abraha ibn [son of] Harith al-Ra'ish, that is, the grandson of Harith al-Ra'ish. In either case Abraha and Harith al-Rashid ruled before him. They said that al-Ra'ish reigned for 125 years and that Abraha reigned for 180 years, so that the start of Afriqash's reign would be 305 years after the start of his brother's reign. So quite apart from the length of his reign he might have lived at their expense for half a century or more! Add to that their differences of opinion about the relationships of one tribe to another. Some of them claim that the tribe of the Anmaz is descended from Qahtan, while some claim that they are descendants of 'Adnan. There is no space for us to record additional examples.

5. Differences about Who Built Particular Buildings

They also disagree about the names of the people who built cities and other buildings. Some say, for example, that the Ma'rib Dam was built by Luqman ibn 'Ad and others, and connect its construction with Queen Bilqis; while others say that it was built by Himyar' and others that it was constructed by Saba ibn Yashjib, who died before it was completed, and that it was finished by the kings of Himyar later. That is what Ibn Khaldun says. If they had built more buildings, there would have been a lot more disputes about their builders. But they seldom erected buildings or built palaces. They claim that 'Abd Shams ibn Ya'rub ibn Yashjib ibn Saba ibn Qahtan built the city of 'Ayn Shams (al-Matariyya) in Egypt and appointed his son Babiliyun to govern it, but it is common knowledge that it was built by the ancient Egyptians and its history is well known.

6. Confusion between Tribes and Individuals

This occurs frequently in their histories, though it seldom appears explicitly in what they say. It is most commonly apparent in their accounts of their kings and great men, especially in relation to their lifespans. If they say that someone ruled for 300 years, for example, it is impossible to explain such a statement except by supposing that what is meant is a tribe or subtribe known by that name, ruled by a succession of rulers in the name of their founder or ancestor, who then became conflated.

This is supported by al-Mas'udi's statement that someone asked the giver of the sacred law about Saba, enquiring whether this was a man or a woman, or a valley or a mountain. He replied: "He was a man, who had ten children, four of whom went north and six south. Similar to this is their confusion between different people. Some said that Jarham was Qahtan, others that he was his son, and others something entirely different. And there are other innumerable examples of the same thing."

Summary

Such is the state of the historical sources that we have to use to determine the facts. We hope that we have the means to examine them carefully, and to distinguish between what is true and what is untrue, through comparison and meticulous research. For a statement, even if it is a myth, may yet contain a fact; and we therefore have to use intellectual discrimination and apply our critical judgment to it. We ask God to inspire us with true judgment and lead us in the paths of truth.

Notes

1. Zaydān, "Tārīkh al-'arab qabla 'l-islām."

2. It really should read "non-Arab people" as there could hardly exist any "non-Muslims" in pre-Islamic times. This *lapsus linguae* illustrates, nevertheless, how difficult the creation of a secular Arab identity, separated from religion, was at the time of Zaidan.

3. Muḥammad Ibn Isḥāq (704–767), author of the first biography of the Prophet, the original version of which is lost. But for a reconstruction for the text see A. Guillaume, *The Life of Muhammad* (London: Oxford Univ. Press, 1955).

4. Abū Muḥammad Ibn Hishām (d. 833), most famous for his biography of Muḥammad.

5. Al-Ṭabarī, Abū Ja'far Muḥammad ibn Jarīr (839–923). Universal historian, Koran commentator; author of the multivolume *Mukhtaṣar tārīkh al-rusul wa-'l-mulūk wa-'l-khulafā' (Summary of the History of Prophets, Kings and Caliphs), EI2,* in the late nineteenth century; M.J. de Goeje edited the work in fifteen volumes.

6. 'Imād al-Dīn al-Iṣfahānī (1125–1201), historian who wrote a history of the Seljuks and a biography of Saladin.

7. Abū al-Fidā (1273–1331), historian and geographer; author of a universal history and a survey of geography.

8. Nūḥ: the biblical Noah.

9. The biblical queen of Sheeba.

10. Azdeshir Bahman; probably meant is Ardeshir I (208–240 C.E.), founder of the Sassanid dynasty, who established himself as Shahinshah in 226 C.E.; he traced his lineage to a mythical Bahman, sometimes identified with Darius III (4th century B.C.) of the Achaemenids.

11. Cyrus the Great or Cyrus II (r. 600 or 576–530 B.C.); see also Esra I:1–11.

◆ ◆ ◆

The Himyarite Kings and Ibn Khaldun

Translated by Paul Starkey

[In response to a question from Shaykh Milad Ahmad al-Tarabulsi al-Azhari]

Al-Hilal: We are pleased that writers and students are starting to research historical facts and to criticize the classical texts, because most of them contain exaggerations, especially in relation to ancient history.[1] It is a good thing for you to have quoted Ibn Khaldun, because he was a critical and precise thinker. *Al-Hilal*, however, was not asserting the correctness of what he said, but simply quoting it in spite of its weaknesses. The truth about this question is obscure, because the ruins of that state are hidden under the sands. It is actually our belief that if those remains were to be excavated, they would confirm as fact much of what we reckon to be myth.

Then again, we should not rely on Ibn Khaldun to completely deny the truth of that assertion, because in this matter he is in the same position as other, later historians. Like them he also lived a long time after the period of the Tubba',[2] whose history had been obliterated many generations before his own time. Historians of this period may be more qualified than he to express an opinion on these matters in view of the historical discoveries made in their time, as well as the reading of inscriptions and remains that Ibn Khaldun and his contemporaries would have regarded as mere talismans; they also would have believed the deciphering of such ruins to be impossible.

As for Ibn Khaldun's idea that the conquest of Africa at the hands of the Tubba' would have been impossible, we do not find the reasons he gives convincing. For the Tubba' could have crossed the isthmus of Suez in a period different from the period of the Amelikites—the sultan of the Amelikites cannot be assigned to a particular period—and, in any event, what would there have been to stop the Amelikites opening a path for them or assisting them, if they were related to them in both ancestry and language? The Egyptians themselves acknowledged that they were subject to a Semitic state that they termed the "Shepherd State." Some historians today think that this was the Tubba' kingdom; others think that it refers to the Amelikites, the 'Adites, and so on. A similar sort of thing might be said about their conquest of Turkey, Persia, or Soghdia. Although we cannot definitely assert the accuracy of those statements because of the lack of convincing evidence, we consider them among the possibilities to be investigated. And there is no way to investigate them except by excavating their remains in Yemen and Hadramawt—and that is impossible except with the support of the Ottoman state.

As for the stories of the Arab historians, we have got used to deriding them because of the exaggerations that permeate them. We do not read anything in these accounts without holding it in contempt, having already made up our minds to disbelieve it. We do not deny that their statements are exaggerated, or that their stories are full of fantasy, but they may point to facts that become clear between the lines, so to speak, and which are not difficult for the expert to understand. Such is the Arabs' statement, for example, about Iram of the Pillars, said to have been built by Shaddad ibn 'Ad[3] in Ahqaf, over an area of ten parasangs[4] by ten. He was said to have made its walls of onyx from Yemen, covered with plates of silver mixed with gold, and inside the city he built a hundred thousand palaces, each palace on pillars of chrysolite and rubies. Each pillar was a hundred cubits high, and in the middle of them he made rivers flow, which he made into streams flowing to the palaces. He made pebbles of gold, jewels, and the like, things beyond all possibility. But whatever is said to denigrate this account, it reveals a truth—at the very least, that the 'Adites built a great city whose buildings were inlaid on some of their walls and columns with precious stones. That is supported by statements of the Greek and Roman historians about the wealth of precious stones in Yemen in ancient times.

There are other ancient stories of a similar kind. The classical Greeks regarded the historical facts contained in Homer's *Iliad* with skepticism, until the archaeological evidence was discovered more than twenty centuries after the time of Homer. We now regard our historians' statements about long-lost tribes and the Tubba' states as a sort of fantasy, but if they excavated the sands of Ahqaf they would discover the remains of the kingdom of 'Ad, just as they found the ruins of Assyria and Babylon in the soil of Iraq. Perhaps they would even find among the ruins of their cities writing like they found in the ruins of Assyria, and they would discover historical facts like those revealed by the remains of Assyria and Babylon. Among these, they discovered buildings and idols that astounded the intellect, in addition to the books inscribed on bricks that they found amid the store rooms. The last of the book stores they discovered was a library whose books may be numbered in the tens of thousands and contain priceless historical treasures. If it had been suggested to people of previous centuries that it would be possible to discover treasures like this in the Iraqi desert, they would have denied it and declared it impossible.

It is no objection that the Torah recorded the greatness of the Assyrians and Babylonians but not that of the Tubba'. For the Torah only concerned itself with matters connected with the history of the Israelites. If the Assyrians had not been mentioned in the Torah, our judgment on the accounts of their science, conquests, and wealth that have been handed down to us would be similar to our judgment on the Tubba'. For at the beginning of the last century the sites in Assyria provided no more evidence than the archaeological remains in Yemen today.

The ruins of the Tubba' cities, however, are not accessible to archaeological societies because of the dangers to which they would be exposed from attacks by Bedouins and highwaymen. Europeans have tried to survey these areas in the same way as they surveyed other ancient sites, but they have failed. The last society to apply itself to this aim was formed several years ago, headed by the famous Orientalist Count Landberg.[5] The expedition traveled to Aden under his leadership, but he was then immediately forced to return for fear of his life and the lives of his colleagues. Had it not been for that, they would have discovered for us the ruins of the Tubba'—just as others rediscovered the Nabataean kingdom, an Arab kingdom contemporary with the final stages of the Tubba' dynasty. Yet others rediscovered the remains of the kingdom of Thamud in Mada'in Salih, which is Hajar. Thamud was a lost tribe, like that of 'Ad. Explorers discovered the remains of temples and palaces in that area, with inscriptions in Nabataean, Himyarite, or similar scripts. People still expect to uncover evidence for the stories of Salih and his people, accounts of which have reached us through religious remains or unbroken historical traditions.

To sum up, the strange nature of the accounts of the Tubba' kings and other ancient Arabs does not give us a license to reject them entirely, but rather invites us to examine them and draw rational conclusions from them. Why should it be odd for the Tubba' to go out to raid Africa, Egypt, or Persia, in the same way as Ramses II raided Syria and Iraq around the fourteenth century B.C.? The accounts of Ramses' raids and wars were disputed until people discovered support for them among the Egyptian sites. Alexander's conquests were of a similar kind: he came from Macedonia, and swept through Egypt, Syria, Iraq, and Persia to India in the fourth century B.C. . Had it not been for the written records left by the Greeks, his story would have been like the story of Tabban As'ad Abu Karab and others. Many other examples could be added from the stories of the ancient kings of Egypt, Babylon, Assyria, Yemen, and other places, some recorded in the Torah and others not.

Notes

1. "al-Ṭabābi'a wa-'bn Khaldūn," *al-Hilāl* 15 (May 1902): 504–8. The Ṭubba' (pl. Ṭabābi'a) refers to the Himyarite rulers who controlled all of southwest Arabia between the third and early sixth centuries B.C. The reader Shaykh Milad Ahmad al-Tarabulsi introduces himself as an amateur historian, interested in the history of the Arabs before Islam, in particular the Tubba'. Confused by the contradictions and improbabilities about the period in the accounts of Muslim historians, he read Ibn Khaldun, who dismisses all the historians writings' as untrue. The reader now turns to Zaidan for clarification, because he is the most knowledgeable scholar about the period.

2. The early Muslim historians considered the term "Tubba'" to be a title; more likely it was a dynasty that ruled after vanquishing the Sabaeans in Yemen around 300 A.D.

3. The 'Ād (pl. 'Adites) are an ancient tribe mentioned frequently in the Koran. Their identity is not clearly established.

4. The reported length of a Parasang, in Persian *farsank,* varies greatly in antiquity. It could be also considerably less than 12,000 human steps.

5. Carlo Landberg (1848–1924) was a Swedish Arabist.

◆ ◆ ◆

Kinship among the Ancient Arabs

A Response to Those Who Argue in Favor of Matriarchy and Totemism among the Pre-Islamic Arabs

Translated by Paul Starkey

Our friend,[1] the great British Orientalist Professor Margoliouth,[2] wrote to us as follows while translating our book *The History of Islamic Civilization* into English:

> There is a considerable gap between what is stated in your book about the genealogies of the Arabs and the views of Orientalists on this matter. If you look at Professor Robertson Smith's book on *Kinship and Marriage in Early Arabia*,[3] you will see that there is a great difference between our well-known views on the subject and what is stated in your own book. The question of matriarchy, for example, has been the subject of numerous volumes, most of whose authors have taken the view that the ancient family did not have any father known as such, but was headed by a mother who had many partners. The rights of fatherhood were an innovation introduced among the Arabs rather later, certainly not much before the time of the Prophet, and the Arab genealogies are all spurious, since the names of the tribes are not names of men who actually lived, as is stated, but are rather, at least for the most part, what are known as "totems" among uncivilized peoples—that is, animals to whom they relate themselves, because they do not understand how nature is organized. From these relationships laws and customs were derived, some of whose survivals are evident among the pre-Islamic Arabs.

Such is the text of the professor's letter. We have examined it carefully, as befits the status of its author, and consulted Robertson Smith's book referred to, which extends to over three hundred pages. We have studied these at length, wanting to acquaint ourselves with those views, because the author is a great Orientalist, and both he and his research writings—those on Semitic religion and other brilliant articles—carry considerable weight in the East. We read his book carefully in the hope of being persuaded of the correctness of this view, since our only aim in what we write is to establish the truth. This is the objective we seek, and if we attain it, we will stand humbly before it; it will be irrelevant whose help we might have had to achieve it. From studying the book, we established how vast a knowledge the man had and how well researched he was in the peoples, languages, and religions of the Semites. Through the evidence of the book, and the strength of the arguments therein, we perceived a conviction and strength of argument that is rare among writers. Indeed, had it not been for that, given the weakness of the view he had taken upon himself to prove, he would not have been able to find a hearing among the best Orientalist researchers, among whom is my friend Professor Margoliouth. Margoliouth's conviction was apparent in the preface to his important book recently published on the life of the Prophet, titled *Mohammed and the Rise of Islam*. However, the professor simply supported the author's view without examining it critically, on the basis of the wide learning for which he is famous. If he had done so, we do not think that he could have had any different feeling from our own, namely, that [Robertson Smith] was mistaken. We shall clarify this in what follows. Perhaps we are just as deluded as he is, for only God is blameless. Nevertheless, I intend to write something on this subject that may be put to the Orientalists. We do not claim to be infallible. It will be enough if the correct points in our remarks outnumber the false ones; even if the opposite is the case, the research may still be useful.

As we shall also be publishing this letter in Arabic, to be read by a group of readers including some still ignorant about matriarchy, totemism, and other new research seldom touched on by Arab writers, we have thought it appropriate to preface our article with a short introduction about the meaning of these terms before proceeding to the subject proper.

1. Totemism among Primitive Tribes Today

"Totem"[4] is a term that entered European languages at the end of the eighteenth century from the American Indian Ojwibi[5] language. It refers to beings revered by certain primitive tribes, each member of the tribe believing that he is related to one of those [beings]. He calls this his totem; and this may be an animal, a plant, or something else. The totem protects him, and he in turn reveres or worships it. If it is an animal, he will not kill it, and if it is a plant, he will not pull it up or eat it. Totemism is different from the worship of animals and plants that is common among certain tribes described as "fetishists." That means worship of an idol in the form of an animal, while totemism means revering and worshipping a certain type of animal or plant.

Totems, in relation to all tribes, are of three classes. The first is the tribal totem, which is public. Everyone participates in respecting it, and it is part of a common heritage. The second is the gender totem, revered by the individuals of one sex in particular, either males or females. It is therefore confined either to the women or the men of the tribe. The third is the personal totem, respect for which is confined to a single individual, and is not passed on to his sons. The first kind is the most significant, and we shall make it the focus of our article.

Tribal Totems

A tribal totem is an animal, plant, or something similar, which is worshipped or revered by every member of a particular tribe. They adopt its name and believe that it was their oldest ancestor, that they are of one blood, and that they are linked by mutual covenants that go back to it. It has two meanings or aspects for them, one religious and the other social. By the religious is meant the mutual relationship between the man and his totem: the man reveres the totem, and the totem protects the man and keeps him safe. As for the social aspect, this consists of the mutual rights between the individuals of that tribe, who are united under the name of that totem, in relation to other tribes, who are linked to other totems. In many cases, these two aspects may differ.

From a religious point of view, the totem may be considered the father of the tribe. The tribe is descended from it, and every tribe has a mythical narrative about its own totem, which they pass on from one generation to another. Most commonly, the focus will be on the method of transmitting it from the animal or plant kingdom to mankind. Among the Iroquois American Indians there is a tribe known as the Tortoise tribe. Its members believe that they are descended from a fat tortoise that found its shell too heavy, so it threw it off its back, and then turned into a man that fathered sons. Then there is the Snail tribe, who believe that they are linked to a snail and a female beaver.[6] A male snail discarded its shell, sprouted two hands, two feet, and a head, and changed into a tall, handsome man, and married the female beaver, through whom he fathered this tribe. In addition, there are tribes related to ducks, geese, and other water birds. In Sénègambie[7] there are tribes related to the unicorn, the hippopotamus, the scorpion, and the snake. All of these animals are considered to be tribal totems, and the tribes are called by their names. The tribes revere and hallow them, and do not harm or kill them. The Duck tribe, for example, will not harm this bird, or kill it, unless a tribe member is consumed by hunger, when he will eat the duck reluctantly, pleading for forgiveness. In the same way, if the totem is a plant, they revere it and avoid trampling on it or eating it. So if someone's totem is wheat, for example, it is forbidden for him to eat it, and if his totem is a tree, it is forbidden for him to burn its branches.

Their respect for the totem is not confined to forbidding them from eating it or harming it. Some people forbid touching it or looking at it. The Stag tribe of the Ohama will not eat the flesh of a stag or refer to a stag; the Gazelle Head tribe will never touch the hide of a gazelle, and may forbid mention of the name of the totem. If they are forced to refer to it, they may resort to metaphor or allusion. Among the Delaware American Indians there is a tribe related to the wolf, another to the tortoise, and another to the turkey. If they are forced to mention one of them, they will use the term "round foot" for the first, "crawler" for the second, and "swallower" for the third. The tribes referred to are themselves known by these metaphorical expressions.

If an animal belonging to the tribe's totem dies, the people celebrate its burial and grieve for it as they would grieve for one of their own. If a man from the Owl tribe in Samoa finds a dead owl, he will sit beside it and start to cry and utter lamentations, striking his forehead with rocks until he makes it bleed. Then he will wrap the owl and take it to the cemetery as if it were one of the members of the tribe. They believe that anyone insulting or harming the totem will be struck down by misfortune, though their precise beliefs vary from tribe to tribe and region to region. Some believe that if anyone eats the totem, the women of the tribe will become infertile, while others believe that they will be struck down by disease, misfortune, or the like. Others imagine that if anyone eats the totem he will be punished by death—the totem staying in his body and continuing to consume it until he dies.

On the other hand, it is believed that the totem will not harm anyone associated with it. For example, people whose totem is a snake are not afraid of snakebites, and believe that snakes will not bite them. Similarly, the Scorpion tribes in Sénègambie believe that poisonous scorpions will cross over their bodies without harming them. The Wolf tribe's beliefs are similar. They often use this as a kinship test for someone who claims to be related to them. So if someone declares that he belongs to the Snake tribe, they will set a snake loose on him, and if it bites him, they will say that he is a deceitful pretender. On this basis, if the totem does not show someone respect and avoid harming him, the tribe will disown him.

However, they are not satisfied that a totem should avoid harming those associated with it or its worshippers. They expect it to bring benefits to them and defend them. The Wolf tribe believes that the wolf will defend it on the battlefield, and most people associated with the totem believe that the totem will warn its adherents of danger before it occurs, through signs or symbols, in the same way as such things are expressed through omens or birds.

One way of drawing closer to the totem, and to seek its favor and protection, is to imitate it in terms of its outward appearance. One may wear its skin or a part of its skin, or take a piece of it to wear around the neck or arm like amulets among other peoples, so that no one is without a charm indicating his relation to a totem.

Among their customs that indicate that they regard themselves as descended from a totem are the celebrations that they hold on occasions such as births, marriages, deaths, and the like. The Red Gazelle tribe, for example, daub a child's back with red when it is born, and if it is from the Wolf tribe, they shout "We have got a little wolf" at its birth and sew into the child's shirt a piece of the wolf's eye or heart. If someone from the Red Dog tribe in Java gets married, they will daub the bride and groom with the ashes of a red dog. The Wolf tribes' beliefs are similar.

As for the sexual totem, this means designating a special totem for either the males or the females of the tribe. Among some tribes in Australia, the males have a totem and the females a totem, both being different from the tribe's totem. The same holds good for the personal totem, for a man may have a special totem, different from the tribe's totem and different from the sexual totem.

From a social point of view, the tribe's totem denotes the cohesion of the tribal members with regard to its relationship to other tribes. The adherents of a single totem are considered as brothers and sisters who collaborate both in good times and in bad, through ties that are stronger than those between family members today. A man may marry a woman from a different tribe and a different totem, and the children may grow up with a different totem, but if war breaks out, the people of one totem will cooperate against the people of the other totem, so that a man may be separated from his wife, and a son from his father or mother.

It is one of the conditions of the totemic system that men of one totem should not marry women of their tribe, nor should women marry men from it. This is what anthropologists call exogamy. Followers of totemism believe that marriage within the same tribe is so harmful to health as to destroy the bones, and they sentence those who embark on it to death or painful punishment. For this reason they take women from other tribes through raids, persuasion, or similar means. Children generally inherit their mother's totem rather than their father's, so kinship is generally through the mother rather than the father, as is generally the custom with us.

The tribe may split into subdivisions of various kinds, related to animal or plant ancestors with a subsidiary relationship among themselves, just as animals can be divided into species and within species into subspecies; or there may be some other relationship between the tribal totem and the branch totems. So the tribe totem might be an animal, and the branch totem might be a plant, eaten by the same animal in a way that cannot be explained here.

Totemism is widespread today in the world of savages. It is the norm among the tribes of Australia, widespread in North America and in Panama, the most widespread totem there being the parrot. South America also retains traces of totemism, on the borders of Colombia and Venezuela, and in Guyana and Peru. Totemism is also of great importance in Africa, for it is widespread in Sénègambie, among the Bagali tribes on the equator and on the Gold Coast, among the Ashanti, among the Damariya and Bakwaniya in southern Africa, and in many other places in the Dark Continent. There are traces of it in Madagascar and some islands of the Maldives. In Asia, there are traces of it among the central Indies, among some of the non-Aryan Bengali tribes, in Siberia and parts of China, and on the Oceanic islands. Most of these tribes have been included by experts under totemism by analogy, because the people revere certain animals or plants, even though they do not take their names.

Summary

Totemism may be summarized as follows:

1. It is widespread today among peoples steeped in savagery.

2. Its basis is that a tribe takes an animal or plant, or some other tangible creature, as an ancestor with whom it believes itself to be linked, and after whom it is named.

3. Every tribe worships or reveres its own totem.

4. Every tribe believes that its totem protects it or defends it, or at least will not harm it, even if it is in the totem's nature to cause harm.

5. Marriage is forbidden between people of a single totem, the basis of procreation among them being through marriage with members of other totems (exogamy).

6. Patriarchy is unknown among them, the basis of kinship being matriarchal.

7. The family has no significance for them, kinship extending only to the totem. Those belonging to a single totem are brothers and sisters, united by one blood.

Origin of This Theory

The theory of totemism in regard to the social system is modern. The first person to articulate it was the British sociologist Dr. McLennan, who died in 1881. He wrote a book on the subject titled *Primitive Marriage*, first published in 1865, and then wrote several more books on the subject and its branches, in which he expounded the origin of his view and the principles on which he based his theory of totemism. No sooner had he published his views than he was criticized by other sociologists, led by the philosopher Spencer and the famous sociologist Sir John Lubbock—particularly the former, who criticized this view at length in his book *The Principles of Civilization* and other writings. We cannot discuss these here, however, for we are concerned solely with the topic at hand, without regard to the correctness or otherwise of this theory; rather, we are investigating what Professor Robertson Smith intended by applying it to the pre-Islamic Arabs.

Smith's View of Arab Totemism

Smith considers that during their earliest period the Arabs traced themselves back to animal and plant ancestors, which they revered and worshipped, and whose names they adopted. In marriage, matriarchy, and other things, their practice was similar to that of uncivilized tribes in Australia, America, and Africa. The general belief that the Arabs could trace their ancestry back to the patriarchs of the Torah, including Isma'il and Qahtan, and that the tribes were linked as commonly understood, was something invented by propagandists at a subsequent date, as late as the first century of the hijra; it was based on the *Diwan* of Imam 'Umar ibn al-Khattab.[8]

In support of this view, he begins by trying to establish the principle of matriarchy among the Arabs, saying that the Arabs in ancient times did not have a family headed by a father, nor were their genealogies established through the father. On the contrary, marriage among them was similar to that in Tibet today. In this so-called Tibetan marriage, a woman marries two or more men, and her children are not related to any one of them but belong to the tribe and are called after its totem, as previously explained. He first tries to adduce proofs to establish that matriarchy was widespread among the ancient Arabs, and when he considers that he has established this, he proceeds to try to prove the existence of totemism, spending an enormous amount of energy in deriving proofs and evidence, which we shall explain, and whose falsity we shall demonstrate.

2. The Ancient Arabs: Their Genealogies and Histories

Before proceeding to investigate Professor Smith's evidence, we shall give a general account of the Arabs, and of their genealogies and history, as background to the investigation.

Anyone investigating the views of this Orientalist advocate of totemism among the Arabs and his supporters will immediately realize that they have been persuaded to adopt these views by two things: first, their lack of trust in the statements of the Arab historians and the ancient stories that they preserved; and second, the enthusiasm of people during the last century for challenging well-established views about the progressive development of the basis of civilization. The spread of that viewpoint in the middle of the century persuaded European writers to attribute everything to natural causes, as Spencer did in attributing religion and most customs to such things. This was also the case for the advocate of Arab totemism. He looked at what Maclennan had written about totemism among savage tribes as an Orientalist well acquainted with the history of the Arabs, but with an unfavorable view of their pre-Islamic past, and contempt for the statements of their storytellers and genealogists. Among the names of the tribes' and subtribes' ancestors, he saw similarities to animal names that he had already imagined must represent the traces of totemism among them. He put this conclusion in front of his eyes and took it upon himself to prove it. And since totemism was based on matriarchy, he sought to prove this, producing some weak evidence, contrived in the extreme, then sought further proof from episodes in Arab history. He turned the exceptional into a principle, while ignoring the established general principles agreed on by the genealogists and storytellers that contradicted the basis of his study. This is strange for an intellectual who had studied the history and myths of many peoples and knew that most ancient history was derived from myths handed down by ancestors, who had purified it of falsehoods and sifted the true from the false, but certainly did not despise myth or deny hearsay. The stories and myths of the gods in Homer's *Iliad* did not stop scholars from examining it closely and distinguishing between the history, religion, and myth in it. The same can be said of the stories of the ancient Indians since the time when a group of Aryans arrived in India, as recorded in their Sanskrit books. The same must also be said of the myths of the Arabs—the stories of 'Ad and Thamud, Tasm and Jadis, the tales of the Great Flood, and so on. Despite seeming farfetched to us, they are not devoid of significant historical facts and the accuracy of many has been revealed with time. We shall quote some small parts of these by way of example:

'Ad and Thamud

The most deeply rooted myths of the Arabs in antiquity, and the ones that seem most farfetched to us, are the stories about the "bygone" Arabs. Until recently, researchers regarded these as myths invented just before Islam, while others thought that they belonged to some other peoples and that the Arabs had memorized them and attributed them to themselves. Then, on the basis of the accounts that people had discovered in the writings of the ancient Greek historians and geographers, such as Strabo, Ptolemy, and others, it became clear that these stories actually contained some solid facts. The most important of the "bygone" Arab tribes were 'Ad and Thamud. It used to be thought that 'Ad was not mentioned in the books of the Greeks, because people had not found any term like it among the names of the Arab tribes, but in an article we wrote on this subject[9] we showed that they mentioned the tribe under the name 'Ad Iram, which they wrote as "Adramitae," to distinguish it from the Hadramawt, which they knew under the name "Xatramotitae." We postulated there it was most likely that this was the same tribe as the tribe of Haduram mentioned in the Torah as being among the Arabs living in the Yemen.

As for Thamud, this tribe was referred to many times in Greek and Roman books. People had already found archaeological sites in the uplands of the Hejaz and deciphered some of the rock inscriptions. Nonetheless, they did not reckon that its history extended back much before the Christian era, until archaeologists found it mentioned in the ruins of Assyria of about the eighth century B.C. in an exposition of reports of wars and conquests. This shows that that tribe was of some significance at that period. In addition to that, there are other accounts of the "bygone" tribes that have been lost over time, or their names have been confused by the Greeks through misreading or something similar. This happened to the Jadis tribe, which the Greeks wrote as "Jolisitai." Most likely, so we believe, this started out as "Jodisitae," but the "d" was confused with an "l"; these are similar in Greek, the "l" being written as ⍰ and the "d" as Δ.[10] This is not to mention the texts in the Torah that support the accounts and genealogies of the Arabs, and the discoveries made, and still being made, in Yemen and elsewhere.

The Arab Genealogists

If this is the situation with the myths of the ancient Arabs, how does it apply to the accounts recorded in books, on which the genealogists in the early period of Islam agreed? The storytellers at that time would not accept a story unless it had been closely checked against a sound chain of transmission. This was because they were accustomed to examine critically the *ḥadīths* of the Prophet and other religious stories at that period. The Arabs may be reckoned as being among the most critical of peoples in regard to storytelling, and among the most precise in memorizing what they recite, especially in the early period of Islam. This was because, for reasons explained in the third part of our book *History of Islamic Civilization,* they relied on memory and ignored writing.

We do not deny that those stories are permeated with invented, disputed, or unbelievable material, but it makes no sense that they should *all* have been made up, since a conspiracy could not be so extensive. And even if we could believe in such a conspiracy, we would have to ask about the time at which it occurred: Was it before or after Islam? If the reply is "before Islam," then what prompted it? We know of no reason for it, and we do not think that the proponent of Arab totemism knows either. Smith, however, would reply "after Islam"—for he stated that the Arab genealogists drew up the genealogies in the early period of Islam, and divided the tribes between the descendants of Qahtan and 'Adnan, before dividing each of these into subgroups, the purpose of this division being to clarify the rights of the tribes in relation to the tribute imposed by 'Umar. But how could that be possible, when we have poems, compositions, proverbs, and tales of the pre-Islamic Arabs, all testifying that they had preserved their genealogies and were careful to trace them back to their ancestors, Qahtan and 'Adnan? Indeed, how could this be said, when Islam, from the time of its appearance to the period of expansion, was built on the Qahtani and 'Adnani lineage, and the caliphs encouraged the Muslims to preserve their genealogies and to investigate them carefully? Among the sayings of the caliph 'Umar was this: "Study genealogy and do not be like the rural Nabataeans. If one of them is asked about his roots, he says that he is from such-and-such a village."[11]

If we suppose that he is right and that the genealogists drew up these genealogies at the beginning of Islam for purposes of tribute, how could the tribes that the genealogists put at a distance from the family of the Prophet have been content with this? They would certainly have received less tribute, or their rights would have been weakened. How could they have failed to protest against that, and how could a whiff of that protest fail to be detected in the words of the historians? But in fact, a conspiracy of genealogists when drawing up the genealogies is unlikely, because they did not actually produce anything themselves but rather went around the desert, collecting the genealogies from oral tradition, then writing them down or memorizing them. A genealogist might collect his information from the people of Najd, Hejaz, and Yemen by asking trusted people in those far-flung places: How could a conspiracy be possible in those circumstances?

The Shu'ubiyya[12] *and Arab Genealogy*

If we admit the possibility that the Arabs did not raise any objection out of respect for the caliph or fear of him, how could the Shu'ubiyya, especially the Persians, have remained silent about this difference from the proud Arab lineage on which the Arabs prided themselves? The non-Arabs would have looked for an argument to put forward for having the Arab nobility extended to them by virtue of being descended from Isma'il and Qahtan. In the early days of Islam, some Persians had called the Arabs descendants of barbarians, and said: "They are like ravenous wolves, and uncouth beasts, eating each other out of jealousy for each other. Their men are bound in the throat of captivity, and their women are slaves, riding on camel litters."[13]

But no one cast aspersions on their lineage either by allusion or through deliberate manipulation, whereas if they had been able to, that would have been their strongest sort of revenge. It cannot be said that they remained silent about it through oversight, or that they simply turned a blind eye to it, because they certainly attacked the Arabs for their different descent and for proselytizing to them, as well as other things connected with genealogy. Buhayr Ya'ir al-'Arab said, in relation to proselytizing:

> You claimed that the Indians were descendants of Khandaf,
> when you yourselves are related to barbarians
> And that Daylam was of the stock of Ibn Dabba Basil
> and that Burjan was a descendant of 'Umar ibn 'Amir
> The Banu al-Asfar al-Amlak are more noble than you
> and the kings of Khosrow are more worthy of our kinship
> Do you want my son-in-law, a loud-mouthed missionary
> without having seen protection from such a one?
> You loudly curse his friends and tribe
> and praise a pure but ignorant man, the son of
> another blameless man. [14]

Despite that, they did not raise objections either to the truth or falsity of their genealogies. The Persian nation had reached the height of its civilization several centuries before Islam. The Arabs had migrated toward them, lived amongst them, and engaged with them in wars and disputes in the pre-Islamic period. Shortly before Islam, the Persians had taken control of Yemen, had settled among the Arabs, and lived among them and mixed with them. They were bound to have known their ways better than anyone else during the pre-Islamic period. If the Arabs had found any reason to doubt the correctness of their genealogies and remained silent, they would have certainly started to take their revenge on the Persians [for that] since the beginning of the first Islamic century. Even stranger is that most of the genealogists themselves were of non-Arab origin; how could they draw up something that could be used as a weapon against them in the hands of their enemies?

Discrepancies in Certain Genealogies

All the information we have about the Arabs depends on the arrangement of their genealogies according to the records in their books or as recited in their poetry. We do not have anything in the way of texts or references to contradict that arrangement, so how can we reject it? There is nothing in what our colleague says about the differences between some genealogists concerning the descent of certain tribes from Qahtan, 'Adnan, Qays, or Kalb, because as we have already explained, ancestry was originally derived from oral tradition in different regions, and "mankind" is a byword for mistakes. It is not unlikely that 'Umar ibn al-Khattab's system, and the imposition of tribute on the basis of lineage, should have made some confusion inevitable, with certain subtribes being related to the wrong main tribes. However, when the genealogists investigated the matter, they distinguished the true from the false as far as they were able. In any case, the existence of such discrepancies does not fundamentally invalidate the principle of genealogy, just as discrepancies between storytellers on the details of a historical event do not prove that it did not happen. If a group had a dispute about 'Amr ibn al-'As' conquest of Egypt, some saying that he took control of it peacefully, while others said that it was by force, or some saying that he brought 4,000 soldiers, while others said that it was 10,000, and others disagreeing over whether the Arabs came on horses or on camels—would that prove that Egypt was not conquered? And if someone said that, wouldn't you accuse him of making a perverse judgment?

Discrepancies among the genealogists may come about because some tribal names are pronounced similarly but have different meanings. This frequently occurs in genealogies. Some genealogists wrote books on the subject such as the *Book of the Differences and Similarities of Tribes* by Abu Ja'far Muhammad ibn Habib,[15] who died in the middle of the third century A.H., which was printed in Göttingen in A.D. 1850. If you look at the encyclopedias of tribes, you will see a number of tribes with the same name, some being traced back to Qahtan, and others to 'Adnan. There are also subtribes from Yemen and others from Qays. The Banu Asad, for example, are a subtribe of Azad, which in turn is a subtribe of Kahlan, a division of Qahtan. The Banu Asad are also a subdivision of Quda'a from Himyar. The Banu al-Aws are a subdivision of the Azad of Qahtan; but the Banu al-Aws are also a subtribe of 'Adnan. The Banu al-Harith comprise several subtribes of various tribes. The Banu Bakr comprise numerous subtribes, some related to 'Adnan and some to Qahtan. The Banu Thaghlib are a tribe descended from Wa'il ibn Rabi'a related to 'Adnan, but there is also another Banu Thaghlib, a subtribe of Quda'a related to Qahtan. The Banu Tamim from Tangier are descended from 'Adnan, but the Banu Tamim are also a subtribe of Hudhayl, related to 'Adnan. The Banu Tha'laba comprise a dozen or so subtribes of various main tribes.[16] Similarly, the Banu Rabi'a, Banu Salim, Banu 'Amir, Banu 'Adiyy, Banu Ka'b, and so on. One name may be shared by a number of subtribes with different origins. Numerous subtribes are found called Banu Umayya. Among the Quraysh, there is Umayya ibn 'Abd Shams ibn 'Abd Manaf, and Umayya ibn Hadhafa, while among the Ansar there is Umayya ibn Zayd ibn Malik ibn al-Aws; in Tayy there is Umayya ibn 'Adiyy ibn Kinana ibn Malik, and among the Quda'a, Umayya ibn Isba ibn Hasis, and so on.

Tribal names may be written similarly but differ in pronunciation and meaning. An example is Jassas, with a double "s," and Jasas, with a single "s." Usually, the confusion between similar names arises from the shape of the letters, ignoring the dots. That was a great source of confusion in pre-Islamic times and in early Islam. Among the Madhhaj, we find 'Anas (with an *n*) ibn Malik ibn Adad, while among the Ghatfan, we find 'Abas (with one *b*) ibn Baghid; among the Azad we find 'Abas (with a *b*) ibn Hawzan ibn Aslam. Similarly with 'Anza: It is pronounced like this among the Rabi'a, where we find 'Anza ibn Asad ibn Rabi'a ibn Nizar. Among the Khuza'a we find 'Ayra (with a *y*), who is also called 'Anzar. Among the Azad there is 'Antara ibn 'Amr ibn 'Awf ibn 'Adiyy ibn al-Azad, and there is also 'Abra (with a *b*), also known as 'Ubra. There is also Ghayra (with a *gh* and *y* and various vowelizations). The same sort of thing can be seen in 'Anz of

Rabi'a, 'Atr of Rabi'a, and similarly Ghabr, Ajram, Akhzam, Ahram, and so on—all of which are of different origins from the others.

These differences in form or pronunciation created some confusion in tribal genealogies. The same might be said about the small number of ancestors in relation to the time span. The reason for this may be that some ancestors have dropped into oblivion or for some other reason; or that the ancestor may be regarded as a tribe with its head rather than a single individual, as is thought to be the case with some of the Jewish ancestors to be found in the Torah. This is another proof of the antiquity of the genealogies from pre-Islamic times, since if someone had simply made them up at a later date, he would have forged them so completely by exaggerating the number of ancestors in order to remove any suspicion of error. On the contrary, the genealogists did not produce anything themselves, but simply transmitted oral tradition that was widespread among the Arabs, preserved in their minds despite its flaws. In addition, consider that among the basic principles for determining rights was that "Origin is innocent of blame." The principle of Arab genealogies is that they should be considered in the form they have come down to us. It is not open to us to object to them or find fault with them except through something at least as trustworthy as straightforward texts, through comparisons that form an uninterrupted chain, and so forth. But relying on exceptional statements or basing one's conclusions on odd pieces of information, and taking the exceptional as a solid base—one simply cannot rely on that. It is a defective sort of investigation; indeed it is not a proper investigation at all, relying on behavior that is contrary to the principles that are followed in research and criticism. The more correct way to establish a case is to proceed gradually from the particular to the general, so that when the parts are confirmed, the whole is confirmed. As for our colleague, he had (or made up) a theory about the whole matter and tried to prove it; and he has not been lacking in scattered reports and information about the Arabs to use as a basis for constructing the weak edifice that he has so skillfully presented as true.

Professor Robertson Smith, the proponent of Arab totemism, became acquainted with Maclennan's views on the totemism of the American and Australian Indians, saw that some Arab tribes had animal names, found that the Arab genealogists disagreed about the origins of some tribes, and leapt to the conclusion that that they represented the vestiges of totemism, as we have previously explained. So he put forward an overall argument that "The Arabs were totemists." Then he started to search in their books for something to support this assertion. It will not be lost on you that there are indeed some odd stories and conflicting accounts. He chose those that he thought would support his statement and ignored the rest. If it were legitimate to proceed in this fashion in relation to proof and evidence, we would be able to prove any argument we posited, however outlandish. If we wanted to believe that women in the pre-Islamic period enjoyed absolute freedom, and enjoyed as high a status in the social structure as in contemporary America, we would certainly be able to find Arab accounts to support this statement. Conversely, if we said that women were treated like cattle in those times, we could find things to support our assertion. But in researching a question like this, the principle must be that *all* the evidence should be examined, and the most likely conclusion drawn, either unanimously or by a majority. In all their stories, myths, poems, history, and customs, the Arabs have never agreed on anything to the extent that they have agreed on these genealogies. How can this be denied, merely on suspicion? Should what is certain be put aside for what is only doubtful? And should we then adopt to a view, not a whiff of which can be found in the tales or histories of the Arabs or in the histories of the other Semitic peoples?

Then again, those genealogies have come down to us, passed on in a continuous chain from the genealogists to the historians despite their different locations and periods. Despite that, the accounts are usually compatible. How could this compatibility be accounted for, if their basis was not correct? If it is argued that this basis was established after the coming of Islam, the man who posited it must have been very influential, so who do you suppose it could have been? And how could his details have remained hidden, given the large number of enemies of the Arabs at that time?

The fact is that genealogies with the Arabs, as with other Semitic peoples, go back a long way, but the Arabs clung to them more tenaciously because of their nomadic lifestyle and the fact that they had no other community to relate themselves to. They went to such extremes in remembering their genealogies that they preserved the genealogies of their horses for several generations past.[17] If you examine the information we have concerning the genealogists, you will be amazed at their care in memorizing their genealogies and their precision in establishing them. When one of them tried to establish a man's lineage, he would trace it back from his father to his subgroup, then to a larger group until he reached his tribe, or in reverse from the tribe to the individual.

Semitic Peoples

In the introduction to his book *The Religions of the Semites*, and in his second book *Genealogies of the Arabs*,[18] which we are now discussing (p. 178), the proponent of Arab totemism held that the Semites had their origins in the Arabian Peninsula, but then branched out. The Hebrews and the Aramaeans migrated from the Peninsula and established themselves in the countries surrounding it, while the Arabs maintained their nomadic lifestyle there. So those two groups should have maintained their totemic system just as the Arabs did. But the author of that book made no such statement. Moreover, even if he were to take this view, we do not think he would succeed in finding anything to support his argument, even superficially, as he did in the case of Arab totemism. The Jews seldom called themselves by the names of animals, for they had come a long way from such a harsh nomadic existence, and so he would not have found anything in the names of the tribes to support such an assertion. If he had found some names, as Professor Cook did in the article[19] that he published two years ago in the *Jewish Quarterly Review*, such as Kalib, Ya'qub, or 'Awrab—then he should have concluded that these were names of people, not of tribes, and it would not have been right to refer to them in order to prove the existence of totemism.

If he had looked at the matter in an objective manner, leaving aside conjectures and assumptions, he would have seen that these Semitic peoples resembled each other in a very obvious and indisputable way, namely that they were all related to the elders of the Torah. The Arabs' descent from Isma'il and Qahtan is proved by the accounts of the ancestry of the nations in the Torah. It will be clear to anyone that studies the matter that

Arab genealogy is a branch of Semitic genealogy, as was established by George Rawlinson in his book *The Origin of Nation*,[20] and by Edward Glaser in his book *History and Geography of Arabia*.[21] We also have an article on the genealogy of the Arabs,[22] in which we described the genealogies of the "bygone" tribes, as well as surviving tribes, by reference to the Torah and to Arab historians, whose accounts are in agreement with the archaeological remains and the texts of the Greek historians.

Arab genealogies are as well established as the genealogies of the Torah, despite the views expressed by some critical researchers that the names of some of the earlier ancestors actually refer to tribes rather than people. If we dismiss them as worthless, we have nothing else available. Can it be right to ignore these genealogies, which have been established over a span of centuries, and adopt a view that has no basis in Eastern writers' books and is not referred to in their myths, customs, religions, or any of the archaeological remains?

What cannot be ignored is that it is simply wrong to compare the conditions and genealogies of the Arabs with those of the barbarous totemic peoples of India, Australia, and America, or with the African negroes, because the Arabs were one of the most advanced peoples intellectually and psychologically—a people with an ancient civilization like that of the most advanced of the ancient peoples. Some researchers working on the antiquities of Yemen and the Hadramawt have taken the view that ancient Arab civilization was the source of the ancient Egyptian civilization, that is, that the Pharaohs borrowed their civilization from Yemen. However correct or incorrect that assertion may be, it does indicate that the Arabs had enjoyed civilization for thousands of years. Even if we ignore the fact that their language was advanced in its structure and expressions—which testifies to the advanced intellects of the people themselves during and before the earliest period of history—does it make sense that they should have traced their ancestors back to plants and animals, like the most primitive peoples of today? The theory of totemism is strange enough in itself, for it is difficult to believe in its existence even among primitive peoples, and we suspect that the theory may be based on defective research. [. . .][23]

Notes

1. Zaydān, "Ansāb al-'arab al-qudamā'," 337–43 and 393–401.

2. David Samuel Margoliouth (1858–1940) taught at Oxford. He translated the fourth volume of Zaidan's *Tārīkh al-tamaddun al-islāmī* into English; see the General Bibliography on Jurji Zaidan and His Works in this volume.

3. William Robertson Smith, *Kinship and Marriage in Early Arabia* (Cambridge: Cambridge Univ. Press, 1885).

4. The word is written in Latin letters in the text.

5. A language of the Algonquian linguistic family; also known as Chippewa.

6. *Jund bādester; bādester* means "beaver" in Persian; *jund bādester* is Castoreum (penetrating smelling substance from the sex glands of the beaver, used in perfumes). Sir James W. Redhouse, *A Turkish and English Lexicon* (Constantinople: A. H. Boyajian,1890).

7. *Sīnghambiyā* or *Sīnīghāmbiyā* (Fr., *La Sénègambie*); African region including Senegal and Gambia. See *al-Munjid fī 'l-lugha* (Beirut: al-Maṭba' al-Kāthūlikiyya, 1969). The term was briefly revived during the 1980s, when both countries joined in a federation: *Le Petit Larousse* (Paris: Larousse, 2002).

8. Smith, *Kinship*, 6; for the issue of totemism in national history see chapter VII.

9. "al-'Ād wa-tārīkhuhum wa-mulūkuhum wa-diyānātuhum wa-lughatuhum." *Al-Hilāl* 6 (Aug. 1898): 889–98.

10. Eduard Glaser, *Skizze der Geschichte und Geographie Arabiens von der ältesten Zeit bis zum Propheten Muhammad nebst einem Anhang zur Beleuchtung der Geschichte Abessiniens*, 2 vols. (Berlin: Weidmannsche Buchhandlung, 1890), 2:259. The reference to Glaser's book appears in Arabic text, without linking it to a specific word. The relevant passage about the "Jolisitai" is on 282.

11. Ibn Khaldūn, 1:109 [footnote in original text]. Rosenthal, *The Muqaddima*,1:266.

12. *Shu'ūbiyya*: "A movement in early Islam that denied any privileged position of the Arabs," *EI2*; the causes for its development and meaning are still much debated.

13. Zaydān, *Tārīkh al-tamaddun*, 135 [footnote in original text].

14. Ibn Abī Rabbih (860–940), *al-'Iqd al-farīd*, 71 [footnote in text]; see also Ibn Abī Rabbih, *al-'Iqd al-farīd*, trans. Issa J. Boullata, *The Unique Necklace* (Reading, UK: Garnet, 2006).

15. Muḥammad ibn Ḥabīb (d. 860) *mawla* of Abū Ja'far al-Baghdādī; author of books on genealogy, literature, language, and poetry; the book referred to is *Mukhtalif al-qabā'il wa-mu'talifuhā*: Ziriklī, 6:307; reprint, Beirut, Dār al-Kutub al-Islāmiyya, 1981.

16. *Nihāyat al-arab fī qabā'il al-'arab*, manuscript [footnote in original text]. It was also available in print: Aḥmad 'Ali Aḥmad al-Qalqashandī (1356–1418), *Nihāyat al-arab fī ma'ārifat qabā'il al-'arab* (Alexandria: Sarkis, 1871): Nuṣayr, 245.

17. *al-Mubarrad al-kāmil*, 454 [footnote in original text]: Muḥammad ibn Yazīd al-Mubarrad, (826–899), *al-Kāmil al-mubarrad* (Cairo: s.n., 1920); Ziriklī, 8:15.

18. W. R. Smith, *Lectures on the Religion of the Semites* (London: A. & C. Black, 1884). With the second is meant his *Kinship and Marriage in Early Arabia*.

19. Stanley A. Cook, "Notes on the Old Testament History," *Jewish Quarterly Review* 17 (1905): 782–99, 788. In vol. 16 of the journal "two years ago" there are eight entries by Cook, mainly book reviews and one about his own work, but neither seems relevant to the point Zaidan makes.

20. George Rawlinson, *The Origin of Nations: On Early Civilizations, on Ethnic Affinities*, 2 vols. (London: Religious Tract Society, 1877).

21. Glaser, *Skizze der Geschichte*, vol. 2, 266 and 421. [This source as well as the *Jewish Quarterly Review* appear in Latin letters as footnotes in the original text.] In the 1890 edition of Glaser's work the relevant chapters are 27 to 29, 404–45.

22. "Nasab al-'arab qabla 'l-islām," *al-Hilāl* 5 (June 1897): 768–78.

23. The article then continues with a debate about matriarchy.

◆ ◆ ◆

The Pre-Islamic Arabs

Translated by Paul Starkey

Preface: The Obscurity of Arab History

The history of the pre-Islamic Arabs continues to be a subject that readers demand, but it is has been a stumbling block for writers from the dawn of Islam until today.[1] Its obscurity and sterile nature have prevented it from being told properly, and the extent of this obscurity becomes particularly apparent to anyone who wants to delve deeply into it and ascertain the truth. Those who do not may simply be concerned to gather together what has been said, despite its deficiencies, without asking about the contradictions and inconsistencies contained therein, even if they are contrary to reason, tradition, and custom. Such has been the case with most of those who have dabbled in the subject since things were first recorded in the Arabic language. Among the hundreds of historians and tellers of tales about the founding of Arab civilization, we do not know of a single one who devoted a special book to this subject, as will be explained in detail in the introduction that follows this preface.

Until very recently, this history remained a collection of odd tales, myth, and exaggeration, passed on from generation to generation without critical examination, becoming more confused and obscure with each transmission. They became even more so in the course of the Middle Ages, in the wake of the deterioration of the Arabs' status and the disappearance of their empire. They [the Arabs] wanted to conceal their weakness with stories of their forefathers, so they resorted to boasting of their conquering ancestors and the Arab virtues they exhibited: they exaggerated their tales or collected and propagated them without correction or precision. Fantasies became more common than facts and anything true disappeared, concealed by falsehood. During that period of darkness people's thoughts and tongues were tied, and they simply related what they heard without deviating from it. If they ever used their brains—except for a very small group of thinkers—they did not go beyond the constraints of tradition that had enslaved their thought and sealed their lips, with no regard for comparison and proof.

When those chains were loosened at the dawn of modern civilization, with scientific discoveries of the laws of the universe and the principles of existence, people returned to reasoned analysis and began to discard anything that contradicted what was rational. A group of critics appeared who subjected history to close examination, including a group who were interested in examining Islamic history. They read the sources for this history and were astonished by what they found there relating to the deeds of the Arabs at the dawn of Islam: how they had swept across the civilized world during that period, conquering the Romans and Persians, though they were themselves only collections of Bedouins, inexperienced and unlettered. In a little over a decade they had conquered these two kingdoms in a way unheard of in the history of nations in either classical or modern times. They then established dynasties, formed governments, and conscripted armies. The investigators became eager to discover the truth about this people, so they began to search in their ancient histories and to measure the tales of the Arabs against what the Greeks and others had recorded. They discovered things that the Arabs themselves had not known, and became even more eager to clarify their history by investigating their monuments, written and unwritten, among the ruins of the Arab cities in Yemen and the Hejaz and on the borders of Syria. However, they were only able to reach those places with a great deal of difficulty, and were therefore only able to examine a few of them, as we shall make clear later. However, even these few raised the curtain on many obscurities and revealed states and nations that neither the Arabs nor the Greeks had known.

Despite this, writers and researchers were still reluctant to write about the history of the pre-Islamic Arabs. More than one person tried but gave up halfway or even before [starting] along this road. People started to regard this subject as a magic form of writing whose secret had been lost and that could not be solved. Only Caussin de Perceval,[2] the famous French Orientalist, ventured to write about this period of civilization in the middle of the last century; he produced a book in three volumes, the first two of which he devoted to the pre-Islamic Arabs. This caused a great stir in the Orientalist world because the author had devoted a lot of effort to arranging and subdividing the book and explaining the problems, but he wrote it before the discovery of the monuments and the deciphering of their scripts. He relied on the Arabs' and Greeks' accounts, which he explained in a way that showed great learning and intelligence, though if he had an opportunity to rewrite it today he would have preferred to write something entirely different rather than revising it.

After Perceval, no one embarked on a book about pre-Islamic history of the sort that we are concerned with, though there were some publications by researchers of inscriptions that they had read about in ruins that they had discovered, and views on some periods of history that were being debated on the basis of Greek accounts or evidence from archaeology. That only made people more impatient for a comprehensive book to appear. About twenty years ago the late Oscar II, King of Sweden, instituted an annual prize to be given to the author of the best book on the history of the pre-Islamic Arabs. This challenge was answered by more than one writer, who submitted their works at the appointed time to the committee charged with evaluating them and selecting a worthy recipient of the prize from among them. The committee decided that there was no book among them worthy of the prize in accordance with the required conditions, but it singled out for honorable mention one of the books submitted, composed by Mahmud al-Alusi, judging it superior to those of his colleagues and giving the author permission publish it. So he published the book in three volumes and regarded himself as having won the prize. This book, titled *The Maturing Needs of the Arabs' Conditions*,[3] contains most of the information about the pre-Islamic Arabs to be found in Arabic books, including their history, famous men, religions, strange events, and customs. He arranged all this in different chapters, but he did not examine it critically and only occasionally approached the study of history and civilization in the modern way.

Meanwhile, we chose the plan we have embarked on for its service to the Arabic language, that is, the publication of history, with its literature and philosophy, and the study of Oriental history, especially the history of the Arabs and Islam, together with literature written in Arabic. We knew that our studies would be inadequate if we did not understand the history of the Arabic-speaking world, which adopted Islam and carried the East forward. The Swedish king's proposal was in accordance with our own wishes. We continued to wait for leading writers to produce something, but when we saw that the proposal had been a failure we decided to study the subject in all its aspects. We therefore studied and tried to understand every single book or communication connected with the subject that had been written by the Arabs and Greeks, or discovered by archaeologists, in addition to the studies and discussions taking place among Orientalists on this subject. Nothing published in English, French, or German escaped our attention; we read them all patiently, so that our research could achieve its goals and scholars would be able to uncover sufficient evidence to clarify that history. Readers repeatedly suggested that we should write the history of Islam, but this history cannot be clear if it is not preceded by the history of the pre-Islamic Arabs. So we asked God for guidance in composing this book.

After examining the material thoroughly, it became obvious to us that one volume would not be enough, so we have divided it into two: the first part, on the history of the Arabs, is published now; while the second, on the literature and customs of the Arabs, will be published next year, God willing.

The Subject of the First Part Is the History of the Arabs before Islam

We have prefaced it with an introduction on the sources for this history, both those in book form and inscriptions written in Arabic, Greek, or Latin. We have mentioned the most important authors, in Arabic, Greek, or Latin, who recorded anything about the Arabs or their country. Some of the sources in the form of archeological inscriptions were found in Arabia, and some outside it. We have detailed the history of archeological discoveries in the Yemen, Hadramawt, Petra, and elsewhere and given an account of the sources in the form of inscriptions outside Arabia in

Babylon, Assyria, and Egypt. We conclude this part with the names of the authors and the books we have consulted in writing this book, arranged alphabetically by year of publication, so that researchers may be able to consult them if necessary.

We have then devoted a special section to the geography of Arabia, in which we describe its boundaries in Classical times, that is, what the ancients meant by *Bilād al-'Arab*, and the original meaning of the expression "Arab" and how it has now changed and expanded. We have investigated who the Arabs are, the location of the "cradle of the Semites," and different views about these matters. Then we have turned to the subject of the book, that is, the history of the Arabs. We have given a good deal of thought as to the best way of dividing it, because the arrangement and classification of a book is the biggest step toward composing it; and we decided to divide it into three periods or phases, as follows.

The First Period

We have called this the "first period," [consisting of] the "desert Arabs" or "northern Arabs" of the first phase. By this layer we mean the most ancient Arab peoples, that is, generally the peoples that the Arabs call "desert Arabs." We mean by this the Arab dynasties that appeared and flourished before the appearance of the Arabs of the Yemen descended from Qahtan.[4] We have also called the Arabs of the first period the "Amalekites" and divided them into two main groups:

1. *The Amalekites of Iraq*. These formed the Hammurabi dynasty in Babylon from the fifteenth century B.C. We have found historical, linguistic, and social evidence that this dynasty was Arab. Confirmation of this is a matter of obvious pride to the Arabs, for if it is true, then the Arabs were the oldest people to draw up a legal code and to institute systems for the advancement of society. We have provided examples of the advanced state of that dynasty.

2. *The Amalekites of Egypt*. These are called by historians "shepherd kings" or Hyksos. We have called them Alshasu.[5] We conclude our discussion of this phase with an account of remnants of the Amalekites such as 'Ad and Thamud, Tamm, Jaddis, and other desert Arab peoples. We add to these two Arab states that were not known to the Arabs themselves,

namely the Nabataeans in Petra and the Palmyran state in Palmyra. We have investigated Petra and its origins in the period of the Edomites; the Nabataeans, their origins, and the question of whether they were Arabs; and we list the names of their kings, with the dates of their rule, their currencies, language, occupations, and civilization. We have done the same for the people of Palmyra: the origin of Palmyra, the history of Zenobia,[6] and Udhayna and its wars, and the question of whether she was Ziba' to the Arabs. We have added a chapter on the ruins of Palmyra, with illustrations of the most important sites, and shown an example of its coinage.

Before moving on to speak about the second layer, we mentioned various peoples in the north of the Arabian Peninsula known to the Greeks. Then we briefly described the peoples who raided Arabia during the period of the first layer. We referred to the Pharaohs, who swept over it between the seventeenth and twelfth centuries B.C., then to the Assyrian kings who raided it—six in all, the first being Taghlart Bilsar in the ninth century B.C. and the last Nebuchadnezzar in the sixth century B.C.—and then to the conquests of the Persians and Romans, which were rather few. For the history of this phase we have drawn a special map.

The Second Period

By the second layer, we mean the inhabitants of Yemen, whom the Arabs call the Banu Qahtan, referring to their states as Himyar or the kingdom of the Tubba'. We preface our discussion with a short geography, and then quote what the Arabs and Greeks say about the kingdoms of the Yemen. After that we turn to archeological discoveries made by people from other nations, and finally we give our conclusions, having gathered together, examined, and compared all these sources of information. We have concluded that the Yemen was ruled by three major dynasties: the Ma'inids, the Sabaeans, and the Himyarites. We have given a detailed account of each dynasty separately with the names of its kings and origins. We have shown how the Ma'inid dynasty had its origins in Babylon and that its founders migrated to Yemen after the collapse of the Hammurabi dynasty. The evidence lies in the similarities between the forms of government, religions, languages, and names of the kings of the Ma'inids and those of the Babylonians. (We have provided the names of the kings of Ma'in.)

We investigated the Sabaean dynasty first in terms of its origins. It seems to us most likely that it is an offshoot of the Abyssinians, whose forefathers came to Yemen in ancient times, settled there, and adopted the customs, language, and culture of the country. Then dynasties appeared among them who ruled at first in the name of Saba, and later of Himyar. We give the names of the kings of both of these, taking them from inscriptions, and we compare the names of the Himyarite kings in the inscriptions with those recorded by the Arabs. We examine these and specify the years of each of the kings along with the factual evidence. We complete the history of the great Yemeni dynasties with a discussion of the Abyssinian period, and we explain the links between the Abyssinians and Yemen from antiquity, until the Abyssinians conquered Yemen at the beginning of the sixth century A.D. We explain the reasons for that conquest, as related by the Arabs and the Greeks.

Then we discuss the minor dynasties of the Yemen, beginning with the Adhwa' and the Aqyal, and demonstrate the existence of kingdoms known to the Greeks but unknown to the Arabs, such as Jaba'iyya, Qatabiyya, and so on. Finally we describe the ancient civilization of Yemen, dividing the discussion into a number of sections: social structure, industry, agriculture, mining, architecture, commerce, culture, religion, language, and writing. We leave a discussion of the last three of these until the second part of this book. As for the rest, we have divided it into chapters, giving examples of the coinage of Yemen, pictures of the city of Ma'rib after its destruction, the remains of Bilqis's palace, and the ruins of Ghamdan. We describe the castles of Yemen and devote a special chapter to the dams, in particular the Ma'rib dam and the famous flood of 'Iram, and we draw a clear plan to demonstrate the architecture of that enormous dam and the reasons for its collapse. We also provide a special map in which we show the territories that were inhabited during this phase.

The Third Period

By the "third period" we mean the Arabs of 'Adnan or Isma'il, or the Arabs of the North in the second phase. We start by describing their origins, and the differences between them and the Arabs of Qahtan, in terms of nomadic or settled lifestyles, language, and religion. We quote the most ancient accounts of the descendants of ‘Adnan from the time of the Torah until the appearance of Islam, and we explain their divisions and links with the family trees of Quda‘a, Rabi‘a, Mudar, and so forth. We mention the dynasties and other information about Quda‘a and the divisions of the rest of the descendants of ‘Adnan.

Before proceeding to their history, raids, and wars, we speak about the Qahtani dynasties outside Yemen, that is, the Ghassanids, Mundharids, Kinda, and others about whose genealogies we express an opinion. We investigate each dynasty carefully, comparing accounts given by the Arabs, Greeks, and Syrians as well as the archeological evidence, evidence from inscriptions, and comparative evidence. We present all this clearly, with maps, drawings, and tables. Finally, we discuss the history and exploits of the desert-dwelling descendants of ‘Adnan and how they freed themselves from domination in Yemen, until Islam appeared. We devote a chapter to the settlement of the Banu ‘Adnan in Mecca. We have drawn a special map for this group to explain the positions of the various tribes in Najd, Hejaz, and the borders of Syria and Iraq. We give the names of the places where battles occurred between those tribes and so on.

We have done our best to write as accurately as possible and to confirm the information we have gleaned by checking the books and inscriptions at hand. We know, however, that the history of these peoples that lies buried under the sand is much fuller than what is available to us. So we will not think it odd if some future discoveries make us change our minds on some of the more obscure points. If this research proves at all useful, the credit will belong to those brave and diligent men who exposed their lives to danger, seeking out archaeological remains and transporting them to the civilized world, and to those scientists and Orientalists who solved their riddles and exposed their treasures.

We should not forget the benefits that we have derived from the Khedival Library and the help extended to us by its director, Dr. Moritz, to consult the relevant books and references and guide us to recent publications.

The most that we can hope for is that this book contains more true facts than mistakes. We could not say that every mistake is a slip of the pen; indeed we acknowledge that what we do not know far exceeds what we do know. Perfect knowledge belongs only to Him who has taught man what he did not know.

The Arabs: Who Are They?

When we talk about "Arabs" today, we mean the inhabitants of the Arabian Peninsula, Iraq, Syria, Egypt, Sudan, and North Africa. In the period before Islam, however, "Arabs" meant only the inhabitants of the Arabian Peninsula, for the population of Iraq and Syria was composed of Syrians, Chaldeans, Nabateans, Jews, and Greeks; the Egyptian population was Coptic; the population of the Maghreb was Berber, Greeks, and Vandal; and the population of Sudan was Nubians, Negroes, and others. When Islam appeared and the Arabs expanded their territory, they settled in these lands and the Arabic language replaced the original languages of those lands, and so their inhabitants were called Arabs.

In ancient history—in the period of the Pharaohs, Assyrians, and Phoenicians—"Arabs" meant the nomadic people in the northern part of the Arabian Peninsula and the east of the Nile Valley, in the land stretching from the Euphrates in the East to the Nile in the West. It included the deserts of Iraq, Syria, and the Sinai Peninsula, together with the adjacent eastern part of the Delta and the eastern desert of Egypt between the Nile and the Red Sea. The Nile Valley was the natural frontier between Libya in the West and Arabia in the East. The Egyptians called the eastern mountains that bordered the Nile in the East *Jabal al-'Arab* or *Bilad al-'Arab*, and they called the mountains to the West the "Libyan Mountains."

In ancient times the term "Arab" was synonymous with "Bedouin" [*badw* or *badiya*] at the time. The meaning of this expression in Semitic languages, including *'arav*[7] in Hebrew, was equivalent to the Arabic *'araba* in Wadi Musa. The Arabs inhabited the desert in particular, and there was no singular of the term, but the Arabs called their peninsula *'Araba*. When some of the Arab tribes abandoned nomadism in ancient times and settled in the cities of Yemen, the Hejaz, Hawran, and other places, the expression "Arab" was no longer restricted to meaning "Bedouin," but its meaning changed just as the people themselves had changed. They were forced to use words to distinguish between the two lifestyles, so they used *ḥaḍar* for townspeople and *badw* for desert dwellers. The expression "Arab" no longer has the connotation "Bedouin" today, except when people use the term *'arabī*, as previously explained. Until Christian times, when the Sabaeans mentioned a settled tribe and its nomads, they would say: "such and such a tribe and its Arabs." The Arabs or Bedouins living in the north of the Arabian Peninsula were divided into groups and tribes both before and after the coming of Islam.

As for the south of the Arabian Peninsula, between the Persian Gulf and the Red Sea, the ancient Greeks reckoned it as part of Ethiopia (Abyssinia), and they counted Abyssinia, Yemen, and the shores of the Persian Gulf as a single region, which they called "Asian Ethiopia." The tribes and peoples that inhabited this region were called by special names such as Sabaeans, Himyarites, Ma'inids, and so on, as will be explained later.

The Greeks soon conquered the Eastern civilized world and settled in Alexandria during the age of the Ptolemys. They changed the nomenclature, called the Peninsula as a whole the "land of the Arabs," and divided it into the three parts already specified. Then the Arabs divided it into five parts and called the population as a whole "Arab," by a process of applying the part to the whole, in the same way as geographers applied the term "Asia" to the whole continent of Asia, which in the Greek period had denoted just Asia Minor. They also applied the term "Africa" to the whole of Africa, whereas before it had been the name for just the northern part. For the same reason, the Greeks applied the term "Saracens" to the people of the Arabian Peninsula, when it was really the name of a tribe living in the mountains in the Peninsula. Some people think that it is derived from the term *sharqiyyīn*, "Easterners,"[8] because the tribe was living to the east of Mount Rat. For a similar reason, the Arabs are known by the Syrians as *Tayya*, from *Tayy*, the name of an Arab tribe. In a similar way, the Arabs call Europeans *Franj*, which was originally the name of a single European people, the Franks. Syrians today are called by names that differ from place to place. In Constantinople, they are called *Halabiyya*, because the first Syrians to migrate there were from Aleppo, while in Iraq they are called *Bayarita*, related to Beirut, and in Egypt *Shawam*, from *al-Sham*, because people from Damascus were the first Syrians to migrate to Egypt.

Where Was the Cradle of the Semites?

Contemporary historians use the term "Semitic peoples" to refer to peoples who communicate in Arabic, Hebrew, Syriac, and Ethiopian and who previously communicated in Phoenician, Assyrian, and Aramaic. This term is derived from Sam, son of Noah, for the Torah states that these peoples were his descendants. Their languages are called "Semitic languages." There is no disagreement about these languages resembling each other in their vocabulary and construction, in the same way as the offshoots of Latin or Sanskrit resemble each other. Italian and Spanish, for example, can be regarded as two sisters whose mother is Latin, and Persian and Urdu as two sisters with Sanskrit as a mother. In the same way, the colloquial languages of Syria, Egypt, North Africa, and the Hejaz are sisters, with classical Arabic as their mother. These "mothers" are still preserved, and their "daughters" can be traced back to them, but the "mother" of the Semitic languages no longer exists. Some philosophers of language have taken the view that they are offshoots of Hebrew, others of Arabic, and others of Babylonian, but their views are no more than guesswork.

There are also different views about the original home of the Semites. Experts have produced on this topic extensive studies, which it would be useless to present here. In general, there may be said to be two basic views.[9] The view of the authors of the Torah was that the cradle of mankind was in Mesopotamia, from where mankind branched out over the earth, so that the Assyrians and Babylonians split off from the Semites in Iraq, the Aramaeans in Syria, the Phoenicians along the Syrian coast, the Hebrews in Palestine, the Arabs in the Arabian Peninsula, and the Ethiopians in Abyssinia. Their evidence for this lies in the words of the Torah, though only a few experts today support this view. Orientalists have researched this question on the basis of language derivation. Some of them have observed similarities between the Semitic languages and the Hamitic languages spoken in Africa and have taken the view that the origin of the Semites lay in Africa. Because of the closeness of Abyssinia to Arabia, both geographically and linguistically, they have said that the origin of the Semites was in Abyssinia. Among the proponents of this view was Salt and Ritter.[10] Another group, led by the Germans Sprenger,[11]

Schroeder,[12] and Winckler,[13] and the Englishman Robertson Smith, have taken the view that the cradle of the Semites lay in the Arabian Peninsula from where they branched out in different directions just as they did in the early days of Islam. They have strong evidence for this view, part linguistic and part social or behavioral. Another group has adopted an extreme form of this theory and restricted this cradle in the Syrian Desert to Najd. Their evidence for the correctness of this theory is that the Arabic language is the closest of the group to the original Semitic language, and that both Hebrew and Aramaic contain vestiges or traces of the nomadic life, which is Arab.

Another group, led by the Italian Orientalist Ignazio Guidi,[14] hold that the cradle of the Semites lay in the southern Euphrates. They base their argument on natural geographical factors relating to the divisions of plants and animals, and their names, in the Semitic languages. Others have taken these sorts of views to an extreme and said that the origin of the Semites lay in Abyssinia, from where they crossed over to the Arabian Peninsula in prehistoric times via the Bab al-Mandab straits to Yemen, where they multiplied before moving from Yemen to the Hejaz, Najd, and Bahrain. From there, a group (including the ancient Palestinians) migrated to Palestine; a group to Iraq (the inhabitants of Iraq at that time being Sumerians and Akkadians, Turanians of the Mongol race who had settled down and adopted a civilized existence); and a group to Phoenicia. The Semites conquered those countries and established the states of Babylon, Assyria, Phoenicia, and Palestine, among others. Proponents of this theory think that the Hebrews migrated from Hejaz, and the Aramaeans from Najd, because Aram means "mountains" and Najd is mountainous. They cite in support of their view Herodotus's statement that the Phoenicians had originally migrated from the coast of the Persian Gulf.

To sum up, it may be said that the question of the "cradle of the Semites" remains obscure, and that it should be put aside until we gain further knowledge through the discovery of further Arab, Assyrian, and Babylonian remains. But whatever the truth about that cradle may be, the peoples who originated there spoke a single language at the time of their dispersal, which we may call "proto-Semitic." This language evolved in the different regions in accordance with the law of evolution, so that their vocabularies and structures began to grow apart while sharing common characteristics that distinguished them from other languages of the Aryan and Turanian families.

Nomadism as the Sustenance of Civilization

Let us move on from research into prehistory and turn to historical times. It seems to us that the oldest Semitic people to settle and leave archaeological remains were the Babylonians. They settled in the third millennium B.C.—the period in which the Phoenicians are thought to have migrated from the Persian Gulf to Syria. Babylon had been a settled and civilized country for several generations before that, inhabited by the Sumerians. The Semites first settled in the west of it, in the deserts of Iraq and Syria; they were nomadic tribes who lived by grazing livestock and raiding, just like the Bedouin there today, and just like the descendants of Lakhm and Ghassan in the early days of Islam. The Sumerians sought their help in fighting their enemies, just as the Persians and Byzantines sought the help of the Lakhmids and Ghassanids, respectively, for in those days superiority lay in physical strength; a settled life brought with it luxury, opulence, devotion to pleasure, and a lazy lifestyle, which would dissipate that strength and cause the people to regress to weakness. A nomadic lifestyle strengthened the body and engendered an independence of spirit, and for this reason settled people and town dwellers would seek the help of the nomads and mountain dwellers when required. When a settled state grew old, it would be conquered by neighboring nomads or mountain dwellers, who would take the place of the previous inhabitants and assume their customs and religions. Before long however, decrepitude would overtake them and they would be replaced by other nomads, as is the usual order of things in God's creation. The nomads or mountain dwellers were the source of sustenance for the cities: they would revive their populations by coming down to the city folk and marrying them, and would raise cattle and other livestock to feed them and for them to ride. The cities were dangerous both physically and mentally: the nomads would come there full of energy and pride, but before long they would settle, and indulge in a life of luxury, until their resolve diminished, to be replaced by weakness as submissiveness spread among them. Then others would come to take their place. Gradually, that nourishing effect would spread as the people of the neighboring mountains descended on the cities, just as happens in Syria to this day: its cities reinvigorate themselves through the Lebanese descending on them, and if you examine the recent revival in Syria, you will see that the majority of those active in it are inhabitants of that energetic mountain.

This has been the case with the world from ancient times until today. Iraq or Mesopotamia was a rich and fertile country, visited in ancient times by the Turanians—nomads or mountain folk that drove out a prosperous people about whom we have no information. They established a fine civilization there, adopted a system of gods and religious laws, and invented a pictorial script that evolved over the generations into the well-known cuneiform script. When they had settled and adopted a life of ease, the Semites arrived from the desert and took over everything they had: they adopted their gods and laws, and developed or improved them, and gradually became more powerful and civilized, as will now be described.

The Semites used to live in the mountains of the Arabian Peninsula. Some of them had camps in the desert between Iraq and Syria, and those of them living near the Euphrates gradually infiltrated the neighboring cities. Those who settled there served the state in war or other activities requiring physical strength, then became assimilated in the population. The inhabitants of those cities called the desert dwellers there "Aramaeans," that is, "mountain people," while the inhabitants of Mesopotamia called them *Amuru*, that is, 'Westerners,' because their territory was situated to the west of the Euphrates, and it was their ancient name in Babylonian. (By *Amuru* they probably meant nomads and settled peoples to the west of the Euphrates as far as the Mediterranean.) They then gave them the name *'Aribī*, that is. "Arabs," which also means "Westerners" in proto-Semitic, and called their territory *Mat 'Aribī*, that is, the "Western" or "Arab" land. Then, as that land was empty desert, the expression "Arab" also came to denote "Bedouin" in the Semitic languages, in the form *'Arav* in Hebrew and *'Arabī* in Arabic, as previously explained. In the same way, the ancient Egyptians also called them "Shasu," that is, Bedouin, or desert people, as will be explained.

The same sort of thing has happened in Egypt. To this day, Egyptians refer to the north of the country as *Bahri* because the sea, *baḥr,* is in the north of their country, and to the south as *Qibli,* which originally meant the direction of the *qibla,* that is, prayer toward the Kaaba in Mecca. Similarly, the eastern part of the Delta is called *Sharqiyya,* "eastern," and the inhabitants Sharqāwiyya, "easterners," while the adjoining area to the west is called *Gharbiyya,* "western." Likewise, the inhabitants of North Africa are called *Maghariba* because they live in the western part of their territory.

This was how the ancients used to name peoples after the places where they lived, by reference to the rising or setting of the sun. So the Jews used to call the Arabs "People of the Mashriq" (*Bnei Qedem*),[15] because the place where they lived in the desert was to the east of Palestine.

Periods of the History of the Arabs

Historians of the Arabs usually divide the history of the pre-Islamic Arabs into two parts: the extinct Arabs and the surviving Arabs. The extinct Arabs are the ancient tribes who disappeared before Islam, while the surviving Arabs have two parts according to their classification: (1) The Qahtan Arabs from Himyar and thereabouts in Yemen, with their various branches; and (2) The 'Adnan Arabs in the Hejaz and adjacent areas. Researchers have differed considerably in their views about these Arabs, but it would be pointless to elaborate.

It has become clear to us from a study of the circumstances and history of the Arabs from the earliest times until the appearance of Islam that they passed through three main phases. In the first or early phase, the leadership was in the hands of the tribes in the northern part of the Arabia Peninsula, most of whom belonged to the extinct Arabs; in the second or middle phase, the leadership fell to the Arabs of the southern part, most of whom belonged to Qahtan; and in the third or most recent phase, the leading role reverted to the north. This phase ends with the appearance of Islam. Most of the tribes at this point were 'Adnan. So we can confidently agree with the ancients in their division, with some necessary correction of terminology, as follows:

1. The extinct Arabs or Northern Arabs;
2. The Qahtan Arabs or the kingdoms of the South;
3. The 'Adnan Arabs or second phase of Northern Arabs.

Notes

1. Excerpts from Zaydān, *Tārīkh al-'arab,* 9–14, 39–45.

2. Caussin de Perceval (1759–1835), Arabist at the Collège de France; the work cited here is *Essay sur l'histoire des Arabs avant l'islamisme,* 3 vols. (Paris: s.n.,1847–1848).

3. Maḥmūd al-Alūsī, *Bulūgh al-ārāb fī aḥwāl al-'arab,* no further data.

4. Qaḥṭān, according to classical Muslim historians and popular consent, is considered the ancestor of all southern Arabs: *EI2.*

5. *Alshāsū* or *al-Shāsū*: not identified.

6. Zenobia, last Queen of Palmyra, defeated in 273 by Emperor Aurelian, who exhibited her in his triumphal procession in Rome, supposedly tied in golden chains. Udhayna was her late husband. *Al-Munjid fī 'l-lugha* identifies her with Zibā'.

7. Actually it should be *'arava.* In the text the word is written in Hebrew.

8. See "Sarazenen" in Nabil Osman, *Kleines Lexikon deutscher Wörter arabischer Herkunft* (München: n.p., 1992); see *EI2,* "Saracenes," for the vagueness of the etymology of the word.

9. Zaidan does not follow his own counting and offers a variety of views but a certain dichotomy develops. Some argue for the Arab Peninsula as the cradle of the Semites; others see their origin outside the Peninsula, with most assuming southern Mesopotamia as that point of origin.

10. Probably Carl Ritter (1779–1856), geographer: Ursula Wokoeck, *German Orientalism: The Study of the Middle East and Islam from 1800–1945* (New York: Routledge, 2009), index.

11. Aloys Sprenger (1813–1893), Oriental and Semitic languages; worked in British colonial administration: Wokoeck, *German Orientalism,* index. See his *Die Alte Geographie Arabiens als Grundlage der Entwicklungsgeschichte des Semitismus* (Bern: n.p., 1875, passim and esp. chap. 3).

12. Leopold von Schroeder (1851–1920), Semitic languages, Sanskrit, comparative linguistics: Wokoeck, *German Orientalism,* index.

13. Hugo Winckler (1863–1913), Assyrian studies: Wokoeck, *German Orientalism,* index.

14. Ignatio Guidi (1844–1935), Italian Orientalist and linguist.

15. In text in Hebrew letters. *Bnei Qedem* actually means "prehistoric people."

◆ ◆ ◆

Ottoman Egypt: Preliminary Remarks

Islamic History Compared with Other Histories and General History

Translated by Paul Starkey

General history consists of events that have befallen mankind from his earliest days until the present.[1] It is a record of the progress or regression that nations have experienced; the movements backward and forward in politics and society; and an exposition of mankind's progress through civilization. As such, it is limited to nations that have played a part in the development of the social fabric.

Some people have defined the study of history by saying that it is philosophy explained by examples, so that the experiences of those who came before can be a warning to those who come later.

General history requires knowledge of human experience from the first days of mankind until today. This is not easy, because what we know of human experience is but a very small fraction of man's history, and mankind only recorded its history after the successful invention of writing. This only happened after several ages of progress, in which nations and states appeared, went to war, and concluded treaties, while wise men in the meantime developed different philosophies. All the information about these events has disappeared, however, and nothing has come down to us, not even the names of those nations. They have all been lost, and we depend for knowledge of their existence solely on the fruits of their achievements, on the tools they invented, or on excavations or ruins.

Historians do not regard that information as history. For this reason, they have given the term "prehistory" to the period that mankind spent before recording his achievements. This is far longer than the period of history proper, and in it mankind made great progress on the ladder of civilization and intellectual advancement. In this period, social structure took shape, the customs of marriage and inheritance were instituted, the family became organized, governments were formed, and religions founded. Likewise the most important inventions were made on which human progress was based in historical times. In this shadowy period writing was invented; man began to cook, bake, weave, sew, and build; and fire and salt were discovered, which are two of the most important discoveries of all.

If someone could tell us who invented pictograms, we would erect a memorial to him, and if someone could tell us who invented the needle we would put up a statue to him. If we knew who discovered fire—that is, the first person to produce fire by friction—we would honor him greatly. But human accomplishments like these in the prehistoric period do not count as history, and there is no way of knowing them except by guesswork.

When we come to the historical period proper, however, we know at least some of the nations, tribes, states, and events concerned, either from books that have come down to us, or from inscriptions that we can read on monuments, or by other means. In length, it is no more than 6,000 years. The first half is patchy, most of it based on guesswork, while the early part of the second half is full of exaggerations and myths, though most of it is accepted, because it is based on historical texts composed after the spread of writing.

What Does the Term "History" Mean?

Before proceeding to describe the different periods of history, let us discuss the origins of the term *tārīkh*, history, in Arabic. There are different opinions on this. Some people have said that it is Persian, while others have said that it is Greek. People have gone to great lengths to formulate an etymology for it, but we do not need this, for the expression is Arabic, and is defined in the dictionary as follows: "The writers dated it, that is, defined its time." Then the meaning acquired an additional significance, so that writers started to use it to mean the "science of history," that is, the narration of happenings and events. Perhaps the reason for the doubt that this word is Arabic is that the Arabs took history from the Persians. They were told that the Persians called it *ma' ruz*, so they arabized it as *mu'arrikh*, then they derived from this the verbal noun *tārīkh*. However, we do not need this explanation, and if we are in any doubt that the expression is Arabic we may look at its cognates in languages related to Arabic. In Hebrew, we have *yareakh*, meaning the "moon"; in Syriac, *yarkha* with the same meaning, and similarly in Chaldean and Assyrian. These words denote a month in their system, for they reckoned by the moon. Similarly, "month" and "moon" in Arabic have the same meaning. There is no significance in the variation between *h* and *kh* between Arabic and its sister languages, for that is normal. Other remnants of *yarh* or *arkh* signifying the "moon" in Arabic are that the Arabs use the expression *rah* to mean "to come or go in the evening," that is, by "moonlight." The meaning simply signifies "in the evening," without specifying "come" or "go," just as with the verbs *aṣbaḥa* or *amsā*. Gradually, however, the meaning "go in the evening" became the usual one, and it then came to mean just "go." The same word may have the meaning of "moon" in one of these languages, and "month" in another: *sahar* [moon], in Syriac, means "month" in Arabic, in the form *shahr*, with a slight modification of the *s*, but it has retained its original meaning in the Arabic *sahur*, which means the moon or its covering. In short, the expression *tārīkh*, meaning "history," is Arabic by origin and derivation.

The Divisions of General History

Historians have differed in their division and classification of history. Most of them divide it into three periods: the first, ancient history, beginning with the most ancient times, and ending with the fall of Rome in A.D. 476; the second, the Middle or Dark Ages, which extend from this date until the discovery of America in A.D.1492; and the third, modern history, from the discovery of America until today.

That is how European writers periodize, though in our view it is a defective classification, being based on sequences of events in Europe and America, with little regard for the history of the East, apart from the ancient civilizations of Egypt, Babylon, and Phoenicia and so forth. They take no account of the great political upheavals that succeeded one another in the East after the passing of those states, each one of which had a great influence on the history of civilization in the other regions of the civilized world.

Our own view is that to take the Eastern nations and states into account, general history should be divided into two main parts, which we may term "Oriental history" and "Occidental history." In general terms, by Oriental we mean Asia, together with the Nile Valley, and those countries beyond it in Africa that were civilized in ancient times. By Occidental, we mean Europe and America and adjoining regions.

Each of these two regions has three phases or periods that are similar in classification but different in time span. Each of them has an ancient period, a middle period, and a modern period, but the East precedes the West both chronologically and in terms of the features of civilization. The ancient history of the East extends from the earliest times to the conquest of Persia by the Macedonian, Alexander the Great, in 331 B.C.; the East's Middle or Dark Ages extend from Alexander's conquest up to the appearance of Islam in 622 A.D., which is the first year of the Islamic calendar. As for the ancient history of the West, it begins with the first appearance of civilization there around the fifteenth century B.C. in Greece, which had taken the basis of its civilization from the ancient nations of the East in Egypt, Phoenicia, Babylon, and so on. It ends with the fall of Rome in 476 A.D., the cause of its disappearance being the attack of the barbarians—the German tribes, or "Bedouins" of Northern Europe—on the Roman Empire. During this period, as has previously been explained, the East moved on into its Middle Ages with the fall of the Persian Empire.

The middle period of Western history—the European Dark Ages, or Middle Ages—begin with the fall of Rome and the barbarian conquest, and extend until the start of modern history with the discovery of America in 1492 A.D. During this period people in the West were heedless of the sciences of their predecessors, the Greeks. Meanwhile the East had awoken from its Dark Ages, with the appearance of Islam and the establishment of the Arab state, so they took those sciences and translated them.

The history of Islam is the history of the modern East. With Islam the East arose from its slumber and regained its glory and vitality. The power of the Muslims extended itself over an area many times larger than the kingdoms of their Oriental predecessors. Their flags flew over the lands of the Pharaohs, Phoenicians, Assyrians, Babylonians, Persians, Armenians, Indians, Turks, Moroccans, and other peoples of North Africa, as well as part of Europe—in Spain, France, and Italy—a development without historical precedent.

The Periods of Islamic History

The history of Islam can be divided into five periods:

1. The age of formation and growth. From the birth of Islam until the end of the Umayyad state in Syria. This was the period of the conquests, or the Arab period [A.D. 622–749].

2. The period of maturity, from the beginning of the Abbasid Empire, *al*-dawla,[2] in A.H. 132 [749 C.E.] until the coup of the Turkish army in 232 A.H. [847 A.D.].[3] This period includes the flowering of the Abbasid Empire, in which literature flourished, and the sciences of the ancients were translated into Arabic. This was the Golden Age of Islam, sometimes known as the "Persian period" because the government was in the hands of Persian ministers.

3. The period of division, from the rise of the Turks until the fall of Baghdad. In this period the state, *dawla*, split into smaller states, *duwal*, comprising different nations, *umam*, in various regions. New states emerged, such as the Fatimid state in Egypt, the Umayyad state in Spain, and the Seljuk state in Syria, as well as Turkish, Persian, Kurdish, and other states [849–1258 C.E.]. [4]

4. The Islamic Ages, from the fall of Baghdad until the beginning of the nineteenth century.

5. The recent Nahda starting from the beginning of the last [the nineteenth] century until today, and derived from modern Western civilization.

History may also be divided into general and specialized. General history includes the history of mankind as a whole, while specialized history includes the particular history of a single subject, like the history of a people, a kingdom, a province, city, state, family, or person. The history of a single person is known as a biography. Of this sort are the *Tarikh al-Ikhlaṣ;*[5] the massacre of the Mamluks,[6] the incident,[7] the appearance of the Mahdi,[8] and so forth.

Specialized history is called by different names, according to its different subjects, for example, Church History, Political History, Legal, Commercial, Literary, Scientific History, and others.

The Merits of Islamic History Compared with Other Histories

Islamic history is a specialized history that deals with nations or states, because it involves repeated patterns of events in the Islamic state, *dawla*, or nation, *umma*. It is equivalent to Roman, Greek, or Persian history and the like, but it is distinguished from them in a number of ways worth considering. The most important of these are:

1. Islamic history is a link between the East and the West, for as the Muslims succeeded in reaching the Far East and the Far West, they were able to link them. It is also a link between ancient Western civilization and modern Western civilization. It preserved the successive changes and adaptations that had occurred in ancient Western civilization in the philosophical sciences and medicine, which the Muslims then used during their civilization, and which there would be no way of knowing except through the study of the history of Islam.

2. Islamic history is distinguished from other states' and nations' history through the inclusion of the histories of various other groups, *'anāṣir,* that were embraced by Islam in Central Asia and elsewhere. These groups had previously lived the lives of nomads or barbarians, but they were drawn to civilization and learning by Islam and subsequently produced scholars, philosophers, politicians, and administrators. The best-known of these groups are the Turks, Mongols, Berbers, and Negroes. This is a point worth dwelling on for a moment, as we say a little about each of these groups.

The Turks. In pre-Islamic times, the Turks were nomads who lived in the steppes of Central Asia, between India, China, and Siberia. They knew only a little about people in the West such as the Romans or Greeks. The Persians purchased them to be slaves or servants, and exchanged them like chattel. When the Arabs came and conquered their lands and enlisted them, they rose up with the others, took control of the provinces, and then established important dynasties in Persia, Iraq, Syria, Egypt, Asia Minor, Constantinople, Afghanistan, and Turkestan. The best known of these dynasties, *dawla*, were the Tulunids, the Ilikids, the Ikhshids, the Ghaznavids, the Seljuks with their various branches, and the Atabegs who succeeded them. The number of legitimate Islamic states rose to more than thirty, and their power grew to such an extent that their cavalry reached Central Europe. Leaders, politicians, religious scholars, and writers emerged among them; they built castles, mosques, and institutes and founded hospitals, schools, and religious lodges. The majority of the surviving Islamic monuments in Egypt, Syria, and Iraq were built by them, and there is no way of knowing about their circumstances except through the study of Islamic history.

The Mongols. The Mongols were nomadic groups living around Lake Baikal in southern Siberia. They only came to prominence after Islam, for before that they had lived by hunting raiding, and looting. When they came into contact with the Muslims in Turkestan, and saw their states and armies, they sought to imitate them. They determined to conquer their territories, which they did in a harsh and barbarous fashion, bringing slaughter, looting, and arson at the hand of Genghis Khan. But they soon became settled because of their proximity to the Muslims in Persia and Iraq. They founded important dynasties, which ruled the East for five-and-a-half centuries, the most famous being the four great dynasties of Aqtay, Talwi, Juji, and Jaghtay.

Other dynasties split off from them and extended their authority, until their flags flew over Zanqaria, Mongolia, Qabjaq, and Turkestan. They conquered the Islamic Empire and penetrated Persia, Iraq, and Syria. Political figures and military leaders emerged among them, and having been idolaters, they converted to Islam and built mosques, schools, and institutes. They founded cities in the Far East, where they erected splendid buildings and towering palaces, and planted gardens and orchards. There is no way of knowing the details of these dynasties except through the study of Islamic history.

The Berbers. By this term is meant the Bedouins of North Africa, who were nomadic tribes. In pre-Islamic times, they were extremely ignorant and uncivilized, idolaters who kept to the mountains and employed sorcerers. They hated civilized life and those who practiced it. The Greeks and the Romans had already suffered greatly from their raids and plundering. They had no other occupations, and the Arabs met with great difficulties in subduing them in the period of the conquests. After they had submitted and converted to Islam, they enlisted in the armies of the caliphs and emirs and conquered much territory, especially in the West. They overran al-Andalus under the leadership of Tariq ibn Ziyad, and they provided great support in the establishment of the Idrisid and Fatimid states. They established the Milaththamid, Almoravid, and Almohad dynasties, as well as those of the Masamida and Alziris, and innumerable others. They raised armies, built fortresses, adopted a civilized lifestyle; and the only way to become acquainted with their story is through Islamic history.

The Zanj. The Zanj were, and the great majority of them still are, carried to the far horizons like cattle and sold like goods. They were subject to the yoke of settled peoples, and worshipped stones or trees. Some of them did not understand the meaning of religion or worship. At the dawn of Islam their homelands were known to have been North Africa and parts of East and West Africa.

When they became subjects of the Arabs through conquest or migration, some of their tribes went to Central Africa, as well as to its coasts. The Zanj adopted the habits of the settled nations, and converted to Islam, then formed themselves into armies, making up units that fought under the banners of the caliphs in the caliphs' territories until they became extremely influential. Some of them took part in government, then formed armies of their own and revolted, just as more advanced peoples did. They formed an army with which they fought the Abbasids for several years, until they had worn it down. They conquered the cities and almost formed a great Islamic dynasty. But instead they set up petty states in central and western Africa and produced leaders and rulers. The best-known of them was Kafur al-Ikhshidi, the ruler of Egypt. More than one poet emerged from them who composed fine poems. They also produced a group of [Koran] reciters and religious scholars. Their history forms a part of Islamic history. We may add to all these groups the histories of the peoples of the North, such as the Karaj, the Armenians, the Kurds, the Khazars, the Slavs, and others.

That is not to mention the Arabs themselves, with their history both before Islam and after it. Were it not for Islam, their history and the history of other Islamic nations would have disappeared. Most of what civilized peoples know about these nations has been taken from the study of Islamic history.

3. The Muslims recorded a period of time whose history would have remained unknown, had it not been for them. This period includes the events surrounding the appearance of Islam, as well as subsequent developments such as the history of the conquest, and later the establishment of civilized life, the spread of knowledge, and the transmission of philosophy and other sciences of the ancients, with all the changes and adaptation that required. These are things of which Europeans would have had no knowledge had it not been transmitted by Islamic civilization.

4. This history extends for a longer period than that of other histories, because Islam included a variety of different Islamic states. When one state disappeared, another arose. We are now in the fourteenth century of the Islamic era, and hundreds of Islamic dynasties have succeeded one another in the various nations of Asia, Africa, and Europe. Many of these dynasties survive until today in these continents, including major states such as the Ottoman and Persian Empires, as well as smaller states in India, the Arabian Peninsula, and Africa.

We know of no other nation whose power has extended over the earth for a similar period. Indeed, Islam has had a long life, and in fact is in the middle of a reformist revival that will help it to flourish for even longer. For this reason, Islam comprises a history longer than any other history.

5. Islamic history is distinguished from other histories by the fact that it includes political, religious, scientific, and legal history, which are features seldom found in conjunction with other histories. The history of Islamic jurisprudence is unparalleled by the history of that of any other nation on earth in the intellectual activity and depth it has generated. The same goes for the history of science, for during the scientific revival in the Abbasid period the Muslims accomplished what no one else had achieved

in any comparable revival. They turned their attention to the sciences of the Greeks, Persians, Indians, Syrians, and others, translated them into their language, and recorded their history and circumstances. This is not to mention the great variety of races of the historians, among whom were Arabs, Persians, Turks, Byzantines, Egyptians, Syrians, Indians, and others. Each nation has its own distinctive quality, and all these qualities came together in Islamic history.

6. Islamic history includes historical examples that are difficult to find united in the history of any other nation, because of the great mixture of races and ethnic groups that converted to Islam, each with its own customs and morality. Among Muslim authors there was a tendency to record events and draw lessons in great detail, although we do not deny that the histories of other nations may also have merits that set them apart from the history of Islam.

The History of Egypt in Comparative Perspective

The history of Egypt is a special sort of history, because it is concerned with Egypt to the exclusion of other countries. It spans a long period, because Egypt is a country with a long history of settled life. Indeed, it is perhaps the oldest of the civilized states, *al-mamālik,* whose history has come down to us. Its history may be divided into two main parts: ancient and modern. The ancient history of Egypt covers the period from the earliest times until the Islamic conquest, including the history of the Pharaonic kingdoms, and ends with Alexander's conquest of Alexandria in 332 B.C. The Ptolemaic period begins with Alexander's conquest and ends with the Roman conquest in 30 B.C., and the Roman period begins with this conquest and ends with the Islamic conquest in 640 A.D. This still continues, and forms the period of Islamic history.

The modern Islamic history of Egypt can be divided into twelve dynasties, all of them Muslim, interrupted by the three-year French occupation under Bonaparte, which we may count as a thirteenth period, as follows:

1. The period of the Rightly Guided Caliphs, A.H.18–41, A.D. 640–661.
2. The Umayyad state, A.H. 41–132, A.D. 661–750.

3. The Abbasid state, first phase, A.H. 132–257, A.D. 750–870.
4. The Tulunid dynasty, A.H. 257–292, A.D. 870–905.
5. The Abbasid state, second phase, A.H. 292–323, A.D. 905–934.
6. The Ikhshids, A.H. 323–358, A.D. 934–969.
7. The Fatimids, A.H. 358–567, A.D. 969–1171.
8. The Ayyubids, A.H. 567–684, A.D. 1171–1250.
9. First Mamluk dynasty, A.H. 684–784, A.D. 1250–1382.
10. Second Mamluk dynasty, A.H. 784–923, A.H. 1382–1517.
11. Ottoman Empire, A.H. 923–1213, A.D. 1517–1798.
12. French Expedition, A.H. 1213–1216, A.D. 1798–1801.
13. Muhammad 'Ali's line, A.H. 1216 , A.D. 1801 –

The Subject of This Book

The subject of this book is restricted to the eleventh of the Islamic dynasties that ruled Egypt, which is the Ottoman Empire, omitting the period 1798–1801, during which Egypt was under the domination of the French. The subject of this book, then, is the history of Ottoman Egypt from the Ottoman invasion of 923 A.H./1517 A.D. until 1213 A.H./1798 A.D., which is the darkest and most disturbed period of modern Egyptian history. The Mamluks had taken control of it, its government had become corrupt, and few writers recorded its history accurately. Nonetheless, we shall make an effort to clarify that history.

Notes

1. Originally preparatory notes for teaching Islamic history at the newly founded Egyptian University. For first publication of this excerpt see: Zaydān, "al-Tārīkh al-islāmī." For the book, based on the lecture notes, see: Zaydān, *Miṣr al-'uthmāniyya*. The translated section is taken from pages 42–51.

2. The term *al-dawla*, pl. *duwal*, may mean dynasty, state, or empire.

3. For the first time the Turkic mercenaries in Baghdad were able to have their choice for the Caliphate appointed: al-Mutawakkil, the tenth Abbasid Caliph. He became utterly dependent on the military that had heaved him to power.

4. Conquered by the Mongols.

5. Not identified.

6. The allusion is to Muhammad 'Ali's massacre arranged in 1811 of his most threatening rivals for power, the Mamluks, who had survived the French invasion of Egypt.

7. Aḥmad 'Urābī Pasha (1839–1911). The 'Urābī rebellion first against Khedive Isma'il Pasha and then against his son Tawfiq, who became minister of defense in 1882, provoking eventually the British occupation of Egypt in 1882. He was exiled after the British occupation of Egypt in the same year.

8. A messianic, nativist movement in Sudan, fighting against Egyptian and the British Imperialism in the late 1880s.

The Syrians and Their Naturalization in America

A Sociological Study

Translated by Hilary Kilpatrick

Our colleague,[1] the editor of the *al-Manazir*[2] (*Panorama*) newspaper in Sao Paolo, Brazil, has written to us in the name of the Syrians in America suggesting we give our opinion about a debate between him and the owner of the *al-Muhajir* (*The Émigré*) newspaper in New York about the future of the Syrians in America. The point at issue was whether they should take the American nationality and become fully assimilated, or whether they should remain Ottomans and maintain their Syrian patriotism (*waṭaniyya*) in order to return to Syria. We have responded to his suggestion and sent our reply to him. But in view of the sociological research this subject entails, we have decided to publish it in *al-Hilal* too.

Dear and esteemed colleague,

I received your letter which suggested, in the name of the Syrians in America, that I give my opinion about the debate between you and our esteemed colleague, the editor of *al-Muhajir*, about the future of the Syrians in America, and specifically whether "they should take the American nationality, *jinsiyya*, and become fully assimilated," which *al-Muhajir* calls for, or whether "they should remain Ottomans and guard their Syrian patriotism, in order to return to Syria," *al-Manazir*'s demand. I am grateful to you both for thinking highly enough of this poor fellow to ask for his judgment about what is one of the most important problems for Syrians. For the answer to this question extends to the situation of the Syrians in all the countries to which they have emigrated in America,

Europe, Asia, Australia, and Africa. If it is right for them to retain their original nationality and return to their country, that must be applicable to Syrians wherever they have settled.

I notice, however, that you give Syrians the choice of following either of these visions, whereas in reality they are obliged by the nature of the process of civilization to follow one of them, as is true for people in all walks of life. If the subject of discussion were "Will the Syrians return from the countries they have emigrated to or stay in them?" it would conform better to the law of history. As the saying goes, "If you want to be obeyed, don't ask the impossible."

I read the respected colleague's letter and saw the discussion which you had in the various issues of *al-Manazir* while I was in al-Raml near Alexandria, a fugitive from inkwells, pens, and notebooks, spending the summer restfully while the crescent moon of *al-Hilal*[3] was hidden. I thought about this important matter while looking out of the window of our hotel, onto the trams coming and going, transporting people between Alexandria and the summer resorts of al-Raml. I watched them carry scores, even hundreds, of passengers, but only a few were native Egyptians. The rest were foreigners, *ajānib,* among them many Syrians, mostly people of rank, wealth, and influence and men of science and letters. I remembered how many Syrians live in Cairo, including highly placed civil servants, holders of administrative and military posts, journalists, merchants, lawyers, doctors, and so on—and there are many like them in the rest of Egypt—and I said to myself: "If *al-Manazir*'s demand were right, all these people would have to return to Syria, and so would the others, coming from the four corners of the earth. They number hundreds of thousands and among them are rich and powerful people. Emigrating has brought them knowledge and experience, they have learned from different nations the best social behaviors and ways of earning a living. They have considerable wealth, as we can deduce by analogy with the wealth of the Syrians in Egypt, which today is reckoned to be 30,000,000 Eg. Pounds, while the community has not more than around 10,000 members. How much wealth must the rest possess, in all the lands to which they have emigrated? They number around 300,000, and even allowing for the fact that the Syrians elsewhere are not as rich as those in Egypt, if we reckon that their fortune is half or a quarter as large, the wealth of all the emigrants from Syria amounts to

> 300,000,000 Eg. Pounds. And it increases as the years pass; ten years ago the Syrian immigrants in Egypt possessed a quarter of the fortune they have now. If the Syrians were to return to Syria with this wealth, that blessed land would rejoice and family and friends would gather there to enjoy the pleasant breeze and refreshing climate—which is the utmost happiness that anyone can hope for in this world. But: "The wind has woven a coat of mail on the water, / What invulnerable armor it would be, were it to turn to iron."

It is not to be expected that this wish will be fulfilled. For the Syrians will stay in the countries to which they have emigrated; they will become assimilated into the population, using its language to communicate with one another and adopting its customs. That is my opinion, which I published in *al-Hilal* some years ago and the editor of *al-Muhajir* also published in his reply. Referring to it would be enough, had your discussion not referred to the homeland and betrayal of it, and to patriotism and its community. These words touch the heart and arouse strong emotions, inhibiting the ability to reach rational conclusions. The discussion in which we are engaged requires that we examine the naked truth and the general interest, so I ask the honored colleagues to allow me to develop in detail what I summarized earlier.

Migration

Migration is as old as mankind, and the oldest reason for it is to earn a living. It is one of the most venerable and firmest pillars of civilization. For human beings descended from a common ancestor and lived in one place; but when that place could no longer support them they migrated to surrounding areas in search of land for farming and pasture. They moved again to different places for the same reason, generation after generation. The oldest account we have of migration is the dispersal of Noah's sons or their tribes from the middle of Asia to the ends of the known world. They are the most ancient races of humanity, and from them are descended the advanced nations known as the Caucasian peoples. Wherever the Caucasians settled during their migration, they found peoples of inferior races, like the Negroes or Indians, whom they conquered, taking their possessions and ruling over them. They founded a civilization that has continued to develop until today. The world was apparently populated thanks to successive migrations of races, some of which were more advanced than others, but ascending over time.

If we look at each region of the world individually, we can clearly see the traces of successive migrations. The Nile Valley's oldest inhabitants were the Negroes. Then came the Nubians, who were more advanced than the former and expelled them toward the south, taking their place. Later the Caucasians arrived, vying with the Nubians and overcoming them; the Pharaohs, founders of the ancient Egyptian civilization, were Caucasians. The same can be said about the coasts of North Africa, where the Caucasian peoples arrived from the east and north, driving the Berbers toward the south. When the Aryans migrated to India, they found the original Indians, who were comparable to the Nubians in Africa, and conquered them, with the Aryans providing the priests (Brahmins) and rulers. The migration of the Aryan tribes to Europe and the Semitic tribes to Syria, Palestine, and the Arabian Peninsula followed the same course.

Apart from that, there have been successive migrations in historical times, especially after the discovery of America, Australia, and other countries of the New World. Europeans (who are Caucasians) migrated to them, expelling the Indian races that lived in them and bringing with them their own civilization. The Indians fled from the Europeans in America and Australia as the Nubians had fled from the Caucasians (Semites) in Africa centuries earlier. The Caucasians are still migrating to the New World from other countries of the inhabited world, and however much their languages, manners, and customs differ, they are all descendants of one man, sharing the same skull shape and superior mental faculties. It is they who established this civilization, spreading it in the Old World and the New, and if they were able to discover other worlds they would migrate to them and settle them.

Peoples vary in their inclination to migrate and their ability to do so, according to differences in climate and character. The Syrians are among those most suited to emigrating and are most keen to do so. From the time of the Phoenicians they were travelers and migrants, settling many of the Mediterranean coasts several centuries before Christ. Their most famous colony was Carthage in North Africa. They also traveled to the lands of ancient civilizations in Assyria, Babylon, and Egypt. They were excellent intermediaries in transmitting their civilizations between those peoples (see vol. 3 of our book *The History of Islamic Civilization*). They did the same thing in the period of Greek and then Roman civilization; they traveled to Greece, Persia, and Alexandria to that end. They have fulfilled the same role during this present phase of civilization. For to seek their livelihood they easily move abroad, and so there are now 200,000 of them in America and large groups in Australia, Tasmania, [New] Zealand, Zanzibar, the Transvaal, Senegal, and other coastal and inland regions of Africa, as well as in India, Persia, China, Japan, and the islands of the ocean [*sic*]. This is apart from Egypt, the Sudan, Tunis, Morocco, and the Syrians living in European capitals. In other words, they are to be found in almost every inhabited country in the four corners of the earth and, with God's help, wherever they settle they prosper.

The Syrians have a trait that distinguishes them from other peoples, *al-umam*; it has become deeply rooted in them thanks to their successive migrations. As well as being energetic and intelligent, they have an extraordinary ability to adapt, to fit their character and habits to the society in which they live, and to learn the language its inhabitants use. Thus when they live in France, for instance, not long passes before they imitate the French so well that you imagine they are themselves French. Likewise, if they live in America or England, you think they are American or English. And you notice they are some of the keenest to stand up for the country they have settled in and the most willing to defend or serve it.

The Homeland and the Patriotic Community

I consider that the esteemed editor of *al-Manazir* exaggerated in relying on the argument of patriotism to support his view, when he counted a Syrian's acquiring American nationality betrayal of the homeland.[4] So I ask him to allow me to explain what "the homeland" and "patriotism" mean where Syrians are concerned. A homeland is a country where people with common interests and reciprocal rights and duties live. Longing for one's homeland is like longing for one's parents; both of them are the product of habit and affection. How can we not long for the country in whose sky we have learned to know the sun, from whose air we have breathed life, on whose animals and plants we have fed, which has sheltered us as children and nurtured us as youths and young men? Our bodies have been formed by elements of it and our characters have been marked by its climate. It brings together our close family and distant relatives; it is where our friends live. Longing for one's homeland is innate, even in dumb animals, and there is no need to prove it. Staying in one's homeland or returning to it is not, however, an imposed duty, just as staying in one's parents' orbit is not a stimulus to civilization nor does it provide a basis for progress except when interest dictates it. When a young man reaches maturity he looks for a livelihood wherever he may find it, even if that obliges him to leave his parents and family. So how can his homeland hold him back? But just as he is expected to remember his family, miss them, and seek their comfort even if he is far from them, likewise if a disaster befalls his homeland, he is required to come to its help in whatever way he can.

This is what the homeland means as far as each individual member is concerned. Where the nation as a whole, *majmū' al-umma,* or the state, *al-dawla,* is concerned, it means the tie of patriotism. In its simplest form, this is the coming together of a country's inhabitants to repel an enemy who wants to attack it. They may be in conflict with each other until danger threatens, but then they unite. That is natural even among dumb animals. Cocks may quarrel and fight, but if you put them in a cage together and starve them, for example, they behave like friends to each other. The inhabitants of a country cooperate in defending it or furthering its welfare through what is called the "bond of patriotism"; this is one of the expressions that we have adopted from the representatives of modern civilization in Europe. They understand it to mean the solidarity of a country's inhabitants in defending its territory and striving for its welfare. It replaces the unifying factor of a common religion or language among other nations. The stronger the state becomes, the more established its authority and the greater the profitable exchanges between the capital and the regions dependent on it, [and thus] the more united the country will be by patriotism. In the earliest historical times, the state was confined to a single city after which it was named, such as Athens, Sparta, and Rome. When the state's authority grew and it expanded through conquest to become a great empire, the empire was named after the city, like the Roman Empire for example, which denotes the city of Rome and the territories belonging to it. And the tie of Roman patriotism waxed and waned with Rome's authority.

In the case of the Arabs, before Islam they were tribes unified by genealogies and tribal solidarity. When they converted to Islam, Islam became their unifying bond. Their state was called "Islamic," not named after a particular city or country. It took the name of its founders or of those of their ancestors who were most closely connected with the Prophet, such as the Abbasids, the 'Alids, the Marwanids, and so on. When the Islamic Empire was divided and non-Arabs came to rule it, the different parts were distinguished according to the origins or languages of their rulers, Turks, Persians, Ḳurds, and so on; these states might also be designated by the names of their founders, like the Zengid and Ayyubid states and the Ottoman Empire. After the Roman Empire had begun to decline and Roman patriotism had weakened, the Europeans established small states that quarreled and fought with each other. Then when the Muslims had become overwhelmingly powerful in the East and the Europeans wanted to wrest Jerusalem from them, they found nothing to unite them except religion. So they came together under the banner of the cross and fought the Muslims. After the end of the Crusades, when the Europeans had begun their recent renaissance and grown stronger, their states began to compete with each other to acquire the main influence on the European continent. Each state sought to unify its people so as to be able to gain the ascendancy. Religion was the greatest unifying bond between them all, as has already been said, and each individual state had no particular factor to unify its members except the homeland or the nation. Thus the French made their unifying factor France or the French people, *sha'ab*; the Germans and the English did likewise. Christianity was divided and no longer served as a unifying bond in Europe, with the emergence of the French, Germans, English, and other people, just as the bond of Islam no longer unified the Muslims, with the emergence of the Persians, Turks, Kurds, and others. If you examine those bonds carefully, you can see that they are in reality based on language and religion. The inhabitants of each Europeans country speak one language, which is that of the rulers, and generally they belong to one religious community which is that of the government.

Patriotism means nothing if there is no state to support or promote it, enlist people to serve it, or bear weapons to defend its independence; in return the inhabitants of the homeland have claims on the state, provided they share a common language. The Syrians, and here the Christians of Syria are meant, are not concerned by all that because they are inhabitants of the Ottoman Empire but they do not serve in its army or defend it, nor do they speak its language. Thus they are not tied by the bonds of Ottoman patriotism; nor does their Syrian homeland have a need of them for such tasks, so if they live far from it, that is neither a betrayal nor a fault. This is all the truer because they were forced to leave Syria in search of a livelihood, after they exhausted all possibilities of making a comfortable living at home. Their homeland seems to have abandoned and expelled them against their will, or as the poet put it:

> If you see a slave who is on the run and not pursued / it is his master
> who is running away from him.

Or, as another poet says:

> If you depart from people who could have kept you from leaving / they
> are the ones who are departing.

The Syrians do not lack the means to progress and they are no less dynamic and gifted than the most advanced of the civilized nations. We have seen them keeping pace with the Europeans even in their own countries. There are Syrian merchants in the largest cities of Europe and America. In addition, they are the leading merchants in Egypt; the largest commercial concerns there are Syrian-owned and there are important lawyers, doctors, writers, holders of government position, and so on among them. They are models of industry, uprightness, and honesty; they are criticized merely for their weak sense of patriotism, but they are not to be blamed for it for the reasons we have mentioned. Moreover there are a multitude of communities and orientations in Syria, and living abroad has increased the Syrians' estrangement from one another because of their inborn ability to adapt their tastes to those of the peoples among whom they live, who are different from one another.

The Syrians' bond with their home country, then, is a bond created by longing and affection, not one of attack or defense [of the country] or of ownership and profit. They are among the nations most attached to their homeland, always remembering it, longing for it even when they have lived abroad for a long time, promising themselves to return to it and making great efforts to do so.

A Syrian's business may expand, he may buy property and build houses in the country he has emigrated to, but he still considers himself a resident there for a limited period at the end of which he will return to his home country. He nourishes that hope because of homesickness—but in reality he will not return. A friend of mine, one of the notables from Hasbayya who settled in Beirut after the well-known catastrophe of 1860, told me that until recently, when his mother needed new cooking utensils, she would ask the coppersmith to put a ring on them so they could be hung on the mules when the family returned to Hasbayya. At the same time, his father was expanding his business, putting up buildings in Beirut and establishing himself there. Several prominent Syrians in this country have a custom, when one of their loved ones dies, to bury him or her in a temporary grave until they can take the remains with them to Syria when they return there. And we know of others in Egypt and elsewhere who send the money they make back to Syria to buy land and build houses there in preparation for their return when they no longer need to live abroad. But they rarely return, and if they do, they seldom remain in Syria. And their descendants in the country to which they have emigrated take the nationality of the country they are born in and grow up among its people, whether their own people like it or not.

They are not to be blamed for becoming naturalized, since they are obliged by the nature of civilization to do so, like other peoples who have migrated to that country. The United States has been settled and cultivated by peoples who have migrated to it from England, Spain, France, Germany, and other countries, mingling with each other, intermarrying, and giving up their original nationality for the American one. Everyone who moves to America, lives among the Americans, and takes their nationality acquires the rights and obligations they have. There is nothing wrong with Syrians preferring to stay in that flourishing country, mixing with its inhabitants and taking their nationality, since their own country can do without them. They, for their part, need the new country because of the sources of income and comfort that it provides, and so they use their talents to work hard and energetically, and every hard worker has his reward.

How I wish from the bottom of my heart that my judgment were wrong, and that I could meet my brethren and friends living in our homeland in comfort, prosperity, and peace. That is the desire of everyone who loves his country. In the meantime, I miss the homeland as a child misses his parents, though I do not consider my remoteness from it as betrayal or disobedience. "My country is dear to me, even when it wrongs me / And though my people wrong me they are noble."

If the Syrians living abroad manage to preserve their language, manners, and customs, as for instance the Germans in America do, that is an achievement. But if they do, it will not be for long, especially in America, given the weakness of Syrian patriotism vis-à-vis American patriotism. For the strong devour the weak, according to God's law in his Creation.

Notes

1. Zaydān, "al-Sūriyyūn wa-tajannusuhum."
2. *Al-Manāẓir.*
3. A pun in Arabic: *al-hilāl* means crescent.
4. *Al-Waṭan wa-'l-jāmi'a al-waṭaniyya.*

◆ ◆ ◆

Through Pressure and Resistance, Hidden Forces Appear

Or, Overcoming Adversity Brings Forth Latent Strengths

Translated by Paul Starkey

Among the best-known laws of the natural sciences is that natural forces, such as gravity, temperature, light, electricity, and magnetism, are all varieties of a single force hidden in matter, and that among the simplest ways of making this force apparent are through rubbing, pressure, or friction, in other words, "resistance."[1] If you look at a piece of iron in its natural state you will see that it is cold, and lacking in light, heat, or electricity, so that you imagine that it is devoid of all these things. But if you knock it with a weight or scrape it with a chisel, it isn't long before you see it warm up and its temperature increase as the pressure of rubbing increases in intensity. The more you increase the pressure, the more the temperature increases, until it turns red, and it may even turn white and give off light. As for producing light through pressure, this process can be clearly seen in the case of the anvil. This involves hitting a piece of iron with a hammer so that a shining spark of light emerges from between them. Before the invention of matches, people used to light their fires with flints or by rubbing pieces of wood hard against one another. There is no difference, except one of degree, between lighting fires with a flint, or rubbing pieces of wood together, or matches; the method is the same. We light matches by rubbing them, but they have a little piece of phosphorous at their end that is quick to ignite, and it requires only a little heat, generated by a little rubbing, to ignite it.

As for the phenomenon of attraction by rubbing, that is most obviously seen when rubbing pieces of amber, red wax, or glass. If you rub a piece of one of these substances with a woolen cloth, it will grow hot. If you hold a small piece of straw or something similar near to it, it will attract it. And if you rub it harder, electricity will be generated. This is well known, as a great number of electrical devices operate solely on the basis of power generated by friction.

It is demonstrable, on the basis of what has preceded, that natural forces are latent in matter, and that these may be brought to light by pressure or resistance and used to satisfy our needs. Otherwise, those forces will remain hidden and be of no use to us at all.

This is also the case in the moral, or ethical, field. A man may be endowed with intelligence, sharpness of intellect, courage, and boldness, but without the adversity that creates pressure and resistance these powers will remain latent in him, so that you would think him stupid and lethargic. Then, when some obstacles stand in his way and he is affected by them, his talents become apparent and the man emerges as a genius, carrying out remarkable deeds. You may well find that the most influential person in terms of advancing the affairs of human society is the one who has been most exposed to adversity and the resulting pressures and struggles. We have the clearest evidence in the form of the biographies of famous men and the histories of nations and societies. It becomes most plain in religious sects. For the persecution suffered by the founders of religions and their followers was their greatest spur and strongest factor in their perseverance and efforts to spread their principles. If they had been left to themselves they would not have achieved a tenth of the success that they had. It is enough to consider the persecution suffered by Christ's Apostles during their mission, for they suffered the worst sorts of torture and the majority of them were put to death.

The same sort of thing applies to the independence of nations. It has often been intense pressure that has acted as a spur to independence. The Americans did not assert their independence from the yoke of the British except to escape from the pressure and injustice they were suffering. When it became too much for them to bear, they bestirred themselves, and the latent forces within them boiled over, so they fought the British and escaped from their clutches. There are many similar examples.

How many men there have been, famous in the fields of politics and administration, with a hold over whole societies, who were idle and listless until driven on by the spur of adversity and the pressure it aroused; at which point, their powers became apparent, so that they rose to positions of prominence in politics, administration, or government, founded parties, and established states. When the late Muhammad 'Ali came to Egypt in the ranks of the Ottoman force sent by the Porte to expel the French, you would not have thought that he wanted to establish a state that would wake the dead of this region through the rule of his successors for several generations. Indeed, we know that when he had made his way through the ranks of the military, reached the rank of *sarshashmah*[2] and become commander of four thousand Albanians, he thought that he had reached an exalted pinnacle. If things had remained as they were and he had not encountered adversity, he would have stayed at that rank or perhaps risen a little higher. But fate challenged him and he revealed his powers until he achieved what he did. The first thing that spurred him to attain real power was a blow that afflicted him from Khosraw Pasha, the governor of Egypt at that time. This governor, who was the first to take charge of Egypt after the departure of the French, expelled the Mamluks, who fled to Upper Egypt. He had secret orders to put them to death, so he mounted a campaign against them using his own soldiers, and ordered Muhammad 'Ali to march with his Albanians in support of the expedition. But Muhammad 'Ali was slow to set off, and the expedition returned defeated before he had arrived. The commander of the expedition complained of this to Khosraw, and attributed the defeat of the campaign to Muhammad 'Ali's tardiness. So Khosraw resented Muhammad 'Ali and made up his mind to have him assassinated. He sent a message to him asking him to come to the citadel at midnight to consider some business, but Muhammad 'Ali realized his intention; his anger was aroused, and a feeling of revenge stirred inside him. He could see no way of achieving his aim except by resorting to the Mamluks. So he made an approach to them, and exchanged secret intelligence with them, while secretly determining to depose Khosraw. He then resolved to take power himself. The Mamluks remained his allies until he succeeded in deposing Khosraw and his successor as governor, and achieved his life's ambition, for which he is well known.

Our argument is also supported by the biography of Luther, the leader of the Protestant community. This man's reform movement at the beginning of the sixteenth century was one of the biggest spurs to modern reform in Europe. Had it not been for Pope Leo X's persecution of him, in the form of deprivation and other forms of harsh punishment, he would not have achieved over several generations what he actually achieved in a few years. The antagonism and "friction" between Catholics and Protestants stirred up the passions of both sides. The Catholics set about restoring unity to their organization, and they set up societies that were a prime factor in aiding the Catholic Church; in the forefront of these was the Society of Jesuits.

There is another proof, nearer to us in time and place than all the others, namely the Sudanese Muhammad Ahmad[3] undertaking his Mahdist missionary campaign. Anyone who studies the history of this man will come to the firm conclusion that had it not been for adversity and persecution he would not have achieved one-hundredth of the fame and extensive power that he gained in his lifetime. If the Egyptian government had left him to his own devices he would not have had the ambition to conquer the Sudan and rule it, nor would his sights have been set on Egypt, Syria, and Iraq. Indeed, we might imagine he would have been content to be a sheikh in his religious order, like al-Sanusi[4] in North Africa, Shaykh al-Mirghani[5] in Sudan, and others.

But if we were to examine the history of this man's life carefully, since the time of his first appearance, we would see that his purpose at first was no more than piety and asceticism. He never had any idea of proclaiming himself as Mahdi. What drove him to this was the great challenge that he encountered from his sheikh, Muhammad al-Sharif. Muhammad Ahmad, who proclaimed himself Mahdi, had grown up keen on a life of asceticism and piety, and studied with many sheikhs in the religious orders. Eventually, he joined the circle of Sheikh Muhammad al-Sharif,[6] the sheikh of the Salmaniyya order. He was extremely pious and religious;

he was also kind and a good companion, well liked by his friends. As he became familiar with the practices of that order, he formed his own separate circle, which was a branch of Sheikh Muhammad al-Sharif's circle, and lived on the island of Aba beyond Khartoum. It happened that one of his disciples was celebrating his son's circumcision. A large crowd attended the gathering and there was singing and dancing in accordance with their customs, for they held that God would thereby forgive them the sins they had committed. But Muhammad Ahmad objected to this and stopped them. They told him that it had been permitted by the head of the order himself, but he replied that what was forbidden by the *shari'a* could not be sanctioned by the head of the order. His words came to the attention of Sheikh Muhammad al-Sharif, who sent for him, so he came to him humbly and submissively and begged his forgiveness in the presence of other sheikhs and learned men. But he did not forgive him; on the contrary, he berated him harshly and expunged his name from the order's register. He left contritely then returned again having adopted an even more submissive pose, putting ashes on his head and a *shu'ba* on his neck (a *shu'ba* being a stick with two branches that is put around the neck as a sign of humility). He went in to Muhammad al-Sharif like that, but this only made him more angry and violent, until he threw him out and insulted him, abusing him for his Dongolese origins. So Muhammad Ahmad left his presence, choked by tears of anger and frustration. That intense humiliation seemed to arouse the intelligence and cunning that had lain dormant inside him. So he entered on a path of criticism of his sheikh, at the same time attaching himself to another sheikh, a rival of Sheikh Muhammad al-Sharif, who accepted him. Muhammad Ahmad began to gather together the various factions, which made Muhammad al-Sharif afraid of him, so he sent a message to try to win him over and promised him forgiveness. Muhammad Ahmad felt the pleasure of victory and became more arrogant and overbearing; he refused his invitation and answered him sarcastically: "I wouldn't want you to demean yourself for a Dongolese like me!" That conversation was relayed throughout the Sudan, and for the first time the man became well known. His mission took off from there: it is clear that had it not been for Sheikh Muhammad al Sharif's challenge he would not have become conscious of his mission or the importance of gathering together the factions. Compare with this numerous incidents that we see every day. We may experience them ourselves, or see them happening to some friends or neighbors, and they are obvious to everyone.

There is one observation that I need to make to conclude the subject, namely that some materials, glass, for example, will not tolerate pressure, resistance, or friction. If you press glass, for example, it will break before showing any sign of heat, and if you rub or press on china it will smash. People are the same: there are some people who will cringe or cower if you pressure them or subject them to stress and adversity. People differ in their ability to bear adversity. There are many obstacles and difficulties that may overtake a man or stand in his way. If they befall a man possessed of latent powers, they can be a reason for him to exhibit them, for he will be strong enough to bear setbacks, work diligently, and demonstrate his talents; but if they afflict a weak man, they will simply increase his weakness until he dies. How many men have embarked on ambitious projects or taken on great deeds, then given up when confronted by difficulties, so that their efforts have been in vain. This was what happened to al-Ta'ayushi, the inheritor of the Mahdist throne in Sudan. He had weak policies and was a bad administrator, so he could not act decisively. So when the Egyptian government opposed him, it took only one blow for his authority to collapse and the apparatus of his government to be destroyed.

How he deals with adversity is what distinguishes one man from another. It makes the strong stronger and the weak weaker, like the friction that heats the iron but smashes the china. But the wisdom of God in his creation cannot be comprehended.

Notes

1. Zaydān, "Bi'l-daght wa-'l-muqāwama yaẓhar al-quwā 'l-kāmina." The Arabic title of this article can be given either a scientific meaning or one related to human character as reflected in the two above alternative English translations. The play on words in the Arabic title conveys the central theme of this article—namely the link between the two that Zaidan tries to establish.

2. Ottoman Turkish: *serçeshmeh,* milit. Rank "officer commissioned to raise irregular troops," Redhouse, 1051.

3. Muḥammad Aḥmad b. al-Sayyid 'Abdallāh, called al-Mahdī (r. 1881–1885); leader of a neopuritanical, nativist movement in Sudan against Egyptian and British imperialism.

4. Muḥammad ibn 'Alī al-Sanūsī (1787–1859), founder of the Sanusiyya order. Having founded his mystic brotherhood in Mecca he moved to the region of today's Libya, where he organized and established his order.

5. 'Uthmān al-Mirghānī (d. 1851), one of the leaders of the Idrīsiyya order.

6. Al-Mahdī joined Muḥammad al-Sharīf in 1861.

◆ ◆ ◆

Salim Saydnawi

Proprietor of the Largest Store in Cairo (1856–1908)

Translated by Hilary Kilpatrick

Our purpose in publishing the biographies of great men is either to record what they did and thus keep their memory alive, out of recognition of their merits and admiration for their gifts, or else to use their lives as examples for others, or for both reasons.[1] The biographies of Bonaparte, Alexander, Mu'awiya, Bismarck, and Gladstone are meant to immortalize those great men's deeds and excite admiration for their achievements. The life stories of Columbus, the discoverer of America, Pasteur, the discoverer of microbes, Gutenberg, the inventor of printing, and others to whom society is indebted are generally intended to record their merits in the pages of history. With the biographies of Disraeli, Palissy, Cellini, Rothschild, and other active and enterprising men who were born into poverty and acquired wealth, knowledge, or skills thanks to their energy and hard work, the aim is to provide an example worth following, as well as to keep their memory alive. The closer their lives are to the readers' concerns, the more useful it is to publish their biographies. The lives of politicians, civil servants, and military men cannot help us at all to progress in our doings as we hope. By contrast, if men of science, trade, or industry have acquired their wealth or fame through their own efforts and integrity, their lives are a good example for young people today. And a penny of example is better than a pound of instruction.

Our writers have generally been accustomed to record the lives of scholars, generals, or politicians. But we are in far greater need of biographies of self-made merchants who have become wealthy by legal means that are bound to lead to success. For trade is the most important source of income in our country. It is a widespread delusion that "wealth cannot be acquired honestly," that "trustworthy, honest men are poor during their lifetime and die destitute," and that "only dishonest, hypocritical tricksters get rich." Sayings, proverbs, and poems exist on the subject. But this is the excuse of those who fail in their undertakings despite their desire to work, their vigilance, and their uprightness. They attribute their failure to their honesty and good intentions, whereas it is due to their lacking some of the prerequisites for success, such as intelligence, knowledge, perseverance, and the like. For honesty, alone, is not enough even if it is accompanied by efforts and vigilance.

As a rule, here are the main qualities a man needs in order to succeed:

The Conditions for Success

1. *Knowledge.* The first thing that someone seeking success in this life needs is to be good in some branch of industry, commerce, or agriculture, or in a profession involving the pen. For instance, he should be a skilled carpenter, a merchant experienced in different kinds of trade or trained in accountancy, a farmer who knows both the theory and practice of agriculture, a clerk familiar with a certain kind of office work or trained in one of the learned professions such as medicine, law, translation, or the art of writing. It is enough for him to know one profession well rather than several professions imperfectly, for a Jack-of-all-trades is master of none, and mastery is needed for success.

2. *Ability to make the right choice.* That means that a person chooses wisely the profession suited to his gifts and practices it in the appropriate place. He does not engage in industry when he is made for commerce, and he does not work in a learned profession if he lacks the necessary specialized knowledge. Nor does he engage in an activity that cannot be expected to succeed, for instance, trading in thick cloth in a hot country, or setting up a factory for goods that are not in demand there or are more expensive than if they were imported from abroad. There are countless other examples which sound sense can be relied on to discern.

3. *Perseverance.* Often a person fails even though he has the necessary knowledge and makes discriminating choices, and that is usually because

he tries to realize the profits from his work too soon. If he does not see the results of his efforts quickly, he gives up, laments his ill fortune, or complains of the times that only favor the ignorant. He may quote obvious examples of people who have succeeded although they know less than he does, but he does not realize that they have done well thanks to perseverance or some other quality needed for success which he lacks.

4. *Integrity.* Small shopkeepers are often heard to say that in this age only hypocrisy sells well and only fraud is in demand; but they say that in every age. And it is not true, for integrity and honesty are among the main conditions for success, especially in our age, the age of truth and freedom. Liars' success lasts a limited time. But integrity alone is of no use, because if you strip an honest man of his knowledge and perseverance, he will become like a dumb animal, which has a good heart and never resorts to cheating but may be robbed or deceived.

5. *Exertion.* A man may be endowed with knowledge, integrity, perseverance, and discrimination and yet have only limited success because he has many competitors in the activity he has embarked on or for some other reason. He will only achieve success by exerting himself and being vigilant. Someone with no more than average intelligence and knowledge may be able to compensate for that through exertion.

6. *Being alert to opportunities.* Seizing opportunities is one of the principal reasons for success, and it is generally the main means to become rich. An opportunity may present itself to someone, and if he notices and seizes it, it will spare him much effort or even open the way to enormous earnings that he could not expect from his ordinary work.

7. *Style of conduct.* This is one of the greatest secrets of success. Someone may be proficient, persevering, honest, hard-working, and vigilant, and yet not have much success because he does not know how to conduct himself well with people or he treats them in a way they do not like. Anyone looking to succeed must be endowed with a pleasant character, cheerful, kind, and sensitive. We know more than one man very well known for proficiency in his work who has failed because he did not behave well toward others. Indeed, a man's success often depends more on fine moral qualities than on intelligence and acumen.

Salim Saydnawi, the subject of our biography, was born poor and acquired great wealth and fame, thanks to his exertion, integrity, perseverance, and good treatment of others, as will be seen in what follows.

Salim's Early Years

Salim was born in Damascus in 1857 into a well-known family. His father, the late Yusuf Saydnawi, was a commercial broker. Salim grew up in his parents' house and learned the rudiments of reading and writing as far as those days allowed. When someone could read the Psalms or the Gospels well and had learned some arithmetic, they used to say, "He has completed his education." Salim's father had thought hard about his two sons' future, believing that a young man could only escape poverty by learning some essential trade. He found an opening for Salim in a European tailor's shop—such shops were new in Syria at the time—and Salim learned the trade and worked as a tailor until he left for Egypt in 1879.

His brother Sam'an, who was two years older, had come to Egypt in 1877. Interested in commerce since childhood, he had worked in a store in Damascus for three years, despite his father's desire for him to learn a craft according to the principle we have mentioned already. He had him apprenticed to a weaver, but Sam'an preferred trade. He arrived in Egypt in 1877 without any capital, but found his uncle, the late Niqula Saydnawi, who was a merchant in the Hamzawi quarter, selling silk wares and notions. Sam'an went to work for his uncle, although he balked at remaining an employee for long. Five months after he started working for his uncle, a Syrian merchant, Ilyas Jahami died leaving underage children. He had a shop in the Hamzawi quarter that the executors wanted to liquidate, and Sam'an seized the opportunity to offer to take care of the liquidation. They agreed, and while he was engaged in winding up the business, he used some of the money he received from sales to buy certain articles and dispose of them with the rest of the goods, on the understanding that he would receive half the profits and the other half would go to the shop. When he was close to completing the liquidation, the profits amounted to 285 Eg. Pounds, half of which belonged to him. He then agreed with the executors to keep the whole sum, paying interest at the legally fixed rate on the other half and on the goods to a value of 140 Eg. Pounds, which were still left in the shop. The shop's capital was 500 Eg. Pounds, two-thirds of which Sam'an owed and on which he paid 200 piastres a month interest.[2]

Sam'an concentrated on seeking success by lawful means. His success was mainly due to the fact that by reflection and vigilance he discovered the original source of the goods he sold, that is, silk wares and handkerchiefs. Egyptian merchants imported them from Constantinople, but he found out that the merchants in Constantinople imported them from Europe. So he imported them from there directly and sold them more cheaply than others. His business flourished and he extended his activities.

When Salim arrived in Egypt, Sam'an was already working in his own shop. Salim first worked as a commercial tailor, going into partnership with Mr. Mitri Salhani in a shop for tailoring and selling clothes; Salim's share of the capital was paid by his brother. Shortly after, the shop burned down and all the capital was lost. There was greater love and camaraderie between Salim and Sam'an than is usual between brothers; it was as though they were one person. The late Sam'an[3] had felt a fondness for his brother since childhood, and when the shop burned down, he disregarded the loss and made him his partner in the rest of his business. They opened a shop in the Muski at the beginning of Mansur Pasha Street, not more than four square meters in area, where Salim worked while Sam'an remained in Hamzawi. They registered the company officially under the name "Salim and Sam'an Saydnawi" in 1879, and set out to work energetically and honestly. They were both bachelors, and they lived in a room in the Ya'qub Bey caravanserai in Hamzawi, which had only one bed and a chair. While one brother slept on the bed, the other slept in the chair. They would eat in a restaurant, choosing the simplest and most economical dishes. We heard them recalling that life after they had attained high standing and great wealth, and they saw no indignity in mentioning it.

The Foundations of Success

Apart from the company, the basis of [the brothers'] success was an event similar to one told in connection with the Rothschild family's success; it indicates the fruits honesty and integrity bring. When Salim was in his aforementioned shop, a maid from Mustafa Pasha Fadil's palace came and bought two lace dresses from him priced at sixteen half-piasters. She had understood that he meant sixteen whole piasters, so she paid that sum and went away without him noticing because he was busy with another customer. Then he counted the money and saw that the woman had paid twice as much as what he asked. He did not know where she lived. The next day she came with another sixteen piasters in her hand and bought two other dresses, so he told her that the price was eight piasters, which was the amount left over from what she had bought the day before, and he gave her the two dresses without taking anything from her. She was amazed at this honesty, which is rare especially in behavior toward the wealthy because people have designs on their money. She recounted the incident to her mistress and news of it spread in the houses of the leading princes and their relatives. Consequently, they all wanted to frequent the honest shopkeeper. Salim knew some Turkish, which made dealing with them easier. Their confidence in his honesty increased every day until they bought furnishings, clothes, or material only from him or on his advice.

His honesty and integrity became well known among the rich and so his earnings increased. The shop grew too small, and in 1881 he moved to larger premises in the Muski, overlooking Port Said Street. (They later expanded the interior, selling carpets and furnishings in an area no larger than half the shop before its expansion.) When he moved to that shop, the brothers joined up to work together while keeping the shop in Hamzawi. Their activities continued to expand and their capital to increase. When the shop became too small, they expanded the facilities until there was no more space. Then they took over a nearby shop, which they turned into the main shop with the records and accounts.

They followed the European market as a guide when fixing prices, which was a major step on their path to success. That started in 1885, when an opportunity arose. The late Salim fell ill and the doctors advised him to go to Europe for treatment. He took advantage of his stay there to contact factories producing the goods he sold and noticed a great difference in prices. So he negotiated with them directly, and that became a principle in setting the prices each year. The brothers divided the work; Salim took over negotiating with suppliers and keeping the accounts, while Sam'an organized the sales department. Their business developed and their work increased, expanded, and diversified until their shop in Cairo became the largest one in the East, employing about 150 people as salesmen and clerks, not counting menial workers and the people they employed on their farms, estates, and other enterprises. In addition, they had branches in Manchester, Lyons, Paris, Alexandria, and elsewhere and a bank that Salim founded as a limited company before he died, Saydnawi, Zarifa, Nahhas and Co. The Ottoman sultan awarded them the title "Bey," "second rank."[4] That year they turned their shop in Cairo into a limited liability company named "Salim and Sam'an Saydnawi Ltd.," while their original company, which continued to deal in real estate and agricultural land, was called "Salim and Sam'an Saydnawi." Their fortune in 1908 was 300,000 Eg. Pounds: two-thirds of it was in real estate and agricultural land, and the remaining third in commerce.

The Calculation of the "Dues or Tithes"

As you see, they founded their company on integrity and honesty, and they surrounded it with a wall of philanthropy; they carried out charitable activities as a duty for which they expected no reward. From the time they founded the company, and while they were still in the small shop, they set aside 5 percent of the profits to be distributed among the poor as alms. At stocktaking each year, when they knew what the profits were, they would take 5 percent to give away. They called this amount the "dues or tithes," to be spent for charity. The Saydnawi family still follows this custom. The amount of the tithes increased as their profits did, so they opened a special account for them in separate registers. The amount may well be 2,000 Eg. Pounds sterling a year now, to be spent on supporting the poor, no difference being made between Muslims, Christians, Jews, and others, with the money going toward clothes, food, housing, or marrying off young girls whose poverty discourages potential suitors. How many families have been protected by their alms, and how many houses would have been ruined without them! The Saydnawis give the money without considering it charity, and if you try to raise the subject they ignore it and may even deny that they engage in philanthropy. But the truth becomes known. It is no wonder that you see the signs of their charity appearing in associations, families, hospitals, schools, and churches. They give an example which the rich would do well to imitate. For few wealthy men are philanthropists, and if they perform some charitable deed, they make a great song and dance about it and publish it in the newspapers out of a desire to enhance their reputation.

His Appearance and Character

Salim, God rest his soul, was of medium height and stout. He was straightforward and spoke the truth, neither swearing nor going back on his word. Patient and long-suffering, he was much inclined to conciliation and forbearance. A persevering worker, he used his time well. He was eager to console the grieving and provide for the poor, and if a father on his deathbed had learned that Salim Saydnawi would be his children's guardian, he would die peacefully. Salim thus acquired many wardships, and he never cared how much of his time or health he spent in dealing with them. He also did a great deal for the Catholic community's pious foundations and as an intermediary to solve problems between business partners, relatives, or friends.

Despite his many cares, Salim greatly enjoyed his family's company and cheerfully stayed at home. His wife, the daughter of his uncle Niqula Saydnawi, who was mentioned at the beginning of this article, was a credit to him because of her intelligence, kindness, prudence, and love of reading. She, for her part, spared no effort for his comfort. When he came home, she lightened his cares with her kindness and gentleness, as a good wife should. Then he would start to play with his children or those of his brother and tease them, his tiredness would disappear and his strength return, giving him more energy to work.

The Lesson to be Learned from This Life

We are on the subject of the late Salim Saydnawi's life, but inevitably we have spoken of his brother too because they cooperated closely in their business and supported each other in their charitable activities. There is a lesson to be learned from the foregoing: these brothers' accomplishments are a cogent argument for the fact that integrity and honesty are necessary for success, and success does not remain assured unless those who achieve it maintain it through almsgiving or charity. If they do, their profits will increase and they will escape the disasters wrought by envy. This is not because envy harms those who are its object. Anyone who improves his position through any kind of work will attract much envy and criticism, and the more important he becomes, the greater the number of those who attack him. Some people do not care what is said about them, they are simply care about becoming richer, whether people like them or not. Others are less concerned with acquiring wealth than with popularity, and they respond to criticism and envy with charity, humility, and politeness. Or they may provide charity for religious reasons, seeking a reward in the world to come. Both these motives are salutary, because they lead to support for the weak and philanthropic activities. Those who are simply concerned to amass wealth, impervious to what is said about them, are an alien growth in the body politic, expanding by sucking up nourishment from it while causing it harm.

The Saydnawi brothers are the best example of how men of wealth and prestige should be. Despite their riches and status their lifestyle was simple and they spent thousands on helping the poor. They are also exemplary for their diligence and energy, working hard from early morning until after the evening meal, as anyone who has visited their shop and has seen the activity in it knows.

Another reason for their success, apart from their integrity, energy, and recognizing opportunities which we have referred to, was their capacity to make the right choices. They chose and divided up the work in accordance with the abilities of each of them, Salim negotiating with suppliers and handling the accounts, while Sam'an managed the sales. Yet another reason was their perseverance. They remained in the same business of selling silk and notions for thirty years, never deviating from it; indeed they expanded it with appropriate subsidiary activities. Their way of treating people was also a contributing factor, for they were renowned for their kindness and unpretentiousness. No buyer or seller ever left their shop dissatisfied.

Notes

1. Salīm Ṣaydnāwī; in Latin letters the name was known as Sednaoui. From Zaydān, *Tarājim* 1, 302–9, published first in *al-Hilāl* 16 (May 1908): 471–78.

2. There are one hundred piasters in every pound.

3. "Salīm" in the text, but evidently "Sam'ān" is meant; translator's note.

4. A rank in the Ottoman administration and army of "two horsetails," three being the highest grade.

◆ ◆ ◆

Community of Interest

The Source of All Other Communities and the Primary Motivation for Undertaking Great Deeds

Translated by Paul Starkey

What Is a Community?

"Community" implies adhering to a principle, belief, or aim, around which a group of people collect, who embrace it and defend it together.[1] Forming groups is natural in man, because man has many needs but cannot fulfill them all on his own, and he is therefore forced to seek help in fulfilling them by joining with his fellow tribesmen or countrymen to cooperate for mutual advantage. He employs various forms of association to bring him together with others, the oldest of which is kinship, or a community based on relationship, which is also known as group loyalty (*'aṣabiyya*). Almost as old is the community of language—for mutual understanding brings together hearts and unites aims.

If a man's relatives multiply and his tribe splits into subgroups, each of them will take up residence in a particular location, and its members cooperate in defense of that location, thus creating a new community based on the homeland. Meanwhile, however, they will continue to share a community of language and of lineage because they all share in a common origin. Usually, the people of a single tribe will profess a single religion. So, however many branches it may have, [the members of the tribe] will also be linked by the bond of religion, quite apart from language and lineage.

It sometimes happens that another people in another country may speak a different language but profess the same religion, and so may be bound to them by the community of religion. There are also numerous other communities. The people in a single country may be divided into groups, some of which are held together by bonds of profession and others by links of sex, color, marriage, or bachelorhood, so that married people form a single group united by the link of marriage, and similarly with bachelors and the middle-aged. Each individual member of one of those groups may, in another capacity, be a member of another group: thus, with others, he will also be a member of a community based on lineage; with others, of a religious community; and with yet others, of a language community. Similarly with regard to profession, customs, age, height, and so forth. So, for example, one might be a doctor and join with other doctors in a professional association, and a lawyer with other lawyers; while a tall man will join with other tall men, a short man with other short men, dark-skinned with dark-skinned, white with white, and so on.

Communities may be opposed to each other and split from others in a remarkable way. The inhabitants of Cairo, for example, are all united by the city of Cairo, but the inhabitant of this city will unite with the inhabitant of Alexandria against a non-Egyptian, and will form a link with the peoples of the East against the peoples of the West. The Egyptian Muslim comes together with the Egyptian non-Muslim in the community based on the homeland, with the Syrian and Iraqi in a language community, and with the Persian and Indian in a religious community. If you consider how such ramifications are found in every country, religion, and language, you will see that such communities are extremely numerous, and that people contribute to them either with or in opposition to others. If we were to draw those relationships as lines between a person and the people he cooperates with, either in a community or otherwise, we would see each of them as a sort of focal point, with lines radiating from it like rays from a radiant body, until they split and merge with the lines radiating from another body in a confused and interrupted way.

There are so many communities that they cannot be counted. A man is bound to participate in a dozen or even more of them, but he will not be aware of this or that community except when he is forced to come together with others for the purpose of attack or defense. If the members of a group or tribe are afraid of an enemy who is attacking them, they will unite against him on the basis of the link of common ancestry, for they are relatives, forming part of a single family. But if that does not benefit them, they will seek help from the ties of homeland, religion, language, or other links.

The Community of Common Interest

If you look carefully at the many communities we have enumerated, you will see that in practice they all go back to a link that has not been mentioned, despite the fact that it is the basis for all the others. This is the Community of Interest or Advantage, which occurs when a group cooperates in a task that will bring them advantage. It is the basis for people to form parties and groups—for if they perceive advantage to themselves in working with a particular group, they will contrive to approach it or use a link to bring them together. But if they see that continuing that relationship will harm their interests, they will abandon that link and adopt a strategy that will link them to another community. For the real community is the community of common interest; history is full of examples of this.

The pre-Islamic Arabs were divided into tribes, all linked by common ancestry, on the one hand the descendants of 'Adnan, and on the other the descendants of Qahtan. The descendants of 'Adnan were divided into dozens of tribes and subtribes, and similarly the descendants of Qahtan. Each tribe or subtribe would unite with its group in solidarity against the rest of the Arabs, and would unite with another subtribe from the same tribe against other subtribes from other tribes. This is well known from the accounts of the raids and wars of the Arabs.

When Islam came, the tribes flocked to it, and made it their main bond. They took no notice of factionalism based on lineage, for the Prophet had said: "Muslims are brothers." In a sermon that he delivered on the day that Mecca was conquered, he said: "O tribe of Quraysh, God has delivered you from the arrogance of the pre-Islamic period, and its pride in ancestry. All men are from Adam, and Adam was from dust."[2] And from the farewell address: "O people, your Lord is one, and your father is one. The most noble of you in the sight of God is the most pious among you. The Arab can only be superior to the non-Arab through piety."[3]

The Prophet was imitated by his first successors, especially 'Umar ibn al-Khattab. It happened that Jibilla ibn al-Ayham, the king of Ghassan, was performing the circumambulation of the Ka'ba after his conversion, when it happened that a Fazzarian trod on his loincloth, so that it came undone. Jibilla raised his hand and struck him and complained of him to 'Umar. 'Umar wanted to smash Jibilla's nose, but he said: "How can that be, O Commander of the Faithful, when he is a member of the rabble and I am a king?' 'Umar replied to him: "Islam has brought you and him together, so that you are not superior to him in anything, except through piety and vitality." Jibilla could not bear that and turned to flee.

Islam brought Arabs and non-Arabs together, just as Christianity in Syria and Egypt brought together Romans, Copts, Nabataeans, Arabs, and others. But people often turned to one of these communities if they saw advantage in it. The Muslims, despite turning their back on the Arab connection, and their adherence to Islam, went back to their former connection to win over some Christian Arab tribes in Syria and Iraq who were siding with the Byzantines and Persians. For their part, the tribes, despite their links of religion and state to the Byzantines and Persians, when they saw that the Arabs were superior, sided with them on the basis of common lineage and language. If they had not seen any advantage for themselves in that alignment, they would have maintained the religious link that tied them to the Byzantines or to the community of homeland that bound them to the Persians. But they were angry at the Persians for the persecution they inflicted on them, so when they saw the power of the Muslims and how their state was advancing, they allied with them through ancestral solidarity and helped them by showing them the Persians' weak spots.

The Arabs of Syria and Iraq often assisted the Muslims in their wars by guiding them, advising them, and giving them information about their enemies. When al-Walid ibn 'Aqaba went out to raid the Byzantines, the Byzantines found him and fought him. Then a Christian Arab came to him and said to him: "I am not of your religion, but I will give you advice on the basis of ancestry. The people will fight you for half the day, and if they see that you are weak, they will kill you, but if you persist, they will flee and leave you!" This advice was very useful to him.

'Umar was not ignorant of that bond. He urged the Muslims to conquer Syria and Iraq, and when he saw the assistance rendered by the Arabs of Iraq, he recognized their merit. When the Muslims were about to impose the poll tax on the client peoples, including the Arabs of Taghlib, Iyad, and Nimr, who were Christians, they refused to pay. This news reached 'Umar, who consulted his colleagues. One of them said to him: "They are Arabs, exempt from the poll tax and they are a people with a grievance, so do not be hostile toward them." That was in accordance with his own sentiments, so he imposed the duty of alms giving on them, as it was imposed on the Muslims, but he made it a condition that they should not bring up their children as Christians.

As Islam became established and the Muslims spread through the land, the Islamic bond became ramified according to country, so that regional rivalries arose among them. The earliest to arise was that between Syria and Kufa during 'Uthman's rule; then, after 'Uthman had been killed, there was a political, regional split. Then under Mu'awiya, there was a split between Syria, the Hijaz, Egypt, and so on, until each country developed a particular solidarity. A single country became a mixture of several peoples: as generation succeeded generation, solidarity based on ancestry disappeared, but the regional ties remained. That is not to speak of the division of the Islamic religious community into Shi'a and Sunni and innumerable Islamic sects derived from the community of interest.

Consider the same phenomenon among the peoples of Europe. At the height of its glory, the Roman Empire bound them together, but when it disappeared, the peoples of Europe split into independent factions. They continued to make war on each other until they embarked on the wars of the Crusades against the Muslims. They undertook those wars using their common religion as a basis for unity and attacked the East on horseback and on foot. Then, when they had completed that task and hurried back to their own countries, they awoke from their indifference and started to form states, each one of which functioned separately, establishing a community that set it apart from the others. We mean, of course, the community of the homeland. In this way were formed the nations of

France, England, Germany, and others, each with its own language and its own territory. Despite this, when necessary they united in accordance with their origins, so that Italy, Spain, and France associated themselves with a Latin link, while Germany, Austria, and England reverted to a Germanic one. However, they only did so when forced to, in search of advantage—which is the real motive for embracing the community [I have called] the community of interest. Indeed, when people appear to be embracing some other community, this is only an attempt to ensure that their influence is brought together. People often create a community that lacks any reality, and connive to use it as a basis for joining people together, because of the advantage that they can see in doing so. This most frequently happens in matters of religion or abstract ideas. In the past, some ambitious rulers would profess adherence to a deity, which they would worship, and use it to play on the sensitive nerve of religion, calling on its adherents to unite in its name and rise up to conquer another people, declaring that they had insulted it. The ruler's followers would heed his call and embark on war and struggle until most of them died. But if they were victorious, the victory would bring glory, and the triumph of victory, to the ruler alone.

Sometimes, an ambitious man will adopt some other abstract idea, whose importance he will exaggerate in the eyes of their followers and use to play on their sense of honor or self-respect. He will declare that his enemies have insulted the honor of his people or party and invite them to restore their honor by the sword, though in fact he is only seeking gain for himself. Most great leaders in every age have done this. They have assembled their men around a scrap of cloth raised on a pole, called it a flag, and made their followers imagine that to defend it was to defend the homeland or their religion. Their followers wear themselves out in its defense until they are victorious, but the victory is the leader's alone.

In addition, there is the glorification of rulers after their death, from a desire to unite around their name and carry out their legacy. They are often elevated to the status of saints, are said to have given speeches that they never made, and have virtues attributed to them that they never possessed. But people do not do this unless they anticipate some benefit for themselves. How many times have people revered men who deserved to be passed over, because they anticipated some advantage by so doing, but passed over men who deserved to be revered, because they saw no advantage in revering them.

What Conclusion Should We Draw from This?

Now that we have discovered that the fundamental motivation for people to stand together in a particular undertaking is a community of interest, and that those undertaking a particular action will only make use of other communities as a means of bringing people together, we will not be misled by the phenomena of appeals in the name of religion, language, or homeland to undertake an action, but will rather look at the true motive for it. If we find in it some real advantage for ourselves and our relatives, equal to the advantage to be gained by those calling for the action, then we will agree to their appeal.

We may also conclude from this that agreement on a public project will not be secured unless all those involved will derive some advantage from its success. There is no objection to our inviting them to be involved in the name of the homeland or religion, or some other community—large or small—once we have made clear to those undertaking it the nature of the personal advantage to each one of them, personally and collectively. If that is made clear to them, they will respond to us in the name of the community we have used to invite them, agree to respect it, and hide any expectation of advantage they may have had, even though this may have been the real motivation for their joining. Anyone who wants to assemble a group to establish a society, to form a company, to found a party, to demand a right, to protest an injustice, or for any other purpose should first consider whether benefits may be expected for those participating. If that is the case, he may invite participants and be sure to succeed; but if not, he may as well throw his project out of the window. He should not be misled by the acceptance he apparently receives at the start of the invitation, especially if he summons them in the name of religion, for it will not be long before he sees them collapsing around him, and the result will be failure.

Notes

1. Zaydān, "Jāmi'at al-manfa'a."

2. An approximate quote from the speech Muhammad gave after the conquest of Mekka, "Two Haddiths of the Prophet" (Sunan Abī DawÙd al-Ḥujarāt); see http://www.darululoom-deoband.com/arabic/magazine/tmp/1326878857fix4sub2file.htm.

3. This quote, somewhat freely formulated, is from Muhammad's Farewell Speech; see www.al-shia.org/ara/ahl/?mod=khotab&id=4.

◆ ◆ ◆

The Future of Modern Civilization and How the East May Advance

Translated by Paul Starkey

Intellectuals of the nineteenth century and later have taken two views of the likely future of this civilization.[1] Some say that it is heading for destruction and extinction, as the worms of corruption gnaw away at its bones. Things will get worse as the peoples of Europe sink into a life of pleasure and luxury and surrender to laziness and idleness, leading to weakness and exhaustion. Then their civilization will suffer the fate of the Greeks and Romans before them. They believe that the same factors that destroyed the civilizations of earlier centuries will destroy the civilization of today. Just as the barbarians in the past toppled thrones, deposed kings, and destroyed whole lands, so in the future a group of people will appear who are even more powerful and bloodthirsty. Those barbarians will range over Europe, bringing its culture and civilization to ruins. By this group they mean the army of laborers who are heading toward poverty and decline because of the tyranny of their employers, who are only intent on gathering wealth. Some people have gone even further. Lord Macaulay said, "The people of [New] Zealand will stand on London Bridge and study history to know who built it." Someone else said: "The nature of civilization itself demands that kingdoms rise and kingdoms fall. So European civilization will come to an end, and culture return to the East, from whence it came."[2]

A traveler stood on the ruins of Baalbek, and wept. When asked about it, he said: "Who knows, a day may come when a man from the East stands on the ruins of London, Paris, and Berlin, just as I am standing now on the ruins of ancient civilization."[3]

We, the people of the East, should not be deceived by the ring of such phrases, which are nothing but poetic fancies, for the correct view about the future of modern civilization is the view of the more reliable authorities. These people say that civilization today is built on a true scientific basis and rests on solid foundations that are capable of progress and reform. It is impossible that what happened to the civilizations of peoples in the past should happen to contemporary civilization, for the causes that led to the disappearance of ancient civilization could not make contemporary civilization disappear, as there is such a large difference between the two.

The Egyptians carried the art of building and architecture to its highest place in history, but they did not excel in other things, and so their civilization was not stable. The Greeks surpassed all other nations of the earth in philosophy, art, and literature, but they were completely ignorant of the natural sciences that protect contemporary civilization from collapse. The Romans created extensive military, political, and religious systems, but they neglected the rest of the sciences. In general, the civilization of past nations paid great attention to the arts, literature, and philosophy, but the natural sciences did not influence them much. Contemporary civilization, however, is based on the natural sciences as well.

Spencer said: "A people, *sha'ab,* are a living, growing body, which has established systems (such as political, religious, and commercial systems) to regulate it. Its functions are its sciences, ideas, and feelings. It is subject to the law of natural selection, and the influence of time and place." Contemporary civilization works to develop these systems to ensure a people's progress and existence, and to render its progress in conformity with its environment and period. For this reason, contemporary civilization will not stand still or cease to function but will continue to progress and move forward.

It is closer to the truth to say that contemporary civilization is stable and becoming more perfect, even though some Western extremists take the opposite view. Europe will not go backward again except as a result of natural factors, such as the return of the Ice Age, which is unimaginable.

Nor is it possible for its civilization to vanish, or to be moved to the East, in the same way as it moved to the West from the East. The only path for Eastern civilization is for it to rise up to emulate the civilization of Europe; otherwise, it will fall prey to the greed of European states. We shall now explain how that may come about.

Japan and the Far East

We are not simply calling on the peoples of the East or encouraging their ambitions to wake up and imitate the Europeans. But we can actually show them a state at the furthest edge of the East that was among the most ignorant of these peoples, but which awoke from its slumber, pulled up its sleeves, and through effort and hard work challenged the most important European states in commerce and dominion, so that it is now counted as one of the world's civilized states. We invite all Easterners to study the circumstance of that nation and to ascertain the reasons for its advance, to study its civilization, and to follow the same path that it did. What the Japanese achieved in a few years no European state achieved, unless with great difficulty and over several generations.[4] Anybody reading what missionaries and travelers wrote about Japan forty years ago will find that it was less advanced than China today. In a third of a century, however, it has been able to emulate the states of Europe and force them to accept it among them. Today we see a constitutional movement in China. Who knows whether another thirty years will see the Chinese rise to the position of their neighbors. As for the factors in Japan's progress, the most important was the love of their king for his people, and vice versa.

After the entry of foreigners in their country, the Japanese people rose up to demand reform. Their princes and wealthy men ceded most of their property to the government. Land ownership there had resembled the feudal system in the Dark Ages that befell Europe. The king made concessions and granted his subjects a constitution by choice and of his own free will. The Japanese did not adopt an attitude of self-sufficiency despite their strong sense of unity, but saw it as their duty to imitate what was good and avoid the bad in foreigners, and this guided their actions. They wanted to reorganize their government and army, so they sent scientific missions to Europe to tour its capitals and study the conditions there and the factors in its progress. They increased savings and plugged their balance of payments deficit, thereby making themselves independent of European finance. They kept themselves free of these traps until compelled by the recent war with Russia. I see nothing to stop any Eastern state from imitating the Japanese in their progress if they follow the same principles.

The Ottoman Empire and the Near East

When the Ottoman Empire progresses, the Near East progresses, and when the Empire falls behind and declines, the Near East does the same. Recent history is the best proof of this. In the eyes of foreigners, the Ottoman Empire continues to be an Oriental state, even if it possessed half of Europe. It controls the most important location, [by which] I mean the impregnable fortress of Constantinople, the link between East and West. If it had been blessed in the past with a good government, it would be today a pool into which the whole world poured its commerce and industry to be distributed on either side. Many people, from both East and West, might think that the proximity of the Ottoman state to Europe would be helpful to it, but the fact is that major damage results from that proximity. If Japan had not been such a long way from Europe, it would have been difficult for it to progress so extraordinarily quickly. How could the Ottoman state progress with Europe watching it, never letting it rest from its problems and worries for a single day? It borrowed millions from Europe only yesterday but has not been able to spend anything to improve its conditions; instead it was forced to spend [the funds] to repair its fleet and equip its armies based on a fear of Europe and the conspiracies and rebellions that Europe would foist upon the Ottoman state.

All the nations of the East are borrowing from Europe today, with the result that tomorrow they will be obliged to return to European domination and accept capitulations[5] that Europe demands of them.

It would be appropriate for the Ottoman Empire to follow the example of the Japanese nation at the beginning of its new life and to send reliable, faithful men to Japan, America, and Europe to study carefully the factors in the progress of those nations and the basis of their civilizations and bring home the advantages, benefits, and ways of behavior that they have acquired. In that way, they would have rendered to the East a memorable service.

There are a great many sources and means of wealth in all parts of the East. We may single out for special mention Iraq and Mesopotamia. If the Ottoman Empire, either on its own or in collaboration with a foreign state, were to extend the Baghdad railway line, and commit to it just half the loan it borrowed from Europe yesterday, it would bring influence, wealth, and a good deal of income to itself and its subjects. These are the countries where Herodotus, the father of history, stood, astonished at their fertility, not daring to give them a full description so as not to be accused of exaggeration.

Notes

1. Zaydān, "Muṣīr al-tamaddun."

2. Not identified.

3. A somewhat free quotation from the eighteenth-century traveler C. F. Volney, *The Ruins: or the a Survey of the Revolutions of Empires* (1811; reprint, Washington, DC: Woodstock Books, 2000), 7: "Who, said I to myself, can assure me, that their [Egypt and Syria's] present desolation will not one day be the lot of our own country? Who knows but that hereafter, some traveler like myself will sit down upon the banks of the Seine, the Thames and the Zuyder Sea where now, in the tumult of enjoyment, the heart and the eyes are too slow to take in the multitude of sensations; who knows but he will sit down solitary, amid silent ruins and weep a people inurned, and their greatness changed into an empty name?"

4. Ever since the Russian-Japanese war in 1904–1905, Japan was greatly admired in the Middle East as the first Eastern nation to defeat a European power.

5. Capitulations (*imtiyāzāt*) is the technical term for treaties between European powers and the Ottoman Empire, concerning rights for trade and protection of Europeans in the Empire. In the nineteenth century they reflected the increasing political and economic power of the Europeans.

◆ ◆ ◆

Only the Fittest Can Survive

Or, Truth Will Prevail in the End

Translated by Paul Starkey

The survival of the fittest is one of the natural laws that is inherent in the Law of Evolution.[1] It is a general principle that applies to everything, whether matters of nature or of ethics and morality. In the same way as it requires some creatures to become extinct because they are not fit to survive in the environment around them, it also requires the disappearance of views or laws that do not suit the social structure, to be replaced by others that are more appropriate. It requires that unsuitable habits or customs be discarded, in addition to other features of society that do not need to be proven at length. My present purpose is to demonstrate another law that is obviously applicable to society or to morality but is also applicable to other natural phenomena, namely the statement, "Only the truth (or what is right) will prevail."

This problem may be counted among natural phenomena; indeed it is among the most reliable of those phenomena, for nature itself knows only what is fit and accepts no adulteration or alteration. In nature, one cause can have only one result. It takes no notice of extraneous phenomena, because it relies on fundamentals and not on accidents. If you bring a piece of iron close to a magnet, the magnet attracts it because it is iron; if you were to put it among dozens of pieces of different metals, it would select it from among them even if the metals resembled each other superficially. It will not be deceived if the piece of iron is given a different color from its original color or its shape is altered. If you painted it white or red or black, if you covered it with paper or cloth, its true nature would not be hidden from the magnet. If you mix a mercury solution with a solution of ordinary salt, a yellow sediment, mercury chloride, will be formed, and that chemical reaction will occur even if the appearances of the two solutions differ in color or consistency. It is the essence and not the form or appearance that nature relies on. It is the same with every other natural reaction in the inanimate world, for the reactions know only what is right, and no other result is possible.

But this law also applies to the plant and animal kingdoms, even if it does not appear as clearly as in the inanimate world, because results are influenced by so many vital factors with so many different causes. Quinine will reduce the temperature of a fever, whether the patient takes it as a liquid or as a solid, as a drink or as an injection. The only condition is that it should be conveyed to the blood. However, its effect is often delayed, weakened, or lost for innumerable reasons resulting from the interaction of vital influences in the body. You can also see that occurring in other physiological or biological phenomena in animals or plants.

If we turn to spiritual and ethical interactions in society, we see that this law is less obvious and slower with regard to results, because it depends on forces that are more confused and mingled. I mean intellectual forces, and other forces that either oppose them, attach themselves to them, or depend on them, such as intellectual passions like the love of fame, envy, love of self, revenge, and so on, which may impede the appearance of the truth so that it is slow to emerge, though it must emerge sooner or later.

How many scientific views have been suppressed by ambition and prevented from appearing for a long time, only to suddenly appear like the sun, so that their originators won the argument—just like those who argued that the earth revolved around the sun, for example, although previous exponents of that view had been accused of heresy. When Darwin and his disciples formulated the Law of Evolution, some men of religion attacked them in a despicable fashion and accused them of heresy, but they then retracted and acknowledged the truth and began to interpret the words of the books of religion in accordance with this Law.

This is also true of reformist views if they stand in the way of traditionalist conservatives with predetermined views. They may remain for several centuries covered in the dust of confusion and fraud, but will eventually appear, even after a considerable time. That has been the fate of most reformers, from the ancient philosophers to the lawgivers and the prophets. Not one of them delivered an opinion without having to wait a lifetime for it to come to prominence. You can also see this in the radical reformers of the present day, of whom there is a group in every country. The closest to us in terms of nationality and period is Muhammad 'Abduh, who taught a doctrine that he intended to be reformist, but it was prevented from appearing as such by those who persisted in the old doctrines. They ganged up against him and accused him of every kind of evil and of weakness of religion. They did that either because of an ingrained belief or because of some traditional goal, but his doctrines inevitably prevailed because they were reformist. You may say the same about Qasim Amin's views on Muslim women, as well as that of others.

Just as true views may be concealed by distortion and not appear for a time, incorrect views may be given life for a time by distortion, so that their falsity only becomes apparent after the passage of several generations. But they will inevitably come to light. Look at those myths to which the human mind was subject for ages, until their falsity became apparent with the advent of the modern scientific method, so that they disappeared into the wind. People today have started to wonder at how their ancestors were duped by those false sleights of hand. Look at the intentional deception in making some people appear different from what they really are by a process of distortion for some personal gain. The closest example at hand is what some flatterers used to say about Abdülhamid II during the period of absolute rule. Among these people was someone who composed a book about the virtues of his glorious age; he attributed to that tyrant a laudable effort to diffuse science and establish schools, and enumerated the reforms he had initiated in the state and nation. People did that out of flattery, seeking thereby a livelihood stained with blood. It may occur to the reader's mind that the true nature of Abdülhamid could not be concealed by such distortion, and that people have always known the true nature of that strange man; but the fact is that many people were taken in by those stories and believed in Abdülhamid's virtue, so that when he was forced to resign after the 13 April incident,[2] some writers objected to setting up the court and rejected what the free men had done. Telegram after telegram arrived at Constantinople from all parts of the Islamic world begging the constitutionalists not to harm the person of the deposed ruler.

What holds true for Abdülhamid also holds true for his leading supporters, and others like them, for some writers in the newspapers pictured them in a most honorable way and attributed to them the most glorious virtues. But when the government was overthrown the truth came out.

Then again, consider the above in light of other things that admit of exaggeration or distortion, such as commercial or industrial achievements. Their initiators announce them and praise them in an exaggerated fashion, but in the end they are only as successful as the truth contained in them. Someone may announce that he is a skilled doctor, a graduate of the greatest schools of France, America, Britain, or elsewhere, and enumerate all he knows of science or diseases he has specialized in; the announcement attracts attention so that he is consulted by the sick. If what he says is true, he will become established and his services will be in demand, but if not, he will be thrown out and sidelined. He may advertise certain drugs for particular diseases. The sick may place most of their faith on the advertisement, and the publication of testimonies and so on, but if the medicine is not beneficial, the advertisement will have been useless. There is no argument that an advertisement may benefit the man that places it, but it cannot conceal the truth: on the contrary, it will hasten its exposure. So it is stupid for certain professionals or merchants to rely on advertising and praise.

Consider also the advertising of books or other fruits of the intellect. They are even more susceptible to deception than other "products," for a man is bewitched by his own ideas. Our writers are still a long way from true criticism in expounding the truth of the works that are presented to them. On the contrary, they devote their efforts to praising the author if he is a friend of theirs, or criticizing his work and its author if it is contrary to their opinions. Very rarely do you find someone free of bias when criticizing a book and clarifying its truth as European writers do.

Sometimes one of the reasons for distortion in describing the fruits of the intellectual may be the wealth of the author, his standing in society, or his influence in the state. So the writer will devote all his attention to praising him out of flattery or respect. Conversely, if the author is suspect in his religion, or stands opposed to the eulogist or the historian in principle, viewpoint, or philosophy, he will begrudge him his rights or actually attack him. This is an old disease in the East that afflicts most historians when they make mention of their contemporary writers or poets. How many an eminent poet has been carried away by his independence of thought or the boldness of his words, thereby rousing the anger of those in power or other eminent people? The result has been that contemporary historians have belittled his merits in order to please those people, or have opposed him because he has deviated from his religion. For example, a group of poets in the early Abbasid period were accused of atheism, while on the other hand historians exaggerated their praise of those poets and intellectuals who were close to the caliphs or their ministers, and even more so when an emir or minister was himself the poet or intellectual in question. The contemporary historian could hardly find in the language an expression adequate for their praise. At times the eulogizer might do this from the best of motives, not intentionally seeking to deceive, but merely carried away by respect, so that he formed an exaggerated view of the poet's or writer's merit. Sometimes the historian might be unable to free himself from the temptations of group loyalty or personal advantage, and this would be apparent through his pen without his realizing it.

Abu Mansur al-Tha'alibi[3] compiled a history of the poets and intellectuals of his time in *Yatimat al-Dahr*, including ministers, princes, and notables among other categories. You may clearly see in his book examples of the influence of the elite that we have been speaking about. When he came to write the biographies of creative artists, for example, he singled out Ibn al-'Amid[4] and al-Sahib ibn 'Abbad[5] for praise. He didn't praise anyone else of the group, despite the large number of people who surpassed them in their craft at that time. He wore himself out compiling expressions of admiration and praise and mentioned nothing negative about the pair of them, even though it is inconceivable that they should have been faultless. Perhaps one of their contemporaries recorded some of their faults but didn't dare to publish them, so they were lost. Some of what survived of such criticism is recorded in Yaqut's[6] *Mu'jam al-Udaba'* of al-Sahib's *saj'*: "It indicates deception. If he had seen a piece of *saj'* that made the king's dignity disappear and the fabric of the state collapse on the spot, it would have been easy for him to abandon it. His writing indicates paralysis, and he is stupid by nature."

A similar view may be taken of other periods up to the present, especially in the East, for their peoples have grown accustomed to flattery, distortion, and groveling for reasons that we have explained elsewhere, to such an extent that students of literature cannot rely on what the newspapers say about any given book. It is very rare for anyone to be inspired to purchase a book solely because of the praise it receives in the newspapers. This is in contrast to readers of European languages, who can have confidence in what the critics say in the leading newspapers. A true estimate of the worth of written works must of course be left to time, which is the sole guarantee of the clear truth. As the generations succeed one another and contemporaries pass away, with all the grudges and envy that they possess, the work remains, and people of succeeding generations can look at it with eyes free from prejudice, assigning it the correct place in terms of neglect or respect, in accordance with the principle of the survival of truth. And this is based on the principle with which we headed this article, namely "truth will prevail in the end."

Notes

1. Zaydān, "Lā yaṣiḥḥ illā 'l-ṣaḥīḥ." The title implies a double meaning. The term *al-aṣaḥḥ* (superlative of *al-ṣaḥīḥ*) is used in the sense of "the fittest" both in a scientific Darwinist and in an ethical or moral sense. Here, as in the essay "Through Pressure and Resistance Hidden Forces Appear," Zaidan aims at establishing the link between the laws of natural science and ethical or moral social behavior.

2. On 13 April 1909, the First Army Corps in Istanbul mutinied against the government. The Committee of Union and Progress of the Young Turks organized an "Army of deliverance" that reached Istanbul ten days later and chased the mutineers out. One of the consequences of this coup attempt was Sultan Abdülhamid's II resignation.

3. Abū Manṣūr al-Tha'ālibī (961–1038), author of *Yatīmat al-dahr fī maḥāṣin ahl al-'aṣr,* a four-volume anthology of poetry and artistic prose: *EI2.*

4. Ibn al-'Amīd the Older (d. 970), vizier and military leader; but known for his patronage of literature and author of at least one work: *EI2.*

5. Ṣāḥib Ibn 'Abbād (d. 995), vizier; man of letters and patron of many poets and literati: *EI2.*

6. Yāqūt al-Rūmī (1179–1229) scholar, geographer, traveler; the work mentioned here is *Mujma' al-udabā', irschād al-arīb ilā ma'arifat al-adīb,* which has not completely survived: *EI2.*

◆ ◆ ◆

How Should We Construct Morality and What Is Women's Influence with Regard to It?

Translated by Paul Starkey

Writers have all taken the view, and the nation's intellectuals agreed with them, that we lack the refined system of ethics necessary for progress in developing a civilized society.[1] By this, we mean truthfulness, faithfulness, moral courage, an acknowledgement of mistakes, and a sense of duty, stability, firmness of character, and so on. Books on etiquette and morality are full of enumerations of good manners and provide copious advice on the best ways to succeed and earn respect. But these statements are seldom acted upon. People simply repeat them and take pleasure in reciting them, just as they find pleasure in pretty poetic fancies. They seldom leave any influence in their hearts; nor is any echo of them apparent in their deeds. It is like when we say to a sick man, "You are sick from a certain disease, as demonstrated by symptoms x, y, z," but we don't prescribe him the medicine that will cure him of the disease. He is pleased to know what the disease is, but the knowledge doesn't help him if it is not accompanied by a prescription and instructions for taking it. If we say that we are in need of a certain ethical value that may gratify us. But it does us no good if we do not know how to create that value and make our actions conform to it. That is what we wish to expound upon in this essay.

How Morality Is Created

In his greatest and most successful discoveries and inventions, man merely imitates nature, using it as his example and deriving inspiration from it. You will hardly find a single important invention that you will not recognize as being based on similar examples occurring in nature around us. So to create an ethical system, we must first discover how that system may be created in man according to the law of evolution, and then imitate nature in creating or forming it.

A consideration of this law tells us that man is the creature of his environment, and that his behavior changes and his morals vary according to the demands of his environment. For this reason, the ethical systems of nations also differ in accordance with their location. Desert peoples do not have the same morality as city dwellers; the morality of mountain dwellers differs from that of plain dwellers, and so on and so forth.

If you consider these morals in the context of their origin and the cause for their appearance, you will see that reason plays a major part in their formation, for it is indeed true what is said, that "a man's morals are the product of his reason and the creation of his environment." To clarify that, let us take an example based on the views of the proponents of the law of evolution concerning the rise of man: Let us imagine man still in an animal state with none of the characteristics of humanity. In our view, it is most likely that his ascent originally began with his intelligence, and that he became differentiated from other animals through consciousness. Then he used his consciousness to form an ethical system in a quest to perpetuate himself and to ward off the forces of destruction that threatened him.

To elaborate a little, we may say that man was created weak among the strong, and found himself exposed to natural influences, a prey to wild animals he could not repel through bodily strength. But what set him apart from them were his mental powers, which he used to defend himself and keep himself alive. Had it not been for that, he would have disappeared from the face of the earth a long time ago, just as other animal species disappeared. But he used his mental powers to protect himself from the cold by making clothes, and to ward off wild animals by making weapons and building houses. Speech helped mankind to socialize, so that tribes and subtribes were formed, which spread over the different regions and areas of the earth. There was great competition among them for resources and supremacy, so mankind became even more in need of his mental faculties than before. The two most important factors in this were self-defense, and the formation of alliances with his brothers to seek their help against his enemies.

The first of these factors—self-defense, either by resisting wild animals or fighting human enemies—created in man the moral values of the desert peoples, such as bravery, heroism, courage, and the like. He was drawn to these by the principles of natural selection and the survival of the fittest. People who live in the desert need these qualities to defend their lives and secure their livelihoods. If they do not have these moral qualities to begin with, they gradually acquire them over the generations, as the weak who are unable to attain them disappear, while the stronger members of the group survive. Those who are not able to acquire those characteristics perish, and the stronger remain. This is also the case with the other moral virtues necessary for mankind to defend itself or secure a livelihood.

As for the second factor—the formation of groups to cooperate against one's enemies—this required another category of moral qualities, based on the exchange of benefits and a knowledge of rights and duties. Mankind's need for social life drove him to acquire the necessary moral qualities for this, and through the use of willpower he gradually became more patient, able to suppress his anger out of a desire to further his own interests. These qualities became habitual; then, with the passage of the generations, they became ingrained. The Bedouin found himself in need of help from his family and neighbors so he started to bring them closer to him by providing what they needed, the most important thing being food. So he was generous in his hospitality, but this requires liberality and openheartedness, so with succeeding generations generosity became one of the virtues of the Bedouin; similarly with faithfulness, kindness, trustworthiness, and so on.

In general, it can be said that need dictates a particular quality and that willpower brings it forth. This is a three-stage process. First, intelligence requires the doing of whatever is required by circumstances, so the will makes it happen under duress. When the action is repeated it becomes a habit. Usually, the process is initiated by one of the wisest and most senior members of the tribe, who is then imitated by his neighbors, because they see advantage for themselves in so doing. Then, over the generations, the habit becomes an ingrained faculty inherited by their successors, and finally it becomes a natural disposition.

In this way, moral qualities were formed over a period of time whose beginnings cannot be ascertained. They vary from nation to nation with differences between environments and other circumstances. For the qualities that the Bedouin requires may not be required by city dwellers. The characteristics of a single nation may vary in different phases of its civilization according to the influences that affect it and force it to adopt habits that it did not require in its initial phases. Then those habits become fixed characteristics. In this way, we can explain the differences between the characteristics of the Arabs in the pre-Islamic period and their characteristics today and between the characteristics of the Romans at the beginning of the Roman Empire and after their civilization had reached its apogee.

The characteristics of a single nation differ according to different environments, and in a single environment the characteristics vary with different phases of civilization. This happens without the people demanding it or even being aware of any transition, because of the progression from habit to faculty, and thence to natural dispositions in accordance with the teachings of evolution.

How to Create a Moral System

If we wish to create qualities within ourselves that we do not have already, we need to imitate nature—but, above all, we need willpower to examine what will benefit us and improve our social circumstances. Once we establish our need for [such qualities], we should work to make it a rule that we have to follow, so that we plan and work on that basis even though we may be reluctant to do so. It will then quickly become a habit, then a faculty, and finally a natural disposition. But the formation of a disposition can only come about over a number of generations, because fixed traits of nations are difficult to eradicate or get rid of except through patience, honesty, and strength of will.

To illustrate: moral bravery is one of the loftiest virtues that we stand in need of. We have first to establish it and believe in it, then make it a basis for our actions, instill it into our children from an early age when they are in the cradle, and give it to them to imbibe with their milk. That is the basis of upbringing, in which we have first to rely on the mothers; before entrusting it to school teachers, and so through the remaining stages of life so that moral bravery becomes a habit to be passed down to one's children, until with the passage of the generations it eventually becomes an ingrained characteristic. Similar observations might be made with regard to other moral qualities.

The Nation Is Woven by Mothers

At first glance, constructing a moral code seems easy. But on further thought you will find it difficult. The reason is that its success depends on two important factors that are difficult to find in ready supply in a nation that needs such reform. These are "a strong will" and "a woman of firm character." Of these, the latter is the more important, because the first step in forging character depends on the mother. If the mother has a strong character, and is entrusted with nurturing ideals in her children, like honesty, knowing one's duty, stability, moral courage, and so on, the nation will achieve its aims and its children will grow up with those qualities. She will also be bringing up the teachers who have to promote those qualities in schools. For this reason we have said elsewhere that "the nation is woven by mothers."

How can we get mothers with strong characters to whom we can entrust this task? If women in our society have become so weak in character through continuous ignorance and subservience over a succession of generations, is there any way to revive them and reform them apart from education? It is no objection that many mothers are good at raising their children despite being ignorant, for strength of character may go together with ignorance, but they will be helped by her environment—that is, the general state of the nation. In the period before Islam, women had strong characters in accordance with the state of the nation at that time; for the Arabs had strong characters and wills then because of the nature of Bedouin life. But when they became settled and inclined to a life of ease, they lost their strength of character, and their women's characters weakened at the same time. Perhaps if they returned to the nomadic life they would regain their strength of character over successive generations.

But our requirement is for strength of character while living in cities, with a modern civilization that we need to adopt together with its moral values. So there is no choice but to bring up women properly so that they can take on the task of leading the nation on the first step toward an advanced morality, while preparing men for work on the second and subsequent stages of the road.

Woman and the Veil

The education of women is the cornerstone of moral education. The interests and social situation of the nation require a sophisticated moral system even more than they do advanced science. For this reason, the education of women has been the most urgent task in promoting civilization. Is there anything more harmful to the social order than people who stand in the way of imbuing women with education and culture, using the argument of the veil or similar arguments? Thank God, there are few people who use this argument. No two intelligent people differ in the matter of the education of women. A large number of eminent people who occupy scientific, religious, and political posts hold that Eastern practice demands the education of women and the removal of the veil. However, while they say this in meetings and indeed practice it themselves by giving their daughters the best education possible and making them understand the true nature of the veil, they do not proclaim these views loudly in the newspapers for legal reasons they find essential to respect.

We know a professor, one of the most eminent men of learning and religion in Egypt, who had his daughter educated in England, where she earned an advanced qualification. When a suitor came forward to ask for her hand, he was unwilling to grant the suitor's request until the professor had arranged for him to see her, and allowed him to converse with her, so that he should be quite clear about the character of the woman who was to be his life's companion. The fact that this sort of spirit exists among the highest class of our nation gives us hope that with time it will become more general.

We do not deny the improvements made in the situation of Muslim women among us, some of whom have become eminent orators, writers, and teachers. But we see this more clearly in the non-Arab Muslim countries, where Muslim girls have started to work in the public sector. The foremost Muslims in this respect are the Turks, whose women have formed a society called "The Society for the Removal of the Veil," in which they call for the education of women and the removal of their chains. Conspicuous in this regard are a group of working women in the telephone company in Constantinople. Turkish women have broken the constraints of the veil and started to improve their position ahead of Arab women, and indeed they played a significant part in the Ottoman reforms.

That is also true of Indian women, for the Indians have formed societies and founded magazines to work for improvements in the position of women, and collected money for their education. The character of Indian women has a firmness that is apparent in various ways. An example is the throne of the Kingdom of Bhopal, which for a full century was ruled wisely and firmly by three queens in succession. The first was Qudsiyya Begum, the widow of Nazzar Muhammad Khan; he had taken control of Bhopal in 1818 but lived for only a short time, so he was succeeded by his wife, who was nineteen years of age. She was wise and decisive; among the things she did, it is said that she sold her jewels in order to relieve her kingdom of its debts. In 1835, she was succeeded on the throne by her daughter Sikandrikum, who was also nineteen years of age. She wanted to emulate her mother in her determined style of administration so she toured the kingdom and examined its condition until she had discovered the faults and other things that marred it and needed to be corrected. Then she came forward with a collection of reforms. She deserves an honorable mention in the history of modern India. In 1863 she made a pilgrimage and wrote a book about her journey that has been translated into English. This Sikandrikum died in the same year, and was succeeded by her daughter Shah Jahan, who has reigned for over fifty years and is still on the throne. She too is famous for her wisdom and determination. On 28 February of last year she delivered a speech on the occasion of the laying of the foundation stone of the Aligarh College; the essence of her speech was to encourage the Indian nation to educate itself and to spend money for this purpose. She addressed the students of the college in a way that demonstrated her lofty ideals and the keenness of her intellect. There is no doubt that she has been an inspiring example for the women of India, who yesterday convened a women's conference, at which she delivered the first speech to promote women's education and advancement.

Women's strength of character appears in different guises according to the different circumstances of different countries. When a nation is at war, it is apparent in their bravery in war, as with Kara Fatima and the Kurds. The Arab woman's strength of character is apparent in the upbringing of her children and the elevation of their spirits; thanks to God, she is acting with this strength. If she continues along the same path, you will be able to congratulate the nation on achieving the superior character that it requires, for mothers are able to plant such seeds in their children from childhood.

Notes

1. Zaydān, "Kayfa naṣnu' al-akhlāq."

The Syrians in Egypt

Translated by Hilary Kilpatrick

Syrians grow up in a country (*bilād*) that has remained since antiquity a cradle of commerce and among a people whose roots go back to the Phoenicians, the first to sail the seas and set out on trading journeys.[1] Those who come from the coastal regions live among merchants and their employees and mix with hundreds of foreigners, from European and other communities, who have come to sell their goods. They thus become practiced in the skills of buying, selling, and haggling. What they see of the nature of their own region renders traveling and roaming the world attractive to them, and no day passes without them hearing of dozens of Syrians emigrating to distant parts in search of a livelihood and wealth. Thus they grow up loving emigration and setting themselves ambitious goals. As the poet says: "Leave the place where injustice rules and let the house mourn its builder / You may find one country instead of another, but never another self / He who is destined to go to one land will never die in another."

In addition, they are keen to master foreign languages. So when a Syrian completes his studies or learns his business well and does not have work that prevents him from traveling, he usually abandons his efforts to support himself in obscurity and [instead decides to] raise his status among his peers. He starts to think hard about possible destinations for emigration. Generally he will prefer Egypt, because after the late Muhammad 'Ali Pasha took power it offered wide opportunities for trade. Syrians began to arrive there in droves, engaging in trade that at the time was extensive because of contacts with the Sudan, the Arabian Peninsula, Persia, and India in the East and Europe and America in the West.

What also made them prefer this "happy country" (*al-qaṭar al-sa'īd*) was the bond of a common language, the prevailing security, and the hospitality and friendliness that they sensed in their Egyptian brothers. Egyptians are amiable and gentle, but they prefer to stay put rather than emigrate and endure traveling because of the fertility with which God has endowed their country (*bilād*) and the good government, security, and manifold possibilities of earning a living easily since the country came under the rule of Muhammad 'Ali's dynasty. Egypt was indebted to these rulers for treating the population well and making it easier for them to earn their livelihood. Thus, living in peace and security, they are not attracted by traveling, and they have no inclination to find out about the situation of different nations. They do not need to, since visitors to Egypt have different religions, attitudes, languages, and costumes. Hundreds, even thousands of foreigners pass through their markets each day, including countless Europeans, Americans, Syrians, Turks, Persians, Indians, Sudanese, Hejazis, and Yemenis, each one feeling safe and confident whether he settles in Egypt or leaves it.

The Syrians became used to living among the Egyptians, going about their commercial business until a number of them became prominent, earning huge fortunes through their application and efforts. Until the last third of the [nineteenth] century they constituted the majority of the wealthy Syrians in Egypt. In recent times, however, Syrians have rarely come to this country for trade, because the opportunities have decreased with the opening of the Suez Canal joining the Mediterranean with the Red Sea. The trade routes to Europe have changed, while Europeans have crowded into Egypt. When former Khedive Isma'il Pasha succeeded to the throne, he made employment in government departments attractive to the Syrians, offering them huge salaries, and so they all favored this career, preferring to receive regular wages. It has taken such a hold on them that, with a few exceptions, they have almost lost the capacity to do business.

So Syrians now generally come to Egypt looking for work in government offices. What a difference there is between their arrival now and that of their forefathers before them! Since they accepted government service they have become lethargic and unenterprising, unable to compete with their predecessors or contemporaries in making money because they are satisfied with the salary they receive at the end of the month. No sooner has the next month begun than they have spent it and perhaps borrowed to help cover their expenses for the rest of the month. It makes no difference whether the salary is high or low, because they inevitably spend it, whether it is less than a hundred piasters or more than a hundred pounds. The general rule is that the salary is spent before the month is over.

We know many of these civil servants, who have high salaries, and we do not imagine, from what we know of their patterns of expenditure, that they need more than half of what they earn, but we see that they have spent everything and borrowed more. This is a situation that should worry them and put them on their guard, because they are spending the most precious years of their life without saving anything they can fall back on in times of need. Besides, they live under the threat of the government dispensing with their services at any time; they know not when. Woe to those who receive the notice of their dismissal when they are in this situation! For, except in rare cases, they will find themselves empty-handed, idle, and facing many expenses because of the wastefulness and extravagance they are used to and the refinement they affect in eating, drinking, and dressing. Yet they cannot work in trade or industry because of the lavish lifestyle they are used to and the way they spend most of their time, either in places of entertainment or in reading novels and other similar activities. They fall prey to perplexity, and despair may lead them to move to a place where no one knows them—that is, if they are not encumbered with a family or there is some other reason forcing them to remain weighed down as they are. I do not know what will become of them if they do not find a place in a government department. After suffering bitterly, ruing the day and lamenting the time they spent in useless pursuits, they will entreat all their acquaintances and enjoin their children and children's children to keep away from such work.

Working in a government office has advantages, especially where Egyptian government departments are concerned, but they do not compensate for even a fraction of the disadvantages A Syrian leaves his country looking for possibilities to earn a good living to compensate for the hardships of his journey and for being far from family and friends. Syrians are skilled in all forms of trade, as experts testify, and the history of their distant ancestors and the position of their country bear out. Present circumstances offer us the most eloquent witness of this; here you have visible proof, so forget what people tell you. There are a great number of merchants in Egypt, coming from different religious communities and nationals, but the Syrians are among the most skillful in business and successful at earning money.

If you look at the Syrians residing here and consider their ways of earning their living, you can see the consequence of working in business or in government service. Those who have saved money have done so through commerce and nothing else. Do not be deceived by promotions, decorations, and titles, which are advantages of government service; the main issue is what you can save for your family and children. You will not see one in a hundred civil servants who has succeeded in saving anything worth mentioning—and if he has, it probably does not come from his government salary.

If a civil servant manages his expenses well and lives economically so as to save part of his salary, together with the indemnity or pension that he receives at the end of his working life, he will have achieved both his aims, enjoying the advantages that government service confers—honor and a splendid situation, which people look up to and are attracted by. At the same time he performs one of the finest public services for the benefit of mankind. But we advise against such work for those who do not know how to carry it out so that it will support them; even if they persevere in it, it may not last.

What is true of Syrians in this respect is also true of Egyptians, although the latter are more entitled to occupy those positions and enjoy the country's advantages. But what we see of their concentration on government employment, on which they pin their hopes and focus exclusively, does not bode well for the future. We advise them therefore to turn their attention to a source of wealth Egypt is well endowed with, and in which few countries can compete with her, namely agriculture. The Nile Valley is fertile and very productive, thanks to the rich earth that the blessed Nile floods bring with it each year. If fathers encourage their sons to pursue careers in agriculture and send them to the College of Agriculture, they will ensure that they have a fine future and the whole country will benefit greatly.

With the foregoing we do not mean that young people should desist from government service, but simply that they should cease to prefer it to any other commercial or agricultural occupation. They should not pin their hopes on and apply in droves for work in government departments until there is no more room for them. Many of them would then remain without work, since, as we have said, they cannot undertake any other activity that would support them. By contrast, if they were to think of other possibilities, work would be satisfactorily distributed, each one would have his rewards, and everyone would share in the advantages.

There is another kind of occupation which is not to be neglected, that is, industry. We are sorry to see that the great majority of young people in Egypt and Syria look down on it, although they read about it in European and American newspapers and see with their own eyes its fruits, such as railways, the telegraph, and the telephone. This should prove to them conclusively that industry is a most noble occupation and most beneficial for the wealth and advancement of the nation. Our exalted government is well aware of that, and it has founded various kinds of industrial schools, the Agricultural School and others, which, it is hoped, will produce the required benefits. And God is the Guide to taking the appropriate action.

Notes

1. Zaydān, "al-Sūriyyūn fī Miṣr." The term "Syrians" does not mean here the citizens of the modern state of Syria. By the middle of the nineteenth century the term "Syrians" (*Sūriyyūn*) replaced the term *shāmī* (pl., *shawām*). At the time of Zaidan's writing, "Syrians" designated people who were subjects of the Ottoman sultan and resided or came from *Bilād al-Shām*, the "geographical Syria" that is bordered by the Syrian Desert in the east, the Taurus Mountains in the north, the Mediterranean Sea in the west, and the Sinai in the south.

◆ ◆ ◆

The Future of the Syrians in America

Translated by Hilary Kilpatrick

New York, S. J.:

We see Syrians thronging to the New World singly and in groups, undeterred by the thoughts of leaving their homeland or by the hardships of the journey.[1] These emigrants now number more than 100,000. Their principal purpose is to earn a living. Will they return to Syria when they become rich? And if not, what fate do you think awaits them?

al-Hilal: We have been asked this question by more than one of our Syrian brothers in America. And we are pleased that they are turning their thoughts to this subject, for it is so important that no Syrian emigrant to America or elsewhere ought to disregard it. Our opinion about the future of the Syrians in the country they have emigrated to is that we do not expect any of them to return to their homeland except for tourism or for relaxation. We say this with great regret, and despite the fact that some of them criticize us for our view, claiming that they will certainly return home and settle down even if it is only after some time. That is what everyone who is far from his homeland and family wishes. It is also the case of the Syrians in Egypt. A great number of them have spent long years in the Nile Valley, engaged in trade, manufacturing, or government service, and since they arrived they have not abandoned the hope that they will return to their hometown or village after a certain date that they fix and then postpone, using temporary obstacles as an excuse. The strange thing is that you see them acquiring property, expanding their trade, and being promoted in government positions while at the same time promising themselves that they will soon return home. How can they do so, when they are becoming ever more firmly established here?

The Syrians who have immigrated to America are full of energy, aiming for success with all their wits about them. They have left family and country in order to earn a living. Some arrived without a penny to their name; most of them did not know the language of the country or the customs of its people. Yet after a short time they have started to compete with the native population in the spheres of trade and agriculture, setting up stores and buying property in the Unites States, Brazil, Canada, and other parts of the Americas. After only a few years have passed, their businesses have expanded and their wealth has increased. Several writers have appeared who have founded newspapers which cover politics, literature, and science. And this in addition to the freedom they have in their work and the increased earnings they hope for as the years pass. It is also true that, because there are so many of them and communications between the places where they live are easy, they compensate for the homesickness which they feel by establishing ties of friendship among themselves.

Some people claim that the only reason for Syrians to emigrate is the present situation in their country, and if it changed and improved, the Syrians would return. It is an idle hope, for that situation is not the main reason for the emigration. Other peoples endure far worse situations and yet never set foot outside their country. But Syrians are naturally inclined to emigrate; they have been used to it for millennia. Perhaps the nature of the country is the reason. It seems not to be able to accommodate the aspirations of its people; if they want to fulfill their ambitions there is not enough room for them to do so. An indication of that is that ever since the time of the Phoenicians they have always been following the trade; there was no known city in those times that they did not settle in, nor a fertile region that they did not cultivate.

The Syrians in America will not return to their homeland, except for those who cannot manage to earn a living—and there are not many of them. While some may not manage to have a comfortable living in the United States, they can easily move to another part of the American continent or else travel to another continent so as not to return to their homeland disappointed.

America is not the only destination to which Syrians emigrate, for there are thousands of them in Australia, Tasmania, New Zealand, the islands in the Ocean [*sic*], in East and Southern Africa, Japan, China, India, and Persia, not to speak of European countries. In Egypt alone they number 80,000.[2]

Syrians have a trait that helps them to succeed in foreign countries. That is, that as well as being energetic, persevering, and intelligent, they are adaptable and easily able to acquire new habits. Thus when they live in France, for instance, you see them taking on characteristics of the French, speaking their language, dressing as they do, and adopting their customs, so much so that you imagine they are French themselves. If they live in England, they acquire the characteristics of the English, so that when you spend time with them or have dealings with them, you begin to wonder if they are not pure English. The same holds true for all other countries.

But this trait is also one of the factors leading to the loss of national consciousness (*ḍayāʿ al-jinsiyya*), which is what we fear will befall the Syrians in America. While we appreciate their remaining in America, we would like them to live there as Syrians, keeping their own customs and moral standards, and not being absorbed into the American people after a few generations, losing their national consciousness, forgetting their language, and modifying those customs and morals.

Our brothers, the Syrians in America, need to be aware of this danger threatening them and act to remove it immediately. The main factor in preserving national consciousness is maintenance of the language, which is the strongest link and the most universal bond. The Syrians in America and other countries to which they emigrate can only keep their national consciousness by maintaining their Arabic language—and how are they to do so?

The answer may be summed up in our saying: "The language is preserved through learning and culture." In other words, Arabic should be the language of science and literature among them. It cannot be the language of commerce, in view of their dealings with foreigners. For clarification, we may say that the methods that must be adopted to keep Arabic alive in America are four in number:

1. Arabic should be the family language, spoken among the members of each family and between Syrian families, on condition that there is a shared foundation. It is a responsibility of the ladies, who are the link between families, especially the mothers, who should feed their children the Arabic language with their milk, not using any other language to talk to them. And Arabic should be the language of family contacts. The children will learn the language of the country in school or from the neighbors.

2. Schools: The Syrians should open Arabic schools in the countries to which they have emigrated to teach the rules of the language and its literature as they are taught in Syria. Thus young people will grow up respecting it and the idea will not occur to them that it is a language of uncivilized people, as some people rashly conclude. On the contrary, they will learn it in order to be able to read it.

3. Journalism: A language only lives by what is written in it. The writings that have the most immediate influence are in newspapers, and there are many of them in America, mostly useful and well-conceived. They should be promoted and encouraged because they provide the best way to help maintain the language, spread it, and raise its prestige. They are also the best means for strengthening the ties of friendship between the residents of America and the rest of the Arab world, Egypt, Syria, Iraq, and so on. Arab journalism in America is one of the clearest indications of the Syrians' energy, intelligence, and love of knowledge, even if part of the Arab press there needs some advice that we may mention elsewhere.

4. Lecture and literary debating societies: They strengthen friendship among young people, open their minds, stimulate their ability to study, and awaken a love for reading in them.

To sum up, the Syrian residents in America will remain there until they are absorbed in the general population and [their Syrian identity] disappears unless they eliminate this danger by the methods I have mentioned. And our help is in God. We invite our respected colleagues, newspaper editors in America, to express their opinions on this subject, for they know better than we do how important it is with regard to the future of the Syrians in the New World.

Notes

1. Zaydān, "Mustaqbal al-Sūriyyūn fī Amrīkā."
2. More likely somewhere between 25,000 to 35,000; see Philipp, *The Syrians*, 86.

◆ ◆ ◆

Egypt and Syria

Cooperation and Relations between Them from the Dawn of History until Now

Translated by Hilary Kilpatrick

What wrong did you do, what wrong did your father do?
Did you oppress them, Egypt, or did they oppress you?
You smiled at the voracious West and its folk,
Giving them more than ever they gave you.
But in the face of the Syrians you frowned—yet
Frown as you may, Syria's a brother to you.

—Hafiz[1]

Introduction: On Immigrants and Natives

Much has been said about "aliens" (*dākhīl*, pl. *dukhalā'*), a term that has appeared repeatedly in some newspapers referring to the Syrians.[2] They mean a group of Syrians who in their opinion are damaging Egypt and the Egyptians, and they claim that the word *dakhīl*, alien, stranger, or visitor, is derived from *al-dakhal*, mental derangement, not *al-dukhūl*, entry. Whatever they may be driving at, we cannot judge their innermost thoughts. But we observe that when the *dukhalā'* are spoken of, people understand the word to be derived from *al-dukhūl* and to refer to the Syrians in general.[3] We would like to say something about the ties between Egypt and Syria, and the cooperation between them from the earliest times until now, to remove the doubts some people have about the fraternal ties between these two countries and spread the idea that Egyptians and Syrians are brothers who are indispensable to each other. Before embarking on our subject, we will comment on the true nature of the Egyptian people, the history of its formation, and the ethnicities it is made up of.

Since ancient times, no country has had more foreigners come to it and blend with its inhabitants than Egypt. This began in prehistory, since it can be inferred from studying the types of people in the Nile Valley that the original inhabitants did not belong to the Caucasian races. The Caucasians entered Egypt in prehistoric times, expelling its inhabitants, settling the country, and cultivating the land before the age of the Pharaohs. Then came the Pharaohs with their different periods and dynasties; they were mostly foreigners who conquered this country, and they founded the ancient Egyptian civilization. They had naturally brought with them soldiers of their own race, whose families then moved to Egypt and settled there under their protection. Some were Semites, others Ethiopians, Hittites, Arabs, and Phoenicians and so on. Some of them occupied the throne and handed it on to their heirs, others engaged in trading, set up workshops, or started plantations. The ancient Persians came in the sixth century B.C. and conquered Egypt. They regarded its inhabitants as a single people, the Egyptian people, and if you had then asked each individual of the nation, they would not have hesitated to describe themselves as Egyptians. The Persians remained and founded families, and they built fortresses, naming them after places in their country. After them came the Greeks, whose numbers increased especially in the age of the Ptolemys. They remained for a long time and established themselves firmly, leaving monuments in the Nile Valley that have survived to this day. The Coptic language is still written in Greek letters today, not to mention the Greek loan words and religious and political terms it contains. Then the Romans conquered Egypt shortly before the beginning of the Christian era. They made it their granary and source of provisions. In the middle of the seventh century A.D. when the Arabs arrived, the lineages of those various peoples had intermingled, the result being known as the Coptic, or in other words the Egyptian, nation. This was distinct from the Byzantine garrison that was in Egypt at the time of the Muslim conquest and that was not assimilated with the Egyptians because of its recent arrival in the country; in fact it closely resembled an army of occupation. But those Byzantines who were born in the country considered themselves as belonging to it, so that al-Muqawqis, the leader of the native Egyptian party at the time, was himself of Greek origin.

When the Arabs established their rule in Egypt, Arab tribes and clans arrived, mingling with the inhabitants. There emerged a class of Arabs of mixed origin who considered themselves Egyptians, only differing from the Copts in religion. After the rise of the Abbasid dynasty, the Persians acquired great influence, taking over the government of the Islamic empire, and a number of them migrated to Egypt. Then, when the Tulunids took control of Egypt in the mid-third century A.H. [868–905 A.D.] the Turks, members of the caliph al-Mu'tasim bi-'llah's[4] suite, came and settled, mingling with the Arabs, Persians, and Copts. The Fatimids arrived in the mid-fourth century A.H. [969 A.D.] from North Africa. They conquered Egypt with an army mainly composed of Berber tribesmen together with mixed-race Arabs from Andalusia, that is, people who had some Spanish or other Frankish blood. During their rule the Fatimid caliphs sought support from Turkish, Kurdish, Daylamite, and Armenian soldiers and black slaves. They would buy or hire them, and these soldiers would live in Egypt, marry, and have children. This was something quite normal; even the caliphs often took concubines from the Turks, the Sudanese, or the Armenians, and the mother of the Caliph al-Mustansir[5] [d. 487 A.H., 1094 A.D.] came from the Sudan. More and more groups of Kurds arrived, especially during the Ayyubid dynasty. Then, under the Mamluk sultans, the numbers of Turks, Circassians, Armenians, Mongols, and others increased. When the Ottomans took power, Janissaries, drawn from various peoples, Albanians, and others were added to the mixed Egyptian nation. Then with the start of the most recent period at the beginning of the last century groups of Turks, Albanians, and North Africans came to Egypt, while the inhabitants of the country at the time considered themselves one people and each person regarded himself as Egyptian. Even the Mamluk emirs were known as Egyptian emirs although they were mostly Circassians or Turks.

This may also be said of Muhammad 'Ali's men, for they settled in the country and had descendants. Although they had only recently left their countries of origin, most of them being Turks, Albanians, and Circassians, they are regarded as Egyptians. There is a large group of them that enjoys standing and influence. We call them people of mixed race, *indimāj al-umam*, in relation to those who merged into the Egyptian nation before them, but in fact all of them are foreigners from abroad. They evolved, however, from being foreigners to being assimilated and then to being part of the Egyptian people. From the foregoing, we can see that the right to belong to the nation in Egypt is acquired only by length of residence and the passing of generations.

The same kind of mixing of the population has occurred in Syria, which has shared Egypt's adversities and good fortune, each one experiencing the same joys and sorrows of conquest, occupation, injustice, or emigration. The relations between the two countries have been very strong, if external incidents are disregarded,[6] and have regularly been renewed as the years have passed. To explain that, we shall divide our discussion of the subject into four parts according to the different types of relations:

1. Relations Resulting from the Natural Environment

With respect to geography, Egypt and Syria constitute one country because they are mutually adjacent without being separated by the sea, desert, or mountains. The one begins immediately where the other ends. Thus they have similar climates where temperature is concerned, the same sky arches over them, and the same atmosphere surrounds them. Their inhabitants are thus close in character and temperament, and they have experienced similar conditions, so that they have come to resemble one another in their customs and morals and in their food, drink, clothing, and houses. At present they are subjects of one sultan, they speak a single language, and their religions resemble each other. In short, the two countries are in fact one divided into two regions: Egypt and geographical Syria, just as Egypt is divided into two regions, Lower Egypt and Upper Egypt, and as geographical Syria is divided into the regions of Damascus, Palestine, and so on. In the eyes of Westerners they are one country, and if they criticize our customs or our morals or praise some of our actions—which they rarely do—they call us "Arabs" or "Orientals," making no distinction between Egyptians and Syrians.[7]

2. Political Cooperation

The closeness of the two countries both geographically and in their natural environment has led them to share the same political situation. If a conqueror had designs on one he would also conquer the other, and when a state controlled either it annexed the other. This can be seen from the time of the Pharaohs, when Ramses II, the ruler of Egypt, coveted Syria and conquered it in the fourteenth century B.C. The Shepherd Kings, who were very likely rulers of Syria, aspired to conquer Egypt and did so. When the Persians invaded these parts, they conquered both countries, as did the Greeks, the Romans, the Arabs, and the Muslim dynasties that followed.

In the time of the Rightly Guided Caliphs, Egypt and Syria were two governorates dependent on the Muslim Empire, whose center was Medina. When the Umayyad state was set up in Syria, Egypt was subjected to it; it was the favorite province, governed by the caliphs' sons and brothers, like 'Abd al-'Aziz ibn Marwan, the brother of the Caliph 'Abd al-Malik,[8] who was governor for twenty-one years; 'Abdallah ibn 'Abd al-Malik, who governed it for five years; and Muhammad ibn 'Abd al-Malik ibn Marwan. When the caliphate passed to the Abbasids and they established their capital in Iraq, Syria and Egypt became two provinces under their banner, experiencing the same fate. Then when Ibn Tulun became independent in Egypt in the mid-third century A.H. [868–905 A.D.], his greatest desire was to annex Syria, and the same can be said about the Ikhshids.

When Egypt became the seat of a ruling dynasty in the time of the Shi'i Fatimids in the mid-fourth century A.H. [969 A.D.], most of Syria fell under its sway until the Seljuks and their Atabeks conquered that country. After the Ayyubid state arose in Egypt following the Crusader conquest of Jerusalem, the first thing Salah al-Din[9] set about doing, when he had driven out the Crusaders and conquered Syria, was to incorporate the country in his domains. When he died, his sons, brothers, and nephews divided his realm, and after a long struggle it emerged as three states, each with its own government, in Aleppo, Damascus, and Cairo. The Crusaders' attacks on Syria and Egypt became more violent then, and so these states helped each other to repel them with men and money. One of the most famous examples of cooperation against the Crusaders occurred in

Egypt during the reign of the Ayyubid al-Malik al-Kamil.[10] The Crusaders had subjected Damietta and the rest of the coast to repeated attacks until they conquered the area, threatening Egypt. Al-Malik al-Kamil defended himself against them, taking up a fortified position in al-Manzala (today's al-Mansura) and calling on the rulers of Syria for reinforcements against them. The Crusaders made Damietta their stronghold and storehouse, and when they marched out to attack the Muslims in their camp at al-Manzala, al-Kamil ordered the Holy War to be proclaimed throughout the land. Soon after, reinforcements arrived from Syria under the command of his brother al-Malik al-Ashraf,[11] while his other brother al-Malik al-Mu'azzam was leading the rearguard. The two armies united and vanquished the Franks, inflicting a crushing defeat on them and saving the country. They called the camp which they had set up at al-Manzala "al-Mansura," that is, the Victorious, to indicate their victory there. One of the pleasant incidents that followed, which illustrates this cooperation, was that al-Malik al-Kamil gave a banquet in al-Mansura at which his brothers Musa al-Ashraf and 'Isa al-Mu'azzam were present (al-Kamil's name was Muhammad). Many notables and high officers of state were present, and when the company was complete, al-Malik al-Ashraf ordered a slave girl to sing these lines, which included an allusion to his bravery fighting the enemy: "When Pharaoh was a tyrant to Acre and its people / And came to Egypt to wreak destruction in the land / Moses went towards them with his staff in his hand / And drowned them in the deep, host upon host."

Al-Ashraf was delighted and said to the girl, "Sing it again, by God!" But al-Malik al-Kamil did not like the words, so he silenced her and told his own slave girl to sing. She picked up the lute and sang: "People of unbelief! Rise up and see / The happenings and novelties of our age / Servants of Jesus! Jesus and his followers and with them Moses / Are lending Muhammad their aid. "[12] (These latter verses are from a poem by Sharaf al-Din ibn Hubara,[13] which begins: "By passion I was forced to spend the night awake.") Al-Malik al-Kamil was pleased with the singing and commanded that both slave girls receive a reward.

After the establishment of the Mamluk sultanate in Egypt, Syria never considered secession for a single day. Then both countries were brought under the authority of the Ottoman Empire at the beginning of the tenth century A.H. [1516–1517 A.D.] by the Ottoman Sultan Selim the Conqueror and they are still ruled by it today. Under Ottoman rule, when the Mamluk governors of Egypt wanted to attack an enemy or revolt against the government, they turned to Syria for help, and the two countries supported each other to preserve their interests, shared or independent. Thus when 'Ali Bey al-Kabir,[14] the Great, the ruler of Egypt, wanted to become independent of the Ottoman Empire, he turned to Sheikh Zahir al-'Umar[15] the governor of Acre, who helped and supported him. Likewise Muhammad 'Ali Pasha, the ancestor of the Khedivial family, sought help from the most important of its rulers, Bashir al-Shihabi,[16] when he sent his son Ibrahim to conquer Syria. The emir aided him, exposing his own position and life to danger in the process. People know what the outcome was and how the emir, after the Egyptian withdrawal from Syria, was expelled from his country and banished, dying far from home.

Ibrahim's most important adviser in that campaign was a Syrian Christian called Bahri Bey.[17] It is said that when Muhammad 'Ali bid farewell to his son the day he set out for Syria, Bahri Bey was with him and Muhammad 'Ali put his hand on his shoulder and said, "Bahri Bey, Ibrahim is going to your country." Bahri Bey bowed to show his obedience, and he carried out his obligations properly.

Moreover the two countries have cooperated in facing natural catastrophes such as diseases or political feuds like revolts and repression. When Bonaparte and his army took the Mamluk emirs by surprise and routed them, a group of them took refuge in Syria, where people provided them with many of their necessities and helped them in their aims, even sending a Syrian to kill General Kléber in his palace in Cairo. And when 'Urabi began his revolt, the Syrian writers settled in Egypt tried their best to dissuade him, fearing the consequences, but he did not listen to their appeal. Then when 'Urabi and his supporters were at the height of their success and this country was aflame with the fire of revolt, the Egyptians found no better refuge from those disastrous events than Syria and Lebanon, where they were given full attention and honors—just as Syrians do today when they settle in Egypt. Furthermore, the people of each country take refuge in the other in times of epidemics like the plague or cholera; usually it is the Egyptians who seek refuge. Being neighbors does not always mean that people live in peace with each other; the wars between Athens and Sparta lasted for years with much bloodshed. But where Egypt and Syria are concerned, no one has heard of the population of either having designs on their neighbors; it was the emirs, sultans, or caliphs who did so, because of their taste for conquest and plunder. The populations suffered terribly as a result, but if they had been left to themselves they would have lived in peace and harmony.

3. Cooperation in Trade and Manufacturing

Egypt is an agricultural country, whereas the Syrians are merchants. Since the days of the Phoenicians, Syrians have been transporting Egyptian goods to distant places and bringing to Egypt the merchandise those places produce, earning a profit from their trading while opening markets for Egyptian produce. Thus there was mutual benefit to both parties since antiquity and in every age since. In the present time of renaissance the Syrians have had the largest share in developing commerce. Most of the Syrians who are famous for their wealth earned their money in trade, a considerable number of them with the trade in Egyptian produce like cotton and grain and the import to Egypt of manufactured goods from Europe, Syria, and Iraq. In the Mamluk period the Egyptian customs were in the hands of Syrians, who received them as a tax-farm[18] from the government, as was the custom then.

The Syrians would bring their wares to Egypt, sell them all, and buy other goods, before going back to where they could sell these, as traveling merchants were used to doing. Rarely did any of them stay for long in the country. It is well known that they began to settle in Egypt from the beginning of the eighteenth century; some Christian families from Damascus belonging to the Greek Catholic community moved to Cairo and Alexandria to expand their commercial or other activities there, and they were followed by members of their own and other communities from the different regions of Syria. They came to be known as *shawām*,[19] that is to say, people from central Syria, Palestine, Aleppo, and Iraq, in other words from the area between the frontier at Gaza and the banks of the Tigris [*sic*]. They worked in trade and manufacturing and began to open shops. They included sellers of broadcloth and notions, brokers, goldsmiths, and weavers. Those who were married lived in their own apartments, while the bachelors would stay in the caravanserais around the Hamzawi quarter.[20] Most of them were Greek Catholics, and their priests accompanied them. They had the greatest difficulty in applying their canon law when it came to personal status, marriage, and inheritance because of the Patriarch of Constantinople's opposition; he wanted to reunite the two communities, Greek Catholic and Greek Orthodox. He had the Sublime Porte issue orders to harass them, so to settle their personal affairs they turned to the *shari'a* courts to get *fatwā*s, which are legal decisions in their favor. We have seen one of these *fatwā*s in a French translation, dated 8 Sha'ban 1196 [30 May 1782] and signed by Sheikh 'Abd al-Raḥman al-'Arishi al-Hanafi, Sheikh Hasan al-Kafrawi al-Shafi'i, Sheikh Ahmad al-Dardir al-Maliki, and Sheikh Salih al-Hanbali.[21] But this is not the place to go into the history of the Greek Catholic community.

When Muhammad 'Ali came to power in Egypt there were 3,000 Syrians in Cairo, 500 in Damietta, 250 in Alexandria, and the same number in Rosetta. They had amassed considerable wealth by acting as middlemen in the trade between Western Europeans and the Mamluk emirs, buying broadcloth, silk, and all kinds of household utensils and furnishings from the Europeans and selling them to the emirs, district prefects, and other notables.

Few Syrians came to Egypt in Muhammad 'Ali's time, because he established his own monopoly over the country's trade, dispatching goods to Europe and elsewhere. The Syrians turned their attention to trade in the Sudan, and many of them settled in Khartoum, Dongola, Berber, and other places, setting up extensive businesses handling ivory, feathers, and gum. When Isma'il became Khedive, he was keen to attract foreigners and infatuated with imitating their civilization and culture. A large number of Syrians, graduates of the school of 'Ayntura and elsewhere who knew French, rose to prominence, since the government needed translators and clerks who knew both Arabic and French in view of the Europeans' involvement with Egyptian government administration. Then Syrians began to enter government service, although they were not naturally inclined to do so because of the attractive salaries. They joined government service in large numbers in Isma'il's time. There followed the 'Urabi uprising and the British Occupation. Then another group of Syrians who had learned English in American or British schools rose to prominence, and they had many chances to find employment in Egypt, after the English language had begun to be used in government administration.

Syrians, however, do not find government service profitable, nor do they have a natural bent for it, so their fortune remained unchanged until the latest financial boom, some ten years ago. This gave them an opening for which they were made—trade and currency dealing. They flocked to Egypt, opening businesses, engaging in speculation, setting up companies, acquiring estates, and building houses. Thanks to their seriousness and hard work, they became rich, like some Egyptians and foreigners. Their wealth increased severalfold, and Egypt witnessed a commercial boom to which they made the largest contribution. Many Syrians in government service resigned and went back to working in trade diligently and honestly—in addition to those engaged in learned professions like the law, medicine, and journalism.

Syrians have engaged in commerce in Egypt as every immigrant from the European or Asian community has done. Native Egyptians are not to be blamed for being offended if foreigners in their country earn what they themselves cannot, because they remain aloof from commerce and work in agriculture and government service. But it cannot be held against those foreigners that they earn money by their own industry and the sweat of their brow, unaided except by their own efforts and honesty. Moreover, when the Syrians earn money in Egypt, it stays in the country, increasing its wealth and strength, for the Syrians have adopted Egypt as a second homeland. If their presence in Egypt were not consonant with the interests of its civilization, they would leave, like the Europeans who go to Syria for trade or some other reason. If a European settles in a town there and opens a shop, soon afterward he sees native Syrians copying him and importing goods from Europe when they have learned how to sell them. The Syrians are better at marketing them because they know the local language and customs. So the European is forced to sell his business to one of his local employees and return to his country. We have eyewitness accounts of such happenings in Beirut, Damascus, and elsewhere. If the

Egyptians were to treat immigrants in the same way they would earn no blame or reproach, for every industrious person has the luck he deserves.

4. Literary and Scientific Cooperation

In the time of the Pharaohs, Egypt was the cradle of science and knowledge, with outstanding philosophers, doctors, and scholars among the most important priests. Egypt's neighbor, Phoenicia, was the link between it and the other civilized peoples of the time in Assyria, Babylon, and so on. The Phoenicians transmitted elements of culture and science from one people to another, as their successors the Syrians did in every later age. They brought to Egypt much of the science, laws, and culture of those nations and took from it many branches of knowledge and crafts. Among these cultural borrowings were two important ones that changed civilization and left a mark in the minds of the different peoples, which time has not destroyed. One was the letters of the alphabet. The Phoenicians derived them from the Egyptian hieroglyphs and then propagated the alphabet throughout the world. The different systems of writing with which the languages of the civilized world on the five continents are written are derived from it, as we have explained in detail elsewhere. The other was the culture the Jews took with them when they left Egypt, which they transmitted over generations, recording some of it in their scriptures. The [Five] Books of Moses[22] contain much of the knowledge, customs, and laws that the Jews adopted from the Egyptian priests. And the laws, rules of society, customs, and morals that are based on those books are well known; their influence is still alive today. In both cases credit is due to Egypt for laying the basis and to the people of Syria for improving on them and propagating that knowledge.

The age of the Pharaohs was followed by that of the Greeks and the emergence of the School of Alexandria established by the Greek community, refugees from humiliation after the loss of their independence in the time of Alexander. They set out for Egypt and Syria, taking their books and sciences with them, and the Ptolemys in Egypt and the Seleucids in Syria encouraged their activities. They founded schools in Alexandria, Antioch, and Beirut, bringing knowledge in the East to life, as they did eighteen centuries later when they left Constantinople after the Ottoman conquest, taking their books and their sciences to Europe and contributing along with its inhabitants to the Renaissance, which was the birth of modern civilization. The School of Alexandria with its scholars and philosophers thrived, becoming a source of learning for seekers of science and knowledge from all parts of the world, and the whole world benefited, including the Syrians, just as the Egyptians benefited from the schools of Syria.

After Islam arose and its banners fluttered over the cities of the East, and after the Muslims set up states with organized governments, there came the phase of culture and civilization. The Muslims undertook to translate the scientific works of antiquity, for which the caliphs had recourse to Syrians because of their previous familiarity with these works and their knowledge of the necessary languages. These scholars translated the scientific works and contributed to them themselves; this is the Arabic scientific Nahda of the Abbasid age. In fact they served the whole Muslim world, and especially Egypt because it was close to them. When that Nahda bore fruit with scholars, Muslims, and others, writing on medicine, pharmacy, natural sciences, history, and literature, the two countries cooperated in the exchange of information and other benefits according to the period and situation. The appearance of prominent scholars, the writing of books, and the founding of schools all happened when the state flourished and developed, and they were all connected mostly with the caliph's palace and the court. When the seat of the caliphate was in Baghdad, scholars emerged more in Syria than in Egypt, but when the Fatimid caliphate was established in Cairo many outstanding scholars appeared in Egypt. The two countries benefited from the exchanges in both cases.

When the scientific movement ended with the decline that overtook Muslim civilization from the seventh century A.H. [thirteenth century A.D.] on, few scholars emerged from the two communities, but their exchanges in the realm of literature did not decrease. Among the most famous writers in Egypt in that period were two Syrians; one was al-Maqrizi,[23] the author of the *Topography*, and the other Ibn Abi Usaybi'a,[24] author of the *Book of Generations of Physicians*, which contains biographies of doctors of the Muslim community from all Muslim countries.

During this period, the main credit for preserving the remnants of Muslim civilization goes to the mosque of al-Azhar, just as the monasteries in Europe preserved the remnants of Roman civilization during the Dark Ages until they could be used to build modern civilization. The University of al-Azhar was a shining beacon in the darkness of those ages, with students attending from all parts of the Muslim world and especially Syria. The Syrians had their own living quarters, *riwāq,* which still exist and are called the Syrian *riwāq* after them. During the period of decline, Syria had a number of scholars who had studied at al-Azhar.

5. The Latest Nahda

In the case of the recent Nahda in the two countries, the credit for it is due in the first place to Egypt, not Syria. It began in Egypt during the period of Muhammad 'Ali with his founding the Schools of Medicine, Pharmacy, and Languages and the Military Academy, and having modern scientific works translated and old texts published. In the middle of the last century, when the Syrians embarked on scientific work, Egyptian books were of the greatest help to them for studying and writing, especially where translation from Frankish languages was concerned. For the Egyptians had gone to great pains to track down scientific technical terms in Arabic books, and so the Syrians had very easy access to them, particularly in books on medicine, pharmacy, mathematics, and the natural sciences. Syrians, however, also contributed to translating books in Muhammad 'Ali's time, for he recruited more than one of them to do so. Generally speaking, Egypt laid the foundation for the renaissance of modern knowledge at the beginning of the last century. At first Syrians used to study the different branches of medicine at the Qasr al-'Ayni Medical School, using the textbooks of its professors and graduates. Then the College in Beirut was established and people's thoughts turned to studying there and using the books of its professors. The mid-nineteenth century saw a good number of scholars in Syria writing on medicine, history, science, literature, and language, and their works were distributed in Egypt.

A very important precursor of this Nahda has been printing. It existed in Lebanon earlier than in Egypt, but where cities are concerned the oldest working printing press is in Bulaq.[25] It was founded at the beginning of the last century to print old texts and modern translations. The man who cast its type, however, was a Syrian called al-Masabiki.[26]

One of the pillars of the Nahda is the Arabic press, which first appeared in Egypt. The first Arabic newspaper was *Egyptian Events*,[27] established by Muhammad 'Ali seventy-seven years ago to publish official information in Turkish and Arabic; later it appeared only in Arabic. Sheikh Ahmad Faris al-Shidyaq edited the Arabic part. Egypt was the first to establish an official press, but Syria had a popular one earlier. The oldest Arabic newspaper *The Answers* was founded by Sheikh Ahmad Faris al-Shidyaq in Istanbul in 1861;[28] it was followed by Abu 'l-Su'ud Effendi's[29] bi-weekly *Wadi al-Nil* (The Nile Valley), started in Cairo in 1867, and the magazine *al-Jinān* (The Gardens), which al-Bustani founded in Beirut in 1870. Subsequently newspapers appeared in both Egypt and Syria.

The second half of the last century saw the emergence in Beirut of some outstanding journalists who moved to Egypt in the days of Isma'il, founding newspapers and reforming journalistic style. Their leader at the time was Adib Ishaq,[30] who brought about a resurgence in journalism for which history will remember him. Credit is also due to the Syrians for bringing the Arabic theater to Egypt, which was introduced there as part of the same movement. Due to this and Egyptian investments in the theater, acting talents emerged.

Egyptian contributions of this kind also involved scientific projects that appeared in Syria itself. Isma'il Pasha was the first to encourage al-Bustani to compile his *Encyclopedia* funding his work and allowing him to use the books of the Khedivial Library, al-Bustani acknowledged this generosity at the beginning of the first volume of that precious work, and the memory of it will live as long as his *Encyclopedia* does.

Isma'il, moreover, financed cultural projects set up by Syrians in Egypt: newspapers, printing presses, theaters, and schools. He would reward a poet for a poem or a writer for a book, which encouraged people and spurred them on to fresh endeavors in the field of literature. So if the Syrians deserve credit for breathing new life into this renaissance and developing it, Egypt can boast of laying its foundations and nurturing it.

Consider another example of this cooperation. The Egyptians are working today to modernize the Arabic language by making it the language of education, newspapers, magazines, and books. The Syrians are working hand in hand with them in Egypt and Syria, because they have a common interest in this endeavor. In addition, the Syrians are publishing this modernized language and its literature in the rest of the world, especially North and South America, through the political newspapers they founded and the cultural societies they set up. A number of writers and poets have emerged in their communities there.

Egypt and Syria are sisters, sharing political, commercial, literary, and scholarly interests and working together in good times and bad. Over the centuries they have had various religions, been ruled by many states, and experienced ups and downs together while living in harmony and that is still the situation today.

With respect to the remarks in some Egyptian newspapers about "intruders," which arouse disagreements: if they refer to the Syrians in general, then it is an error we hope they will correct, after they have understood that the Syrian is a faithful worker, serving the country he lives in energetically and honestly. He is more useful and less harmful to it than the other elements making up the Egyptian population and better equipped to serve its interests through his knowledge, his opinions, or his wealth. He is also the closest friend the Egyptians have, related to them through ties of language, homeland, geography, religion, morals, manners, and customs, as well as trading, cultural, and scientific interests.

Notes

1. Zaydān, "Miṣr wa-'l-Shām."

2. Ḥāfīẓ is the pen name of the Egyptian poet Ḥāfīẓ Ibrāhīm (1871–1932); translator's note.

3. For the use of the term *dukhalā'* in the rhetoric of Mustafa Kamil, see Steppat, 260.

4. Al-Mu'taṣim (r. 813–833). First Abbasid Caliph to rely more on slave troops, typically of Turkish origin, than on various Arab military formations. But he also ruled a generation before the Tulunids rose to power in Egypt. Perhaps meant are either Musta'īn bi-'llāh (r. 862–866) or Mu'tazz (r. 866–869); both had close relations with the Turkish Ibn Ṭulūn clan.

5. Al-Mustanṣir billāh, last Abbasid Caliph but one (r. 1226–1242); his mother was Turkish. Zaidan must have meant al-Muqtadī (r.1075–1094).

6. Possibly a reference to the "Aqaba incident" in 1906, concerning the border between Egypt under British occupation and the Ottoman Syrian Provinces to the north.

7. However, see pp. 403–7.

8. 'Abd al-Malik ibn Marwān fifth Umayyad Caliph (r. 685–705). Muḥammad ibn 'Abd al-Malik ibn Marwān and 'Abdallāh ibn 'Abd al-Malik were his sons.

9. Ṣalāḥ al-Dīn al-Ayyūbī (r. Egypt and Syria 1169–1193), a.k.a Saladin; of Kurdish origin; vigorous defender of the Muslim realm against the Crusaders; probably the most popular Muslim personality in Western Europe since the Middle Ages.

10. Al-Malik al-Kāmil Naṣr al-Dīn ibn al-'Ādil al-Ma'ālī Muḥammad (1180–1238), nephew of Ṣalāḥ al-Dīn; ruled Egypt and defended it against the Crusaders: *EI2*.

11. Malik al-Ashraf Mūsā ibn al-'Ādil, and al-Malik al-Mu'aẓẓam 'Īsā.

12. These verses play on the fact that the three brothers bear the names of the founding figures of Judaism, Christianity, and Islam, Moses (Mūsā), Jesus ('Īsā), and Muḥammad; translator's note.

13. Sharaf al-Ḍīn ibn Ḥubāra. Possibly meant is Sharaf al-Dīn Abū 'l-Wafā', b. Ismā'īl al-Ḥillī (1174–1230); court poet of the Ayyubid Abū 'l-Fatḥ al-Ghāzī, son of Salāḥ al-Dīn: Brockelmann, *Supp.* 1, 457.

14. 'Alī Bey al-Kabīr (r. 1760–1767,1768–1773) Mamluk ruler of Egypt, tried to forge an alliance with Ẓāhir al-'Umar and the Russians to fend off his overlord, the Ottoman sultan.

15. Ẓāhir al-'Umar (1690–1775) carved out a semi-independent realm around the city of Acre, financed by the cotton exports from there to France: Thomas Philipp, *Acre: The Rise and Fall of a Palestinian City 1730-1831*(New York: Columbia Univ. Press, 2001).

16. Bashīr Shihābī II (1767–1841), emir of Lebanon, succeeded to establish his authority above all the other Druze and Maronite feudal clans and create a certain political unity under his rule. He sided with Muhammad 'Ali when Egypt invaded Syria.

17. Ḥanna Baḥrī Bey (d. 1843), from a powerful Greek Catholic Family in Damascus, immigrated to Egypt and returned as the chief civil administrator for Damascus under Ibrahim Pasha, when the latter conquered Syria in 1831. See Philipp, *Syrians*, 66ff.

18. A financial arrangement by which the estimated annual revenues of any specific source of income were advanced to the government by rich individuals for the privilege to collect the sums and in addition the profits over the following year.

19. Originating from Bilād al-Shām.

20. Where the largest of Cairo markets is located.

21. Sheikh 'Abd al-Raḥmān al-'Arīshī al-Ḥanafī, Sheikh Ḥasan al-Kafrāwī al-Shāfi'ī, Sheikh Aḥmad al-Dardīr al-Mālikī, and Sheikh Ṣāliḥ al-Ḥanbalī. They were the representatives of the four Schools of Law in Sunni Islam. The first was also the head of the Syrian student dormitory in al-Azhar and was considered *Shāmī*. Al-'Arīsh in Sinai was considered part of *Bilād al-Shām*.

22. Pentateuch.

23. Tāj al-Dīn Abū 'l-'Abbās al-Maqrīzī (1364–1441); meant is *al-Mawā'iẓ wa-'l-i'tibār fī 'l-khiṭāṭ wa-'l-āthār*. Other important works are *al-Sulūq li-ma'rifat duwal al-mulūk*, also a

history of Egypt, and a biographical dictionary of Egypt *Kitāb al-Muqaffā*: Brockelmann, *GAL* 2, chapter 2.

24. Ibn 'Abū Uṣaybi'a (ca. 1195–1233) *'Uyūn al-anbā' fī ṭabaqāt al-aṭibbā'*, some 380 biographies of physicians: *EI2*.

25. The first presses in Lebanon were in monasteries and restricted to printing liturgies and church texts.

26. Niqūlā al-Masābikī; Maronite from Aleppo; sent in 1815 by Muhammad 'Ali to Italy to study the art of printing; after his return in 1819 he established the Būlāq Press and directed it until 1830. Jamāl al-Dīn al-Shayyāl, *Tārīkh al-tarjama wa-'l-ḥaraka al-thaqāfiyya fī 'aṣr Muḥammad 'Alī* (Cairo: Dar al-Fikr al-'Arabi, 1951), 198.

27. *Al-Waqā'i' al-Miṣriyya*, the Egyptian official gazette.

28. *Al-Jawā'ib*; it actually was a weekly, founded in July 1860: di Ṭarrāzī 1:61.

29. 'Abdallāh Abū 'l-Su'ūd (1828–1878), Egyptian; attended school founded by Muhammad 'Ali; worked in government administration; translator, author, known poet; he edited *Wādī al-Nīl* until his death, when it was closed: Ṭarrāzī 1:47, 69, 130–31.

30. Adīb Isḥāq (1856–1885) grew up in Damascus, attended the Lazarist school there, worked for a short while in Beirut, and migrated to Egypt where he dedicated himself to writing and publishing.

◆ ◆ ◆

The Syrians in the Americas

Translated by Hilary Kilpatrick

Alexandria, Butrus Effendi Ilyas Sam'an:

How many Syrian immigrants to America are there, how much does their fortune amount to, and does remaining in America benefit their own country?

Al-Hilal: This question was raised coincidentally when our friend Amin Effendi Ghurayyib, owner of the New York paper *al-Muhajir*, was staying in Cairo.[1] So we asked him to answer this question because he is one of the most knowledgeable people about all aspects of the situation in America. Here is his answer:

> It is not known how many Syrian immigrants there are in America. It is very difficult even to have an approximate idea of the number; in fact it is impossible for significant reasons. The figures of emigration from Syria are the only reliable and truthful source for the numbers of those who have gone to America, but emigration is neither legal nor accurate[ly known].
>
> Perhaps three quarters of those who leave for the New World do so secretly without informing the government, out of fear that it will withhold permission to travel. And although there are an enormous number of Syrians in America today, we do not think that the government registers in Beirut, Lebanon[2] or Constantinople[3] indicate the presence there of more than a few thousand souls.
>
> Enormous obstacles await those who would take an official census of the Syrians in America. One is that the Syrians are extraordinarily

scattered throughout the different countries, and so it is difficult to track them down.[4] Another is that some of them in some places, especially in the United States, have become fully assimilated to the Americans, and no longer bother to mention their Syrian origin, for in the American view what counts are a man's own deeds and standing, not his relationship to other people.

I remember that about seven years ago some Syrian clergy in America tried to count the members of their various parishes, but huge difficulties stood in their way and their efforts bore no fruit. An estimate based only on conjecture in this matter is unreliable, for the difference between such an estimate and the real number may be very large, varying by a factor of two. Here is an example: an American church society in New York wanted one day to help the Syrians in that city by producing a booklet with figures about them, their occupations, and how they earn their living. This [is done], in order to distribute it among the Americans so that ordinary people would know something about this community living among them. Despite the Americans' capacity for study and perseverance and the aid given by New York Arabic newspapers the society experienced immense difficulties in carrying out the count, for most ordinary Syrians did not understand the reasons for doing so. As a result the booklet was incomplete. After all the society's efforts in sending out investigators and pollsters, the booklet noted that that the number of Syrians in New York ranged between five and ten thousand.

If this is the situation in the most developed city in the whole of America, so that taking a census should be easier there than elsewhere, you can imagine what it would be like to count those who have taken up residence as foreigners in the thousands and thousands of cities in the lands of Columbus. I will, however, give some preliminary estimates, from which the intelligent reader can draw conclusions if he wishes.

Emigration from Syria to America really began fifteen years ago [in the early 1890s]. In other words, before that time emigration was not numerically significant. It increased gradually until the number of Syrians entering the United States last year was 6,000 persons, when the figures are adjusted. But we cannot make any comparison with prior years, because we do not know the size of the increase from year to year, and also because the American Immigration records are of no use, since not all Syrians are registered as such. There are "Turks," "Arabs," "Egyptians" and so on, who may include Syrians as well as others.

It is said that the United States is the land of the largest emigration. The newspapers of the communities in North and South America agree on this. In other words, the Syrians in the United States are more numerous than anywhere else; people even say, for what it is worth, that there are between 100,000 and 150,000 Syrians in the United States. Personally I reckon them to be 100,000. Even if exaggeration on this subject is possible and even likely, anyone who travels through Washington's country cannot consider that figure excessive. For he will rarely enter one of its countless cities or towns without coming across traces of Arabic speakers. Researchers and those immigrants, who know their community well, agree that the return from America to Syria is not large enough to affect this estimate of their numbers. The increase, by contrast, is continuous and bears witness to an extraordinary growth.

Brazil follows the United States in terms of the number of Syrians living there. There are those who contest this opinion and believe that there are as many Brazilians among our brothers as Americans, if not more. (By Americans we mean Syrians living in the United States.) The obstacles impeding the counting of Syrians in the great republic in the north are multiplied in Brazil. Thereafter come the Argentine Republic in the south, Mexico in the north and so on.

In short, the number of Syrians who have emigrated to America is unknown and cannot be known. But it is possible to state that the New World as a whole has around 400,000 of them. We know, however, that this statement needs to be corroborated, and we will be most grateful to anyone who produces another estimate which has been verified.

Unfortunately less is known about their wealth than about their numbers. In the city of New York alone, there are about a hundred Syrian traders, whose total business activities in imports and exports amount to not less than 10 million riyals a year. The profits vary between 5 and 10 percent, but nowadays this equals personal expenditure. The present financial year, which ends in the United States in the month of June, will show that the Syrians in New York suffered heavy losses because of the financial crisis that drastically reduced economic activity and led to bankruptcies. In the interior of the United States [beyond New York] profits are usually higher than in the city and expenses are lower. There are some individual Syrians who are well off, but no one, as far as we know, dares to express an opinion about how much the aggregate wealth of the community is. Their businesses are varied, handling all kinds of activities everywhere. And the amount of capital cannot be deduced from merely observing business activities. Much money is deposited in banks, some of it resting in a deep, motionless sleep, giving no sign of its existence. While one man operates with 10,000 riyals and makes a profit of 1,000 riyals annually, another operates with just 1,000 and makes a profit of 2,000. A man who has 50,000 riyals may live in a style which does not indicate that he has any money, while another may live like a millionaire without you knowing from where he gets his money. In fact the people of Babel were not less ignorant of each other's affairs, after God had vented his wrath on them, than we are in America, when the time to draw up official statistics comes round.

If you ask whether the bees that have left the Syrian hive to suck the juice of flowers East and West return home or send what they have harvested to their original hive, the present course of events shows that Syria has received her due share from the New World and she should be satisfied with it. Emigrants to America have bought vast estates in Syria which they have not been able to cultivate. They have built many houses which they could not inhabit. They have yearned for the land of their ancestors as camels yearn for water, but they have not been able to live in it. And from now on, thoughts are changing on the opinion expressed by a poet: "A man's only homeland is the place which accords with him / and only his friends are his nearest and dearest."

Even if we were to reckon that the intense desire to return from America to Syria, hidden in the hearts of wealthy Syrian immigrants, is something which could gradually be turned into a serious plan to pack up and return, we would find that the plan itself needs a period of no less than a lifetime to wind up the business satisfactorily. I know many merchants, and one of them may say, "When I wind up my business I'll be satisfied with the loss of 1,000 *lira*, if I can manage that." The person who hears that knows, first, how difficult it is to wind up a business, and second, how much he will hesitate to accept the loss of 1,000 *lira*. As is well-known, money is like children; "the more there are, the dearer they become."

We cannot draw any conclusion from the return of some individuals to Syria and their settling there. First, they are only a drop in the ocean compared to the total number of emigrants. Second, their presence in Syria as people of wealth is like an electric current which strikes at their neighbors' hearts, provoking them to travel to America following their example. If an individual emigrant brings back from America to Syria 1,000 *lira*, Syria will no doubt benefit from that money, but in exchange it will lose the strength of a hundred men whom the arrival of this money causes them to want to travel.

Notes

1. Zaydān, "al-Sūriyyūn fi Amrīka."

2. Beirut was not part of the province, al-*mutaṣarrifa,* of Mount Lebanon at the time; translator's note.

3. Lit., "what is there?" (*mā hunālik*). *Mā hunālik* is the title of Ibrāhīm al-Muwayliḥī's satirical account of life in Constantinople, which was published in Cairo in 1896. The author of this article seems to be indicating the Ottoman capital allusively by the same expression; translator's note.

4. A more serious problem is that U.S. immigration had no classification of "Syrian" but only "Ottoman" and/or "Caucasian."

◆ ◆ ◆

Egyptian Patriotism

Translated by Hilary Kilpatrick

Cairo: Muhammad Effendi Mustafa al-Husayni:[1]

In the introduction to the biography of the late al-Barudi,[2] you mentioned that throughout the history of Egypt a part of its population has always been of mixed blood, from as far back as the Pharaohs to the Circassian Mamluks. I wish you would expand on this, mentioning the peoples who have settled in the Nile Valley and mixed with its inhabitants, so that we can see who has the most right to be considered Egyptian.

al-Hilal: Since ancient times, no country has seen more foreigners migrate and mix with its inhabitants than Egypt. That began in prehistory, as emerges from the study of the various types of people in the Nile Valley. Its original inhabitants did not belong to the Caucasian peoples, but the Caucasians conquered Egypt in prehistoric times. Expelling its inhabitants, they took their place and made the country prosper before the age of the Pharaohs. Then came the Pharaohs, with their different periods and dynasties; they were mostly foreigners who conquered this country, and they founded the ancient Egyptian civilization. They naturally brought with them soldiers of their own race, whose families then moved to Egypt and settled there under their protection. Some were Semites, others Ethiopians, Hittites, Arabs, Phoenicians, and so on. Some of them occupied the throne and handed it on to their heirs; others engaged in trading, set up workshops, or started plantations. The ancient Persians came in the sixth century B.C. and conquered Egypt. They regarded its inhabitants as a single people—the Egyptian people. Individual members at that time would not have hesitated to describe themselves as Egyptians. The Persians remained and founded families, and they built fortresses, naming them for places in their country. After the came the Greeks, whose numbers increased especially in the age of Ptolemy. They remained for a long time and established themselves firmly, leaving monuments in the Nile Valley that have survived to this day. The Coptic language is still written in Greek letters today [and consists of many] Greek loan words, religious terms, and political-technical terms (which the language absorbed). Subsequently, the Romans conquered Egypt shortly before the beginning of the Christian era. They made it their granary and source of provisions. In the middle of the seventh century A.D. when the Arabs arrived, the lineages of those various nations had intermingled; the result became known as the Coptic nation, that is, the Egyptian nation. This was distinct from the Byzantine garrison that was in Egypt at the time of the Muslim conquest and that had not been assimilated with the Egyptians because of its recent arrival in the country; in fact, it closely resembled an army of occupation. But those Byzantines who were born in the country considered themselves to belong to it, so that al-Muqawqis, the leader of the native Egyptian party at the time, was himself of Greek origin.

When the Arabs established their rule in Egypt, Arab tribes and clans arrived and mingled with the inhabitants. There emerged a class of Arabs of mixed origin who considered themselves Egyptians, only differing from the Copts by their religion. After the rise of the Abbasid dynasty, the Persians acquired great influence, taking over the government of the Islamic empire, while a number of them migrated to Egypt. Then, when the Tulunids took control of Egypt in the middle of the third century A.H. [868 A.D.], the Turks, members of Caliph al-Mu'tasim bi-'llah's suite, came and settled, mingling with the Arabs, Persians, and Copts. The Fatimids arrived from North Africa in the middle of the fourth century A.H. [969 A.D.]. They conquered Egypt with an army mainly composed of Berber tribesmen together with Arabs of mixed race from Andalusia, that is, people who had some Spanish or other Frankish blood. During their rule, the Fatimid caliphs sought support from Turkish, Kurdish, Daylamite, and Armenian soldiers and black slaves.

They would buy or hire them, and these soldiers would live in Egypt, marry, and have children. This was something quite normal; even the caliphs often took concubines from the Turks, Sudanese, or Armenians, and the mother of Caliph al-Mustansir (d. 487 A.H. [1094 A.D.]) came from the Sudan. More and more groups of Kurds arrived, especially during the Ayyubid dynasty. Then, under the Mamluk sultans, the numbers of Turks, Circassians, Armenians, Mongols, and others increased. When the Ottomans took power, Janissaries (drawn from various peoples), Albanians, and others were added to the mixed Egyptian nation. Finally, with the start of the most recent period at the beginning of the last century, groups of Turks, Albanians, and North Africans came to Egypt. The inhabitants of the country at the time considered themselves one people and they all regarded themselves as Egyptian. Even the Mamluk emirs were known as Egyptian emirs although they were mainly Circassians, Turks, or others.

This may also be said of Muhammad 'Ali's men, for they settled down in the country and had descendants. Although they only recently left their countries of origin—most of them being Turks, Albanians, and Circassians—they are regarded as Egyptians. Many of them have status and influence. We call them "people of mixed race" compared to those who merged into the Egyptian nation before them, but in fact all of them are foreigners. They evolved, however, from the category of foreigners to that of those who were assimilated and then to being part of the Egyptian people. From the foregoing, we can see that the right to belong to the nation in Egypt is acquired only by length of residence and the passing of generations.

Some writers, however, consider religion as connected with national sentiment and thus regard those who belong to the state religion (Islam) as being closer to having the right to belong to the nation. Thus a Turk, Syrian, or Circassian who settles in Egypt and raises children, if he is a Muslim, is considered Egyptian, whereas if he is a Christian or a Jew he remains an immigrant or foreigner in their eyes. This is an odd opinion, incompatible with the principles of civilization, for national sentiment is one thing and religion is another, as is obvious.

Notes

1. Zaydān, "al-Waṭaniyya al-miṣriyya."

2. Maḥmūd Pasha Sāmī al-Barūdī (1840–1904) was an accomplished Nahda poet who also had a military and political career. He became a close collaborator of Aḥmad 'Urabi Pasha during the 'Urābī rebellion: *Al-Hilāl* 13 (Feb. 1905): 257–64.

◆ ◆ ◆

Arabs and Turks before and after the Constitution

Translated by Hilary Kilpatrick

Many people have written to us asking our opinion on the debate carried on in the newspapers on the mutual relations or rivalry between Arabs and Turks.[1] We have therefore decided to write a chapter on these relations from the beginning of Islam to the present.

1. Arabs and Turks before the Constitution

How the two peoples encountered each other: The Arabs and Turks had no contact in pre-Islamic times. They were both nomadic peoples (*ahl al-bādiya*), given to war and raiding, but they never met because of the enormous distances separating them. The Arabs lived in the Arabian Peninsula while the Turks lived in the Altai Mountains (Mountains of Gold) in Central Asia between India, China, and Siberia; and deserts, valleys, and mountains lay between Arabs and Turks. The Turks differed greatly from the Arabs in physical appearance, character, customs, and language. It was impossible for them to understand each other because of the distance in structure and vocabulary between the original Turkish language and the Arabic language; Turkish had no Arabic words and Arabic had no Turkish ones, not to speak of differences in styles of expression.

When the Arabs embraced Islam and began to build an empire through conquest or other means, their horses' hooves trod the lands of the Turks, which they called *Mā wara' al-nahr*,[2] and they conquered Bukhara, Samarqand, Ferghana, Ashrusana, and other parts of Turkestan during the Umayyad caliphate. The inhabitants of those regions were tribes ruled by princes or kings bearing titles such as Khaqan or Ikhshid, and they were still idol worshippers. Entering the Muslims' realm brought them into contact with the civilized world of the time, and when they embraced Islam their hidden attributes were revealed. Great generals appeared among them, and they established dynasties that ruled the Muslim world for successive centuries. The relation of the Turks with the Arabs in Islamic times may be divided into two periods—the first the age of service and the second the age of rule. We understand by the age of service the Turks' entry into the service of the Arabs in the early Islamic period and by the age of rule the Turks' subsequent domination of the Arabs.

Arab Domination in the Early Islamic Period

The Arabs were proud and independent by nature, and when they embraced Islam and conquered the known world they became even more arrogant, believing that they were superior to all other people, *nās*, and made of different clay. The Arab considered he could lord it over the non-Arab and regarded himself as born to command and others as born to serve. For this reason the Arabs only concerned themselves with matters of politics and government in the early Islamic period, leaving everything else to others. No one contested their rule, and so they became increasingly arrogant, particularly toward the non-Arab Muslims, whom they called *mawālī*,[3] meaning that these Muslims had been their slaves and they had freed them. (They were different from the *dhimmis*.[4]) Persians, Turks, and other non-Arab Muslims were all counted as *mawālī*. The Arabs were so haughty that they disliked praying behind a "freedman" and if they did so, they said, "We do that out of humility before God." They did not address them respectfully as "Father of" but only used their names and nicknames; nor did they walk alongside them or precede them in processions. And there are other instances set out in detail in the *History of Islamic Civilization*.[5]

The Arabs were intoxicated with the wine of sovereignty and victory, because they had advanced from herding camels to administering kingdoms in only a few dozen years. They imagined that they had some innate virtues and qualities which no one else possessed, just as the Romans had done before them, and as the members of some dominant nations in this age do, which is to assume they are distinct from the rest of humanity thanks to their inborn nature. The Arabs' superiority was regarded as self-evident, needing no proof. So when the Umayyads took their contempt for non-Arabs to extreme lengths, after the wonder at the Prophet's mission faded, the non-Arabs began to express their discontent, supporting the descendants of 'Ali and other enemies of the Umayyads. A party that did not recognize the Arabs' superiority arose. It was called the *Shu'ubiyya*, and it only appeared during the Abbasid period after the Arabs' influence had waned.

The Arabs' power began to diminish especially after the conflict that emerged between al-Amin[6] and al-Ma'mun,[7] since al-Ma'mun sought the Persians' help against the Arab supporters of his brother, and he was victorious. The Arabs' influence decreased and the caliphs thereafter came to rely on the help of non-Arabs, especially Turks, whom they enrolled in their armies.

The Turks' Service in the Muslim Army

The period of service began with the conquest of Turkestan in the Umayyad period. Whenever the generals conquered a city or region they would bring the captives, men and women, to their own people or sell them to others who would transport them to different regions and sell them as slaves. When the Abbasids took power, Turkistan was paying the land tax and the poll tax on non-Muslims. As part of the poll tax the tax collectors would take children from the nomadic tribes and sell them into slavery. Most of these children were prisoners of war or booty from raids, as was the custom in those times. The governors would take the best of them for themselves, to serve in their palaces with slaves drawn from other peoples. They were known as Mamluks.

The Turks stood out from the other peoples who submitted to the Muslims because of their physical strength, courage, skill in archery, endurance of hardships during journeys on horseback, and steadfastness on the battlefield. Gradually the caliphs used them to form an army. The first caliph to enroll them in the army was the Abbasid al-Mansur,[8] but they were just a small troop without any importance in the state, for the main role then was played by the Khurasanians (Persians) and the Arabs. When competition between Arabs and Persians increased in al-Rashid's[9] time and the Arabs lost power as al-Amin's authority declined, the Persians, al-Ma'mun's supporters and his relatives on his mother's side, gained the upper hand and ruled despotically. The comforts of civilization had been harmful to the Muslims, depriving them of the will and ability to conquer and be victorious. Al-Mu'tazim,[10] al-Ma'mun's brother, reflected on this before he became caliph; his mother was Turkish and he had inherited many of the Turks' characteristics we have mentioned. Moreover he was partial to them because they were his maternal relatives, just as al-Ma'mun favored the Persians.

Al-Mu'tazim observed the Persians' boldness and effrontery after his brother al-Amin had been killed, and he began to fear them. He had no confidence in the Arabs since they had lost their sense of tribal solidarity, become accustomed to the comforts and luxuries of civilization, and lost their vigor. So he decided to reinforce his position by using the Turks, who at the time were still nomadic and violent, courageous in war, and enduring a life of hardships. He took to selecting the strongest of them, buying them from their masters in Iraq or searching for them in Turkestan and other places. He collected several thousand fine-looking, healthy men; gave them garments of silk brocade, gilded belts, and gilded accoutrements to wear; and clad them in a uniform that distinguished them from the rest of the army. He took special care to train this force of his, built the city of Samarra for them, and awarded them pensions. They converted to Islam and settled down. Al-Mu'tazim did not only buy slaves, but he attracted many commanders and princes toward him. Thus the Turks became powerful and influential; they dominated affairs of state, especially after they had rescued the empire from the rebel Babak al-Khurrami and conquered 'Ammuriyya during al-Mu'tazim's reign. Power that had been held by Persian ministers was transferred to the Turks. After al-Mu'tazim the reins of state were firmly in their hands, especially when al-Mutawakkil[11] began to combat the Shi'a. He gave the Turks preference because they supported him. Al-Mutawakkil's son al-Muntazir incited them (or they incited him) to kill his father, which they did; that was the beginning of their contempt toward the caliphs. They made al-Muntazir caliph, but his reign did not last more than a few months until he died full of remorse. He was succeeded by al-Musta'in bi-'llah in 248 A.H. [862 A.D.][12] and al-Mu'tazz in 251 A.H. [865 A.D.]; by this time the Turks had acquired immense power. One of the stories illustrating their tyrannical behavior toward the caliphs is that when al-Mu'tazz[13] became caliph his close companions invited the astrologers to court and asked, "How long will the caliph live and how long will he hold power." A wit who was present remarked, "I know better than they do how long his life and his caliphate will last." "How long do you think?" "As long as the Turks want!" And everyone in the room burst out laughing.

Al-Mu'tazz was murdered in the most horrible way. They dragged him by his legs to the door of the room, beat him with clubs, and tore his shirt, with the sun shining into the house. He would raise one foot and lower the other because the sun was so hot, while one of them slapped him with his hand. They pulled out al-Mustakfi's[14] eyes and threw him into prison, where he died. Al-Qahir[15] was so poor that when they imprisoned him he was wearing a cotton robe and had wooden clogs on his feet. It is no wonder, then, that the caliphs became a plaything in the hands of the Turks. When they struggled for power the caliph took the winning side, and after the commanders had sworn obedience to the caliph, the caliph swore obedience to them. In such conditions the Arabs' prestige collapsed. It was said of them: "An Arab only succeeds if he has a prophet with him to help him." Meanwhile, the Turks became more and more powerful, moving from dominating the caliphal palaces to setting up independent states. Thus they graduated from serving in states ruled by the Arabs to ruling over Arabs and others.

Turkish Rule in the Middle Ages

Turkish rule began with the setting up of principalities in the shadow of the Abbasids, the oldest one being that of the Tulunids, followed by the Karakhanids, the Ikhshidids, and the Ghaznavids. Then they established empires, the first of which was the Seljuk Empire with its ramifications in Fars, Turkestan, Asia Minor, Syria, Iraq, and elsewhere. This was followed by the empires of the Mamluk sultans in Egypt and Syria, and finally the Ottoman Empire, *al-Dawla al-'uthmāniyya*, with which Islamic history enters a new phase. Before then, the Muslim world was fragmented and weakened by the shocks it had endured from invaders such as the Mongols. The Ottomans appeared when they were needed, conquering Constantinople, which the Muslims had despaired of taking after several attempts. The Ottomans made war on the greatest rulers of Europe, routing and pursuing them as far as Hungary; besieging Vienna, the Austrian capital; forcing the Archduke Ferdinand to pay tribute; and raiding in the Mediterranean as far as the Spanish coast. Europe trembled in fear of them. They conquered the eastern Arab world as far as Iraq, then turned south and west to conquer Syria and Egypt, where the remnants of the Abbasid state had survived. The Abbasids ceded the caliphate to them, and during the time of Sultan Sulayman (926–974 A.H. [1520–1566 A.D.]) their empire extended from Budapest on the banks of the Danube to Aswan on the banks of the Nile; and from the Euphrates in Iraq to the Straits of Gibraltar. All the western part of the Muslim world came under the authority of the Ottoman Empire, as it does today. The fact that caliphate and temporal power were combined[16] is one reason why the Ottoman Empire has survived longer than the Muslim empires that preceded it. This includes the Abbasids despite the length of time they ruled, because their authority had become merely nominal three centuries after they established their state. The Ottoman Empire is the first non-Arab Muslim state to have combined the caliphate with sovereign power that was accepted by the Muslims.

The Arab ethnic element, *al-'unṣur al-'arabī*, in that period was weak, except in Andalusia for a certain length of time. The Arabs sought to regain power without success during Fatimid rule in Egypt; but no sooner had they done so than the Kurds and Turks conquered the country. From then on they put up no resistance, except for the uprising of some tribes in Arabia and elsewhere, inspired by a political or religious message, like the Wahhabi movement in the Nejd and the Mahdist movement in the Sudan. When Muhammad 'Ali Pasha, the founder of the Khedivial dynasty, decided to set up a great Muslim state at the beginning of the nineteenth century, he appealed to Muslim solidarity for support. At that time there was a strong sense of solidarity, *'aṣabiyya*, in Egypt among the Turks and the Arabs. But the Turks' solidarity was with the Ottoman Empire, so Muhammad 'Ali Pasha chose to appeal to Arab solidarity. He came to personify the hope for an Arab revival, especially after his war with the Wahhabis and meeting with the Sherif of Mecca and tribal leaders. The schools and printing presses that were established and the books that were published revived the Arab ethnic element and sense of identity, *'aṣabiyya*. But the Arabs did not help him achieve his political aims; these were thwarted by the ambitions of Western European nations in the Muslim world. However, the revival was of great cultural and practical benefit to the Arabs of the East, preparing the way for the Nahda we are now experiencing.

2. Arabs and Turks after the Constitution[17]

Community of Shared Interest[18]

As has become clear from the foregoing, in the period of despotism the ruler used to accede to the throne over the bodies of members of his own group, who saw nothing strange or unjust in that because they were thoroughly subservient. They firmly believed that they had been created to follow the ruler, at whose complete mercy they were. By contrast, in this age of constitutions and freedom, the nation, *al-umma*, has acquired a voice where the ruler's authority is concerned and an opinion on the way his government is run. It is time for people to renounce blind loyalties. We do not believe that solidarity, *'aṣabiyya*, or real union, *al-jāmi'a al-ḥaqīqiyya*, is based on anything but common interest. By this we mean that a person does not seek a union unless it is in agreement with his interests or those of his nation, *umma*. Just as rulers breathed life into the chauvinism that they exploited to defeat their enemies, so the nation, which has become sovereign thanks to the Constitution, should only accept unions that are in harmony with its interests.

Each of us has many different ties linking him with various communities, *al-jāmi'āt*, and he turns to the group loyalty that he considers useful in a given situation. A Syrian Christian, for instance, shares the tie of religion with Europeans and Copts and the tie of patriotism, *jāmi'at al-waṭan*, with the Muslims, Jews, and other communities of Syria. The tie of language links him to the Muslims of Egypt, the Hejaz, North Africa, and Iraq, that of belonging to the Empire to the Turks, Armenians, and

Greeks, and that of being an Easterner to the people of India and Persia. If he is a merchant he is counted a member of the group of merchants, while if he is a journalist he belongs to the community of journalists, linked together by journalism. The same is true for other sections of society. Take for example the Turkish Muslim in Egypt. He shares the tie of religion with the Egyptian Muslims, the tie of language with the inhabitants of Anatolia, Turkistan, and Constantinople, and the tie of belonging to the same state with the people of Syria, Iraq, Armenia, and Macedonia. The Greek from Macedonia, likewise, shares the tie of religion with the Christian peoples of Europe and a common national identity, *jāmi'at al-jins*, with the Greek state, while belonging to the same state, *jāmi'at al-dawla*, unites him with the Turks, Syrians, Armenians, and so on.

All these people and those in similar positions are free to choose the solidarity or common ties that they consider useful or of greatest benefit in the light of existing conditions. This is what we meant with the saying that the real community is the one of "shared interest"[19] but it appears to people, *al-nās*, in the garb of some other form when serving it. A man may change from one form to another as circumstances require. At the beginning of Islam the Arabs existed on the basis of religious and tribal loyalties, but when they settled down in cities, a tie of loyalty to a territorial community developed among them, producing the factions of the Hejazis, the Kufans, Basrans, Syrians, and so on.

During the Ottoman Empire the Turkish sultans gave prominence to ethnic solidarity, *'aṣabiyyat al-jins*, out of a desire to rally the Turks to them and expand their state through conquests. They appealed to Arabs and other Muslims, using religious loyalty, while their subjects were obedient and submissive. But when this state's laws became corrupted and its inhabitants, *al-sha'b*, enlightened with modern civilization, each group, *ṭā'ifa*, took refuge in the loyalty that it thought would rescue it from that injustice. The Muslims disregarded loyalty, *'aṣabiyya*, of religion because it linked them with the ruling class which they blamed for wronging them; they turned instead to nationalities and languages. The Arabs considered their interest lay in Arab solidarity, *'aṣabiyya*,[20] because it links the inhabitants of the Arabian Peninsula, Egypt, Syria, Iraq, North Africa, the Sudan, and so on, and together they make up millions. They began to speak about it, and Muhammad 'Ali in particular gave it new life, as has already been mentioned. The Armenians found their interest lay in ethnic solidarity ,*al-jāmi'a al-jinsiyya,* so they came together in the name of all Armenians, and then they moved closer to Europe because of religious solidarity, hoping it would protect them in the name of a common religion. The Syrian Christians sometimes also appealed to certain European countries *duwal,* pl. of *dawla,* to protect them in the name of religion. These people were all linked by one bond, "Ottoman patriotism," *al-jāmi'a al-'uthmāniyya,* but it was not effective because of bad government and suspicion between the ruler and his subjects.

Ottoman Community

The Ottoman ruler is Turkish, but his misrule has affected all his subjects, even the members of his own people, *abnā' 'aṣabiyyatihi,* the Turks. They have become estranged from him and contested his rule, and he has grown suspicious of them. Wishing to reduce their influence, rein in their ambitions, and weaken their say in affairs, he turned to other groups to support him against them, causing the relations between them and the Turks to deteriorate. This occurred after he had feared for his position because of the other group's, that is, the Arabs', discussions about the caliphate. He gave some Arabs important positions, and they went along with him, supporting his ideas. Intelligent Turks realized that their affairs would never prosper or their state flourish unless they created new loyalties and extended the ties of solidarity in the Empire. They realized that the ties of religion or nation only serve despotic monarchs to control peoples, *al-umam.* Having been exposed to civilized people in Europe and seen how they advocate the tie of patriotism, *al-jāmi'a al-waṭaniyya,* in the name of the state, they chose Ottoman patriotism, *al-jāmi'a al-'uthmāniyya,* as their form of solidarity. This embraces Turks, Arabs, Armenians, Greeks, Albanians, and others. They proclaimed it and their influence grew. Foreign countries approved of their efforts and encouraged them until they achieved the promulgation of the Constitution in the name of the Ottomans. The Turks, the pillar of the state, announced that they would give up their nationality, *jinsiyya,* and relinquish their political rights, only recognizing the tie of Ottomanism, *al-jāmi'a al-'uthmāniyya,* out of their belief that if they did not do so, their state would be torn apart and collapse. The Arabs agreed, although some did not believe in the sincerity of the Turks' promise, because they were unaccustomed to sincerity from the Turks or other Eastern peoples. Some of them joined that union out of desire for a position or some other advantage, and when their expectations were not met, they held it against the Turks and accused them of acting in bad faith. Some partisans of the Arabs attacked the Committee of Union and Progress (CUP), imputing extreme nationalism, *al-ta'aṣṣub al-jinsī*, to it and charging it with using Ottoman patriotism merely as a cover for restoring Turkish solidarity and Turkish privileges and being insincere in pursuing other aims. This was a cause of dissension and disturbances.

The strongest argument they adduced in this matter was that the elections to the Parliament were not free and independent but organized under the control of the Committee of Union and Progress. Consequently there were far fewer Arab deputies than their numbers warranted, and they included only one Christian. The CUP had the majority and only issued the decrees it wanted. The Constitution lays down equal rights for the various communities, so the government should have appointed some Arabs to the most important positions, like governorships and ministries, but it did not do so. At first sight these objections appear sound, but they are not.

Our concern is of course with the Arab cause, because we belong to them, speak their language, and share their character. We are particularly concerned with this cause because of our personal interest, since we stand up for the Arabs and concern ourselves with their literature and history. We do our utmost to advance their affairs and one of our greatest wishes is that the Arabs should have a powerful state.[21] Therefore what we say in this matter can only be interpreted as arising out of a sincere desire for the true public interest. Here is our opinion.

The Committee of Union and Progress's Despotic Rule

It is undeniable that the CUP used its influence in the elections to ensure its party gained the majority, thus becoming the most powerful voice in the Parliament, and failed to appoint Arabs to the highest offices. But we ascribe that not to its desire to monopolize power to the detriment of the Arabs or others. For the Committee, which has astonished the world with its rational behavior, wisdom, and honest intentions in seeking reform, includes the best writers, men of science, and philosophers. It has achieved deeds that history will immortalize for as long as the Constitution remains: it transformed the government in a way that no one else had done, as history from the earliest times to this day bears witness and as is attested by prominent contemporary statesmen. It is incomprehensible that the Committee which has achieved this should violate its own policy thus, knowing that that would only lead to a weakening of the state or even destroying it. Its use of discernment and rational behavior in all its actions is proof of that. It carried out the acts it is reproached with, out of a desire to maintain the state's security and in order to protect the Constitution, which had been established with great efforts, from being undermined if others were to take over the government.

How dare we blame the CUP (the Turks) for their suspicion of us, since we have not given them proof of our desire to unite with them heart and soul? The supporters of the autocratic government were Arabs. When the regime changed, the Constitution was proclaimed and the Turks announced that they were renouncing their nationality and privileges out of a desire to conform to Arab demands. Apart from supporting the establishment of an Arab league, these Arabs set up the Arab Brotherhood Society in Istanbul. (We have criticized this society in another issue of *al-Hilal*.) They founded newspapers to defend the Arabs, denigrate the Turks and boast of Arab glory, Arab empires and Arab science. Others wrote articles calling for a Syrian (Arab) union, seeking administrative autonomy and appointing themselves the Syrians' spokesmen, unbeknownst to the Syrians themselves. How can the Turks be blamed for their suspicion of the Arabs after that? What right do we have to reproach them for delaying appointing Arabs to high positions—if it is true that they did that intentionally? The reason for that might be their belief that Arabs cannot now occupy political or administrative positions, not because they are incapable of doing so but because they have not had the necessary preparation that the Turks have had through their centuries-old experience of government. Anyone who wants to preserve the Ottoman Empire, while it is in the process of developing, will agree that offices should be entrusted to those Turks or members of other Ottoman peoples, *al-umam*, who are experienced in administration and government. Arabs and others need to prepare themselves for these tasks—and that will not happen overnight.

There is no disagreement that the Turkish elite is better equipped than ours for administration and government. In this time of transition the state needs experience, skill, and intelligence in politics while its structures become firmly established. It is not wise for us to rely on inexperienced men in that context.

It may be objected that the CUP's autocratic use of power goes against the spirit of the Constitution. But we would reply: how splendid autocracy is, when it is the autocracy of the intelligent and the just! Sensible people agree that the East will never achieve its renaissance except under a just and wise autocratic ruler. In fact this is the best form of government for every people, and the ruler's power is only limited through a constitution because there are so few intelligent and just men. How different is the situation now, when we have been fortunate enough to have a Committee bringing together the best of the wise and the just! If it is autocratic, its autocracy goes hand in hand with consultation, because it is made up of scores or hundreds of members. Hence it is less likely to make mistakes when exercising autocracy than an individual would be. If we were given the choice, we would prefer that this Committee manage the affairs of state by itself without consultation for several years, until the foundations of the structure it has worked so hard to set up have become firmly established. And if it made a mistake or wrought harm on the Arabs or anyone else, wisdom would require that we restrain ourselves and overlook it, out of a desire to serve the interests of the state—unless we had real proof of bad faith and not merely suspected it.

We therefore propose that our Arab brothers have confidence in their brothers the Turks, rejecting the loyalties of the age of despotism, which are those of pre-Islamic times, and focusing on the tie of common interest, which today means Ottoman patriotism, *al-jāmi'a al-'uthmāniyya*, through which we have obtained the Constitution, and through which alone we will be able to preserve and strengthen it. We must reach an agreement, and agreements are only reached between two parties when one of them is wronged but, being wiser, he tolerates this injustice magnanimously and broad-mindedly, out of a desire for an agreement that will benefit both of them. What is true for individuals is also true for groups. Agreement is essential for the survival of our state, and the wise man will overlook his friend's immoderate behavior so long as he does not fear it will harm the common good; he will argue with him amicably and discuss with him as an intelligent partner. When this state stands firmly on its feet, with its affairs in order, everyone can demand their rights with the utmost insistence. Until then, it is unwise for us to accuse our partner of betraying us on a mere conjecture or to call him to book for a fault that, even if committed intentionally, does not harm the public good. This is all the more so since the partner is the originator of the project, establishing its foundation and setting out its main lines, with us providing little help in its development. After the its completion, he invited us to join him and benefit from it, giving us a co-equal share, on condition that we help to preserve it. Should we not then forgive him for preferring some of his companions, while he does not prevent us from enjoying this state of affairs? This, after we had spent our lives regretting that we would never obtain one-hundredth as much?

Notes

1. Zaydān, "al-'Arab wa-'l-Turk qabla 'l-dustūr wa-ba'duhu." Especially in the second part it becomes evident how fluctuating the terminology for "nation," "people," "community," etc. are still in the Arabic at the time of Zaidan: The term *al-jāmi'a*, for instance, may mean "community" or the loyalty to that community, or an ideology and movement as in *'al-jāmi'a al-islāmiyya*, pan-Islamism.

2. Literally: "what is beyond the river," i.e., Transoxiana; translator's note.

3. *Mawlan*, pl. *mawālin*, freedman; translator's note.

4. Members of protected non-Muslim monotheistic communities; translator's note.

5. Zaydān, *Tārīkh al-tamaddun al-islāmī.*

6. Amīn, sixth Abbasid Caliph (r. 809–813).

7. Ma'mūn, seventh Abbasid Caliph (r. 813–833).

8. Al-Manṣūr, second Abbasid Caliph (r. 754–775).

9. Harūn al-Rashīd, fifth Abbasid Caliph (r. 786–809).

10. Al-Mu'taẓim, eighth Abbasid Caliph (r. 833–842).

11. Al-Mutawakkil, tenth Abbasid Caliph (r. 847–861).

12. Where the author only gives the dates according to the Muslim calendar, the dates of the Christian era have been added in square brackets; translator's note.

13. Al-Mu'tazz, thirteenth Abbasid Caliph (r. 866–869).

14. Al-Mustakfī, twenty second Abbasid Caliph (r. 944–946).

15. Al-Qāhir, nineteenth Abbasid Caliph (r. 932–934).

16. Zaidan represents here a view, widespread in his time, that the caliphate had only a spiritual authority, using the church-state model of the European West. In early Islam the caliphate encompassed both spiritual and temporal power.

17. This part of the article is not published in the *Mu'allafāt Jurjī Zaydān al-kāmila*: 18, 575.

18. *jāmi'at al-maṣlaḥa.*

19. See the *Anthology*, "Community of Interest: The Source of All Other Communities and the Primary Motivation for Undertaking Great Deeds."

20. A key concept in Ibn Khaldun's theory of history: *ésprit de corps* or group loyalty that becomes the *agens historiae.*

21. The term is *dawla*, meaning here the Ottoman and not a future Arab state.

◆ ◆ ◆

Are the Syrians Arabs? Or What Are They?

Translated by Hilary Kilpatrick

Since the proclamation of the Constitution, the newspapers have written at length about the Syrians and whether they are Arabs. Different views have been expressed on the subject, and more than one reader has written to us to ask for our opinion, which we now give.[1]

The Syrians before Islam

What is generally meant by "the Syrians" are the inhabitants *(ahl)* of Syria, Iraq, the Jazira, and Palestine.[2] It is difficult to determine their origins because of the many governments which they have lived under in ancient and modern times. In the oldest historical times these regions were inhabited by Semitic peoples *(shu'ūb,* plural of *sha'b)* who were closely related by descent and language. Before the arrival of the Semites, they were the abode of peoples of unknown origin. The Semites were more powerful than them and so they conquered their lands and settled them; the earlier peoples died out gradually, several centuries before the Christian era. The area was inhabited by Semites in the following order from north to south: the Aramaeans (Syriac speakers and Chaldeans), the Phoenicians, the Hebrews, and the Nabateans. Other non-Semitic peoples mingled with them, living among them in different parts of their countries, in addition to the remnants of the original peoples; it would take too long to explain this situation. The Semites, however, overcame them all, and their religions, manners, and customs prevailed.

The central geographical position of this region made it a target for the ambitions of conquerors among the ancient nations (*al-umam*), such as the Hittites, Egyptians, Assyrians, and Persians, who invaded and overran it in turn, with their peoples trickling into it. No government in Syria, however, achieved such stability as that of the Greek successors of Alexander. That great conqueror invaded and penetrated deeply into Syria in the fourth century B.C., and his successors turned it into a Greek country, with Greeks emigrating to it, settling, and intermarrying with its inhabitants, especially after the rise of Christianity. It came under the sway of the Romans, but the Greek element remained predominant, being most visible on the Mediterranean coast and gradually diminishing toward the interior.

Despite this intermingling, the Semitic peoples kept their manners, customs, and languages. The Jews in particular, despite the oppression and captivity they suffered, preserved the same customs and religion as they had had in the time of David and Solomon, apart from the changes which their language underwent during the Babylonian captivity. Then [their language] mingled with Syriac and Chaldean and became known as the Aramaic or Chaldean language—the language in which the Talmud is written. The Jewish people itself divided into Jews and Samaritans. As for the other Semitic peoples, especially the Aramaeans, they converted to Christianity and developed their own manners and customs. Most of them lived in Iraq, the Jazira, and the Syrian highlands as far as Palestine. On the western frontier of Syria, the Mediterranean coast, the Greek element predominated, while on its eastern frontier, the desert, the Arab element prevailed. From the early fourth century B.C. there was an Arab people known as the Nabataeans (*Anba'* or *Naba'*). They lived to the southeast of Palestine among the remnants of the Edomites in the kingdom of Petra, whose history we have set out in detail in our book *The Arabs before Islam.*[3] They were in contact with the inhabitants of Syria and Palestine for successive generations. When their power waned, new Arab tribes appeared to take their place on the borders of Syria and Iraq, and the Persians adopted them as allies to repel the raids of their brothers in the desert or to help them in the wars that broke out between the two empires—Persia and Byzantium—before the rise of Islam. The Byzantines' allies, the Ghassanids, lived in the Hawran, and the Persians' allies, the Lakhmids, lived on the banks of the Euphrates in al-Hira. When war broke out between Byzantium and Persia, the Ghassanids were mobilized with the former and the Lakhmids with the latter, each of them defending their allies. The Arabs settled on the frontiers between Persia and Byzantium in the Jazira and Iraq for similar reasons; they included clans of Iyad and Rabiʿa.

Thus at the rise of Islam, Syria and Iraq were mostly inhabited by the remnants of the original Aramaeans in the north and east, the Jews and Samaritans in the south, and the surviving Nabateans in the southeast, with the Ghassanid and Lakhmid Arabs bordering them and the tribes of Iyad and Rabiʿa in the Jazira. Mingling with them were scattered groups of other peoples such as the Mardaites in the Amanus Mountains, the Jaramiqa in Mosul, and groups of partly Greek or Byzantine inhabitants on the Syrian coasts and partly Persian and Kurdish inhabitants in the north.

The Syrians after the Rise of Islam

When Arab rule became firmly established in Syria and Iraq, the Arabs intermarried with the population there and settled in the cities. Other people migrated there in search of a livelihood and settled in the countryside. With the foundation of the Abbasid state, the Persians' influence increased and they took over running the administration; some of them moved to Syria and Iraq. Then an increasing number of Turks began to serve in the army, and there was a large Turkish migration to these two countries. The government also used to enlist Kurds, Daylamites, and Armenians. The Kurds were especially numerous in the days of the Ayyubids, while the Turks and Circassians preponderated in the age of the Seljuks, the Zengids, and the Mamluk sultans. After Ottoman rule was established, Janissaries from many different backgrounds, Albanians and others, came to join the population. In addition, there was the migration of Franks during the Crusades and afterward, including people from France, England, Germany, and Italy. They flooded into the frontier areas and the Holy Land and stayed for a long time in a kingdom that was reinforced by the Christians from Europe who came there. Some of them stayed in Syria, settling down and founding families.

Syria's neighbors living on the Mediterranean coasts in the west and in the desert in the east have been migrating to the country continuously. This is especially true of the Greeks and the Arabs of the Hawran, whose migration is still continuing. And many of the Christian families in Syria trace their descent back to one of these two peoples.[4]

Where origin is concerned, Syrians today are divided into two large groups, Muslims and Christians. Let us look at the lineage of each group separately. (The Jews have preserved their lineages, which have undergone little change.) [Regarding] the Muslim lineages in Syria: these mostly go back to the Arabs, because they are the first Muslims who settled in Syria after the conquest, as has already been said. The Arabs later mixed with other Muslim nations, such as Turks, Circassians, Kurds, Persians, and Daylamites, and those of the Christians, Jews, Greeks, and others who embraced Islam. Among those who have preserved their Arab lineage are the Khalidi, Husayni, and Makhzumi families. And some families have an admixture of Aramaean, Greek, or Jewish blood.

The Syrian Christians' Lineages

It is the Christians of Syria who have been the object of the discussion filling the newspapers. When Islam appeared, most of them were Aramaeans, Arabs, and Greeks, as has been shown. The Aramaeans are the original inhabitants of the country; the Greeks joined them by sea from the west and settled the coasts of the Mediterranean, while the Arabs, most of whom belonged to Ghassan in the Hawran and to Iyad and Rabi'a in the Arab peninsula, entered the eastern and southern regions. At the rise of Islam these tribes were Christian, but the tribes of the Jazira helped the Arabs because of the common bond of race or language and out of resentment of the Persians, and the Arab Muslims recognized that as a virtue in them. When the Muslims set out to impose the poll tax (*jizya*) on the protected non-Muslim communities (*dhimmis*) after the conquest, the tribes of Taghlib and Iyad objected and refused to pay it. 'Umar ibn al-Khattab heard of this, and appealed to his advisers. One of them said: "They are Arabs who are too proud to pay the poll tax, and they can cause harm. Don't give your enemy a weapon against you." That corresponded with what was in his own mind. He imposed the alms tax on them as it was imposed on the Muslims, but he made it a condition that they should not bring up their children as Christians. That naturally led to the tribes becoming Muslim. ʻUmar was extremely vigilant in preserving the sense of Arab identity, *al-jāmiʻa al-ʻarabiyya,* not allowing the Arab Christians to penetrate into Byzantine territory. If they did so, he tried to get them back, taking the matter up with the Byzantine emperor, because he considered that he had a right to do so. They say that when al-Walid ibn ʻUqba marched out to conquer Iraq and al-Jazira, the Arab Christians joined him except for the tribe of Iyad, who migrated into Byzantine territory. Al-Walid wrote to inform ʻUmar of that, and ʻUmar wrote to the Byzantine emperor: "I have heard that an Arab tribe has left our territory and entered yours. Expel them, by God, or else we will expel our Christians to you." So the emperor sent them back.

Among the Arabs in Syria after the Muslim conquest, the only ones to remain Christian were some of the Ghassanids in the Hawran and a few followers of the Lakhmids from among the Iraqi Arabs or members of Kinda and other tribes who had joined them.[5] The Arab blood or lineage among the Christians of Syria mostly goes back to the Ghassanids. The Arab conquerors who settled in Syria and Iraq were all Muslims, and few of them had been Christians before. Thus nothing from the conquerors' lineages entered those of the Syrian Christians, nor did any element of the lineages of the Muslim peoples who settled in Syria after the Arabs, such as the Turks, Kurds, Persians, and Circassians. By contrast, many lineages of Christian peoples who settled in Syria, like the Armenians, the Greeks, and the Franks from the time of the Crusades and later, mingled with those of the Syrian Christians. For when they arrived and settled down, they multiplied. Their lineages were forgotten; they spoke Arabic and adopted the Syrians' character and customs, and they merged into them.

The Syrian Christians' lineages today go back to those of the original inhabitants, the Aramaeans (Syriac and Chaldean), and those of immigrants, the oldest and most widespread of whom on the Mediterranean coast are the Greeks. From the earliest historical times the Greeks came to Syria and mingled with its inhabitants, settling on the coast. After the age of Alexander this migration increased until Syria became a second country to them, as has been said. They continued coming to it after the

Muslim conquest, and they still do so. There are many families in Syria with Greek origins, and their names indicate that: for instance, the Yanni, Bauli, Katsiflis, Babadulus, and Filibidhis families. Some families have changed their names, adopting Arabic ones, but kept the memory of the genealogy among the family members, like the Mishaqa family of Damascus, who trace their origin back to Yusuf Batraki[6] from Corfu in Greece. He settled in Tripoli and traded in filtered silk (*mushāqa*), and that is what he came to be known by. Another example is the Masarra family, a branch of a Greek family originating in Trebizond; their ancestor moved to Diyarbekir and then Aleppo, and the family expanded in Damascus and Cairo.

The Arab lineages among the Syrians are also ancient, but most of them are in the east and south of the country bordering on the Arabian Peninsula. The inhabitants of the Peninsula often used to move to the nearby villages and adopted a settled way of life. But those ancient roots are now lost, and most of what is known of the Arab lineage among the Syrians goes back to the Ghassanids. It was already established in Syria before Islam, and then successive generations of Ghassanids entered Syria, mixing with its inhabitants, either seeking a livelihood from farming or some other activity or fleeing from the Arab Muslims into the hills of Syria. The most recent event they mention, connected with their coming to Syria, is their migration in the mid-fifteenth century following a dispute that which broke out in the Hawran and forced them to take refuge in cities. They scattered through Syria and a large number of them settled in southern Lebanon. Many of the Greek Orthodox and other Christians of this region trace their descent from the Ghassanids. Some of them settled in cities and begot progeny. There are also large Christian tribes whose origins are found in the Hawran; the shaykhs of the Khazin family in Lebanon claim an origin in Hawran and say that their ancestor came from Adhru' in that region in the mid-fifteenth century. Likewise the Mutran family in Ba'albek and Zahleh is originally from the Hawran community. The same thing goes for the Jabbara, Ghannam, Hawrani, 'Atiyya, Shuqayr, Trad, Haddad, Sfayr, and Ghusn families and their like.

Among the other Christian lineages are the Armenian ones, of which there are many. They are all considered as Syrian, like the Hindiyya, Khayyat Pasha, Abkariyus, Wartabit, and Qarabit families.

Then there are the lineages of Frankish origin, the names of most of which have been lost except for a few like the Abayla (Abela) family from Spain, the Italian Tasu (Tasso) family, and the English Sharshil (Churchill) family. The Karam family in Ehden goes back to a French colonel, and the Tarabays in Tripoli trace their origin back to the French from the time of the Crusades. The same goes for all the Christian peoples that have settled in Syria and intermarried with its inhabitants, but that would take too long to explain.

The Christian Syrians, then, are not Arabs as far as lineage goes, even if they have some Arab blood; they are a mixture of different peoples. But they are considered Arabs because they speak Arabic. Successive generations of them have been born in Arab lands and they have adopted Arab moral values. Syria became Arab after the Muslim conquest because Muslim Arabs settled in it and adopted it as their country, spreading their language, manners, and customs in it, so Syria's people are considered Arabs even if their lineages do not go back to Arab tribes.

Seen in this way, the Arabs fall into three classes: (1) The desert dwellers who belong to Arab tribes and still preserve their genealogies. (2) The Muslim Arabs who settled in the countryside, mingling and intermarrying with non-Arabs and also incorporating other Muslim non-Arab peoples. They inhabit the cities of Syria, Iraq, Egypt, and North Africa and are united by Arabic language and the Muslim religion. (3) The mixed-race Arabs, that is, those affiliated to the Arabs, the Christian inhabitants of these countries, who are considered Arabs because of their language, manners, and customs but not because of their descent. They include the various Christians of Syria and Iraq and the Copts of Egypt. By analogy, the Anatolian Christians who speak Turkish are counted as Turks, although most of them are Greek by origin. And other such cases exist.

Notes

1. Zaydān, "Hal al-sūriyyūn 'arab aw mā hum?"

2. That Iraq is included seems surprising. Al-Jazira is today the region between Euphrates and Tigris that belongs to Syria. In earlier times the eastern parts, east of the Upper Tigris, in today's Iraq and Turkey, were also considered part of Bilad al-Sham. In the original 1916 Sykes-Picot agreement between France and England, staking out the territorial claims of the French and the British, the area east of the Tigris was included in

the French claim. Only in the Lloyd George–Clemenceau agreement of 1918 was the area added to the British territorial claims to Mesopotamia. Zaidan uses here the term *bayna 'l-nahrayn*, meaning literally "Mesopotamia," an expression that usually is applied to the whole Euphrates-Tigris region. The term "Iraq" meant originally the southern part of this region. Zaidan himself seems not quite sure about the terminology when he speaks further down about Syria and Iraq.

3. See General Bibliography on Jurji Zaidan and his Works, *al-'Arab qabla 'l-islām*.

4. Zaidan's family being one of them; see Zaidan, *Autobiography*, 19–20.

5. This seems to contradict squarely his observation further down that "the Christian Arabs, then, are not Arabs as far as lineage goes, even if they have some Arab blood."

6. "Barakā" in the text; translator's note.

PART THREE

◆ ◆ ◆

General Bibliography on Jurji Zaidan and His Works

◆ ◆ ◆

General Bibliography on Jurji Zaidan and His Works

Comments on the Bibliography

The date when each work was first published in Arabic appears after the title. Of the twenty-two novels Zaidan wrote, only one is not a historical work but rather a "romantic" novel.

Most information concerning the publication of each work comes from collections in the Widener Library, Harvard University; the Firestone Library, Princeton University; and the Library of Congress. The novels enjoyed an enormous popularity and were repeatedly reprinted and newly edited, sometimes with different titles. These issues and the lack of enforcement of copyrights make it difficult to track all the publications.

From the holdings of the Widener Library at Harvard University, the following information has emerged.

Regarding *Dār al-Hilāl:* The name was changed from *Maṭba'at al-Hilāl* sometime between 1939 and 1942. Published editions of all the novels came out in 1932/33, 1949/50, and 1965/66. In addition, an unknown number of reprints were issued, including reprints published in 1966 by Dār al-BayrÙt in Beirut. In 1989 reprints were published by Dār al-Ma'ārif in Sousse, Tunis. Also in the 1980s, ManshÙrāt Dār Maktabat al-Ḥayāt in Beirut reissued the works in five volumes. During the same decade Dār al-Jīl in Beirut published the *Collected Works* of Jurji Zaidan and *Mu'allafāt Jurjī Zaydān al-kāmila*. The latter reissue also included the novels, which were published between 1981 and 1983. Individual novels were time and again published by small publishers in Beirut.

Information on the publication of the novels comes from two additional sources:

1. The list in the introduction by Muhammad Ḥarb to Zaidan's *Miṣr al-ʿuthmāniyya*. Such information is marked by *.

2. The list in Kamran Rastegar, "Literary Modernity between Arabic and Persian Prose." Such information is marked by †. For both titles see listings below.

In 1925 the calendar in Iran was changed from an Islamic lunar calendar, H.Q. (Hijra Qamarī), to an Islamic solar one, H.S. (Hijra Shamsī). In the years immediately following it is not always clear which calendar is used. In such cases two C.E. years are given as possibilities.

Translations of the novels are identified by their language at the end of each source. Altogether almost one hundred translations were identified including reprints and new editions. Their distribution between various languages is as follows: one each in Russian and German; one, possibly two in Uzbek; two each in Spanish and Indonesian; three each in Javanese and Urdu; four each in French, Ottoman Turkish, and Azeri Turkish; six in English; seven in Uighur; and, by far the most translations, sixty-two or close to two-thirds in Persian, many of them reprints. Zaidan mentions in passing in his journal, *Al-Hilāl*, that several people were working on translations into other languages such as Tamil and Russian, which we were unable to trace. He also complains about translators who "forget" to mention the name of the author. As one reader wrote him, "Thanks be to God that the translator does not sue you for transgressing his copyright because you composed the novel before it was translated!" A truly comprehensive listing of all translations and editions would need research in various national libraries.

Historical Novels

al-Mamlūk al-Shārid. 1891. Cairo: Dār al-Hilāl, 1965.

Der letzte Mameluck und seine Irrfahrten. Trans. Martin Thilo. Barmen: Klein, 1917. German.

Asīr al-Mutamahdī. 1892. Cairo: Dār al-Hilāl, 1966.

Asīr al-Mutamahdī. Trans. N. N. Tehran: s.n., n.d. Persian *.

Istibdād al-Mamālīk. 1893. Cairo: Dār al-Hilāl, 1965.
Istibdād al-Mamālīk. Trans. N. N. Tehran: s.n., n.d. Persian *.

Jihād al-Muḥibbīn. 1893. Cairo: Dār al-Hilāl, 1965.
Jihād al-Muḥibbīn. Cairo: Dār al-Hilāl, 1950.
Jihād al-Muḥibbīn. Trans. N. N. Tehran: s.n., n.d. Persian *.
Ashiq - māshuqlar majirasi. Trans. Mayil Qadir. Urumchi, China: Khālq Nāshriyati, 1998. Uighur.

Armānūsa al-Miṣriyya. 1896. Cairo: Dār al-Hilāl, 1965.
Armānūsa al-Miṣriyya. Sousse/Tunis: Dār al-Ma'ārif, 1989.
Armānūsa Miṣrī. Trans. 'Abd al Ḥusayn Mīrzā ibn Mu'ayyad al-Dawleh. Tehran: s.n., 1322/1904, or 1943. Persian * .
Dukhtar-i Nīl. Trans. Muḥammad 'Alī. Shīrāzī. Tehran: Afsun, 1381/2002. Persian †.
Armānūsa Miṣri. Trans. Ja'far Qazyan. Tehran: s.n., n.d. Persian *.

Fatāt Ghassān. 1897–98. Cairo: Maṭba'at al-Hilāl, 1933 and 1966.
Fatāt Ghassān. Beirut: Dār Bayrūt, 1966.
Fatāt Ghassān. Sousse/Tunis: Dār al-Ma'ārif, 1989.
Hatem Shāmī. Trans. 'Abd al-Ḥusayn Mīrzā bin Mu'ayyad al-Dawleh. Tehran: s.n. 1330/1911 or 1951. Persian *.
Ghassan Hint. Trans. Aḥmad Buyuk Cinar and Karīm-i Tekin. Istanbul: s.n., 1330/1951 C.E. Turkish.
Rahasia tjintjin Nukman. Trans. A. Fuad Said. N.p.: s.n. 1965. Indonesian.
Ghāssan qizi. Trans. Yalqun Ismail. Urumchi, China: Shinjang Khālq Nāshriyati, 1993. Uighur.
Dūshīzah-i shāmī. Tehran: s.n., 2006. Persian.
Dilāvaran-i 'arab. Trans. Muḥammad 'Alī Shīrāzī. Tehran: Nashr al-'Ilm, 2008. Persian.

'Adhrā' Quraysh. 1899. Cairo: Dār al-Hilāl, 1965.
'Adhrā' Quraysh. Trans. Mir Mehmet Karim al-Hajj Mir Ja'farzadeh. Baku: s.n.1325/1907. Azeri *.
Dushizih-yi Dilir. Trans. 'Abd al-Ḥusayn Mīrzā. Tehran: Nashriyat-i Muhsin, 1329/1911. Persian †.
Azra Ghuraysh. Trans. M. 'A. Shīrāzī. Tehran: s.n., 1337/1958. Persian *.
Azra Ghuraysh. Trans. M. 'A. Shīrāzī. Tehran: Afsun, 1380/2001. Persian †.
Marvān. Trans. Ra'īs Aḥmad Ja'farī. Karāchī: Nafīs Ikaiḍaimī, 1989. Urdu.
Qurāish qizi. Trans. Mamut Sabit. Urumchi, China: Shinjang Khālq Nāshriyati, 1986. Uighur.

Quraish qizi. Trans. Abdildabāk Aqishtai uli Narbutin. Urumchi, China: Shinjang Khaliq Baspasi, 1999. Uighur.

Sab'at 'ashar Ramaḍān. 1900. Reprint, Cairo: Dār al-Hilāl, 1966.

Sab'at a'shar Ramaḍān. Cairo: Dār al-Hilāl, 1949.

Sab'at 'ashar Ramaḍān. Bayrūt: Dār Bayrūt, 1966.

Sab'at 'ashar Ramaḍān. Sousse/Tunis: Dār al-Ma'ārif, 1989.

Malḥamat al-Imām 'Alī: maqtal al-Imām 'Alī wa-basṭ ḥāl al-khawārij wa-tatimmat al-fitna ilā isti'thār banī umayya bi-'l-khilāfa wa-'l-khurūjihā 'an ahl al-bayt. Written by the publisher of *Al-Hilāl* in the year 1900; prepared by Muḥammad al-Rāwī; edited by Hidāya Shukr. Beirut: Dār al-Yūsuf, 2003.

Sab'at 'ashar Ramaḍān. Trans. Mir Mehmet Karim al-Hajj Mir Jaf'arzadeh. Baku: s.n., 1328/1910. Azeri.

Ramizanning on yāttisi. Trans. Mamut Sabit. Urumchi: Shinjang Khālq Nāshriyati, 1982. Uighur.

Faje'eh-yi Ramazan. Trans. M. 'A. Shīrāzī. Tehran: s.n., 1335/1956. Persian †.

Hivdahum-i Ramazan. Trans. Javad Fazi. Tehran: Kitabha-yi Jibi,1342/1963. Persian †.

Faje'eh-i Ramazan Ganjinih. Trans. M. 'A. Shīrāzī. Tehran: s.n.,1361/1982. Persian †.

Quṭām va naqsh-i dar shahādat-i Imām 'Alī. Trans. and corrected by Īraj Muttaqīzādah and Ibrāhīm Khānah'zarrīn. Qum, Iran: Mu'assasah-yi Farhangī-yi Intishārātī-i A'imah, 1375HS/1996. Persian †.

On I'eddi Ramazan. Baku: Daneshe Ḥamidun Nāshri'aty, 2003. Azeri.

Ghādat Karbalā'. 1901. Cairo: Dār al-Hilāl, 1966.

Ghādat Karbalā'. Bayrūt: Dār Bayrūt, 1966.

Ghādat Karbalā'. 2nd ed. Sousse/Tunis: Dār al-Ma'ārif, 1991.

Tārīkh-i Salm'a. Trans. 'Abd al-Ḥusayn. Tehran: 1903/1321HS. Persian †.

'Arusih Karbala. Trans. 'Abd al-Ḥusayn Mīrzā bin Mu'ayyad al-Dawla. Tehran: 1329/1950. Persian.

Faji'ih-yi Karbala. Trans. M. 'A. Shīrāzī. Tehran: s.n., 1337/1948. Persian †.

al-Ḥajjāj ibn Yūsuf. 1902. Cairo: Dār al-Hilāl, 1965.

al-Ḥajjāj ibn Yūsuf. Trans. 'Abd al-Ḥusayn Mīrzā bin Mu'ayyad al-Dawleh. Tehran: s.n., n.d., Persian †.

al-Ḥajjāj ibn Yūsuf. Trans. M. R. Tehran: Nashriyat-i Muḥsin, 1329 HQ/1911. Persian †.

Intiqām-i Khun-i Ḥusayn. Trans. M. 'A. Shīrāzī. Tehran: Afsun, 1381 HS/2002. Persian †.

Fatḥ al-Andalus, aw Ṭāriq ibn Ziyād. 1903. Cairo: Dār al-Hilāl, 1965.
Fatḥ-i Andalus. Trans. Ibrahim Nesh'at. Tehran: s.n., 1323/1905. Persian *.
Fatḥ-i Andalus. Trans. M. 'A. Shīrāzī. Tehran: Kanun-I Ma'rifat, n.d. Persian †.
Penaklukan Andalus. N.p., s.n. 1964. Javanese.
The Conquest of Andalusia. Trans. Roger Allen. Washington, DC: Zaidan Foundation, 2012. English.

Shārl wa-'Abd al-Raḥmān. 1904. Cairo: Dār al-Hilāl, 1965.
Shārl wa-'Abd al-Raḥmān. Sousse/Tunis: Dār al-Ma'ārif, 1989.
Sharl va 'Abd al-Muḥsin. Trans. 'Abd al-Raḥīm Khalkhalī. Tehran: s.n., 1333/1915 or 1954. Persian †.
Sharl va 'Abd al-Muḥsin. Trans. M. 'A. Shīrāzī. Tehran: s.n., 1338/1959. Persian *.
Sharl va 'Abd al-Muḥsin. Trans. M. 'A. Shīrāzī. Tehran: Afsun, 1381/2002. Persian †.
The Battle of Poitiers, Charles Martel and 'Abd al-Rahman. Trans. William Granara. Washington, DC: Zaidan Foundation, 2012. English.

Abū Muslim al-Khurasānī. 1905. Cairo: Dār al-Hilāl, 1965.
Ebu Müslim Horasani. Trans. Zeki Majamez. Istanbul: Kanaat Matbaası, 1330/1911. Ottoman *.
Abū Muslim Khurāsānī. Trans. 'Abd al-Ḥusayn Mīrzā bin Mu'ayyad al-Dawleh. Tehran: s.n., 1333HQ/1915. Persian *.
Abū Muslim Khurāsānī. Trans. Ḥabīb Allah Amuzegar. Tehran: s.n., 1318HS/1939–40. Persian *.
Abū Muslim Khurāsānī. Trans. Rukn al-Din Humayun Farukh. Tehran: 1323/1906 or 1945. Persian.
Abū Muslim Khurāsānī. Trans. M. 'A. Shīrāzī. Tehran: s.n., 1339/1960. Persian *.
Abū Muslim Khurāsānī. Trans. M. 'A. Shīrāzī. Tehran: s.n., 1353/1974. Persian †.
Abū Muslim Khurāsānī. Trans. M. 'A. Shīrāzī. Tehran: s.n., 1363/1984. Persian †.
Abū Muslim Khurāsānī. Trans. Muhammad Riza Mar'ashi. Tehran: s.n., 1371/1992. Persian †.
Abū Muslim Khurāsānī. Trans. M. 'A. Marsha'ipour. Tehran: s.n., 1371/1992. Persian †.
Abū Muslim Khurāsānī. Tehran: s.n., 1372/1993. Persian.
Abū Muslim Khurāsānī. Trans. M. 'A. Shīrāzī. Tehran: Afsun, 1381/2002. Persian †.
Abū Muslim Khurāsānī. Trans. M. 'A. Shīrāzī. Tehran: Dunya-yi Kitab, 1384/2005. Persian †.
Bendera hitam dari Churasan. Trans. Mahjuddin Sjaf. Djakarta: Balai Pustaka, 1953. Javanese.

al-'Abbāsa ukht al-Rashīd: aw nakbat al-Barāmika. 1906. 6th printing. Cairo: Maṭba'at al- Hilāl, 1932.

La Soeur du Caliphe. Trans. Michel Beytar. Paris: Fontemoiny, 1912. French.

'Abbase. Trans. Ḥasan Badr al-Dīn. Istanbul: s.n., 1342 H.Q./1923–24. Ottoman.

'Abbāsa ukht al-Rashīd. Trans. Mīrzā Ibrāhīm Ghami. Tehran: s.n., n.d. Persian *.

'Abbasa va Barmakiyan. Trans. M. 'A. Shīrāzī. Tehran: s.n., 1332/1953. Persian *.

'Abbasa Khāhar-i Hārūn al-Rashīd. Trans. Muḥammad Taqi Sharī'atī Muzinani. Mashhad, Iran: s.n., 1334/1915 or 1955. Razdegar has 1323/1944. Persian *.

'Abbasah va Barmakiyan. Trans. M. 'A. Shīrāzī. Tehran: s.n., 1381/2002. Persian †.

al-Abbasa la hermana del califa. N.p., s.n., 1940. Spanish.

Sestra Kharuna ar-Rashida. Trans. and comments by I. Lebedinski. Leningrad: Khodozh,1970. Russian.

Harun Rāshidning singlisi. Trans. Hörmātjan Abudrakhman Fikret from an Uzbek version. Urumchi, China: Shinjang Khālq Nāshriyati, 2000. Uighur.

The Caliph's Sister: Harun al-Rashid and the Fall of the Persians. Trans. Issa J. Boulatta. Washington, DC: Zaidan Foundation, 2012. English.

al-Amīn -Ma'mūn. 1907. 5th reprint. Cairo: Maṭba'at al-Hilāl, 1932.

al-Amīn wa-'l-Ma'mūn. Cairo: Dār al-Hilāl, 1965.

Amīn va Ma'mūn. Trans. 'Ali Asghar Hikmet. Tehran: s.n., Persian *.

Amīn va Ma'mūn. Trans. Ishraq Khavari. Tehran: s.n., 1310/1931. Persian * †.

Amīn va Ma'mūn. Trans. M. 'A. Shīrāzī. Tehran: Naqsh-i Jahan, n.d. Persian †.

Amīn va Ma'mūn. Trans. M. 'A. Shīrāzī. Tehran: Ganginih, 1364/1985. Persian †.

Amīn va Ma'mūn. Trans. M. 'A. Shīrāzī. Tehran: Afsun, 1380/2001. Persian †.

The Caliph's Heirs: Brothers at War and the Fall of Baghdad. Trans. Michael Cooperson. Washington, DC: Zaidan Foundation, 2012. English.

'Arūs Farghāna. 1908. Cairo: Dār al-Hilāl, 1965.

'Arūs-i Farghāna. Trans. Sayyid Izhār Ḥusain 'Arsh. Bombay: Maṭba'i Karīmī, n.d. Urdu.

Jihan Khatun Farghana. Trans. N. N. Istanbul: s.n., 1927. Ottoman.

'Arūs-i Farghāna. Trans. Amīr Ghuli Amīnī. Isfahan: s.n., 1334 HQ/1915/16. Persian *.

'Arūs-i Farghāna. Trans. M. 'A. Shīrāzī. Tehran: s.n., 1954. Persian *.

Novia de Fargana. Trans. Malatios Khouri. Intro. Dr. Enrique de Gandía. Buenos Aires: Editorial del Diario Siriolibanés, 1946. Spanish.

Dibawah rajuan setan. 2nd part of 4. Trans. N. N. Arūs Fargāna: n.p., s.n., 1964. Indonesian.

'Arūs-i Farghāna. dastan-i tarikhi akhlaqi 'ishqi. N.p., s.n., n.d. Persian.

Pengantin Fergana. N.p., s.n., 1965. Javanese.

Farghona kelini. Trans. Shoikrom Shoislomov. Illus. Inna Sandler. Tashkent: Sharq, 2005. Uzbek.

Pārghanā qizi. Trans. Tahir Talip and Muhāmā Polat. Urumchi, China: Shinjang Khālq Nāshriyati, 1994. Uighur.

Aḥmad ibn Ṭūlūn. 1909. Cairo: Dār al-Hilāl, 1965.

Aḥmad ibn Ṭūlūn. Trans. Mir Sayyid Ja'far. Tehran: s.n., 1328/1949. Persian *.

Aḥmad ibn Ṭūlūn. Trans. M. 'A. Shīrāzī. Tehran: s.n., 1344/1965. Persian.

Aḥmad ibn Ṭūlūn. Trans. M. 'A. Shīrāzī. Tehran: Afsun. 1381/2002. Persian †.

'Abd al-Raḥmān al-Nāṣir. 1910. 4th reprint. Cairo: Maṭba'at al-Hilāl, 1933.

Dastan-i 'Abd al-Raḥmān Nāṣir. Trans. Amir Quli Amīnī. Isfahan: s.n., 1311/1932. Persian † *.

al-Inqilāb al-'Uthmānī. 1911. Cairo: Maṭba'at al-Hilāl, 1966.

al-Inqilāb al-'Uthmānī. 5th reprint. Cairo: Maṭba'at al-Hilāl, 1932.

al-Inqilāb al-'Uthmānī. Cairo: Dār al-Hilāl, 1966.

Inqilāb-i Osmani. Trans. 'Ali Akbar Ghum. Istanbul: s.n., 1329 HQ/1911. Persian *.

'Uthmanli Inqilabi. Trans. 'Ali 'Abbas. Baku: s.n., 1332HS/1913. Azeri *.

Inqilāb-i Osmani. Trans. M. 'A. Shīrāzī. Tehran: s.n., 1336-1343. Persian *.

Inqilāb-i Osmani. Trans. M. 'A. Shīrāzī. Tehran: Majalla-yi Mah-i Naw, n.d. Persian †.

Allah veuille. Trans. M. Y. Bitar and Thierry Sandre. Paris: Flammarion, 1924, serialized in *Le Figaro* in 1923. French.

Fatāt al-Qayrawān. 1912. Cairo: Dār al-Hilāl, 1965.

Fatāt al-Qayrawān. Sousse/Tunis: Dār al-Ma'ārif, 1989.

Banu-yi Qiravan. Trans. Ishraq-i Khavari. Tehran: Nashriyat-i Muḥsin, 1329/1950. Persian †.

La demoiselle de Kairouan. Trans. Nadia Ramzi. Paris: Alteredit, 2005. French.

Ṣalāḥ al-Dīn al-Ayyūbī. 1913. Cairo: Dār al-Hilāl, 1965.

Ṣalāḥ al-Dīn wa-makā'id al-Ḥashshāshīn. 4th reprint. Cairo: Maṭba'at al-Hilāl, 1933.

Ṣalāḥ al-Dīn al-Ayyūbī wa-Ismā'iliyān. Trans. Mujbatabi Minuvi. Tehran: s.n., 1304HS/1925. Persian * †.

Ṣalāḥ al-Dīn Ayyūbī va Ismā'ililer. Trans. Zaki Maghamiz. Istanbul: s.n., 1927. Ottoman Turkish *.

Ṣalāḥ al-Dīn al-Ayyūbī wa-Ismā'iliyān. Trans. M. 'A. Shīrāzī. Tehran: Majalla-yi Mah-i Naw, 1334/1955. Persian * †.

Ṣalāḥ al-Dīn û fêt beng kêşekan. Trans. Kurdı A. B. Hewrı. Bexda [Baghdad]: Ġapxaney Me'rif, 1957. Kurdish.

Ṣalāḥ al-Dīn al-Ayyūbī wa-Ismā'iliyān. Trans. M. 'A. Shīrāzī. Tehran: Ganjinih, 1363/1984. Persian †.

Ṣalāḥ al-Dīn al-Ayyūbī wa-Ismā'iliyān. Trans. M. 'A. Shīrāzī. Tehran: Afsun, 1381/2002. Persian †.

Selaheddînê Eyyûbî. Trans. Emîn Narozî. Stockholm: Nûdem, 2003. Kurdish.

Saladin et les Assassins. Trans. Jean-Marie Lesage. Paris: Paris—Méditerranée, 2003. French.

Saladin and the Assassins. Trans. Paul Starkey. Washington, DC: Zaidan Foundation, 2012. English.

Shajarat al-Durr. 1914. 4th reprint. Cairo: Maṭba'at al-Hilāl, 1932.

Shajarat al-Durr. Sousse/Tunis: Dār al-Ma'ārif, 1989.

Malikeh Islam. Trans. Ḥabīb Allāh Amuzegar. Tehran: s.n., 1298 HS/1915-16. Persian * †.

Tree of Pearls, Queen of Egypt. Trans. Samah Selim. New York: Syracuse Univ. Press, 2012. English.

Works on History

Tārīkh al-māsūniyya al-'āmm. Cairo: Maṭba'at al-Hilāl, 1889.

al-Tārīkh al-'āmm mundhu 'l-khalīqa ilā hādhihi al-ayyām: mu'assas 'alā 'l-jughrāfiyā wa-mūḍaḥ bihi 'alā ṭarīqa mustaḥditha tusahhil fahmahu wa-'ḥifẓahu. Vol. 1. Beirut: s.n., 1890.

Kitāb Tārīkh miṣr al-ḥadīth min al-fatḥ al-Islāmī ilā hādhā 'l-'aṣr: ma'a fadhlaka tārīkhiyya fī tārīkh miṣr al-qadīm. 1889. 2 vols. 3rd reprint. Cairo: Maṭba'at al-Hilāl, 1925.

Tārīkh miṣr al-ḥadīth. 1889. New edition, intro. and indexed by Naẓīr 'Abbūd. Beirut: Dār al-Jīl, 1982.

Tārīkh miṣr al-ḥadīth: ma'a fadhlaka fī tārīh miṣr al-qadīm. 1st ed. Cairo: Maktabat Matbūlī, 1991.

Miṣr al-'uthmāniyya. 1st ed., researched and edited by Muḥammad Ḥarb. Madīnat Naṣr. Cairo: Dār al-Āfāq al-'Arabiyya, 2002.

Tārīkh al-yūnān wa-'l-rūmān. Cairo: Maṭba'at al-Hilāl, 1899.

Tārīkh inklītirā. Cairo: Maṭba'at al-Hilāl, 1899.

Tārīkh al-tamaddun al-islāmī. 5 vols. Cairo: Maṭba'at al-Hilāl, 1902–6.

Tārīkh al-tamaddun al-islāmī. 5 vols. Newly edited by Dr. Ḥusayn Mu'nis. Cairo: Dār al-Hilāl, 1958.

Tārīkh-i tamaddun-i islāmī. Trans. 'Abd al-Ḥusayn Qājār. Ṭehran: Maṭba'a-'i Ḥal al-Matīn, 1911. Persian.

Tarikh-i tammadun al-islami. Vol. 2. Trans. Zaki Bey Maghamiz. Istanbul: Dar Aqdam, 1911. Ottoman Turkish.

Tārīkh tamaddun-i islām. Trans. Muḥammad Ḥalīm Ansārī Rudaulvī. Karachi: Shaykh Shaukat 'Alī, 1964. Urdu.

Umayyads and 'Abbásids. Vol. 4 of Jurjí Zaydan's *History of Islamic Civilization*. Trans. D. S. Margoliouth. Leyden: E. J. Brill, 1907. English.

Umayyads and 'Abbásids. Vol. 4 of Jurjí Zaydan's *History of Islamic Civilization*. Trans. D. S. Margoliouth. New Delhi: Kitab Bhavan, 1978. English.

Umayyads and 'Abbásids. Vol. 4 of Jurjí Zaydan's *History of Islamic Civilization*. Trans. D. S. Margoliouth. Westport, CT: Hyperion Press, 1980. English.

al-'Arab qabla 'l-islām. Cairo: Maṭba'at al-Hilāl, 1907/8.

Kitāb al-'Arab qabla 'l-islām. 2nd printing. Cairo: Maṭba'at al-Hilāl, 1922.

al-'Arab qabla 'l-islām. 3rd printing. Cairo: Maṭba'at al-Hilāl, 1939.

al-'Arab qabla 'l-islām. Newly edited by Ḥusayn Mu'nis. Cairo: Dār al-Hilāl, 1957.

Ṭabaqāt al-umam aw al-salā'il al-bashariyya. 1912. Reprint, Beirut: Dār al-Turāth, 1969.

Works on Language and Literature

al-Alfāẓ al-'arabiyya wa-'l-falsafa al-lughawiyya. Beirut: Maṭba'at al-Qiddīs Jāwiriyūs, 1886.

al-Falsafa al-lughawiyya wa-'l-alfāẓ al-'arabiyya. 2nd ed. Fajjāla, Cairo: Maṭba'at al-Hilāl, 1904.

al-Falsafa al-lughawiyya wa-'l-alfāẓ al-'arabiyya. Newly edited by Murād Kāmil. Cairo: Dār al-Hilāl, 1958.

al-Falsafa al-lughawiyya wa-'l-alfāẓ al-'arabiyya. 2nd ed. by Murād Kāmil. Cairo: Dār al-Hilāl, 1969.

al-Falsafa al-lughawiyya wa-'l-alfāẓ al-'arabiyya. 2nd printing by Murād Kāmil. Beirut: Dār al-Ḥadātha, 1982.

al-Lugha al-'arabiyya bi'tibārihā kā'in ḥayy khādi' li-nāmūs al-irtiqā'. 1904. New ed. by Murād Kāmil. Cairo: Dār al-Hilāl 1960.

Tārīkh al-lugha al-'arabiyya. 1st printing. Intro. 'Issām Nūr al-Dīn. Beirut: Dār al-Ḥadātha, 1980.

Tārīkh ādāb al-lugha al-'arabiyya. 4 vols. Fajjāla, Cairo: Maṭba'at al-Hilāl, 1911–1914.

Tārīkh ādāb al-lugha al-'arabiyya. 4 vols. New ed. by Shawqī Ḍayf. Cairo: Dār al-Hilāl, 1957–195?.

Other Works

Ansāb al-'arab al-qudamā'. Cairo: Maktabat al-Hilāl, 1906.

Bunāh al-nahḍa al-'arabiyya. Cairo: Dār al-Hilāl, 1957.

'Ilm al-firāsa al-ḥadīth/kayf ta'raf nafsaka wa-ta'raf al-nās. 1901. Reprint, Cairo: Dār al-Hilāl, 1954.

Kitāb 'ilm al-firāsa al-ḥadīth, aw al-istidlāl 'alā 'l-akhlāq al-nās. Cairo: Maktabat al-Thaqāfa al-Dīniyya, 2003.

Kitāb 'ajā'ib al-khalq. Cairo: Maṭba'at al-Hilāl, 1912.

Mukhtaṣar jughrāfiyyat miṣr. Cairo: Maṭba'at al-Ta'līf, 1891.

al-Mukhtaṣar fī tārīkh ādāb al-lugha al-'arabiyya. Cairo: Maṭba'at al-Hilāl, 1924.

al-Mukhtaṣar fī tārīkh ādāb al-lugha al-'arabiyya. Cairo: Dār al-Hilāl, 1946.

Tarājim mashāhīr al-sharq fī 'l-qarn al-tāsi' 'ashar. 1907. 2 vols. 3rd reprint. Cairo: Maṭba'at al-Hilāl, 1922.

Tarājim mashāhīr al-sharq fī 'l-qarn al-tāsi' 'ashar. Beirut: Dār Maktabat al-Ḥayāt, 1970.

Autobiographical

Riḥlat Jurjī Zaydān ilā ūrubbā, sanat 1912. Cairo: Idārat al-Hilāl, 1923.

Riḥla ilā ūrubbā 1912. 1st printing. Ed. and intro. Qāsim Wahab. Abu Dhabi: Dār al-Suwaydā li'l-Nashr wa-'l-Tawzī', 2002.

Mudhakkirāt Jurjī Zaydān. 1st printing. Ed. Ṣalāḥ al-Dīn al-Munajjid. Lebanon: Dār al-Kitāb al-Jadīd, 1968.

The Autobiography of Jurji Zaidan. Including four letters to his son, translated, edited, and introduced by Thomas Philipp. Washington, DC: Three Continents Press, 1990.

Letters by Zaidan to His Son Emile. Unpublished collection. Copies were made in 1973 by the present author in Beirut in the office of Salah al-Din al-Munajjid. The letters should be in the holdings of the archive of the American University Beirut, but cannot be located there. The Zaidan Foundation has copies of them.

Collected Works

Mu'allafāt Jurjī Zaydān al-kāmila. 21 vols. Beirut: Dār al-Jīl, 1981–1983.

Al-Hilāl. Periodical. Cairo: vol. 1 (1892) through vol. 22 (1914) under J. Zaidan's management. The journal has been continuously published until the present day.

Studies and Critiques of Zaidan's Works

Abū Khalīl, Shawqī. *Jurjī Zaydān fi 'l-mīzān*. Damascus: Dār al-Fikr, 1981.

Āl Kāshif al-Ghiṭā, Muḥammad al-Ḥusayn. *Kitāb al-Mu'ālamāt wa-'l-murāja'āt wa-'l-nuqūd wa-'l-rudūd*. 2 vols. Beirut: al-Makṭaba al-Ahliyya, 1913/1331.

Alkhayat, Hamdi. "Ǧurǧi Zaidan, Leben und Werk." Ph.D. diss., Univ. of Cologne, 1973.

Amin, Ahmad. "Jūrjī Zaydān al-mu'arrikh wa-'l-adīb." In *al-Kitāb al-Dhahabī li'l-Hilāl*. Cairo: Dār Al-Hilāl, 1942.

Arāsilī, Almān. *Jūrjī Zaydān wa-'l-riwāya al-tārīkhiyya fī 'l-adab al-'arabī*. Trans. Muḥammad Yūnis. Baghdad: s.n., 1969.

Arasly, E. G. *Dzhirdzhi Zeidan i arabskii istoricheskij roman*. Moscow: Nauka, 1967.

'Ārif al-Zayn, A. "Tārīkh ādāb al-lugha al-'arabiyya." In *al-'Irfān 4* (Rajab 1330, June 1912): 253–55.

al-Ashmāwī, 'Abd al-Raḥmān. *Waqfa ma'a Jūrjī Zaydān*. Riyadh: Maktabat al-'Ubaykān, 1993.

Baydas, Kh. " Jurjī Zaydān." *al-Nafā'is* (Sept. 1914): 392–96.

Ben Lagha, Zaineb. "Le Personnage Historique Dans l'Œuvre Romanesque de Ǧurǧī Zaydān: Entre Figure Exemplaire et Personnage de Roman." Ph.D. diss., Institut National des Langues et Civilisations Orientales, Paris, 2006.

Ben Lagha, Zaineb. "Le Roman Historique." In *Histoire de la Littérature Arabe Moderne 1800–1845*. Vol. 1. Ed. Boutros Hallaq and Heidi Toeller, 205–20. Paris: Actes Sud, 2006.

Cheikh Moussa, Abdallah. "L'Écriture de soi dans les Mudhakkirāt de Ǧurǧi Zaydān." *Bulletin d'Études Orientales* 37.

Dār al-Hilāl, madrasat al-tanwīr. Ed. Maḥmūd Izzat. Alexandria: Bibliotheca Alexandrina, 2010.

Dupont, Anne Laure. *Ǧurǧī Zaydān 1861–1914: Écrivain reformiste et temoin de la renaissance Arabe*. Damascus: IFPO, 2006.

Dupont, Anne Laure. "Transformations sociales et culture arabe réformiste dans les Mudhakkirāt de Jūrji Zaydān." In *al-Ṣiyar al-dhātiyya fī Bilād al-Shām*, ed. Maher Cherif and Kais Ezzerelli, 145–68. Damascus: IFPO, 2009.

Dupont, Anne Laure. "Usages et Acculturation de la Franc-maçonnerie dans le milieu intellectuel Arabe à la fin du XIXe siècle à travers l'exemple de Jurji Zaydan." *Cahiers de La Méditerranée* 72 (June 2006): 331–52.

Dupont, Anne Laure. "What Is a Kātib al-'āmm? The Status of Men of Letters and the Conception of Language according to Jurji Zaydan." *Middle Eastern Literature* 13 (Aug. 2010): 171–81.

Elshakry, Marwa. "The Gospel of Science and American Evangelism in Late Ottoman Beirut." *Past and Present* 196 (Aug. 2007).

Elshakry, Marwa. "Knowledge in Motion: The Cultural Politics of Modern Sciences Translations into Arabic." *Isis* (History of Sciences Society) 99 (2008): 701–30.

Ḥarb, Jūzif. *Jūrjī Zaydān; rijāl fī rajul*. Beirut: Bayt al-Ḥikma, 1970.

Ḥasan, Muḥammad 'Abd al-Ghanī. *Jūrjī Zaydān*. Cairo: al-Hay'a al-Miṣriyya al-'Āmma li-'l-Ṭa'līf wa-'l-Nashr, 1970.

al-Ḥulwānī, Amīn ibn Ḥasan. *Nabsh al-hadhayān min tārīkh Jūrjī Zaydān*. Ed. and anno. Māzin Muṭabbaqānī. Medina: Maktabat Ibn al-Qayyim, 1989.

Ḥusayn, Ṭāhā. "Zaydān kama 'araftuhu." In *al-Kitāb al-Dhahabī li-'l-Hilāl*. Cairo: Dār al- Hilāl, 1942, 133–35.

Jayyusi, Salma Khadra. *Trends and Movements in Modern Arabic Poetry*. Leiden: Brill, 1977.

Jeha, Shafiq. *Darwin and the Crisis of the Medical School in 1882*. Beirut: AUB Univ. Press, 2004.

Jindī, Anwār. *Jūrjī Zaydān, munshi' al-Hilāl*. Cairo: Maktabat al-Anjilū al-Miṣriyya, 1958.

Al-Karmalī Pere Anastās Marī. "Naqd kitāb tārīkh ādāb a-lugha al-'arabiyya." In *al-Lugha al-'Arabiyya* 1, no. 1 (Apr. 1912): 392–97, 447–49; 1, no. 2 (Aug. 1912): 52–62; 3, no. 2 (Aug. 1913): 73–82.

Kratshkovski, I. U. "Der historische Roman in der neueren arabischen Literatur." *Welt des Islams* 12 (1930): 51–87.

Kratshkovski, I. U. *Istoricheski Roman b Sovremennoy Arabasksoy Literatur*. Petersburg: n.p., 1911.

Massad, Joseph A. *Desiring Arabs*. Chicago: Univ. of Chicago Press, 2007.

Moosa, Matti. *The Origins of Modern Arabic Fiction*. London: Lynne Rienner, 1997.

al-Muḥs, 'Abd al-Jawād Muḥammad. *Riwāyāt Jūrjī Zaydān: dirāsāt tārīkhiyya*. Cairo: Maktabat al-Nahḍa al-Miṣriyya, 2004.

Naṣr, Anīs. "Jurjī Zaydān." *al-Ḍād* 2 (1938).

al-Nu'mānī, Shiblī. "Naksh tārīkh al-tamaddun al-islāmī." *al-Manār* 15 (1912): 58–67; (Apr.): 270–80; (May): 343–52; (June): 415–27.

Philipp, Thomas. "Approaches to History in the Work of Jurji Zaidan." *Asian and African Studies* 9 (1973): 63–85.

Philipp, Thomas. *Ǧurǧī Zaidān: His Life and Thought*. Beiruter Texte u. Studien 3. Beirut: F. Steiner, 1979.

Philipp, Thomas. "Language, History, and Arab National Consciousness in the Thought of Jurji Zaidan." *International Journal of Middle East Studies* 4 (1973): 3–22.

Philipp, Thomas. "Women in the Historical Perspective of an Early Arab Modernist." *Welt des Islams* 18 (1976–77): 65–83.

Rastegar, Kamran. "Literary Modernity between Arabic and Persian Prose." *Comparative Critical Studies* 4, no. 3 (2007): 359–78.

Sheehi, Stephen. *Foundations of Modern Arab Identity*. Gainesville: Univ. Press of Florida, 2004.

Zaidan, George C., and Thomas Philipp, eds. *Jurji Zaidan's Contributions to Modern Arab Thought and Literature: Proceedings of a Symposium Held in June 2012 at the Library of Congress*. Washington, DC: Zaidan Foundation, 2013.

Zaydān, Jūrjī. *Radd ranān 'alā nabsh al-hadhayān*. Cairo: Maṭba'at al-Ta'līf, 1891.

"Zaydān, Jurjī." In Ilyās Zakhūrā, *Kitāb mirāt al-'aṣr fī tārīkh wa-rusūm akābir rijāl al-maṣr*. 3 vols. Cairo: s.n., 1914–1917, 3:65–80.

"Zaydān, Jurjī." In Yūsif As'ad Dāghir, *Maṣādir al-dirāsa al-adabiyya*. 2nd ed. Beirut: Maktabat Lubnān, 2000, 442–48.

Arabic Novels Referring to Jurji Zaidan

al-Ḍa'īf, Rashīd. *Tablīṭ al-baḥr*. Beirut: Riyāḍ al-Rayyis li-'l-Kutub wa-'l-Nashr, 2011.

Dhāk [Naṣīb 'Abdallāh Shiblī al-Lubnānī]. *Riwāyat al-baṭalayn*. Beirut: s.n., 1889.

Khātir, Nūr. *Al-Farāsha al-zarqā'*. Beirut: Al-Thaqāfī al-'Arabī, 1996.

Glossary of Arabic Terms

◆

Bibliography of Sources Quoted in This Book

◆

Index of Names

◆ ◆ ◆

Glossary of Arabic Terms

ʿabqariyya. genius
ādāb. literature and culture
adab. refinement, belles-lettres
adnā. lower
ahl al-bādiya. Bedouins
ʿālim. scholar, scientist
ʿāmma. the masses, lower classes
ʿarab al-bādiya. nomadic Arabs
ʿaṣabiyya. group loyalty, esprit de corps
ʿaṣabiyyat al-jins. racism
arqā. higher, more refined, or from a superior class
al-aṣlaḥ. the fittest
bilād. land, country
Bilād al-Shām. geographic Syria; the Levante
bulūgh. maturity
dawla. pl. ***duwal***, dynasty, government, state, empire
al-dawla al-ʿuthmāniyya. Ottoman Empire
Dār al-Hilāl. publishing house
al-dukhalāʾ. s., ***dakhīl***. intruder
al-hātif. noncorporeal voice
ʿilm, pl. ***ʿulūm***. knowledge, science
ʿilm al-ādāb. the human and social sciences
ʿilm wa-tarbiyya. science and education
al-insān al-kāmil. perfect human being
al-Jāhiliyya. time of ignorance, i.e., before the revelation
dhimma. non-Muslim monotheist communities with protected status, subject to a Muslim ruler
Dhimmī. member of a non-Muslim monotheist community

dīwān. collected works, poetry

ḥadīth. sayings of the Prophet Muhammad

hijra. exodus of the prophet from Mecca to Medina and the beginning of the Islamic calendar Anno Hijra

al-Ḥizb al-Lāmarkaziyya al-'Uthmāniyya. Ottoman Decentralization Party

indimāj al-umam. mixture of people

inkhiṭāṭ. decline, fall

inqilāb. reform or revolution

irtiqā' wa-'nḥiṭāṭ. rise and fall

irtiqā'. rising and growing

isnād. chain of transmitters of the *ḥadīth*

al-jāmi'a al-ḥaqīqiyya. "true" or real community

al-Jam'iyya al-'Ilmiyya al-Sūriyya. Syrian Scientific Society

jāmi'at al-dawla. state

jāmi'at al-jins. ethnicity

jami'at al-manfa'a or *maṣlaḥa*. community of usefulness or benefit

jāmi'at al-maṣlaḥa al-'āmma. community of common interest or common good

al-jāmi'a al-'uthmāniyya. Ottoman community or nation

jāmi'at al-waṭan or *al-jāmi'a al-waṭaniyya*. patriotism

jinsiyya. nationality, race, ethnicity

jizya. head tax on *dhimmi*s

jumhūr al-qurrā'. literate public

kātib 'āmm. public educator

khāṣṣa. elite

khurāfa. superstition, fairy tale

Koran, Koranic. Holy book of Islam; pertaining to that Holy book

kufr. heresy

al-madaniyya. civilization

Madhhab al-nushū' wa-'l-irtiqā. Darwinism

al-Majma' al-'Ilmi al-Sharqi. Eastern Scientific Society

majmū' al-umma. national community

mamlaka, pl. *mamālik*. kingdom, state, empire sovereignty

ma'qūl. rationally acceptable, reasonable

al-maṣlaḥa al-'āmma. common good

Maṭba'at al-Hilāl. publishing house of *al-Hilāl*

miṣriyyīn. Egyptians

mu'allifūn. authors

mu'arrikh. historian

muqtabasa. acquired, adopted, or borrowed

muṣannifūn. compilers

al-musta'ribīn. assimilated Arabs

al-muta'arribīn. arabized people

mutarjimūn. translators, biographers

muwaṣṣil. mediator

nadā' iqlīmī. local chauvinism

al-Nahḍa. Arab Awakening

al-nahḍa al-urubbiyya. European Renaissance

nāmūs, pl. ***nawāmīs.*** law, principle

nāmūs al-irtiqā'. law of evolution

nāmūs al-ṭab'īa. law of nature

nawāmīs al-ḥayāt. laws of life

numū'. growth

nushū'. rising and growing

al-qurūn al-islāmiyya al-wuṣṭa. Islamic Middle Ages

quṭr, pl. ***aqṭār.*** limited territory, territorial section

rawāj. marketability

rūḥ al-'urūba. the spirit of Arabism

Shams al-Birr. branch of the British YMCA

Shu'ūbiyya. movement in early Islam, denying any privileges to Arabs Muslims

ta'akhkhur. backwardness

al-ta'aṣṣub al-jinsī. racism

ṭabaqāt. classes, groups of people, layers; in Arabic literature it signifies a particular genre of books: the bio-bibliographic dictionaries

ṭabaqāt. bio-bibliographical dictionaries

tafarru'. ramification and branching off

takāmul. perfection, completion, in Persian "evolution"

takawwun. formation, becoming

tamaddun. civilization

al-tamaddun al-qadīm. ancient civilization

taqaddum. progress

taraqqin. progress

tārīkh. history

tarjama. translation or biography

tasalsul. descent

tasha''ub. ramification and branching off
taṭawwur. development, progress, evolution
al-'ulamā al-ṭabī'īn. natural scientists
umma. community
al-umma al-'arabiyya. Arab nation
al-umma al-miṣriyya. Egyptian nation
ummat al-'arab. nation of the Arabs
ummat al-lugha. community of language
ummat al-mu'minīn. community of believers
al-'unṣur al-'arabī. Arab element, ethnicity
waṭan. homeland, fatherland
waṭaniyya. nationalism, patriotism

◆ ◆ ◆

Bibliography of Sources Quoted in This Book

General

Abū Khalīl, Shawqī. *Jūrjī Zaydān fī 'l-mīzān*. Damascus: Dār al-Fikr, 1981.

Amīn, Qāsim. *Taḥrīr al-mar'a*. Cairo: Maktabat al-Taraqī, 1899.

Anderson, Benedict. *Imagined Communities: Reflections on the Origin and Spread of Nationalism*. 2nd ed. London: Verso, 1991.

Annual Reports: Board of Managers, Syrian Protestant College, 1866/67–1901/02. Being the reports by President Daniel Bliss to the Board of Managers of the SPC.

Annual Reports: Board of Managers, Syrian Protestant College, 1866–1922. Beirut: s.n.,1961–1965.

Antonius, George. *The Arab Awakening*. 2nd ed. New York: Capricorn Books, 1965.

al-Arsūzī, Zākī. *al-Mu'allifāt al-kāmila*. 4 vols. Damascus: Maṭābi' al-Idāra al-Siyāsiyya li-'l-Jaysh, 1972–1976.

Arsuzi-Elamir, Dalal. *Arabischer Nationalismus in Syrien: Zakī al-Arsūzī und die arabisch-nationale Bewegung an der Peripherie Alexandretta/Antakya*. Hamburg: Lit Verlag, 2003.

Asad, Talal. *The Formation of the Secular: Christianity, Islam, Modernity*. Stanford: Stanford Univ. Press, 2003.

al-Ashmāwī, 'Abd al-Raḥmān. *Waqfa ma'a Jurjī Zaydān*. Riyadh: Maktabat al-'Ubaykān, 1993.

Azouri, Najib. *Le réveil de la nation Arabe*. Paris: Plon Nourrit, 1905.

Barzun, Jacques. *Darwin, Marx, Wagner*. New York: Doubleday, 1958.

Bayat, Mangol. *Mysticism and Dissent*. New York: Syracuse Univ. Press, 1982.

Barrū, Tawfīq 'Ali. *al-'Arab wa-'l-turk fī 'l-'ahd al-dustūrī al-'uthmānī*. Cairo: Jām'at al-Duwal al-'Arabiyya Ma'had al-Dirāsāt al-'Arabiyya al-'Ālamiyya, 1960.

Brown, L. Carl. *The Surest Path: The Political Treatise of a Nineteenth-Century Muslim Statesman*. Harvard Middle Eastern Monograph Series 16. Cambridge, MA: Harvard Univ. Press, 1967.

Büchner, L. *Sechs Vorlesungen über die Darwin'sche Theorie von der Verwandlung der Arten und die Entstehung der Organismenwelt, sowie die Anwendung der Umwandlungstheorie auf den Menschen, das Verhälnis dieser Theorie zur Lehre vom Fortschritt und den Zusammenhang derselben mit der materialistischen Philosophie der Vergangenheit und Gegenwart*. Leipzig: T. Thomas, 1868.

Canovan, Magret. "On Being Economical with the Truth: Some Liberal Reflections." *Political Studies* 38 (1990): 5–19.

Cheikh Moussa, Abdallah. "L'Écriture de soi dans les Mudhakkirāt de Ǧurǧī Zaydan." *Bulletin d'Études Orientales* 37–38 (1985–1986): 23–50.

Cleveland, William L. *The Making of an Arab Nationalist: Ottomanism and Arabism in the Life and Thought of Sati' al-Husri*. Princeton: Princeton Univ. Press, 1971.

Cook, Stanley A. "Notes on the Old Testament History." *Jewish Quarterly Review* 17 (1905): 782–99.

Cox, Harvey. *The Secular City*. New York: Macmillan, 1965.

Dawn, C. Ernest. *From Ottomanism to Arabism: Essays on the Origins of Arab Nationalism*. Urbana: Univ. of Illinois Press, 1973.

Dawn, C. Ernest. "The Rise of Arabism in Syria." *Middle East Journal* 16 (1962): 145–68.

Demolins, E. *A quoi tient la supériorité des Anglo-Saxons?* Paris: Firmin Didot, 1897.

Dupont, Anne-Laure. *Ǧurǧī Zaydān 1861–1914: Écrivain réformiste et témoin de la Renaissance arabe*. Damascus: IFPO, 2006.

Dupont, Anne-Laure. "What Is a kātib al-'āmm? The Status of Men of Letters and the Conception of Language according to Jurji Zaydan." *Middle Eastern Literature* 13 (Aug. 2010): 171–81.

Dupont, Anne-Laure. "Transformations sociales et culture arabe réformiste dans les Mudhakkirāt de Jurji Zaydān." In *al-Ṣiyar al-dhātiyya fī Bilād al-Shām*, ed. Maher Cherif and Kais Ezzerelli, 145–68. Damascus: IFPO, 2009.

Dupont, Anne-Laure. "Usages et Acculturation de la Franc-maçonnerie dans le milieu intellectuel Arabe à la fin du XIXe siècle à travers l'exemple de Jurji Zaydan." *Cahiers de La Méditerranée* 72 (June 2006): 331–52.

Elshakry, Marwa. "Knowledge in Motion: The Cultural Politics of Modern Science Translation into Arabic." *Isis* 99 (2008): 701–30.

Fawaz, Leila Tarazi. *An Occasion for War*. Los Angeles: Univ. of California Press, 1994.

Florian, Jean. *Numa Pompilius, Second roi de Rome*. Paris: Didot, l'aîné, 1786.

Gibb, H. A. R., and H. Bowen. *Islamic Society and the West*. 2 parts. London: Oxford Univ. Press, 1962.

Glaß, Dagmar. *Der Muqtataf und Seine Öffentlichkeit.* 2 vols. Würzburg: Ergon, 2004.

Glaser, Eduard. *Skizze der Geschichte und GeographieArabiens von der ältesten Zeit bis zum Propheten Muhammad nebst einem Anhang zur Beleuchtung der Geschichte Abessiniens.* 2 vols. Berlin: Weidmannsche Buchhandlung, 1890.

de Goeje, M. J. "Review of Zaidan's Tārīkh al-tamaddun al-islāmī." *Journal Asiatique* 10, no. 3 (1904): 356–58.

Granara, W. "The Historical Poetics of Jurji Zaidan's Andalusian Fictional Cosmos." In *Jurji Zaidan's Contributions to Modern Arab Thought and Literature,* ed. George C. Zaidan and Thomas Philipp. Washington, DC: Zaidan Foundation, 2013.

Greenfeld, Liah. *Nationalism: Five Roads to Modernity.* Cambridge, MA: Harvard Univ. Press, 1993.

Gusdorf, G. "Conditions and Limits of Autobiography." In *Autobiography: Essays Theoretical and Critical,* ed. J. Olney, 28–48. Princeton: Princeton Univ. Press, 1980.

Haeri, Niloofar, *Sacred Language, Ordinary People.* New York: Palgrave Macmillan, 2004.

Haim, Sylvia. "The Arab Awakening: A Source for the Historian." *Welt des Islams* 2, no. 4 (1952): 237–50.

Haim, Sylvia, ed. *Arab Nationalism: An Anthology.* 2nd ed. Los Angeles: Univ. of California Press, 1976.

Hanssen, Jens. *Fin de siècle Beirut.* Oxford: Oxford Univ. Press, 2005.

Harper, R. F., ed. *The Code of Hammurabi, King of Babylon.* Chicago: Univ. of Chicago Press, 1904.

Hawting G. R. *The Idea of Idolatry and the Emergence of Islam.* Cambridge: Cambridge Univ. Press, 1999.

Hourani, Albert. *Arabic Thought in the Liberal Age.* London: Oxford Univ. Press, 1962.

al-Hulwānī, Amīn ibn Ḥasan. *Nabsh al-hadhayān min tārīkh Jurjī Zaydān,* ed. and anno. Māzin Muṭabaqqanī. Medina: Maktabat ibn Qayyim, 1989.

Ḥusayn, Ṭāhā, "Āthār al-Hilāl wa-munshi'hi." In *al-Kitāb al-Dhahabī 1892–1942,* 133–35. Cairo: Dār al-Hilāl, 1942.

Ḥusayn, Ṭāhā. *al-Ayyām.* Cairo: Maṭba' Amīn 'Abd al-Raḥmān, 1926.

Ibn Khaldūn, *The Muqaddima.* 3 vols. 2nd ed. Trans. Franz Rosenthal. Princeton: Princeton Univ. Press, 1968.

Ibn Abī Rabbih. *al-'Iqd al-farīd.* Trans. Issa J. Boullata. *The Unique Necklace.* Reading, UK: Garnet, 2006.

al-Jabartī, 'Abd al-Raḥmān. *'Ajā'ib al-āthār fī tarājim wa-'l-akhbār.* 4 vols. Cairo: Boulaq Press, 1879–1880.

Jarār, Ma'mūn Fāris. *Khaṣā'iṣ al-qiṣṣa al-islāmiyya.* Jidda: Dār al-Manāra, 1988.

Jayyusi, Salma Khadra. *Trends and Movements in Modern Arab Literature.* Leiden: Brill, 1977.

Jeha, Shafik. *Darwin and the Crisis of 1882 in the Medical Department.* Beirut: Univ. Press of the American University of Beirut, 2004.

Keddie, Nikki. *Sayyid Jamāl al-Dīn al-Afghānī.* Los Angeles: Univ. of California Press, 1972.

Kedourie, Elie. *Nationalism.* London: Hutchinson, 1960.

Khalidi, Rashid, et al., eds. *The Origins of Arab Nationalism.* New York: Columbia Univ. Press, 1991.

Khuri-Makdisi, Ilham. *The Eastern Mediterranean and the Making of Global Radicalism, 1860–1914.* Los Angeles: Univ. of California Press, 2010.

Kurzman, Charles. *Democracy Denied: 1905–1915: Intellectuals and the Fate of Democracy.* Cambridge, MA: Harvard Univ. Press, 2008.

Lennhoff, Eugen. *The Freemasons.* 1934. Reprint. London: A. Lewis, 1978.

Letters by Zaidan to His Son Emile. Signifies a Collection of Handwritten Letters by Zaidan to His Son Emile and Other Family Members. Copies available through the Zaidan Foundation.

Lutfi al-Sayyid, Afaf. *Egypt and Cromer.* London: Murray, 1968.

Marical, R. "La Critique de Textes." In *L'Histoire et ses méthodes, 1247–1360,* ed. C. Samaran. Encyclopédie de la Pleiade 11. Paris: Gallimard, 1961.

Massad, Joseph A. *Desiring Arabs.* Chicago: Univ. of Chicago Press, 2007.

al-Mas'ūdī (pseudonym). "al-Dawla al-'uthmāniyya fī lubnān wa-sūriyya." *Al-Hilāl* 25 (Dec. 1916): 183–92; (Jan. 1917): 292–301; (Feb. 1917): 385–93; (March 1917): 461–69; (Apr. 1917): 573–81; (May 1917): 643–50; (June 1917): 747–53; (July 1917): 807-–12.

McLennan, John Ferguson. *Primitive Marriage.* Edinburgh: A & C Black, 1865.

Mishāqa, Mikhā'īl. *Muntakhabāt al-jawāb 'ala 'qtirāḥ al-aḥbāb.* Beirut: al-Maṭba' al-Kāthūlikiyya, 1955.

Mishāqa, Mikhā'īl. *Muntakhabāt al-jawāb 'alā 'qtirāḥ al-aḥbāb.* Trans. Wheeler Thackston. In *Murder, Mayhem, Pillage and Plunder.* Albany: SUNY Univ. Press, 1988.

Mubārak, 'Alī. *al-Khiṭaṭ al-tawfīqiyya al-jadīda.* 16 vols. Cairo: Boulaq Press, 1886–1889.

al-Muḥs, 'Abd al-Jawād, Muḥammad. *Riwayāt Jūrjī Zaydān.* Cairo: Maṭba' al-Nahḍa al-Miṣriyya, 2004.

Musa, Salama. *The Education of Salama Musa*. Trans. L. O. Schuman. Leiden: Brill, 1961.

Nāṣir al-Dīn, 'Alī. *Qaḍīyat al-'arab*. Beirut: Manshūrāt 'Uwaydāt, 1946.

Nu'mānī, Shiblī. "Naqd tārīkh al-tamaddun al-islāmī." *al-Manār* 15 (Jan. 1912): 58–67; (April 1912): 270–80; (May 1912): 343–52; (June 1912): 415–27.

Ozouf, Mona. *Composition Française: retour sur une enfance bretonne*. Paris: Gallimard, 2009.

Philipp, Thomas. *Ǧurǧī Zaidān: His Life and Thought*. Beiruter Texte und Studien 3. Beirut: Franz Steiner Verlag, 1979.

Philipp, Thomas. "Class, Community, and Arab Historiography in the Early 19th Century." *International Journal for Middle East Studies* 16 (1984): 161–75.

Philipp, Thomas. *The Syrians in Egypt 1725–1975*. Berliner Islamstudien 3. Wiesbaden: Franz Steiner Verlag, 1985.

Philipp, Thomas. "The Autobiography in Modern Arab Literature and Culture." *Poetics Today* 14 (Fall 1993): 573–604.

Philipp, Thomas. "Copts and Other Minorities in the Development of the Egyptian Nation-State." In *Egypt: from Monarchy to Republic*, ed. Shimon Shamir, 131–50. Boulder, CO: Westview Press, 1995.

Philipp, Thomas. *Acre: The Rise and Fall of a Palestinian City 1730–1831*. New York: Columbia Univ. Press, 2001.

Philipp, Thomas. "Creating the Enemy." *Welt des Islams* 48 (2008): 50–57.

Philipp, Thomas. "Progress and Liberal Thought in al-Hilāl, al-Manār and al-Muqtaṭaf before World War I." In *Nationalism and Liberal Thought in the Arab East*, ed. Christoph Schumann, 132–44. London: Routledge, 2010.

Pichon, Frédéric. "Du vieux avec du neuf: histoire et identité d'un village chrétien de Syrie: Ma'lula (XIXe–XXI siècles)." Ph.D. diss., Univ. Sorbonne, Paris, 2009.

Rawlinson, George. *The Origin of Nations: On Early Civilizations, on Ethnic Affinities etc*. 2 vols. London: Religious Tract Society, 1877.

Reichmuth, Stefan, and Florian Schwarz, eds. *Zwischen Alltag und Schriftkultur: Horizonte des Individuellen in der arabischen Literatur des 17. und 18. Jahrhunderts*. Beiruter Texte und Studien 110. Würzburg: Ergon, 2008.

Riḍā, Rashīd, ed. *Kitāb intiqād tārīkh al-tammadun al-islāmī*. Cairo: s.n., 1912.

Rihbany, A. M. *A Far Journey*. New York: Houghton Mifflin, 1914.

Robinson, Ronald. "The Eccentric Idea of Imperialism with or without Empire." In *Imperialismus and After*, ed. Wolfgang Mommsen and Jürgen Osterhammel, 269–89. London: Allen & Unwin, 1986.

Rosenthal, Franz. "Die Arabische Autobiographie." *Analecta Orientalia* 14 (1937): 1–40.

Sābāt, Khalīl. *Tārīkh al-ṭibā'a fī 'l-sharq al-'arabī*. Cairo: Dār al-Ma'ārif, 1966.

Schumann, Christoph. *Radikalnationalismus in Syrien und Libanon: Politische Sozialisierung und Elitenbildung 1930–1958*. Hamburg: Deutsches Orientinstitut, 2001.

Schulz, Reiner. "Islam und Judentum im Angesicht der Protestantisierung der Religionen im 19. Jahrhundert." In *Judaism, Christianity, and Islam in the Course of History: Exchange and Conflicts*, ed. L. Gall and D. Willoweit. 139–66. Schriften des Historischen Kollegs, Kolloquien 82. München: Oldenburg Verlag, 2011.

al-Shayyāl, Jamāl al-Dīn. *Tārīkh al-tarjama wa-'l-ḥaraka al-thaqāfiyya fī 'aṣr muḥammad 'ali*. Cairo: Dār al-Fikr al-'Arabī, 1951.

Sheehi, Stephen. *Foundations of Modern Arab Identity*. Gainesville: Univ. Press of Florida, 2004.

al-Shudūdī, As'ad Ibrāhīm. *Kitāb al-'arūs al-badī'a fī 'ilm al-ṭabī'a*. Beirut: al-Maṭba' al-amīrikānī, 1873.

Smiles, Samuel. *Self-Help*. London: John Murray, 1856. Trans. Ya'qūb Ṣarrūf as *Sirr al-najāḥ, The Secret of Success*. 1880. Reprint. Beirut: al-Maṭba' al-amīrkī, 1913, 1922.

Smith, William Robertson. *Kinship and Marriage in Early Arabia*. Cambridge: Cambridge Univ. Press,1885.

Smith, William Robertson. *Lectures in the Religions of the Semites*. Edinburgh: A&C Black, 1889.

Spencer, Herbert. *Education: Intellectual, Moral, Physical*. New York: Appleton, 1860. Trans. Najīb Shukrī. *Afyad al-kitāb fī 'l-tarbiyya*. Cairo: s.n.,1903.

Sprenger, Aloys. *Die Alte Geographie Arabiens als Grundlage der Entwicklungsgeschichte des Semitismus*. Bern: Huber & Co., 1875.

Steppat, Fritz. "Nationalismus und Islam bei Mustafa Kamil." In *Welt des Islams*, n.s. 4, no. 4 (1955): 241–341.

Stern, Fritz. *The Politics of Cultural Despair*. Los Angeles: Univ. of California Press, 1974.

Sūdā, Yusuf. *Fī sabīl al-istiqlāl*. Beirut: Dār al-Riḥānī, 1967.

Suleiman, Yasir. *The Arabic Language and National Identity*. Washington, DC: Georgetown Univ. Press, 2003.

al-Tanāḥī, Ṭāhir. "al-Hilāl fī niṣf qarn." In *al-Kitāb al-Dhahabī 1892–1942*, 148–51. Cairo: Dār al-Hilāl, 1942.

Tibi, Bassam. *Nationalismus in der Dritten Welt am arabischen Beispiel.* Frankfurt: Europäische Verlagsanstalt, 1971.

Tomiche, N. "Naḥda." *Encyclopedia Islamica.* 2nd ed. Leiden: E. J. Brill, 1960–2005.

Voigt, Rainer. *Die infirmen Verbaltypen des Arabischen und das Biradikalismus Problem.* Veröffentlichungen der Orientalischen Kommission 39. Stuttgart: Franz Steiner Verlag, 1988.

Volney, C. F. *The Ruins: Or a Survey of the Revolutions of Empires.* 1811. Reprint. Washington, DC: Woodstock Books, 2000.

Wielandt, Rotraud. "Zeitgenössische ägyptische Stimmen zur Säkularisierungsproblematik." *Welt des Islams* 22 (1984): 117–33.

al-Yāzijī, Ibrāhīm. *Lughat al-jarā'id.* Cairo: 'Alī Maḥmūd al-Ḥaṭṭāb, 1910.

al-Yāzijī, Nāṣif. *Kitāb majmā' al-baḥrayn.* Beirut: Maṭba' al-Ābā' al-Yassū'iyyīn, 1856.

Zakhūrā, Ilyās. *Mir'āt al-'aṣr fī tārīkh wa-rusūm akābir al-rijāl bi-maṣr.* Vol. 2. Cairo: Maṭba'at Ilyās Zākhūrā, 1916.

Zurayq, Qusṭanṭīn. *al-Wa'y al-qawmī, naẓarāt fī 'l-ḥayāti al-qawmiyya al-mutafattiḥa fī 'l-sharq al-'arabī.* Beirut: Dār al-Makshūf, 1938.

Zaydān, Jurjī: Articles Authored by Him in *al-Hilal*, Quoted in This Study

Note: An asterisk (*) following the entry indicates that the article is translated in the *Anthology*.

"Ajyāl al-duwal aw i'māruhā qadīman wa-jadīdan—al-dawla wa-'l-umma." *Al-Hilāl* 21 (May 1913): 451–66.

"'Allamuhum wa-'trukuhum." *Al-Hilāl* 7 (Oct. 1898): 9–14.

"Ansāb al-'arab al-qudamā': ridd 'alā al-qā'ilīn bi-'l-umūma wa-'l-ṭutamiyya 'inda 'arab al-jāhiliyya." *Al-Hilāl* 14 (March 1906): 337–43, (April): 393–401 (May): 473–82.*

"al-'Arab qabla 'l-islām." *Al-Hilāl* 3 (March 1895): 534–41.*

"al-'Arab wa-'l-turk qabla 'l-dustūr wa-ba'dahu." *Al-Hilāl* 17 (April 1909): 408–17.*

"Arkān al-'ulūm al-ṭabī'iyya aw khulṣa abḥāth al-'ulamā' al-ṭabī'iyyīn." *Al-Hilāl* 3 (April–July 1895): 605–13, 647–54, 729–38, 764–72, 810–15, 846–52.

"Bi-'l-daght wa-'l-muqāwama taẓhar al-quwā al-kāmina." *Al-Hilāl* 7 (Dec. 1898): 171–75.*

"Diyānat al-būdhiyya." *Al-Hilāl* 8 (Feb. 1900): 290–95.

"Diyānāt ahl al-ṣīn." *Al-Hilāl* 7 (May 1899): 484–88.

"al-Dīn wa-'l-'ilm." *Al-Hilāl* 8 (March 1900): 329.

"al-Dīn, al-'ilm wa-'l-tamaddun." *Al-Hilāl* 8 (Aug. 1900): 676–77.*

"al-Dīn wa-'l-'umrān." *Al-Hilāl* 16 (Feb. 1908): 310.
"Falsafat al-nushū' wa-'l-irtiqā' li-'l-duktūr Shiblī Shumayyil." *Al-Hilāl* 18 (June 1910): 565–67.*
"Hal fī 'l-wujūd 'ālam ākhar?" *Al-Hilāl* 17 (May 1909): 470–76, 476.*
"Hal al-Sūriyyūn 'arab aw mā hum?" *Al-Hilāl* 17 (April 1909): 425–32.*
"Ibn Khaldūn wa-'l-ṭabāb'ia." *Al-Hilāl* 10 (May 1902): 504–10.*
"Ithbāt wujūd Allāh." *Al-Hilāl* 1 (Dec. 1892):114–23.*
"Iḥtifāl al-miṣriyyīn bi-'l-jāmi'a al-miṣriyya." *Al-Hilāl* 17 (Jan. 1909): 242–43.
"al-Ijtimā'iyyūn wa-'l-ishtirākiyyūn." *Al-Hilāl* 16 (Feb.1908): 265–82.
"Jāmi'at al-manfa'a." *Al-Hilāl* 19 (Feb. 1911): 280–85.*
"al-Jāmi'a al-miṣriyya." *Al-Hilāl* 15 (Nov. 1906): 81–88.
"al-Jāmi'a al-miṣriyya wa-'l-ta'līm al-lāzim li-'l-bilād." *Al-Hilāl* 17 (Feb. 1909): 272–79.
"al-Jinn wa-'stiḍār al-arwāḥ wa-'l-mā'ida al-nāṭiqa." *Al-Hilāl* 13 (Dec. 1904): 173–77.*
"al-Katātīb aw madrasa kulliyya." *Al-Hilāl* 14 (Oct. 1905): 18–22.
"Kayfa naṣn'a al-akhlāq wa-ta'thīr al-mar'a fī 'ṣṭinā'ihā." *Al-Hilāl* 22 (May 1914): 585–91.*
"Kuttāb al-'arabiyya wa-qurrā'uhā." *Al-Hilāl* 5 (Feb.–May 1897): 448–59, 489–99, 529–37, 731–36; 6 (Oct. 1897): 126–32; 7 (April 1899): 393–400.*
"Kutub al-dīn 'inda 'l-ṣīn." *Al-Hilāl* 7 (May 1899): 538–42.
"Lā yaṣiḥḥ illā 'l-ṣaḥīḥ." *Al-Hilāl* 20 (May 1912): 476–80.*
"al-Lugha al-'arabiyya al-fuṣḥā wa-'l-lugha al-'āmma." *Al-Hilāl* 1 (Jan. 1893): 200–204. *
"Madrasa kulliyya miṣriyya hiya ḥājatunā al-kubrā." *Al-Hilāl* 8 (Feb. 1900): 264–67.
"al-Marā' fī 'l-jāhiliyya." *Al-Hilāl* 7 (July 1899): 585–91.
"al-Marā' qabla 'l-ḥijāb waba'duhu." *Al-Hilāl* 22 (Dec. 1913): 163–76.
"Maṣīr al-tamaddun al-ḥadīth wa-kayfa yurtaqī al-sharq." *Al-Hilāl* 19 (April 1911): 419–22.
"Miṣr wa-'l-shām." *Al-Hilāl* 16 (Oct. 1907): 15–26.*
"Mustaqbal al-sūriyyūn fī amrīkā." *Al-Hilāl* 9 (Jan. 1901): 210–14.*
"Nasab al-'arab qabla 'l-islām." *Al-Hilāl* 5 (June 1897): 768–78.
"Qidam al-arḍ." *Al-Hilāl* 16 (June 1908): 554–59, 554.
"al-Riwāyāt al-islāmiyya." *Al-Hilāl* 7 (May 1899): 489–93.
"Sālim Saydnawī: "Ṣāḥib akbar maḥall tijārī fī 'l-sharq (1856–1908)." *Al-Hilāl* 16 (May 1908): 471–78.*
"al-Shābb al-sharqī." *Al-Hilāl* 6 (Jan. 1898): 333–40.

"Sharī'at hammurābī malik bābil: aqdam sharā'i' al-'ālam." *Al-Hilāl* 13 (Jan. 1905): 195–216.

"al-Sūriyyūn fi amrīka." *Al-Hilāl* 15 (April 1908): 424–27.*

"al-Sūriyyūn fī miṣr." *Al-Hilāl* 1 (April 1893): 271–75.*

"al-Sūriyyūn wa-tajannusuhum bi-'l-jinsiyya al-amirīkiyya." *Al-Hilāl* 13 (Oct. 1904): 14–20.*

"al-Ta'aṣṣub al-dīnī wa-'l-ta'aṣṣub al-siyāsī." *Al-Hilāl* 19 (Oct. 1910): 54–55.

"al-Ṭabāb'a wa-'bn Khaldūn." *Al-Hilāl* 5 (May 1902): 504–8.*

"al-Ṭabī'a wa-'l-ṭabī'iyyūn wa-'l-kutub al-muqaddasa." *Al-Hilāl* 4 (Oct. 1895): 139–42.

"Tārīkh al-'arab qabla 'l-islām: wa-mā fīhi min al-ashkāl wa-'l-ibhām." *Al-Hilāl* 3 (March 1895): 534–41.*

"al-Tārīkh al-islāmī bi-naẓar ilā sā'ir al-tawārīkh." *Al-Hilāl* 19 (Dec. 1910): 154–61.*

"Tolstoi." *Al-Hilāl* 19 (Jan. 1911): 195–210.

"Watar al-dīn ḥassās, yastawalī bihi al-khāṣṣa 'alā al-'āmma." *Al-Hilāl* 19 (Jan. 1911): 241–44.*

"al-Waṭaniyya al-miṣriyya." *Al-Hilāl* 13 (March 1905): 349–51.

Dictionaries and Encyclopedias

Brockelmann, Carl. *Geschichte der Arabischen Literatur.* 2 vols. and 3 vols. Supplement. Leiden: Brill, 1937–1949.

al-Bustānī, Buṭrus. *Dā'irat al-ma'ārif.* 11 vols. Beirut: s.n., 1867–1870.

al-Bustānī, Buṭrus. *Muḥīṭ al-Muḥīṭ*. 2 vols. Beirut: s.n., 1867–1870.

Dāghir, Yūsuf. *Maṣādir al-dirāsa al-adabiyya*. 2nd ed. Beirut: Maktabat Lubnān, 2000.

Encyclopedia of Islam. 2nd ed. Leiden: Brill, 1970–2007.

Kaḥḥāla, 'Umar Riḍā. *Mu'jam al-mu'allifīn*. Beirut: Mu'assasat al-Risāla,1985.

Lane, E. W. *An Arabic English Lexicon*. 2 vols. London: Williams & Norgate, 1863.

Le Petit Larousse. Paris: Larousse, 2002.

al-Munjid fī 'l-lugha. Beirut: al-Maṭba' al-Kāthūlikiyya, 1969.

Nuṣayr, 'Ā'īda Ibrāhīm, ed. *al-Kutub al-'arabiyya allatī nushirat fī miṣr fī 'l-qarn al-tāsi' 'ashar.* Cairo: Qism al-Nashr bi-'l-Jāmi'a al-Amrīkiyya, 1990.

Osman, Nabil, ed. *Kleines Lexikon deutscher Wörter arabischer Herkunft*. München: Beck, 1992.

Redhouse, Sir James W. *A Turkish and English Lexicon*. Constantinople: A. H. Boyajian,1890.

Ṭarrāzī, Fīlīb dī. *Tārīkh al-ṣaḥāfa al-'arabiyya*. 4 vols. Beirut: al-Maṭba'a al-'Arabiyya, 1913–1933.

Wokoeck, Ursula. *German Orientalism. The Study of the Middle East and Islam from 1800–1945*. New York: Routledge, 2009.

Zakhūrā, Ilyās. *Mir'at al-'aṣr fī tārīkh wa-rusūm akābir al-rijāl bi-maṣr*. Cairo: Matba'at Ilyās Zakhūrā, 1897.

Ziriklī, Khayr al-Dīn al-A'lām. *Qāmūs tarājim ashhar al-rijāl wa-'l-nisā' min al-'arab wa-'l-muta'arrabīn wa-'l-mustashriqīn*. 5 vols. Cairo: Maṭba'at Kūstātsūmās, 1954–1959.

Index of Names

Comment on indexing Arab names:

An alphabetical listing of Arabic names is notoriously problematic. No "family name–first name" dichotomy exists. In addition to a personal name the full name can contain a patronymic part, a kinship or tribal link, or the assertion of the geographical origin and other ascriptions. The part of the name under which the person actually becomes known varies from case to case; for instance, you will never find Ibn Khaldun under his full name 'Abd al-Rahman ibn Muhammad ibn Khaldun al-Tunisi al-Hadrami. An attempt has been made to place the known part of the name in the alphabetical order, when known.